Selected Letters of Henry James to Edmund Gosse, 1882–1915

Henry James, 1913, detail of painting by John Singer Sargent
Trustees of the National Portrait Gallery

Edited by Rayburn S. Moore

Selected Letters of Henry James to Edmund Gosse 1882–1915

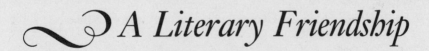 *A Literary Friendship*

Louisiana State University Press   *Baton Rouge and London*

97 96 95 94 93 92 91 90 89 88   5 4 3 2 1

Designer: Patricia Douglas Crowder
Typeface: Linotron 202 Janson
Typesetter: Focus Graphics
Printer: Thomson-Shore, Inc.
Binder: John H. Dekker & Sons, Inc.

LIBRARY OF CONGRESS CATALOGING-IN-PUBLICATION DATA

James, Henry, 1843–1916.
    Selected letters of Henry James to Edmund Gosse, 1882–1915: a
literary friendship / edited by Rayburn S. Moore.
        p. cm.
    Includes index.
    ISBN 0-8071-1439-1 (alk. paper)
    1. James, Henry, 1843–1916—Correspondence. 2. Gosse, Edmund,
1849–1928—Correspondence. 3. Authors, American—19th century—
Correspondence. 4. Authors, American—20th century—
Correspondence. I. Gosse, Edmund, 1849–1928. II. Moore, Rayburn
S., 1920–   . III. Title.
PS2123.A44 1988
813'.4—dc19
[B]   88-1392
                                                                          CIP

The author gratefully acknowledges Alexander R. James, holder of the copyright on
Henry James's correspondence, for permission to reprint the letters herein.

This publication has been supported by the National Endowment for the Humanities,
a federal agency which supports the study of such fields as history, philosophy,
literature, and languages.

The paper in this book meets the guidelines for permanence and durability of the
Committee on Production Guidelines for Book Longevity of the Council on Library
Resources.∞

For Margaret and in memory of Max and Sammie Moore

Contents

Illustrations

Acknowledgments

It is a pleasure to record here the obligations I have incurred in editing these letters. I am grateful to Mattie Russell, curator emeritus of manuscripts at the William R. Perkins Library, Duke University, for calling my attention to James's letters to Gosse in the manuscript department and for making them available to me; to H. Montgomery Hyde, a collateral kinsman of Henry James, who encouraged me to examine the entire body of letters from James to Gosse and put me in touch with Alexander R. James, present holder of the James family's copyrights, who graciously allowed me to collect and edit this correspondence for publication; to Jennifer Gosse, Edmund Gosse's granddaughter, who looked with favor upon the project and offered generous encouragement; to David Masson and C. D. W. Sheppard, sublibrarians in charge of the Brotherton Collection, the Brotherton Library, University of Leeds, the main repository of James's correspondence with Gosse, each of whom, in turn, kindly made the manuscripts and the facilities of the Brotherton Collection available to me; to Leon Edel, the author of the standard biography of James and the editor of a recent edition of James's general correspondence, who offered advice and cooperation and assured me our separate editions would not conflict; to Ann Thwaite, the author of the standard treatment of Gosse's life and career, who helped me in various ways and answered my questions about Gosse; and to Philip Horne, University College, London, who kindly made me aware of several important transcripts of James's letters at the Houghton Library, Harvard University.

Some of the letters in this collection are published with the permission of the Huntington Library, San Marino, California; the Princeton

University Library; the Collection of American Literature, the Beinecke Rare Book and Manuscript Library, Yale University; and the Henry James Collection (#6251), Barrett Library, University of Virginia Library. Many other libraries have also generously allowed me to use their holdings and have furnished photocopies of manuscripts: the British Library, London; the Brotherton Library, University of Leeds; the Cambridge University Library; the Miller Library, Colby College; the William R. Perkins Library, Duke University; the Houghton Library, Harvard University; the Library of Congress; the Archibald Stephens Alexander Library, Rutgers University; and the University Research Library, University of California at Los Angeles.

Many librarians have also been helpful, among them Brooke Whiting and Anne Caiger, University Research Library, University of California at Los Angeles; A. E. B. Owen, Cambridge University Library; J. Fraser Cocks, III, and Patience-Anne W. Lenk, Miller Library, Colby College; the late Benjamin E. Powell and J. P. Waggoner, Florence Blakely, Mary Canada, Elvin Strowd, Emerson Ford, and Robert L. Byrd, William R. Perkins Library, Duke University; Christine Burroughs, Claire Columbo, Marie Ellis Stephens, and Robert M. Willingham, Jr., Ilah Dunlap Little Library, University of Georgia; Rodney G. Dennis and Elizabeth A. Falsey, Houghton Library, Harvard University; Sara S. Hodson, Huntington Library, San Marino, California; John C. Broderick and James H. Hutson, Library of Congress; Jean F. Preston, Princeton University Library; Clark L. Beck, Jr., and Bonita Craft Grant, Archibald Stephens Alexander Library, Rutgers University; Edmund Berkeley, Jr., Barrett Library, University of Virginia; Donald Gallup and Christa Sammons, Beinecke Library, Yale University.

Correspondence previously published in *Henry James Letters*, edited by Leon Edel, is reprinted by permission of Harvard University Press and is copyright 1980, 1984 by Alexander R. James. For permission to reprint other letters, I am grateful to the *Colby Library Quarterly*, Farrar, Straus, and Giroux, Inc., *Journal of the Rutgers University Library*, Charles Scribner's Sons, the *Southern Review*, the University of Texas Press, and Adeline Tintner.

For various scholarly courtesies, I am grateful to Robert L. Gale, Adeline Tintner, Lewis P. Simpson, Glenn Horowitz, Steven Ozment, George O. Marshall, Jr., Walter Gordon, and Margaret B. Moore. For research assistance, I am pleased to thank Ann Burroughs, Deborah

Skinner Davis, Young-Min Kim, Tim Marsh, and Arjuna Parakrama.

I am also indebted to Dean William J. Payne of the University of Georgia for making it possible for me to devote parts of each year to this work. John Algeo, James B. Colvert, and Coburn Freer, department heads in English, provided travel funds and summer support; and the late Robert C. Anderson, former vice-president for research, the late Charles J. Douglas, assistant vice-president for research, William O. Burke, assistant vice-president for research, Jean-Pierre Piriou, associate vice-president for research, and S. William Pelletier, former provost, all offered help of one kind or another. Larry Dendy and Walker Montgomery, public relations, kindly provided copies of photographs for use as illustrations.

For typing James's letters and helping me to decipher his often difficult scrawl, I am grateful to Kathleen DeMarco, Mary Adams, Laura Mashburn, Virginia Seaquist, and Florence Whitmire. Mrs. Whitmire deserves special praise for typing various drafts of the manuscript.

The editorial staff of Louisiana State University Press has been unfailingly helpful. Beverly Jarrett encouraged me from an early stage of the research for this edition; Catherine Barton advised me about preparing the manuscript for publication; and Catherine Landry diligently and expertly copy-edited the manuscript. Last but not least, Linda Webster indexed the volume with professional skill.

Selected Letters of Henry James to Edmund Gosse, 1882–1915

A Note on Editorial Principles

Of over 400 letters of Henry James to Edmund Gosse and his family, I have selected 317, of which 224 have never been printed in full before. I have been concerned mainly about literary content, but I have included some correspondence that may be considered, in James's own well-known phrase, "mere graciousness of twaddle," in order to illustrate the flavor and character of James's friendship with Gosse and his family, especially Mrs. Gosse, and also to indicate other aspects of the lives and careers of the two writers.

In preparing the letters for print, I have based the texts in this edition upon the original manuscripts and upon the collation of photocopy and manuscript , and I have indicated the location of the manuscript of each letter in abbreviated form above the text of each letter. When the present text is based upon any other source, I have acknowledged the same in the notes. Although ninety-three of the letters printed herein have appeared before in one form or another, I have, with rare exception, used the manuscript as my text even when I print letters I myself previously edited and published. I have included such letters in order to offer in one place as complete a coverage as possible of James's correspondence with Gosse and to provide texts consistently based upon manuscripts.

I have tried throughout to follow James's epistolary practice with regard to a letter's content. I have retained his ampersands, reproduced *etc.* as *&c*, kept his punctuation within parentheses, maintained his dashes, and, in short, been diligent about respecting what James has written. On rare occasions I have silently closed a parenthesis or completed a dash, but in general I have tried to correct neither his spelling nor his punctuation (in a few instances I have provided a period in brackets). When I have inserted something, I have indicated such additions by brackets, and when I concluded that a Jamesian idiosyncrasy might confuse the reader, I used *sic*, but not often. Nor have I indicated titles of works (books, plays, or other literary publications) or foreign phrases by italics unless James has done so. (In the notes, of course, my practice follows the usual scholarly standards.) Fortunately, James makes few mistakes in spelling or grammar, and though he occasionally gets lost in the jungle of his syntax and dashes (especially as his style grows more complex in the so-called major phase), he is normally in firm control of what he is writing, whether it be grand manner or twaddle.

As to epistolary form itself, I have consistently placed addresses and dates in the upper righthand corner (this is James's normal practice, but this information sometimes follows his signature at the end), even when the address is printed top-center on personal stationery. I have retained the words and punctuation on the stationery even when I have regularized the address in regard to position. I have also used italics to indicate James's underscoring of *th* and *d* in dates, though I have omitted his erratic underlining of day, month, and year, and I have followed faithfully his way of indicating dates, inconsistencies and all. Dates of letters are sometimes a problem. I have been helped by typed copies of the originals at the Brotherton Library, the Library of Congress, and the William R. Perkins Library, Duke University, and a few elsewhere that were presumably authorized by John Alexander Symington, librarian of the Brotherton Library in Leeds. When James gave only a day, Symington, Philip Gosse, or, rarely, Edmund Gosse himself wrote the date in pencil on the manuscript. These dates are usually accurate, though I have discovered that some are wrong for one reason or another. All possible questions about dates are discussed in the notes, including disagreements with dates of letters already printed. The typed copies, in addition, have helped me decipher James's hand, a formidable task at best and one made even more daunting by James's own admission on occasion that his scrawl was "illegible." In the final analysis, however, I have based all decisions upon the manuscripts, not upon the copies. As for salutations and closes, I have tried to follow James's erratic practice as much as possible. His most frequent salutation is followed by a period, but a comma or dash is not unusual, and at times the salutation becomes part of the first sentence of the letter itself. Complimentary closes, similarly, are often incorporated in the last sentence of the text, and only James's name is dropped below the last line—frequently with a flourish or a period that I have seen no need to include.

My main intention is to offer a text that is as close to the original as possible and that is accessible to the printer, the scholar, and even the wary general reader. I am assuredly aware of the problems of space and have in some instances—especially in matters of addresses—presented in one or two lines matter that may have been given in two or three.

Annotation is another matter. I have aimed primarily at an academic audience—scholar and student alike—and have tried to offer as much information and elucidation as will make James's comments, asides, allusions, and references accessible to readers of the present. Such readers, then, may consistently assume when annotation is not provided that either it is available in normal sources of reference or, alas, I am not able to supply it.

Chronology

1843	HJ, second son of Henry James, Sr., and Mary Robertson Walsh James, born April 15 in Washington Place, New York City.
1845–1860	HJ educated by governesses and in day schools in New York City and Albany and in various schools in Switzerland, France, and Germany.
1849	EWG, only child of Philip Henry Gosse and Emily Bowes Gosse, born September 21 in London.
1855–1866	EWG educated at home by father and mother and at day schools, and, after the death of Emily Gosse in 1856, by Eliza Brightwen Gosse, his stepmother. Family moves to Devon in September, 1857. EWG attends Thorn Park Classical and Mathematical School, Teignmouth, 1863–1866.
1862	HJ attends Harvard Law School.
1864	HJ's first contributions to magazines: *Continental Monthly*, *North American Review*.
1866	EWG accepts position in the cataloging department of the British Museum and begins work in January, 1867. Associates with Richard Garnett, Théophile Marzials, and other young writers.
1868	EWG's first magazine contribution printed October 10 in *Athenaeum*.
1869–1870	HJ journeys to Europe: England, France, Switzerland, Italy. EWG's *Madrigals, Songs and Sonnets* (with John Blaikie), his first book (1870), ap-

	pears. EWG meets Robert Louis Stevenson.
1871	HJ's "Watch and Ward," his first novel, serialized in the *Atlantic Monthly*. EWG visits Norway and purchases Ibsen's *Digte*.
1872	EWG's review of *Digte* appears in the *Spectator*, followed by three other articles introducing the Norwegian writer to Britain. EWG begins to translate Ibsen's *Love's Comedy*, but finds no publisher. HJ returns to Europe for two-year stay.
1873	*On Viol and Flute*, EWG's next collection of poems, appears.
1875	EWG accepts position as translator for the Board of Trade, marries Ellen (Nellie) Epps, daughter of Dr. George Napoleon Epps and pupil of Ford Madox Brown, and begins friendship with Austin Dobson and Swinburne. HJ's first books, *A Passionate Pilgrim and Other Tales* and *Transatlantic Sketches*, appear. HJ returns to Europe to live; takes rooms in Paris for year and meets Turgenev, Flaubert, Maupassant, Daudet, and Zola, among others. "Roderick Hudson" published in the *Atlantic Monthly* (January–December) and subsequently in November as HJ's first novel in book form. EWG's *King Erik*, a verse tragedy, appears in December.
1876	EWG rents house at 29 Delamere Terrace, near Regent's Park Canal, his home for the next 25 years and the scene of many Sunday afternoons "at home." HJ's "The American" begins in the *Atlantic Monthly* in June, and book publication follows in May, 1877. HJ "emigrates" to London and takes flat in Piccadilly in December at 3 Bolton Street, his base for almost 10 years.
1877	HJ publishes reviews in the *Nation* and elsewhere, and essays and articles on English topics and scenes in the *Galaxy* and *Lippincott's*. EWG continues contributions to *Fraser's*, the *Spectator*, and the *Academy*; begins collecting books and

receives as gift from John Addington Symonds, friend of two-years' standing, some first editions of Massinger. Emily Teresa Gosse (Tessa), second child and first to live, born September 14.

1878   HJ's *Watch and Ward* published in book form, followed by *The Europeans* and *Daisy Miller*. EWG's *The Unknown Lover* (play).

1879   HJ's *An International Episode, Confidence*, and *Hawthorne* appear, as do EWG's *Studies in the Literature of Northern Europe*, essays on Scandinavian writers, and *New Poems*. Philip Henry George Gosse, EWG's only son, born August 13. HJ and EWG meet in September at a luncheon that also includes Stevenson and Andrew Lang.

1880   HJ's *Washington Square* out in book form.

1881   Laura Sylvia Gosse (Sylvia), EWG's last child, born February 14. EWG becomes the *Century*'s first "London agent." HJ returns to the United States in October, and *The Portrait of a Lady*, after runs in *Macmillan's* and the *Atlantic Monthly*, is published in November.

1882   Mary Walsh James dies January 29. HJ dramatizes *Daisy Miller* (privately printed); returns to England in May but, upon illness of HJ, Sr., rushes back to Cambridge in December only to find father dead. First extant letter to EWG August 2. EWG's *Gray* published in English Men of Letters series.

1883   HJ settles father's affairs and returns to England in August. EWG's *Seventeenth-Century Studies*, a collection of essays on poetry for the *Cornhill Magazine*, appears, and *On Viol and Flute* brought out in New York by Henry Holt. First collected edition of HJ's work (14 volumes) published in London in November and *Portraits of Places* (mostly in Italy, France, and England) in December.

1884   HJ's "The Author of Beltraffio," "The Art of Fiction," and *A Little Tour in France* published.

EWG edits edition of Gray's works (4 volumes) and lectures in America (December to January, 1885); appointed Clark Lecturer, Trinity College, Cambridge, October 1, a post held until 1889.

1885   HJ's *Stories Revived* (3 volumes) and EWG's *From Shakespeare to Pope* and *Firdausi in Exile and Other Poems* published. EWG receives honorary M.A. from Cambridge.

1886   HJ's *The Bostonians* and *The Princess Casamassima*, after serialization in the *Century* and the *Atlantic Monthly*, respectively, appear; he moves to 13 De Vere Mansions (later refined to 34 De Vere Gardens, his street number) in March. EWG's *Raleigh* published and "The Unequal Yoke," his first novel, serialized in the *English Illustrated Magazine* for April, May, and June (to be dedicated to HJ if published in book form). *From Shakespeare to Pope* attacked by John Churton Collins in the *Quarterly Review* for October. HJ's liberal sympathy contributes to ripening of friendship.

1887   HJ in Italy from December, 1886, to July; essays on Constance Fenimore Woolson and John Singer Sargent appear in *Harper's Weekly* and *New Monthly*, respectively. EWG, "down on [his] luck," begins life of Congreve for Walter Scott's Great Writers series. Stevenson, good friend to both HJ and EWG, leaves for America in August.

1888   EWG's *Life of William Congreve* appears, and Philip Henry Gosse dies August 23. HJ brings out *Partial Portraits*, *The Reverberator*, and *The Aspern Papers*.

1889   HJ's *A London Life* and EWG's *A History of Eighteenth-Century Literature (1660–1780)* published.

1890   HJ's *The Tragic Muse* appears, and he turns to playwriting. New edition of EWG's *On Viol and Flute* and his *Life of Philip Henry Gosse, F.R.S.* and

Northern Studies (revision of *Studies in the Litera-ture of Northern Europe*) issued.

1891   HJ dramatizes *The American* with moderate success (privately printed by William Heinemann) and publishes "The Pupil" and other stories. EWG collects magazine essays in *Gossip in a Library*, publishes first book with Heinemann, and translates Ibsen's *Hedda Gabler*.

1892   Alice James, HJ's sister, dies March 6 in London. *The Lesson of the Master* and *The Secret of Narcisse*, EWG's second novel, appear.

1893   HJ's *The Real Thing and Other Tales*, *The Private Life*, *The Wheel of Time*, *Picture and Text*, and *Essays in London and Elsewhere*, and EWG's *Questions at Issue*, miscellaneous articles, published.

1894   HJ contributes to the *Yellow Book* and brings out *Theatricals*. EWG offers *The Jacobean Poets* and *In Russet and Silver*, a collection of poems dedicated to Stevenson, who receives the book shortly before he dies December 3.

1895   *Guy Domville* produced January 5 (and subsequently) with disastrous results to HJ's career as play-wright and general peace of mind; his *Theatri-cals: Second Series* and *Terminations* (tales) appear.

1896   HJ's *Embarrassments* (tales) comes out, and he returns to the novel with "The Old Things" in the *Atlantic* (published in book form in 1897 as *The Spoils of Poynton*). EWG's *Critical Kit-Kats*, essays on Elizabeth Barrett Browning, Whitman, Stevenson, *et al.*, dedicated to Thomas Hardy.

1897   HJ's *The Spoils of Poynton* and *What Maisie Knew* appear. EWG's *A Short History of Modern English Literature* (dated 1898) issued, the first of many printings.

1898   HJ's "The Turn of the Screw" (later included in *The Two Magics*) and *In the Cage* published. HJ moves into Lamb House, Rye (leased in 1897). EWG edits new edition of Fielding (12 volumes).

1899   HJ's *The Awkward Age* appears in book form, and

	EWG's *The Life and Letters of John Donne* (2 volumes) comes out.
1900	HJ's *The Soft Side* (tales) published.
1901	HJ's *The Sacred Fount* (no prior serialization) and EWG's *Hypolympia; or, The Gods in the Island: An Ironic Fantasy* (verse) appear. HJ takes room at the Reform Club, London. EWG moves to 17 Hanover Terrace, his home for the rest of his life. Sundays "at home" continue.
1902	HJ's *The Wings of the Dove* (no prior serialization) appears.
1903	HJ's *The Better Sort* (tales), "The Ambassadors" (serialized in the *North American Review* from January to December), and *William Wetmore Story and His Friends* (2 volumes) appear. EWG's *English Literature: An Illustrated Record* (4 volumes, written with Richard Garnett) published.
1904	HJ returns to U.S. in August to prepare for *The American Scene*; visits William James at Chocorua, N.H., and Edith Wharton at Lenox, Mass.; and spends some time in Cambridge and Boston. *The Golden Bowl* (no prior serialization) appears in New York in November. EWG becomes librarian of the House of Lords in February; publishes *Jeremy Taylor* (English Men of Letters series) and *French Profiles* (periodical essays).
1905	HJ travels to New York, Philadelphia, and Washington, through the South to Florida, and subsequently to Chicago, St. Louis, and California; lectures on "The Lesson of Balzac" and "The Question of Our Speech" (published together in October); returns to England in August. HJ's *English Hours* (travel articles) out in October. EWG's *Coventry Patmore* (Literary Lives series) and *Sir Thomas Browne* (English Men of Letters series) appear.
1906	HJ revises fiction and writes prefaces for New York Edition; works on text of *The American Scene*. In

the fall EWG begins to edit literary supplement
of *Daily Mail*; continues until April, 1907.

1907   *The American Scene* appears and is reviewed by EWG
in *Daily Mail*, February 1. The first volumes of
the New York Edition come out in New York in
December and the last in July, 1909. EWG's
Ibsen and *Father and Son* published.

1908   HJ's *The High Bid* (play) produced in Edinburgh in
March (again in London in February, 1909), and
Views and Reviews (criticism) appears. EWG
writes *A History of the Library of the House of Lords*
(introduction to the catalog of the library).

1909   HJ's *Julia Bride* and *Italian Hours* (travel sketches) and
EWG's *The Autumn Garden* (poems) appear.

1910   HJ has long nervous illness, beginning in January.
Goes to Germany with William James, also ill,
and subsequently to United States in August,
where William dies August 26. *The Finer Grain*,
last collection of tales, published in October.
Academic Committee of Royal Society of Literature established, with HJ and EWG both elected
members.

1911   HJ remains with brother's family, recovers from
nervous depression, receives honorary degree
from Harvard, and returns to England in August; *The Outcry* appears. EWG brings out last
volume of verse, *Collected Poems*, and *Two Visits to
Denmark, 1872, 1874.*

1912   HJ at Reform Club during first months of year but
returns to Lamb House in summer, receives
honorary degree from Oxford June 26, and
contracts shingles in September. EWG awarded
C.B. in January. EWG's *Portraits and Sketches*
appears.

1913   HJ leases flat at 21 Carlyle Mansions in Chelsea (with
help of EWG) and takes possession in January.
His *A Small Boy and Others* published in March.
Honored by British friends (largely arranged by
EWG) on seventieth birthday, April 13, with

silver-gilt porringer and portrait by Sargent. EWG's *The Future of English Poetry* published as English Association pamphlet number 25; receives French Legion of Honor.

1914 HJ's *Notes of a Son and Brother* and *Notes on Novelists* published. Britain enters World War I August 4, and both HJ and EWG defend the Allied cause with pen and service. EWG retires from librarianship of the House of Lords September 26.

1915 *Uniform Tales of Henry James* (14 volumes) begins to appear in April. HJ works on *The Ivory Tower* and returns to *The Sense of the Past*; with help of EWG, takes out British citizenship July 26; has "slight stroke" December 2, followed by a more severe one December 3. Mrs. William James sails from America to take charge. EWG publishes *Two Pioneers of Romanticism: Joseph and Thomas Warton*, British Academy Warton Lecture on English Poetry, number 6.

1916 HJ awarded O.M. on New Year's Honours List. Dies at 21 Carlyle Mansions February 28. Funeral service in Chelsea Old Church, London, and ashes interred in family plot in Cambridge, Mass. Discussion of edition of HJ's letters begins. EWG ruled out as editor by James family, though he eventually serves as consultant to Percy Lubbock, the chosen candidate. EWG's *Inter Arma* (essays) appears.

1917 EWG's *Life of Algernon Charles Swinburne* issued. HJ's *The Ivory Tower* and *The Sense of the Past*, both incomplete, come out simultaneously in September, and *The Middle Years*, unfinished autobiographical fragment, follows in October.

1918 War ends November 11.

1919 EWG's *Some Diversions of a Man of Letters* and HJ's *Within the Rim and Other Essays* published. EWG presented with letter on seventieth birthday from over 200 prominent friends (Barrie, Conrad, Hardy, Housman, and Kipling among them), informing him that a portrait bust of himself by Sir William Goscombe John, R.A., will commemorate occasion. Begins to write regularly for *Sunday Times* and continues until death in 1928.

1920   *The Letters of Henry James* published in April. EWG contributes essay on HJ to *London Mercury* and *Scribner's Magazine* in April and May. Awarded honorary doctorate by Cambridge in June. Bust of EWG shown at Royal Academy and presented to honoree November 9. Sponsoring friends include former prime ministers Asquith and Balfour, the archbishops of Canterbury and York, and Barrie, Bennett, Conrad, Galsworthy, Hardy, Kipling, Shaw, the Sitwells, and Walpole, among other writers.

1921   EWG president of the English Association; publishes *Books on the Table* (articles from *Sunday Times*). *The Novels and Stories of Henry James* (35 volumes, edited by Percy Lubbock) begins to appear in January and is completed in November, 1923.

1922   *Aspects and Impressions* (periodical essays, including one on HJ published first in 1920) and *The Continuity of Literature*, EWG's presidential address printed as English Association pamphlet number 54, are published.

1923   In January EWG has "cardiac seizure," but recovers by March. His *More Books on the Table* (further articles from *Sunday Times*) appears.

1925   EWG's knighthood announced in New Year's Honours; made commander of the French Legion of Honor and awarded honorary degree by the Sorbonne. His *Silhouettes* (more articles reprinted from *Sunday Times*) is published.

1926   EWG's *Poems* (last collection) appears.

1927   *Leaves and Fruit*, EWG's last collection of essays, is published; EWG seriously ill from typhoid in August and September, but recovers.

1928   Thomas Hardy dies January 11, and EWG serves old
               friend as pallbearer at Westminster Abbey, Janu-
               ary 16. *Selected Essays* (2 volumes for Heinemann's
               Travellers' Library) appears. EWG dies May 16
               of "acute bronchitis and retention of urine";
               funeral at St. Marylebone Parish Church, Lon-
               don, May 21.

Abbreviations

BHJ	Leon Edel, Dan H. Laurence, and J. Rambeau. *A Bibliography of Henry James* (3rd ed.; Oxford, 1982).
British Library	British Library, London
Cambridge	Cambridge University Library, Cambridge University
CLQ	Richard C. Harrier (ed.). "Letters of Henry James." In *Colby Library Quarterly*, 3rd Ser. (May, 1953), 153–64.
Colby	Miller Library, Colby College
Duke	William R. Perkins Library, Duke University
EG	Ann Thwaite. *Edmund Gosse: A Literary Landscape, 1849–1928* (London, 1984).
Harvard	Houghton Library, Harvard University
HJ	Leon Edel. *Henry James*. Vol. I: *The Untried Years, 1843–1870* (Philadelphia, 1953); Vol. II: *The Conquest of London, 1870–1881* (Philadelphia, 1962); Vol. III: *The Middle Years, 1882–1895* (Philadelphia, 1962); Vol. IV: *The Treacherous Years, 1895–1901* (Philadelphia, 1969); Vol. V: *The Master, 1901–1916* (Philadelphia, 1972).
HJL	Leon Edel (ed.). *Henry James Letters* (4 vols.; Cambridge, 1974, 1975, 1980, 1984).
Huntington	Huntington Library, San Marino, California
LC	Library of Congress
Leeds	Brotherton Collection, Brotherton Library, University of Leeds

LHJ	Percy Lubbock (ed.). *The Letters of Henry James* (2 vols.; New York, 1920).
LL	Evan Charteris. *The Life and Letters of Sir Edmund Gosse* (New York, 1931).
N	F. O. Matthiessen and Kenneth B. Murdock (eds.). *The Notebooks of Henry James* (1947; rpr. New York, 1961). The most recent edition, Leon Edel and Lyall H. Powers (eds.), *The Complete Notebooks* (1987), appeared after my edition was in press.
Princeton	Princeton University Library, Princeton University
Rutgers	Archibald Stephens Alexander Library, Rutgers University
SL	Leon Edel (ed.). *The Selected Letters of Henry James* (1955; rpr. Garden City, N.Y., 1960).
SR	Rayburn S. Moore, ed. "A 'Literary-Gossippy Friendship': Henry James's Letters to Edmund Gosse," *Southern Review*, XX (Summer, 1984), 570–90.
TC	Typed copy
TD	Paul F. Mattheisen and Michael Millgate (eds.). *Transatlantic Dialogue: Selected American Correspondence of Edmund Gosse* (Austin, 1965).
TLS	Typed letter signed
UCLA	University Research Library, University of California at Los Angeles
Virginia	Barrett Library, University of Virginia
Yale	Beinecke Library, Yale University

Introduction

Henry James met Edmund Gosse in 1879, and by 1883 the two were good friends and, though both lived in London, correspondents. James, by then forty and with the death of his parents immediately behind him, and having achieved a reputation in both England and America as the author of *The American* (1877), *Daisy Miller* (1878), and *The Portrait of a Lady* (1881), had settled in Bolton Street, Piccadilly. Gosse, six years younger, married, and living on Delamere Terrace, Westbourne Square, had worked in the cataloging section of the British Museum from 1867 to 1875, at which time he became a translator for the Board of Trade. He had come to know well Algernon Charles Swinburne, Robert Louis Stevenson, Thomas Hardy, Austin Dobson, and Dante Gabriel Rossetti, among others; and had published three volumes of poems and his first biographical and critical books. He had contributed essays and criticism to such periodicals as *Fraser's*, the *Cornhill Magazine*, the *Academy*, *Saturday Review*, and the *Athenaeum*, for which he had achieved some standing as a man of letters and, particularly, as an interpreter of Henrik Ibsen and other new Scandinavian literature. In the three decades before James's death in 1916, the friendship between the two writers deepened and survived such trials as John Churton Collins' attack on Gosse's *From Shakespeare to Pope* in 1886 and James's difficulties with the drama in the 1890s. Unfortunately, only one side of the correspondence remains available, for James in the last decade of his life had a "gigantic bonfire" in which apparently many of Gosse's letters, among others, were consumed. Fewer than twenty-five are extant. Gosse, on the contrary, saved James's letters, including those to his wife and children, and close to four hundred are presently available in collections. Consequently, this consideration of the relationship between James and Gosse is based primarily upon James's letters, and though Gosse's opinions and experiences are culled from many sources, including his few letters to James that remain, this collection is composed of 317 of James's letters to Gosse (17 are to Mrs. Gosse), 224 of which have not heretofore been printed in full.[1]

The first letter now available, dated August 2 [1882], declines an invitation (James will be "out of town") to attend one of Gosse's already well-established Sunday "at homes." The second, dated December 10, 1882, offers some insight into the friendship in its early stages. James writes Gosse that he is sailing for "America on Tuesday, summoned by the critical condition of my father, who is dangerously ill," and asks him to inform two other friends, William Dean Howells and George Du Maurier, of his plans. Henry James, Sr., died before James arrived in Boston, but after his return to London in the summer of 1883, the friendship with Gosse continued to ripen.

A significant factor in this increasing intimacy between the two writers was the critical response to Gosse's *From Shakespeare to Pope* (1885), a collection of lectures he had delivered in both America and England. In October, 1886, John Churton Collins, a friend of Gosse's and lecturer in English for the London University Extension Society, contributed an article to the *Quarterly Review* in which he assailed the study's inaccuracies, damned literary puffery, and observed of the book: "Not the least [of] its mischievous characteristic[s] . . . is the skill with which its worthlessness is disguised." Touched to the quick, Gosse replied in the *Times* on October 19 from Trinity College, Cambridge, where he was Clark Lecturer, and in the ensuing exchange of letters and unpleasantnesses, even Swinburne, an old friend, took occasion to write a few unkind things about Collins.[2]

James did not enter the lists in public, but in a series of six letters beginning October 22 and continuing until November 8, he offered comment, advice, and sympathy. On October 22, he applauded Gosse's letter of October 19.

It is perfect in tone & taste & temper, it is highly to the point as a vindication, & the last few lines are a gem. You have said neither too little nor too much, & what you have said you have said excellently well. You have been graceful without being evasive, sportive without being flippant, effective without being violent. . . . All that will remain of the fray a short time hence will be a general impression that you were ponderously & maliciously attacked by an old friend & that it came out—by which I don't mean it had been hidden before—that you were remarkably clever. . . . I predict you an "ovation" at Cambridge.

On October 26 he expressed his distress that Gosse "should continue to be overturned by this whole beastly business," yet assured him of his understanding and concluded: "I really don't see the smallest necessity for your *knowing* a word more about this odious matter, nor for your reading the newspapers. I can't too earnestly recommend you not to *look* at them—for an instant; I urge this upon you as one who has himself been tried. . . . Long ago I determined simply never to glance at such stuff & both as a man & an artist je m'en porte à merveille. Avert your eyes—& your nose—& the rest will take care of itself." At the same time, James realized, as he wrote Howells, that Gosse was paying a "penalty" for his "false position" at Trinity (presumably the lectureship, for which he had limited qualifications), but James nevertheless predicted on October 29 that Cambridge would be "robustly" with Gosse, and on November 3 he acknowledged Gosse's telegram about Cambridge's response: "I hope it isn't too late to express to you my *great* satisfaction. . . . I knew it would be so—& so may it continue."[3] Finally, on November 8, James expressed his pleasure in receiving news "pitched in the key of resurrection—by which I mean of a return to normal life."

In the meantime, Gosse had supplied James with the donnée for "The Author of Beltraffio" and, to James's delight, praised the story when it appeared in 1884. "You obey," James admitted on June 9, "a very humane inspiration whenever you murmur *bravo*! in the ear of the much-attempting & slowly-composing, easily-discouraged & constantly dissatisfied fictionist." James, in turn, characterized Gosse's edition of Thomas Gray's work, published in 1884, "as a very beautiful & (evidently) very perfect book," and on August 28, 1886, he reported that he was reading Gosse's *Raleigh*, published in 1886, "with breathless admiration & interest. It seems to me," he added, "wondrous well done."

The next literary crisis occurred in the 1890s, when James temporarily abandoned the novel for drama. Discouraged by the reception of *The Tragic Muse* (1890) and tempted by the money to be made in the theater—to say nothing of his lifelong interest in it—James turned *The American* into a play for the Compton Comedy Company in 1890 and suffered through its run in the provinces in 1891 and subsequent seventy appearances in London. Gosse was assiduous in offering sympathy and consideration. On January 3, the day of the first production of the play in Southport, James thanked Gosse for his "*petit mot*," remarked on "the vulgar ordeal of tonight," and concluded: "I am yours & your wife's while yet I *may* be. After 11 o'clk. tonight I *may* be the world's—you know—& I may be the undertaker's. I count upon you both to spend this evening in fasting, silence & supplication. I will send you a word in the morning—wire you if I can—if there is anything at all to boast of."[4] On the following day, James wired Gosse: "Complete and delightful success universal congratulations to which I venture to add yours and your wife's." But the play, though not a failure, proved in the end neither a financial nor a critical success. The disaster was yet to come.

In addition to *The American*, James wrote plays—none produced—for Augustin Daly, Edward Compton again, Ada Rehan, and Ellen Terry. In the summer of 1893 he wrote *Guy Domville* for George Alexander, the manager of St. James's Theatre in London. Since Alexander was committed to another play, *Guy Domville* did not go into rehearsal until December, 1894, with the first performance to occur on January 5. James's letters of December to Gosse, filled with pain over the recent death of Robert Louis Stevenson, their mutual friend, also refer to "the demoralizing & exhausting & incongruous ordeal I am daily going through at the theatre." On December 27, James explained that complimentary tickets would soon be forthcoming and expressed his pleasure that W. E. Norris, a fellow novelist and another mutual friend, would be attending the play with Gosse, but admitted his concern that Norris would be "making that midwinter journey [from Torquay] to such an end. . . . Yes," he concluded, "I should like much to talk with you. The ghost of poor R.L.S. waves its great dusky wings between me & all occupations. . . . I am unable to say whether Friday or Saturday will be free evenings for me—the damnable theatre is now given over to nocturnal as well as diurnal rehearsals. But I shall probably know to-night."[5]

Discussion with Gosse led James to plan to while away the hours of the first performance at a pub in the neighborhood, but by January 3 James had changed his mind and decided on seeing another play, Oscar Wilde's *An Ideal Husband*, at the Haymarket. Leon Edel has provided full-scale accounts in several places, especially in his introduction to *Guy Domville*, of what followed. The play received a mixed reaction from its audience—the boxes and stalls for the play, and the pit and gallery against it—and James, returning from the Haymarket, was led on stage by Alexander for a curtain call after the performance. He faced both applause from the "cultivated majority" and scorn from a "handful of rowdies," as Bernard Shaw later described the audience's reaction. After seconds of speechlessness, according to Gosse, James "bowed and spread forth deprecating hands and finally vanished." Gosse was sympathetic and supportive, and immediately penned a defense for which James expressed his gratitude on January 13: "All thanks for your graceful and humorous defense of Poesy, or of Comedy (it comes to the same thing.) It would do much for the case, if the thing had not been, from the first, mortally wounded. I am none the less grateful for your wit & eloquence. This I shall express to you better some evening soon— I will come in. I have had a very tired & tiring week." The irony is, of course, that *Guy Domville* actually had a fairly good press and even ran for forty performances (not enough, however, for Alexander to break even), but James concluded, as he later informed Elizabeth Robins, that the whole experience had been "one of the most detestable incidents of my life." Gosse eventually characterized the night of January 5, 1895, as "the most tragical in Henry James's career."[6]

Subsequently, the friendship grew even more intimate, and when James moved to Lamb House in 1898, the visits between Rye and Hanover Terrace (Gosse himself moved in 1901) were frequent and cordial, and the correspondence expanded accordingly. James had, on occasion, written notes to Nellie Gosse—"Mrs. Nelly," as he frequently referred to her—and eventually as well to the children, Tessa, Philip, and Sylvia. This is not to suggest that all went along perfectly smoothly. Gosse chafed when James failed to respond adequately to letters or neglected to invite him to Rye—accused James of being an "artful creeper into rabbit-holes" and wrote a "piercing shaft" of a letter that James acknowledged to W. E. Norris almost "put the fat on the fire." James, in turn, grew restive over Gosse's "levity," his zest for social climbing among "dukes and duchesses," and the elaborate celebration of holidays and the unceasing social amenities of Hanover Terrace.[7]

Still, the two friends continued to discuss each other's work in public and private. On November 10, 1907, for example, James praised *Father and Son* as "extraordinarily vivid and interesting, beautifully done, remarkably *much* done and deserving to my sense to be called . . . the very best thing you have ever written." Gosse, of course, was immensely pleased and gratified. Earlier in 1907, he, in turn, had given James "extraordinary pleasure" on February 2, "more," according to James, "than any Appreciation of any book of mine has *ever* given me," in a "beautiful notice" of *The American Scene* in the *Daily Mail*. And on December 29, 1908, James acknowledged the pleasure he had "extracted" from Gosse's letter about the New York Edition, "one of the very handsomest I ever received. . . . 'One of' indeed, I say?—*the* most precious pearl rather of my crown of recognition. None other, whatever, begins to approach it in lustre or loveliness. The Edition has been a weary grind (such a mass of obscure & unmeasurable labour,) but I feel all you say as the most delightful consequence of it. So I am tenderly grateful for your brave & generous words." James returned the compliment on June 4, 1909, when he characterized Gosse's essay on Swinburne in the latest *Fortnightly Review* as "admirable—delightfully done & very *interesting*; the best, on the whole, I think of your portraits in that kind."

The two friends also exchanged confidences that were not literary in nature though they were frequently of considerable personal importance to each. Both men were forthright about the European political situation prior to and after the beginning of World War I, and it was in this context that James shared with Gosse his decision to become a British citizen and requested that his friend support him with his signature and influence in this move, one of the most important of his life. On June 25, 1915, James took Gosse into his confidence:

The force of the public situation now at last determines me to testify to my attachment to this country, my fond domicile for nearly forty years (40 *next* year,) by applying for naturalization here: the throwing of my imponderable moral weight into the scale of her fortune is *the geste* that will best express my devotion—absolutely nothing *else* will. Therefore my mind is made up & you are the 1st person save my Solicitor (whom I have had to consult) to whom the fact has been imparted. Kindly respect for the moment the privacy of it. . . . But the point, please, is this: that the process for me is really of the simplest, & *may* be very rapid, if I can obtain 4 honourable householders to testify to their knowledge of me as a respectable person, "speaking & writing English decently" &c. Will you give me the great pleasure of being one of them?—signing a paper to that effect? I should take it ever so kindly. And I should further take kindly your giving me if possible your sense on *this* delicate point. Should you say that our admirable friend the Prime Minister would perhaps be approachable by me as another of the signatory 4?—to whom, you see, great historic honour, not to say immortality, as my sponsors, will accrue. I don't like to approach him without your so qualified sense of the matter first—& he has always been so beautifully kind

& charming to me. I will do nothing till I hear from you—but his signature
. . . would enormously accelerate the putting through of the application.[8]

Gosse responded the same day.

I read your letter with the liveliest emotion. It is splendid of you, and
beautifully like yourself, to make this sacrifice for us. You give us the most
intimate thing you possess. It is most moving, and most cheering, a grand
geste indeed.

Now as regards Asquith, I am as sure as I can be about anything that he
will rejoice to be your sponsor. I cannot conceive an objection, and I can
think of no occasion on which he would more certainly desire to express his
own natal citizenship. Don't hesitate to ask him.[9]

James immediately wrote the prime minister and received his consent.
Gosse made his "Statutory Declaration" on July 9, for which he
claimed from James only a signed copy of his "declaration of faith," and
James informed his friend on July 26 that "since 4.30 this afternoon I
have been able to say Civis Britannicus sum!" Four months later, on
December 2, James suffered a stroke, the beginning of his last illness,
and died subsequently on February 28, 1916, less than two months
before his seventy-third birthday.

Gosse's response was immediate and characteristic. On March 4, the
day after James's funeral in Chelsea Old Church, he wrote the *Times*
about James's "incomparable brain" and his "noble and tender heart,"
and concluded, "He was a supreme artist, but what we must remember
and repeat is that he was a hero . . . an English hero of whom England
shall be proud."

Subsequently, Gosse continued to promote James's work and reputation. He was proposed by Max Beerbohm as a prime candidate for the
editing of James's letters and, except for Mrs. William (Alice) James's
opposition, might have edited the correspondence that Percy Lubbock
eventually published. He ended up serving as a consultant to Lubbock.[10] He had saved "more than 400" of James's "precious" letters to all
members of his family, and in 1920 he contributed essays on James to
London Mercury and *Scribner's Magazine*, the bases for a chapter on James
in his *Aspects and Impressions* (1922). He knew the value of James's work
from the 1870s onward and, until his own death in 1928, seldom missed
an opportunity to espouse or promote James in the London literary
world, a scene in which he became an important authority. Gosse was
one of the first important critics to appreciate James consistently
throughout his career and continued in the vanguard, with Howells,

Lubbock, Edith Wharton, and others, after James's death. Their friendship, to quote Edel, may have been a "literary-gossipy" though "genuine" one, but it turned out to be a significant one to both writers for over three decades, a period covering most of their careers.[11]

-*-

James's letters to Gosse have appeared chiefly in Percy Lubbock's edition (1920) and, more recently, in Leon Edel's (1974–1984). Lubbock's includes 28 letters to Gosse, a number of which are excised in part, and Edel's contains 41, 14 of which had appeared in Lubbock's collection. Others have appeared from time to time, but the present edition contains 224 hitherto unpublished letters of James to Gosse.

The letters discuss matters important to both writers, as well as the "mere twaddle of graciousness." Topics vary from grave to gay, and the style from the relative forthrightness of the early eighties to the complexities of James's late manner—from the directness of James's mention of his father's critical condition in 1882 to the ornate description of his decision to seek British citizenship in 1915. The diction is often informal, as when James tells Gosse that his poem will "tickle the old man [O. W. Holmes] in his tenderest part" and even after the diction and sentence structure become more ponderous, as when James alludes (with a twinkle) to the rewards possible to those who support him in his quest for naturalization—"to whom," he remarks, "great historic honour, not to say immortality, as my sponsors, will accrue." Indeed, throughout the correspondence James's use of the vernacular of the day—British and American slang and idiom in particular—demonstrates a wide knowledge of and familiarity with fresh currents in language. He is "under the weather," "real sick," or "feeling poorly," he takes a "great shine" to someone, he keeps his "eye peeled" and becomes "mortally tired," and he knows about "dudes" and "billionaires." He frequently "sits tight," "holds on tight," or "sticks fast" to Lamb House or wherever he may be; he "puts up with" all sorts of inconvenience, and craves a "really endless jaw" or "a good grumble" with Gosse and hopes he is "up to the scratch." Even his characteristic closings of letters are seldom merely the usual trite terms but are instead related in some way to the text of the missive or to his mood at the time. He moves from "very truly yours" and "ever yours" to such personal conclusions as "yours & wife's always-participating" in the late 1880s. By the 1890s, the conclusion is frequently related to some part of the body of the text, as in "yours, if I may safely say so!, ever," though there are still occasional endings of "Always yours" or "Ever your H.J." And during this decade and subsequently, James usually reserves a line for greetings to Mrs. Gosse, as in "a thousand things above all to her who palpitates at your side, from your distant but perfect palpitater in sympathy."

The reader of these letters learns a great deal, not only about Henry James and Edmund Gosse (from James's point of view, of course) and about their lives and careers, but also about the English literary and, to a lesser extent, social and political worlds of the period. All of this is imparted in a style that is consistently and constantly characteristic of the writer and at the same time is clearly sensitive to his correspondent, a style that continues to charm and beguile readers of later generations for whom neither the form nor the substance was devised. Even readers who are not quite those "upon whom nothing is lost" may still test the author's execution and end up appreciating it, even if not quite liking it. For many, indeed, it provides "solidity of specification" for a particularly fascinating part of the human spectacle.

1. For James's published correspondence, see *LHJ, SL, TD*—this collection contains eleven letters of James to Gosse—and *HJL*. See also *LL*, H. Montgomery Hyde, *Henry James at Home* (New York, 1969), and *EG*. In this edition, I am quoting throughout from originals and photoduplications of manuscripts except where noted, even when letters have hitherto been published.

2. My account of the Churton Collins attack is based, in part, upon *LL*, 190–97, and *EG*, 277–97. Gosse also defended himself in an article in the *Athenaeum*, October 23, 1886; Swinburne's views appeared in the same periodical on November 6.

3. James's letter to Howells is quoted in *EG*, 288.

4. Although this letter is printed in *HJL*, III, 316–17, I have quoted from the original (Leeds). The wire that follows is also at Leeds.

5. My account of the production of and response to *Guy Domville* is based, in part, on "The Last of the Domvilles," in Henry James, *Guy Domville*, ed. Leon Edel (Garden City, N.Y., 1960), 78–108. The letters by James quoted in the Introduction, including the one dated December 27 (*HJL*, III, 502), are printed herein.

6. The comment to Elizabeth Robins is quoted in James, *Guy Domville*, 108; Gosse's remark appears in *Aspects and Impressions* (London, 1922), 33. During the period James devoted to the drama (1890–1895), he also produced some of the best short fiction he ever wrote, including "The Pupil" (1891), "The Real Thing" (1892), "The Middle Years" (1893), "The Death of the Lion" (1894), and "The Coxon Fund" (1894).

7. For Gosse's comment, see his letter to James of June 14, 1896 (*TD*, 236) and for James's reference to the "piercing shaft" of Gosse's letter, see James's letter to William Edward Norris (1847–1925) of September 22, 1900. James's exasperation with Gosse's "levity" and the family's social activities is frequently expressed in letters (1899–1913) to Norris at Yale. Many of these letters were printed in *LHJ*, but the passages referring to Gosse were excised, presumably because Gosse himself recommended such editing. There is also a suggestion that James later "betrayed" Gosse. See Thwaite for Arthur C. Benson's report that, in 1915, James lamented Gosse's "grostesque theory of intimacy, his intolerable levity, his application of flippancy to all relations, his dreadful juvenility," yet concluded that "the tragedy of it is that he cares—he cares" (*EG*, 470). Two

months later, however, James approached Gosse first among his many English friends for help with his request for British citizenship, a matter vital to his well-being, which brought him "deep & abiding peace." And two days before his first stroke, James visited Gosse at Westminster on November 29, "the last time he went out" (Gosse, *Aspects and Impressions*, 53).

8. This letter has previously appeared in *LHJ*, II, 480–81, in *TD*, 288–89, and in *HJL*, IV, 762–63, but the present text is based upon the original in LC.

9. *TD*, 290.

10. See *HJL*, I, xvi–xix.

11. *HJ*, III, 83–84.

3 Bolton St. W
                                                              Aug 2*d* [1882][1]

Dear Gosse.

   I am very sorry I go out of town tomorrow, to remain till Tuesday—that is, with the interval only of Friday in town. I am unable,
therefore, to accept your kind invitation for Sunday. But shall come
& see you after I return.

                                             Very truly yours
                                                H. James

   1. Though this is presumably not James's first letter to Gosse, it is, as far as can
now be ascertained, the earliest one extant. Gosse has, early in the friendship,
invited James to one of his already well-known Sundays "at home." James appeared
for the first time at a Gosse affair the following December. See "The Book of
Gosse," a record of guests kept by Gosse from 1875 to 1920. A copy of this
guestbook is available at Leeds. The original is at Cambridge.

3 Bolton St.
                                                              Piccadilly W.
                                                              Dec. 10*th* [1882][1]

Dear Gosse.

   If you haven't already sent me that MS. don't send it. I sail for
America on Tuesday, summoned by the critical condition of my
father, who is dangerously ill.[2] Give me your good wishes across this
wintry *Atlantic*. I don't know the length of my absence—it may be
short, it may last till the summer. Will you kindly communicate my
departure to Howells, & tell him I will write him from Boston?[3] Will

you also please say a very friendly word to Du Maurier for me, & tell him I shall come & see him as soon as I return?[4] I will do the same to you. Excuse my haste—I have still everything to do, & I leave London tomorrow afternoon. This is always my address.

Very truly yours
H. James

P.S. If you have already sent the MS. (i.e. yesterday,) it will be re-delivered to you here on your calling or sending for it, —or rather, I forget, that in that case it will come tomorrow a.m., & I shall have time to send it back.

    1. This letter is printed in *SR*, 571–72.
    2. Henry James, Sr., died December 18. James sailed December 12 and arrived in New York December 21, the day of his father's burial in Cambridge. Since James had been named executor of his father's estate, he remained in the States until the following August.
    3. William Dean Howells, former editor of the *Atlantic Monthly* and author of *A Modern Instance* (1882), was one of James's oldest literary friends.
    4. George Du Maurier (1834–1896) was an illustrator for *Punch* and another old friend who subsequently won considerable attention as the author of *Peter Ibbetson* (1891) and *Trilby* (1894). James wrote an article on him that appeared in the *Century* for May, 1883, and was later reprinted in *Partial Portraits* (1888).

3 / MS Colby

131 Mount Vernon St.
Boston. April 2*d*. [1883][1]

My dear Gosse.

    I ought already to have thanked you for the *Viol & Flute*, which your American publishers sent me down [a] fortnight ago.[2] But I waited, so that I might read the book; which I have now done, with much satisfaction. It seems to me full of art and feeling and fancy, & all sorts of things which I, who never in my life succeeded in turning a couplet, consider with admiration, wonder & envy. It is very modern, as we say, nowadays; too modern I almost think, for poetry— which should always be at a certain distance from us—that is, behind us. Your subjects are antique, but your ingenuity is of the present— which makes me wish all the more that I had but a fraction of it. I am almost terrified by your "culture"! Still, I venture to thank you again, familiarly.

    I hardly know when to think I shall see you. It is probable I shall not leave America before midsummer, & at that time you will be botanizing & poetizing by some eligible stream.[3] But I shall look you up with the return of the dusky season.

I hope you hear sometimes from Howells, from whom I have received but one short note, with no information (to speak of) about himself.[4] I shall be sorry to be absent from London during the weeks that he (as I suppose) intends to pass there & I delegate you, that is, would if I dared, my paternal duties toward him. I will repay you later. I hope your winter has passed happily, & remain with kind remembrances to Mrs. Gosse—

Yours very truly
H. James

1. Printed in *CLQ*, 154. My text, however, is based upon a photocopy of the original and differs in several substantive ways.
2. *On Viol and Flute* (New York, 1883) was Gosse's first collection of poems and had been published in London in 1873.
3. James actually returned August 29, 1883.
4. For Howells, see letter 2, note 3.

4 / MS Colby   3 Bolton St. W.
Nov. 7th 1883.[1]

My dear Gosse.

You & Gilder & the pictures (partially) make a seduction; but I am afraid not an irresistible one. I don't see my way to Dublin within any appreciable period, & I hesitate much to make an engagement which will hang over my head for months & give me bad dreams of printer's devils with a violent brogue.[2] I don't think that *for Dublin* I should be first-rate. (Observe the limited character of that emphasis.) Please therefore excuse me—unless you can postpone the thing till next summer, which isn't likely. I shall console you for my inflexibility the next time I see you—which will be the 1*st* Sunday I don't go out of town.

Yours very faithfully
Henry James

1. Printed in *CLQ*, 158–59.
2. Richard Watson Gilder (1844–1909) was editor of the *Century*, to which magazine both Gosse and James were contributing during this period. The irony of James's reference to "printer's devils" is that he is at this time working on three tales for the *Century*: "The Impressions of a Cousin" (November, December, 1883); "Lady Barberina" (May–July, 1884); and "A New England Winter" (August, September, 1884). See James's letter to Gilder of February 1 [1884], *HJL*, III, 23–24.

5 / MS Leeds

3 Bolton St.
Piccadilly W.
Dec. *26th* [1883?]¹

My dear Gosse.

Your note of yesterday—or rather, I should say, your copious &
friendly letter—gives me real pleasure. It is very good of you to say
to me all those ingenious & appreciative things. I appreciate them, in
my turn, heartily, & am your debtor for that sort of sympathy that
does one good, & which, in fact, when one meets it, is one of the
best things of life.

I am glad you find the paper on Turgénieff something of a pic-
ture.² He was a noble, a really inspiring model, & I am almost feel
[*sic*] as if what I had *not* managed to say in my article was the most
essential & characteristic thing. But if it has an aroma of admiration
& tenderness, it has some justification. He was a pure, beautiful,
delightful mind; & I have never known any one who made upon me
the same kind of impression. The thing, alas, is full of errors, from
my having seen no proof; e.g. Mme Pauline *Pierdot*!—for Viardot.
Yes, I too like what I read the better when I know (& like) the author.
That is partly why I have read your letter with so much pleasure. I
shall look you up again some proximate Sunday. Noël, Noël! Ever
faithfully yours

Henry James

1. Printed in *HJL*, III, 19.
2. Turgenev had died in 1883, and James's "Ivan Turgénieff" had appeared in the
Atlantic Monthly in January, 1884, and was collected later in *Partial Portraits* (1888).

6 / MS Leeds

Paris. Feb. *7th* [1884?]

My dear Gosse.

Excuse the brutal brevity with which I enclose you a small cheque
for the subscription to the gentle Gray.¹ I am for two or three weeks
in this strange land, & have so many things to do that I must wait, to
be loquacious, for the return to London (when I will come & see
you) of yours very faithfully,

Henry James.

P.S. I saw yesterday Edm. de Goncourt, who made use of such a
charming & amusing phrase in speaking of Gustave Flaubert, his

slowness of work, long hours at his table & u fi a tution [?] for the
same. "Il faut vous dire que dans sa journée il y avait innormèment
[*sic*] *de coucheries et d'école buissonière!*"

1. James paid £3 as a subscription to a memorial sponsored by Gosse in behalf of
Thomas Gray. The Gray Memorial, a statue executed by Gosse's friend Hamo
Thornycroft (1850–1925), was unveiled at Pembroke College, Cambridge, in May,
1885. See *EG*, 263.

7 / MS UCLA   3 Bolton St. W.
                                          June *5th* [1884?]¹

Dear Gosse.

I wonder if you can tell me—I don't know—whether I can have a
friend invited for a month to the Savile? The friend is J. S. Sargent,
the painter, who comes over from Paris in a day or two, & to whom
the said Savile will be convenient. (He is to be here a few weeks,
painting some portraits.) I don't know whether one can do this at the
Savile, nor how one does it—& if my young man needs a seconder,
would you very kindly stand as such? and would you still more
kindly drop me a line of instruction? I thank you in advance, & am
ever yours

Henry James

1. According to Leon Edel, James met Sargent in the winter of 1884 (*HJ*, III,
108–13). Sargent's arrival in England followed hard upon the controversy raised by
the appearance of his portrait of Madame X (Madame Gautreau) at the Paris Salon
in May. See Carter Ratcliff, *John Singer Sargent* (New York, 1982), 79–89. According
to James, Sargent was to be in London "for the month of June" (*HJL*, III, 42).

8 / MS Leeds   3 Bolton St. W.
                                          June *9th* [1884]¹

My dear Gosse.

Thanks—many—for your note about *Beltraffio*.² I am delighted
you see some life in it & have an appetite for the rest. Of course it is
tragic—almost (I fear) repulsively so. But the 2d part is better written
than the 1st, & I agree with you in thinking the thing is more solid
than many of my things.³ I feel it to be more *packed*—more complete.
But I shall do much better yet! Meanwhile you obey a very humane
inspiration whenever you murmur *bravo!* in the ear of the much-
attempting & slowly-composing, easily-discouraged & constantly dissatisfied fictionist. Your ever grateful

Henry James

P.S. Perhaps I *have* divined the innermost cause of J.A.S.'s discomfort—but I don't think I seize, on p. 571, exactly the allusion you refer to. I am therefore devoured with curiosity as to this further revelation. Even a post-card (in covert words) would relieve the suspense of the perhaps-already-too-indiscreet—H.J.

1. This letter is printed in *SR*, 572–73.
2. Gosse had provided the donnée for James's "The Author of Beltraffio," a tale that was currently appearing in *English Illustrated Magazine* for June and July, 1884. See *N*, 57–58.
3. Gosse had known John Addington Symonds (1840–1893) and had told James about Symonds' differences with his wife over the eduction of their son, which provided the germ of James's tale. He had also suggested something about Symonds' homosexuality, the presumable cause of Symonds' "discomfort" mentioned in the postscript; the paginal reference is apparently to the first installment of James's story as it appeared in *English Illustrated Magazine*, I (June, 1884), 563–73. See *HJ*, IV, 125–27. James had written Symonds on another matter on February 22, 1884. See *LHJ*, I, 106–107.

9 / MS Colby   3 Bolton St.
                                                  June 24*th* [1884?][1]

Dear Gosse.

   I am greatly obliged to you for seconding my young man in the face of your scruples, & feel that my request was truly indiscreet. When I made it I had not the least idea it was irregular—or of course I would have forborne. I supposed that seconding (for a short introduction) was a mere matter of form, & that knowing the proposer, for the seconder, was tantamount to knowing the individual invited. This is the case at the Reform, where my limited observation of club-manners has mainly been acquired, & where, since I have been a member no one that I have proposed has (so far as I recollect) been seen either before or after by the member seconding. In a smaller club, however, it doubtless matters more—as it should do, & I shall be more regular in the future. Thanks again for your stretching the point. My invité shall be taught to dissimulate—or, rather, to simulate, & I think I can promise you that no catastrophe will ensue.

   I was just about to answer your note about Sunday next. I have promised to pay about—"29 distinct damnations," as Browning says, on that afternoon—but am not without hope of arriving, more blessedly, at Delamere Terrace, & somewhat latish.[2] I will bring Sargent if I can put my hand on him, & at any rate you must come & meet him at dinner as soon as I can get him to name a day.[3] I will then propose it to you.

Yours ever
Henry James

1. This letter has been printed in *CLQ*, 160–61, but since it is there incorrectly dated and contains several other errors, I have used a photocopy of the manuscript as text. For the dating of this letter about John Singer Sargent, see letter 7, note 1.

2. "Twenty-nine distinct damnations" is referred to in "Soliloquy of the Spanish Cloister," l. 51. Gosse lived at 29 Delamere Terrace, Westbourne Square, from 1876 until he moved to 17 Hanover Terrace, Regent's Park, in 1901.

3. See letter 10 for James's dinner invitation that would bring Gosse and Sargent together.

10 / MS Leeds

3 Bolton St.
Piccadilly
July 18*th* [1884]

My dear Gosse.

I hope very much indeed that you can dine with me on *Monday* next at 8, at the Reform Club, Pall Mall. I expect only two other men, Sargent & Paul Bourget[,] an amiable Frenchman who has written books.[1] Excuse the shortness of my notice—Bourget is the cause of it. Do come.

Ever yours
Henry James

1. Bourget (1852–1935), a novelist whose *Cruelle Enigme* (1885) would soon make him well known in France, was introduced to James by Sargent.

11 / MS Colby

Dover, 15 Esplanade.
Sept. 9*th* [1884][1]

My dear Gosse.

Being in town for a few hours yesterday I found your poetical tribute to Dr. Holmes which you had been so kind as to send me (it hadn't been forwarded) & which I read with much applause.[2] It is charmingly ingenious, very felicitous, quite true enough, & altogether a very pretty idea very prettily rendered. It will tickle the old man in his tenderest part, & he will embrace you, in Boston—if fate is still to carry you there. I am immersed in unsociable seclusion, & (I am happy to say) sadly belated work, at this agreeably-dull little place, where I have a delicious absence of acquaintance & a still more delicious presence of leisure for a pressing task.[3] I shall remain here (unless bad weather drives me away) for the greater part of this month. I wonder whether you wouldn't come down & spend 36 hours with me? I can offer you a lonely cot & a simple, wholesome victual: in short a very modest but very cordial hospitality; almost any date would suit me. I fear you are in town (from something you said to me of your plans) pegging away at lectures & much driven by the same. Kindly remind me of your date of sailing for the U.S. I must see you before that, even if it be sooner than I suppose (my supposition placing it in *November*?)[4] I hope you are well—& "sustained" under pressure. Thanks again for the elegant verses—I envy you your rhyming touch!

Yours ever
H. James

1. Printed in *CLQ*, 159–60. Internal evidence—the dates of the poem to Holmes and Gosse's trip to America—indicates that the year is 1884.
2. Edmund Gosse, "An Epistle to Dr. Oliver Wendell Holmes, on his Seventy-fifth Birthday," *Critic*, n.s., August 30, 1884, p. 102. See also *TD*, 30.
3. James was working on *The Bostonians*, a novel that was to appear in the *Century* (February, 1885, to February, 1886) and then in book form (1886). By October 1 he had sent the first installment to the magazine (*HJ*, III, 121).
4. Gosse delivered a series of winter lectures at the Lowell Institute in Boston and was in America from November 29, 1884, to January 27, 1885. See *TD*, 10–19.

12 /MS Harvard   15 Esplanade Dover
Sept. 18th [1884?][1]

My dear Gosse.

Your note alarms & distresses me & makes me wish doubly that you might smoke a cigarette on my balcony. I am very sorry indeed to hear that you are so abominably overworked. Your account of the time you have lacked a decent holiday is quite appalling & makes me fear for your health & reason!—makes me also value still more my own privilege—to which you allude—of carrying my scribblement to the seaside or elsewhere.[2] If I had the competence for which you express a wish, I should be almost capable, in my sympathy, of dying to bequeathe it to you—or of living to share it with you.[3] I won't add another pang to your condition by saying that the weather, the sea, the breeze just now, here, are enchanting & that if you should feel on Saturday afternoon more free than you have been, & wld. telegraph me a little in advance, I shld. be delighted to help you to rest till Monday. It is all I can do for you here but that heartily. I have a little room & a little plate for you. Yours ever

Henry James

There is a train from Victoria at 4.20 & one from Charing X at 4.30.

1. Several facts point to 1884 as the year of this letter. James spent most of September, 1884, in Dover, and though he also spent part of September in 1885 at the same address, he was in Paris, too, during September, 1885. Gosse, moreover, as Thwaite points out, "spent a hard-working, almost holidayless year in 1884" (*EG*, 147). During the summer and early fall, he was preparing the lectures he delivered at Cambridge, beginning October 25, and at the Lowell Institute in December and at Johns Hopkins in January, 1885. Finally, the content of letter 11 relates closely to that of letter 12.

2. James often took his work "elsewhere" until he eventually acquired Lamb House and moved there in 1898. Despite his complaint, Gosse traveled frequently throughout Britain and on the Continent, and though he was not always "on holiday," he often was.

3. Gosse may have thought that James's share of his father's will was greater than it was. Actually, however, part of James's inheritance was put in a trust for his brother Wilky's family, and his share of the annual income from the estate he "made entirely over" to his sister Alice (*HJ*, III, 64–65).

---

13 / MS Leeds   3 Bolton St. W.
                                                     Jan. 28*th* [1885]

Dear Gosse.

I don't know exactly when you are due, but I send a word, at a venture, to welcome you back to old England, & to beg you to send me a line of notification that you will dine with me at the Reform Club, at 7.30, alone, one of your 1*st* free evenings (any one you fix) to relate your adventures.[1] Perhaps you are even now on the bounding main—*felicissimo ritorno*! & the same to Mrs. Gosse.

Ever yours
Henry James.

1. Gosse had sailed from America on January 27. See letter 11, note 4. He wrote Howells on February 15 that he had dined with James "last week" (*TD*, 164).

---

14 / MS Leeds   3 Bolton St. W.
                                                     Feb. 7*th* '85

Dear Gosse.

I am delighted to have news of you & to re-iterate my welcome.[1] I

am engaged to dine every day till *Wednesday*; but I shall look for you
on that day, *11th*, at *7.30* at the Reform Club. Don't dress, unless you
prefer it. I will come in for tomorrow afternoon for ½ an hour if
humanly possible; but if I don't turn up please know that I have a
dozen urgent visits to make which I can only achieve on Sunday
afternoon. Kind greetings to Mrs. Gosse.

Yours ever
H. James

1. See letter 13. The subsequent remark about dress is the first of many later
statements about attire.

15 / MS Leeds   3 Bolton St. W.
Feb. 25*th* [1885]

Dear Gosse.

Your *Gray* is a very noble & munificent present, as well as a very
beautiful & (evidently) very perfect book.[1] I thank you for it in all
friendship. It will be jolly to read over the letters (I have some of
them in a little Pickering edition) on your handsome little page. But
what a devil of a work your *4th* vol. must have been! Bravo & merci!

Ever yours
Henry James

1. Gosse's edition of *Works of Thomas Gray* (4 vols.; 1884) had recently appeared.
The fourth volume contains notes and commentary on Plato and Aristophanes.

16 / MS Leeds   3 Bolton St. W.
April 16*th* [1885]

My dear Gosse.

I leave town on Saturday for 2 or 3 months—so that I am very
sorry to say I shall not be able to come in on Sunday. I am not going
abroad, but into the country & for all sorts of reasons. I think I told
you this before. For the same cause I shall not be able to be at Cambridge the 26*th* of next month.[1] It would be rash in me to undertake
it: my immediate future is too obscure. Will you express to the Master & Fellows of Pembroke, my many thanks, my great sense of the
honour they do me, & my extreme regret at not being able to lunch
with them? I shall be infinitely obliged to you. I have lately read over
in the beautiful copy you so munificently gave me, all Gray's let-

ters—with a high & renewed sense of his delightful mind & style, & an admiring wonder at your industry & care as an editor. What an arduous piece of work the 4 vols. must have been, & what a relief when you had got rid of them.[2] I am very sorry not to see you again before I depart, and I shall make it up later. I have been reading American statistics about Miss Murfree—that she is 4 ft. 7 inches & ¾'s in stature, &c.[3] Who shall say we don't live in a literary age! I shall be the next fortnight (or less) at Bournemouth, & shall see Stevenson.[4] All my greetings & regrets to your wife. Ever your

Henry James

1. The date of the unveiling of the Gray Memorial at Pembroke College. James had subscribed to the project. See letter 6, note 1.
2. James refers to the Gray edition in letter 15.
3. Mary N. Murfree (1850–1922) had since 1878 published fiction in the *Atlantic Monthly* under the name of Charles Egbert Craddock, and her *In the Tennessee Mountains* (1884) had been well received by critics and public alike. Miss Murfree's identity as the author of the stories by Craddock had been revealed a few weeks earlier at a dinner given in her honor in Boston by the Thomas Bailey Aldriches (Aldrich was the editor of the *Atlantic Monthly*). See Edd W. Parks, *Charles Egbert Craddock (Mary Noailles Murfree)* (Chapel Hill, 1941), 124–25. See also William Dean Howells to Gosse, March 9, 1885, in *TD*, 167.
4. James had met Robert Louis Stevenson in 1879, presumably at the same time he met Gosse, and their friendship by this time was close and warm. See James's letter to Thomas Sergeant Perry, September 14, 1879, in *HJL*, II, 255. Gosse had known Stevenson since 1870, though their friendship actually began in 1874 (*EG*, 91).

17 / MS Leeds

St. Alban's Cliff
Bournemouth
May 27th [1885]

My dear Gosse.

Many thanks for the photographic memento (admire that phrase) of your brilliant function of yesterday, from which I was so reluctantly & mournfully absent. The speeches were most graceful, & the whole affair must, I think, have wafted a balmy breath to the present mansion of the beloved Thomas. Thornycroft's bust strikes me as a charming, refined creation, & if he wasn't like that he certainly ought to have been.[1]

Your allusion to the donative Americans (in the circular) is in your best style, & I am especially grateful to you for your kind mention of my (as I suppose) beauty!

R. L. Stevenson, here, is the consolation of my existence, &

l'emptor de mes soirées, in rather a sad episode. He is presently going up to town for a week, to Colvin's.[2] Consumptively, I take him to be really much better than at former periods: conversationally, he can't improve. Do let me know if you hear anything of interest from W.D.H. about his connection with the Osgood infamy.[3] I hope you are in health & prosperity—I am looking out for your return. Ever yours very faithfully

H. James.

1. Hamo Thornycroft's bust of Thomas Gray, the so-called Gray Memorial, had been unveiled on May 26. See letters 6 and 16, note 1.
2. Sidney Colvin (1845–1927) was one of Stevenson's closest friends. He subsequently edited an edition of Stevenson's works (1894–97) and his letters (1899, 1911).
3. The failure of the firm of James R. Osgood and Company, a Boston house that published work by both James and Howells, led to losses for James (*HJ*, III, 145), but Howells, according to Edwin H. Cady, "lost nothing" (*The Realist at War: The Mature Years of William Dean Howells, 1885–1920*, [2 vols.; Syracuse, 1958], II, 1–2).

18 / MS Leeds

3 Bolton St. W.
Nov. 21*st* [1885]

Dear Gosse.

I am back in London, this 2 or 3 weeks, & despair of seeing you very soon unless you have the courage to dine with me alone some day next week. Thursday or Friday would suit me best, if either of them suit you. Do come—I want to have a crack with you—& we shan't need any one else's society. I have been until the other day in Paris. I wish Mrs. Gosse could dine at a club; in that case I shld. perhaps persuade her to honour me. *Reform Club*, 7.30, Thursday or Friday; & don't dress unless you have a prejudice that way.

Yours ever, dear Firdausi[1]
Henry James

1. Gosse's collection *Firdausi in Exile and Other Poems* appeared in 1885, though the title poem itself had been completed in 1881 and first published in 1883. See *LL*, 509, and *EG*, 229, 231.

19 / MS Leeds

3 Bolton St. W.
January 28*th* [1886]

My dear Gosse.

Your kind note should have been answered yesterday, but that I was unwell and couldn't put pen to paper.

I have indeed kept watch & ward over Saturday week *6th*, & shall be delighted to dine with you at Trinity on that day, at 7.15. I shall take the last train to Cambridge that will bring me in time—without running it unduly close—for that function. You, I assume, will already be there.[1]

I will come in with pleasure on Sunday if it is humanly possible. I have about 375 social duties to perform on that afternoon, but shall strain toward Delamere Terrace. Ever faithfully

Henry James

1. Gosse had been appointed Clark Lecturer at Cambridge in 1884 and had begun his two-year appointment on October 1 of that year. His lodgings were in Trinity College. See *EG*, 248.

20 / MS Leeds   34, De Vere Gardens, W.
                                  Saturday a.m. [August 7, 1886]

My dear Gosse.

I throw myself on your charity for the hour. I received last night a telegram from Sidney Colvin, which I haven't yet answered, telling me that Louis Stevenson is staying with him & asking me to dine with them either tonight or tomorrow.[1] I am engaged in the country tomorrow, & there remains only tonight to see the seductive Louis. Would you be much inconvenienced by my proposing that we put off *our* dinner till next week, when, at any rate, independently, of our tête à tête I want you—on *Thursday 12th*—to dine with me to meet Guy de Maupassant?[2] I hope you are not to be absent after Sunday. I am to remain in town all this month & next; & shall find frequent occasion to repair my loss of tonight—for which I shall propose a very early compensation. I don't specify that date now, as I go away on a 48 hours' visit on Monday—& shall count upon you for the Maupassant dinner for Thursday. I will apprise you before that of the hour & place of the latter. I have a vague idea of Greenwich.[3] Think me not rude—I should have been too sorry not to see Stevenson at all—& believe me ever faithfully yours

Henry James

1. For Sidney Colvin, see letter 17, note 2.
2. James had known Maupassant (1850–1893), the well-known French fictionist, since the mid-seventies.
3. The dinner took place in Greenwich on Thursday, August 12. See letter 21 for guests and other details.

21 / MS Leeds   34 De Vere Gardens
                                                    Thursday noon. [August 12, 1886]
My dear Gosse.

I will explain to you this evening the cause of my delay in letting you know time & place for dinner. They are connected with uncertainties on Maupassant's part; but it is now settled that we go to Greenwich;—& I beg you therefore to find yourself at the Westminster Bridge steamboat pier at *5.15 sharp*, for this purpose. I will meet you there. I hope this tardy notification will not inconvenience you—as you will want to take your overcoat. No dressing, of course. We shall be ["]Du Maurier, Maupassant, one of the French (or rather Italian) Bonapartes, vous & moi."[1] *Give my messenger a word to show you twig.*

                                                    Ever your
                                                    H. James

1. The dinner had been mentioned in letter 20. For Du Maurier, see letter 2, note 4. The Bonaparte was Count Joseph-Napoléon Primoli (1851–1927), a grandson of Napoleon's brother. See *HJ*, III, 174. James refers to this occasion many years later in letter 296, dated January 21, 1914.

22 / MS Leeds   13 De Vere Mansions West, W.
                                                    Aug. *28th* [1886][1]
My dear Gosse,

Would Tuesday or Wednesday night, next, 31*st* Aug. and 1*st* Sept., do for our dinner? I shld. be very happy on either occasion, or on Thursday 2*d*, either. Tout à vous.

                                                    Henry James

I am reading your *Raleigh* with breathless admiration & interest. It seems to me wondrous well done.

1. The days and dates given by James in the first paragraph of this letter are correct for 1886; this year also seems the likely one since he is reading Gosse's *Raleigh*, a book that appeared in 1886 in London.

23 / MS Leeds   34, De Vere Gardens, W
                                                    October 22*d* 1886.[1]
My dear Gosse.

I heartily applaud your letter—it is perfect in tone & taste & temper, it is highly to the point as a vindication, & the last few lines are a gem.[2] You have said neither too little nor too much, & what you have said you have said excellently well. You have been graceful without being evasive, sportive without being flippant, & effective without being violent. (I am almost imitating, methinks, the style that Mr. Collins would recommend!) It will do you great good, & do none whatever to your critic, who on the whole, distinctly, will mainly have succeeded in making you (especially when the dust of the battle has subsided a little) a *plus gros Monsieur* than you were before. Calmez-vous, then, soignez-vous, gird up your loins, do your work & do it better than ever; cease to count your bruises, & be conscious only of the life that is in you. All that will remain of the fray a short time hence will be a general impression that you were ponderously & maliciously attacked by an old friend & that it came out—by which I don't mean it had been hidden before—that you were remarkably clever. Also that all your old friends were not ponderous & malicious. I predict you an "ovation" at Cambridge, & am ever faithfully yours

Henry James

Oh, my asinine compatriot, in last night's *P.G.*![3]

1. Printed in *SR*, 573–74.
2. Gosse's letter had appeared in the *Times* on October 19, 1886, in response to John Churton Collins' slashing review of Gosse's *From Shakespeare to Pope* (1885), a collection of lectures delivered at Cambridge. Collins (1848–1908), a graduate of Balliol College, Oxford, a teacher, and a friend of Gosse's, attacked Gosse's scholarship and critical judgment in the *Quarterly Review* for October, 1886. Despite his comments in this letter, James's usual advice during this period is, as he expresses it on October 26, "never to glance at such stuff." For a full account of this affair, see *LL*, 191–97, and *EG*, 276–97.
3. This is apparently a reference to an "American Correspondent" in the *Pall Mall Gazette* who had written, "At home we do not employ government clerks to teach literature." See *EG*, 293–94.

24 / MS Leeds   34, De Vere Gardens, W.
                                                   October 25*th* [1886]

My dear Gosse.

Would *Thursday* or *Friday* suit you to come & dine—at 8? I should be delighted to see you if either day is possible. I hope you are less & less bothered—in spite of the brutality of the P.M.G.[1] It does you— in the world—positive good—disgusting people with your assailers &

exciting a tender interest in you as one on whom they have let themselves loose.

> Ever yours
> *Henry James*

1. The *Pall Mall Gazette* was printing letters and comment on the *From Shakespeare to Pope* disagreement, and Collins himself (as Oxoniensis) appeared in its columns on October 25 (*EG*, 293–94).

25 / MS Leeds   34, De Vere Gardens, W.
                                                         October 26*th* [1886][1]

My dear Gosse.

I was afraid you wouldn't be able to dine with me—but I sent a word on the chance.

I am infinitely distressed that you should continue to be overturned by this whole beastly business—& yet I understand it, for iteration will drive any man frantic.[2] It is a matter of sensibility, & sensibility is much. All the same, sensibility apart, I really don't see what you have to consider except your own attitude—which I take to be simply that of continued & confirmed interest in your work, & ambition & purpose in regard to the literary life. Don't despair of that or of yourself—& the rest will be of course disagreeable, but still simple & superficial, like having been pushed without warning into a dirty pond, in which one splashes a moment & loses breath. The moment may seem long—especially if one is pushed again—but one scrambles out, as soon as one recovers one's surprise, without having left any vital part whatsoever behind. I repeat that the whole mass of the public *d'élite* feel the greatest sympathy for you as having been made to an almost unprecedented degree the subject of a peculiarly atrocious & vulgar form of modern torture—the assault of the newspaper—which all civilized & decent people are equally interested in resisting the blackguardism of. As for the *stupid* public, one must simply mind that at one time as little as at another. It is always there & is always a perfectly neglectable quantity, in regard to any question of letters or of art. Above all, however, what I wanted to say to you most especially is that I really don't see the smallest necessity for your *knowing* a word more about this odious matter, nor for your reading the newspapers. I can't too earnestly recommend you not to *look* at them—for an instant; I urge this upon you as one who has himself been tried. Under what earthly necessity are you, for

instance, to know what idiotic rubbish on the subject may be shov-
elled out in America? Long ago I determined simply never to glance
at such stuff & both as a man & an artist je m'en porte à merveille.
Avert your eyes—& your nose—& the rest will take care of itself. I
shall come in & see you, if you have time, on Thursday evening
(night)—being engaged tonight & tomorrow. Take my advice, & your
nerves will bloom again like roses in June. Ever, my dear Gosse,
yours most faithfully

Henry James

1. Printed in *SL*, 81–82, and in *HJL*, III, 136–38.
2. This "whole beastly business" refers to the controversy with J. Churton Collins over Gosse's *From Shakespeare to Pope*. See letter 23, note 2.

26 / MS Leeds   34, De Vere Gardens, W.
                                   October 29*th* [1886]
My dear Gosse.

Good for Trinity—good for the Vice Master—good for you. Bad,
on the other hand, for your assailants. I am glad so sad a mistake has
been undone. You will find that Cambridge is robustly with you—
&, as I told you, I shall be much interested to hear *how* you find it.
May this lovely day be a portent of calmer hours. I wish your wife
might be at Cambridge with you, to get the good of it: but I fear she
isn't.[1]

I haven't seen R.L.S. for 2 or 3 days, but I yesterday took his step-
son (it's so queer his having a step-son) to the American legation to
get a passport for the foreign parts to which he is happily being
shipped.[2] Coragio! pazienza!

Ever very faithfully
Henry James

1. The Cambridge response is described in *LL*, 195–97, and *EG*, 294–95.
2. Stevenson's step-son was Lloyd Osbourne (1868–1947), who became a writer,
contributed introductions and prefaces to volumes in several editions—Biographical
(31 vols., 1908–12), Vailima (26 vols.; 1922–23), and South Seas (32 vols., 1925),
among others—and penned *An Intimate Portrait of Robert Louis Stevenson* (1927).

27 / MS Leeds   34, De Vere Gardens, W.
                                   Wednesday morning. [November 3, 1886]
My dear Gosse—

I came home last night from a three day's absence to find your tele-

gram (I never have things forwarded when I go away for 2 or 3 days.)
Your success at Cambridge will by this time be ancient history to
you—but I hope it isn't too late to express to you my *great* satisfaction in it.[1] I knew it would be so—& so may it continue. I trust it has
driven the blue devils—& the others, the black ones, away. I hope
the new Master—do you know him? (I wish he wasn't a parson) will
"distinguish" you.[2] If he wishes to back up his college he will. I
should have been delighted to go & see your wife on Sunday—but
was 150 miles away. Sunday next I also fear to be absent—but I shall
probably call before that. Let me hear more. Bien à vous

H. James

1. For Gosse's "success at Cambridge," see *LL*, 195–97, and *EG*, 294–95. James
had predicted for his friend an " 'ovation' at Cambridge" in his letter of October 22.
2. William Hepworth Thompson (1810–1886), master of Trinity, had offered the
Clark lectureship to Gosse in May, 1884 (*LL*, 161). He died October 1, 1886, and was
succeeded by Henry Montagu Butler (1833–1918).

28 / MS Leeds   34 De Vere Gardens.
                                                   [November 8, 1886]
My dear Gosse.

It is very pleasant to get news of you pitched in the key of resurrection—by which I mean of a return to normal life. (I regard you as
on terra firma again.) I should have liked to hear more about the
Cambridge air—but you must tell me of this when you come back.
Swinburne's diatribe gave me joy—mingled a little with the fear that
his hyperbole might compromise a little his effect. But it is a fine
scalding bath of contempt.[1] Yes, the notice in the Athenaeum of my
"Princess" is singularly discreditable. But this sort of thing is a very
old story to me—I have nothing more to learn about it—& j'en ai pris
mon parti (the *parti*, generally, of unconsciousness, or at any rate of
quick oblivion,) though it disillusionizes one for art & letters.[2] Come
& see me when you return & believe me ever faithfully

Henry James

1. This is James's last known letter of the year regarding the celebrated Collins-
Gosse affair. In responding to Gosse's defense in the *Times* of October 19, 1886, Collins had in the *Athenaeum* for October 30 referred to previous criticism he had made
of Swinburne's work; Swinburne, in turn, had attacked Collins in the *Athenaeum* on
November 6.
2. For the "notice" of the *Princess Casamassima* (1886) in the *Athenaeum*, see No.
3080 (November 6, 1886), 596–97.

29 / MS Huntington

Villa Bricchiere
Bellosguardo
Florence
April 14 [1887]

Dear Mrs. Gosse.[1]

I received some time a friendly card of invitation from you, which made me conscious of the weak side of my present situation. I am on a beautiful hill top, in a picturesque, a vast & vaulted old villa, just out of one of the gates of Florence—& the loveliest view on earth lies before & beneath me, while the divine Italian spring, in its first freshness, gives what, if I were affected, I should call an accent to the scene. None the less I languished for your social circle on the 1st, & this is a word to express my vain regret. I languished the more because at that moment I was in Venice, whose pestilent if romantic emanations had made me ill for a month—so that I had a double reason for wishing I might have exchanged the grand for the little canal.[2] Now that I am on terra firma—& high as well as firm—I am quite as well as my perverse nature ever lets me be. I scarcely expect to be back in London for a couple of months more—but I oughtn't to tell you this, it has such a crowing, tantalizing nasty sound. Unless indeed, it may irritate your husband into answering me back which is just what I desire. I don't write to him directly, because, as I should like so much to hear from him that would seem indelicate. In truth I should welcome any news from your house, which has been hidden from me for so long. I feel very far from London, & though I like it where I am, as they say in Massachusetts, I should like it still better if I could say to myself here that you & the Clark lecturer[3] have not completely forgotten yours very faithfully

Henry James

1. On occasion from the 1880s until his death, James wrote Ellen (Nellie) Epps Gosse (1850–1929), and where the context is significant enough, these letters have been included. The address given is a villa leased by Constance Fenimore Woolson (1840–1894), an American novelist and friend, who sublet it to James in December, 1886. After January 1, 1887, she moved into the villa herself, and James "descended into Florence." In February he went to Venice, but in April he returned to Florence and to Miss Woolson's villa to take the lower apartment while she lived in the upper (*HJ*, III, 200–13).

2. The Gosse home on Delamere Terrace overlooked Regent's Park Canal (*EG*, 165).

3. Gosse remained Clark Lecturer until 1889.

30 / MS Leeds

Villa Bricchiere[1]
Bellosguardo
Florence
April 24*th* [1887]

My dear Gosse.

This won't be much of a letter—but let us make of it what we can.
I made much of yours which came to me three days since. It was
good of you to call back to me—across Alps & channels—so
promptly & cheerily. Apropos of channels how was it that you were
"nearly drowned"? I palpitate for the items & heave a general *soupir*
of relief. Il faut me raconter cela! I have really nothing to relate to
you save that I sit here making love to Italy. At this divine moment
she is perfectly irresistible, & this delicious little Florence is not the
least sovereign of her charms. I am fixed, till June 1*st*, in a villa
which in England would be suburban, but here is supercelestial,
whence the most beautiful view on earth hangs before me whenever
I lift my head—which is one reason why I can only write short letters. The spring is in its flower & Florence is sweet à faire pleurer—
but really, that is my only news. There is nothing personal or literary in the air. The only intelligent person in the place is Violet
Paget—who is so, however, with a vengeance.[2] She has one of the
best minds I know—is almost worthy to be French—& makes one a
little less ashamed of the stupid English race. She is disputatious &
paradoxical, but a really superior talker. I suspect, however, that as a
writer she has gone through all her paces—some of them very lively.
She is trying to throw herself into fiction—for which she has not a
distinct faculty. I will go & see Miss Marzials if I can—but she lives
miles away from me—& *calls* are the scourge of Florence. I have a
vivid recollection of her & her clever talk one evening, at supper at
your house. I met in Venice that queer, uncanny person her brother,
who made, in sooth, a disagreeable, painful impression on me.
Someone mentioned to me that you used to know him well—& you
must tell me, some time, how he comes to be so.[3]

I hear from Howells that he is coming this summer to Paris; but
(once he has put his boy at the Beuxarts) que fera-t-il dans cette gal-
ère? *Mont Oriol* has the supreme quality of *life*—but I don't think it is
du meilleur Maupassant—any more than *André Cornélis* is du
meilleur Bourget.[4] It has no idea—no donnée—except the smutty
one of the waters operating on the sterility of the young wife through

the (*robinet*—I won't use a plainer English word though in connection with water it would be exact,) of the young lover. And that has served many times. Your "crude" compliments to the Princess are quite delicate enough to tickle.[5] I am delighted the air of your life is clear again—I *did* foresee it would be. One has only to hold fast, & it always is.[6] I shall scarcely be in London before July *1st*, but I shall give you a sign as soon as I am.

Ever faithfully yours
Henry James

1. See letter 29, note 1.
2. Since 1884 James had known Violet Paget (1856–1925), an Englishwoman who wrote books under the name of Vernon Lee and lived much of her life in Florence (*HJ*, III, 115). It is worth noting that Constance Woolson is not mentioned. See letter 29, note 1. Apparently James described his living arrangements with Miss Woolson only to a few mutual friends. See, for example, *HJ*, III, 199ff.
3. Gosse had known the Marzialses for some years. Théophile (1850–1920), the poet and composer, he had known since British Museum days in the 1860s, and he had given Émilie, Théophile's sister, the manuscript of his life of Gray (1882) for a Christmas present in 1883 (*EG*, 233).
4. Maupassant's *Mont Oriol* and Bourget's *André Cornélis* both appeared in 1887.
5. Although *The Princess Casamassima* had been serialized in the *Atlantic Monthly* from September, 1885, until October, 1886, it had been published in book form in London on October 22.
6. A reference to Churton Collins' attack on Gosse's *From Shakespeare to Pope*. See letters 23, 24, 25, 26, 27, and 28.

31 / MS Leeds

34 De Vere Gardens W.
August 3*d* [1887]

My dear Gosse.

You gave me leave to put off our meeting of Friday in case of some urgent reason having turned up. I am ashamed to say that I *am* in one of those tight places & that it will ease me off materially if you will allow me to take a day next week, instead, for our dinner.[1] I am not yet able to specify that day—but will propose it to you, with the alternative of one or two others, as early as possible. As we are both to be (as I understand you) straight away in London occasion will not fail. Don't trouble to answer this, but await the further overture of yours disappointedly

Henry James

1. James had returned from Italy July 21 and was "just beginning" *The Tragic Muse*. See his letter of July 23, 1887, to Grace Norton in *HJL*, III, 195–98. The "tight place" may refer to a conflict of social engagements.

32 / MS British Library   34 De Vere Gardens
                                              August 17th [1887]

Dear Gosse.

I went to-day to R.L.S.'s ship, which is at the Albert Dock, about 20 minutes in the train from Fenchurch St.[1] Its sailing has been put off till Monday forenoon, so there is more time to do something. I couldn't, after all, get *on* the ship—as she stood off from the dock, without a convenient approach, & both the captain & the steward, (whom I wanted to see,) were not there, as I was told by a man on the dock, who was seeing some things being put on by a crane, in which I couldn't be transferred. The appearance of the vessel was the reverse of attractive, though she is rather large than small. I write tonight to Mrs. Stevenson, to ask if they are really coming up to to [*sic*] sail—that is if nothing has interfered at the last moment. If they are, there is nothing to be done to deter them, that I see. I shall ask her to *telegraph* me an answer. I shall feel that I must go again (to the ship) as I don't very well see how things are to be sent there. I will telegraph you what she telegraphs me & what I decide to do. Ever yours

                                              H. James

1. This letter is also printed in *LHJ*, I, 129–30. For James's efforts to see Stevenson, see also letter 33.

33 / MS Leeds   34 De Vere Gardens W.
                                             Aug. 19*th* [1887]

Dear Gosse.

I just return home (after telegraphing you) to find your note. I am sorry to learn that my offering is superfluous—for substantial reasons. It will be—literally—champagne upon the waters—which is a worse place for champagne than even for bread!

I doubt whether I shall see poor Louis—having been unable to obtain after various efforts, either sight or sound of Mrs. S. I don't know how to get at him—nor where: which, however, may very well be exactly the state of affairs that he desires to bring about. I know he wishes, at this last crisis, to be left awfully alone.[1]

—Requiescat!—

Do tell me *where* I may see or find the protest of the pure French

Youth. I shall be sorry to miss it. But isn't it all a preconcerted *truc*—
a refinement of advertising?—

Bien à vous
H. James

1. Stevenson embarked for America on August 21, and his ship put in at Le
Havre, whence he wrote James on August 22. See Janet Adam Smith (ed.), *Henry
James and Robert Louis Stevenson: A Record of Friendship and Criticism* (London,
1948), 120.

34 / MS Leeds   Red Barns
Coatham, Redcar.
Thursday.[1]
Aug. 31*st* [1887]

Dear Gosse.

I have been out of town for many days, & your pleasant letter
found me yesterday at Whitby. I should long ago have given you my
news in the shape of a solicitation to dine with me had it not been for
these repeated absences. I expect to be away (coming back to London
but for a few hours) till the 8*th* or 9*th*. Hadn't you better make a note
of it & dine with me at 7.30 on the 9*th*—if you go away yourself on
the 10*th*? I hope your absence is to be brief. After that I shall be,
with God's help, straight away in town, for long. I am charmed with
this fine Yorkshire coast scenery—& Whitby is a delight. I have had
walks almost as good as that famous one last summer.[2] Yes, we will
talk of many things,—including R.L.S.'s verses. It (the vol.) has
some few things of high charm—but I only ½ like his publishing it—
& the verses on me are a source of simple anguish to your more than
ever privacy-loving[3]

H. James

1. Thursday occurred on September 1 in 1887. James often wrote letters after
midnight, and from time to time he confused days and dates. The year is apparently
correct.
2. James had spent some time in 1885 and 1886 with Gosse, Sargent, and a few
other English and American artists in Broadway in Worchestershire. There they
worked "desultorily and took tremendously long walks" (*EG*, 267). For Gosse's own
account of the visit in September, 1886, see *LHJ*, I, 88–89.
3. Stevenson's *Underwoods* (1887) contained "Henry James" and "The Mirror
Speaks," in which James is referred to as "the Prince of men."

35 / MS Leeds   34 D.V.G.W.
                                                   Dec. 24*th* [1887][1]

My dear Gosse—

An impulse not morbid I trust, leads me to send you three words on this (supposedly) genial Xmas eve, in correction of my plaintive accents of last night. Let them serve as a Xmas greeting, & a friendly cheer, to my own address as well as, particularly, to yours. I feel as if I had whined & am ashamed of it—having, as I am resolved, a considerable future in my (as your friend O. B. Frothingham's critic would say,) guts![2] So have you—don't doubt of that! It is a good thing from time to time, in the floundering gallop of existence, to have to take a fence: let us therefore, at these moments, exchange jovial & stimulating cries. There is in all difficulties an excitement which it would be poor to be without. So, in short, I still propose to succeed, & let me have the pleasure of observing that you do the same. Even this dim morning is garish enough to flout, as I recall them, my lamplit remarks, on the celebrated "clique."[3] What I meant was so little that it was scarcely worth meaning at all;—the tongue magnifies things as it wags, & it is all accidental. Heaven bless them all, I wish them, vague as I am about their identity, every compliment of the Season. The same, my dear Gosse, to your intelligent & virtuous house—Greet your wife for me, end the year with me on a fine rich note, & believe me ever much-intendingly yours

Henry James

P.S. If you *should* speak to Besant I don't mind, after all [,] your telling him it is for me you do it. If I profit, in fact, by any suggestion of his, it is better that he should know I owe it to him.

1. Although this letter is filed with the letters of 1888 in the Brotherton Collection, it obviously belongs with those of 1887, as references in letter 36 make clear.
2. Octavius Brooks Frothingham (1822–1895), a Boston Unitarian clergyman, was a founder of the Free Religious Association. James is apparently referring to a discussion of the poor sale of his books and of the possibility of hiring a literary agent. Gosse recommended A. P. Watt. See letter 36, note 2.
3. A reference to the Society of Authors (see letter 46, note 1), an organization James did not much admire, though he and Gosse both were members. Walter Besant, mentioned in the postscript, was a founder of the society. For Besant, see also letter 46, note 1. Besant's pamphlet on fiction in April, 1884, had occasioned James's "The Art of Fiction."

36 / MS Leeds   34 De Vere Gardens W.
                                   January 3*d* 1888.[1]

My dear Gosse.

I went yesterday to thank you for your excellent, friendly service, but found only your most amiable lady. I don't know why, indeed, I should say "only," for I had so charming a chat with Mrs. Gosse that, after the first bitterness of disappointment I was really quite consoled for your absence—especially as my fancy was led on to picture you at a bright convivial scene. I hope you have not returned from it in too cynical a mood to care for my very grateful sense of your quick, kind action in the matter of Mr. Watt. It was immensely obliging of you to take the field with so little delay & I appreciate your benevolence. You are right in supposing that my talk with you the other night made me feel better! It quite set me up, as if I had received a cheque for £1000. I tremble on the verge of Mr. Watt—but shan't write to him till I can ask you, viva voce, 2 or 3 questions about him—as for instance whether I might interview him in a purely experimental or tentative manner, without putting myself in his hands.[2] I am beset with certain doubts & fears. I shall be delighted to come to you *any* evening next week that you may designate—I have very few engagements now. Let me beg Mrs. Gosse graciously to help you to choose one & believe me ever faithfully yours

Henry James

1. This letter is included in *HJL*, III, 210–11.
2. James was dissatisfied with the way his work was being handled by editors and publishers. See, for example, letter 35 and also his letter to Howells of January 2, 1888 (*LHJ*, I, 134–36). James had asked Gosse for his suggestions concerning an agent, and Gosse had proposed, as mentioned in letter 35, note 2, A. P. Watt (d. 1914), one of the first literary agents, who represented, among others, Walter Besant and Wilkie Collins. James subsequently hired Watt, but changed to Wolcott Balestier in 1890 and eventually to James B. Pinker (1863?-1922) in 1899.

37 / MS Leeds   34 De Vere Gardens W.
                                   Jan. 9*th* [1888]

My dear Gosse.

Alas, alas, I mourn for Morison—& am exceedingly touched by his caring to see me at such a time.[1] Of course I will go with eagerness. It so happens that Thursday will be a good deal better day for me than Wednesday: I have promised on Wednesday to take Mrs. Kemble to the afternoon performance of a d—d, or rather damnable, play.[2] On Thursday at 4 I shall be very, very glad to see the poor fellow. Will you kindly say so to him & thank him for the chance?

Ever yours
Henry James

1. James thought J. A. Cotter Morison (1832–1888), British author, "a very charming and clever man." He added in a letter of January 10 [1888] to Grace Norton (1834–1926), Charles Eliot Norton's sister and a favorite correspondent, "Though I have never seen much of him, I have always like him and feel much touched at his sending me a message to come" (*HJL*, III, 214). Gosse was visiting the dying Morison "every second day" (*EG*, 308). For additional references to Morison, see letters 38, 39, and 41. Morison died February 26, 1888. This letter is also included in *HJL*, III, 219.

2. Frances Anne Kemble (1809–1893), daughter of Charles Kemble, was a famous Shakespearean actress who had married Pierce Butler and lived on a Georgia plantation in the 1830s. She had been introduced to James in Rome in December, 1872 (*HJ*, II, 84–85).

38 / MS Leeds   34 De Vere Gardens W.
January 19th [1888][1]

My dear Gosse.

I ought yesterday to have answered your good note about Morison—that is, to have thanked you for it.[2] But when ½ my morning had gone in note writing I had to turn to mercenary composition—& I treated you as familiarly postponable. I went to see the pauvre malade on Tuesday—& found him visibly brighter & seemingly stronger—moving about, making little exertions &c. It is only a vain lure, of course, but one feels as if it were a little gain—a little respite in the *conscious* process of dying. I shall probably go to him again tomorrow. I found Jusserand with him—& he talked to us both vigorously for ¾'s of an hour, & to me (as he had done to Jusserand before I came,) for twenty minutes afterwards.[3] I liked very much the bright little spark of France: just big enough to glow. What opposite poles they represent: the Frenchman three feet long, vivified & vitalized to his finger-tips, & the large Englishman, with a surface like a domain, whose central fire doesn't reach to it or to his extremities, his expressive parts. The Gaul is like one of those squeezed flowers that emit their odour. Excuse these flights of fancy—you will think I take you for a magazine. I have good hope of being able to come in about 5 on Sunday.

Ever yours
H. James

1. This letter is printed in *HJL*, III, 219–20.
2. See letter 37, note 1.
3. Jean Jules Jusserand (1855–1932) and James became good friends. He was, as James observed to Grace Norton on February 5 [1888], "remarkably intelligent and pleasant" and "the *conseiller* of the French Embassy" (*HJL*, III, 216). Jusserand subsequently served as French ambassador to the United States from 1902 to 1925.

39 / MS Leeds   34 De Vere Gdns. W.
                                                   January 25*th* [1888]

My dear Gosse—
  Thank you very much.
  How wretched—how dark & darkening. If he could only pass away![1] It gave me a dismal sense that he was worse (in spite of his walk) his not being able to see me on Monday—knowing how much it is to him to see one. I shall probably go tomorrow, but I scarcely expect to see him. I think we shall scarcely see him more. It is too miserable simply to watch him die.
  Yes I will come in, some evening, soon; & meanwhile note your absence.

                                                   Ever yours
                                                   Henry James

1. The reference is to J. A. C. Morison; see letter 37, note 1.

40 / MS Leeds   [34 De Vere Gardens W.]
                                                   Jan. 30*th* [1888?][1]

Dear Gosse
  I forgot last night to ask you, as I had intended, whether you would not lend me, or send me, the *parts* of the story of yours, in the E.I.M. which you mentioned to me sometime since, & which afterwards I found, on looking for them, I hadn't preserved.[2] I suppose I had them originally—but every now & then I have a closing-out of old magazines. I should particularly *like* to con the tale; & will carefully return you the sheets. If you have them only in the magazine form, (i.e. not detached,) so that they may be too bulky to send by post, I can easily send for them.

                                                   Yours ever
                                                   Henry James

P.S. Further reflection on the Gray-Lowell matter, in the light of what I remember him to have said to me, only confirms my conviction that the Princeton article was an old Harvard lecture of his, written years ago & simply printed *tel quel*.[3] And his essential indolence, which is a vice but not a crime—especially as he is nearly 70 years of age—may very largely account for his not having added anything to it for the occasion.

    1. Although this letter is included with those of 1889 at the Brotherton Library, the year is more likely 1888. January 30 occurred on Monday in 1888, and James frequently visited the Gosses on Sunday night during this period. Moreover, letter 55 is dated January 29 [1889] and obviously does not fall the day before the present letter. Finally, James notes in letter 39 that he will "come in, some evening, soon."

    2. This "story" is Gosse's anonymously published short novel, "The Unequal Yoke," *English Illustrated Magazine*, [III] (April, 1886), 500–12, (May, 1886), 562–76, (June, 1886), 604–15. James's loss of the text of the novel is ironic since, in his effort to persuade the Macmillan firm to publish the magazine text in book form, Gosse indicated he wished to dedicate the work to Henry James. See *The Unequal Yoke (1886)*. Introduction by James D. Woolf. (Delmar, N.Y., 1975), 4.

    3. For James Russell Lowell's article on Thomas Gray, see the *New Princeton Review*, Ser. 5, I (March, 1886), 153–77. When it was collected in *Latest Literary Essays and Addresses* (1891), Charles Eliot Norton observed in a prefatory note to the volume that the "essay was in large part written more than ten years before it was printed in the 'New Princeton Review.'" Lowell became seventy on February 22, 1889.

41 / MS Leeds   34 De Vere Gdns., W.

February 27*th* [1888]

Dear Gosse.

    I heard of the end of Morison's trouble last night from Jusserand, whom I met at dinner.[1] You will already know, probably, that he died yesterday noon— This is a word to say that as *you* will probably receive some information about the funeral, I shall be very grateful if you will communicate it briefly to me.

    —Requiescat. It's a relief—a blessing—but also full of a certain dolorous woe. One is doubly glad, now, of the presence of that nice son, whom I saw & liked 5 days ago. —[2]

    I have designs of looking in at you nocturnally some day at the end of this week. Ever yours

H. James

    1. See letter 37, note 1. Morison died February 26; there was no public funeral. For Jusserand, see letter 38, note 3.

    2. Theodore Morison, presumably. See letter 43, note 1.

42 / MS Leeds   34 De Vere Gdns W
                                   Feb. 28*th* [1888]

My dear Gosse.

Many thanks for your note: I assent heartily to all you say about Morison.[1]

I gather (or rather I definitely understand,) that you won't be in town on Sunday eving [*sic*]. Saturday was the night I was going to propose to you. Friday wd. be impossible for me & Thursday difficult. My 1*st* free day after Sunday wd. be Wednesday of next week. If you *are* in town on Sunday I will come then. Otherwise I will wait. Excuse the incoherence of haste: I *do* understand that you are not in town on Sunday.

Please don't fail to give me any sign that may come to you about Morison's funeral.[2]

> Ever yours
> *Henry James*

1. See letter 37, note 1. Gosse's opinion of Morison is also expressed in a letter of January 16, 1888, to George A. Armour (1856–1936), a Scottish engineer and businessman who lived in Chicago: "The worst news is that Cotter Morison, whose health has long been failing, has now completely broken down. His death, indeed, is now a question of days. . . . In certain ways I shall never see his like again" (*TD*, 209).
2. See letter 43, note 1.

43 / MS Leeds   34 De Vere Gdns. W
                                   February 29*th* [1888]

My dear Gosse—

It's well, & perfectly comprehensible though the poor young Theodore doesn't phrase it à la Sainte Beuve.[1]

Moreover, it's a relief, for the ghastliness of the thing would have been great—& I am very glad you too are spared it.

I am proportionately sorry to see you speak of yourself as "very unwell"—which strikes me as a strange state of things on yr. part. May it speedily pass into something more congruous. I will manage [to see] you one of the 1*st* evenings of next week.

> Ever yours
> *Henry James*

1. The reference, apparently, is to Theodore Morison (1863–1936), son of J. A. Cotter Morison (see letter 41), who had been a student at Trinity College, Cam-

bridge, when Gosse was Clark Lecturer there in the 1880s. See *LL*, 197. Young Morison has probably informed Gosse and James that there will be no public funeral ceremony for his father, a well-known Positivist.

44 / MS Leeds   34 D.V.G.
                                                                May 22*d* 1888

My dear Gosse—

You have my great sympathy in the present tension of your situation. I had not felt "neglected"—pour quoi me prenez-vous?—but had hoped things were well & smooth with you. You show me they are not, so long as the terrible *process* of your poor father's extinction goes on. It is not death that's bad—it's dying. Why can't we be dead—or even be living—without it? I rejoice with you in the change of your father's feeling—or manner; it must make the thing very different. I wish him & you equally the End—& I wish you & your wife nerves & spirits & resistance till it comes—[1]

I go down or up to Cambridge on June 2*d* to spend Sunday with the F. Myerses—may I not hope to find you at Trinity?[2] It will be a specimen of our cross purposes else. But of course you can't say—from one day to another. I have spent this wanton Whitsuntide in town, very peacefully, thank goodness. I passed up to Hampstead on Sunday afternoon & on the way stopped to say a word to Morison's daughters, if they were there.[3] One of them *was* (the younger,) & in the highest gaiety & bloom. They give up the house presently & move into a smaller in the same quarter. I have this a.m. a most characteristic letter from Bourget, who has gone to Venice to write a "grand morceau de vie cosmopolite" with an anglo saxon heroine "ne m'en déplaise." [4] He wants books (peerages, &c) to help him to construct a noble English family, & to know what is the equivalent in England of la retraite dans un couvent. What is?—can you tell him? I fear his anglo saxon (from that) has the same old tendencies. Il ne revient pas from an English girl's, in Paris, having said to him that now Mary is to be married "Vernon cherche une autre amie." He can't get over it, & sees depths within depths in it. And it does somehow make one laugh: even ones so justly lugubrious as you & me— me who am yours & wife's always-participating

Henry James

1. Philip Henry Gosse (1810–1888), the well-known naturalist, died on August 23.

2. Frederick Myers (1843–1901) was the author of the volume on Wordsworth (1881) in the English Men of Letters series, a founder of the Society for Psychical Research, and a friend of William James.
3. J. A. Cotter Morison had died the previous February. See letter 37, note 1.
4. For Paul Bourget, see letter 10, note 1.

45 / MS Leeds   34 De V.G.
                                                        June 4th [1888]

My dear Gosse—
   I return this a.m. from Cambridge to find your charming & impracticable proposal for yesterday. I went for the Sunday to the F. Myerses—& found Cambridge divine.[1] Dined on Saturday eve. with the Master of Trinity &c.[2] Should like so to talk with you of it all— but am engaged *every* blessed night this week. How long, oh Lord, how long—? Shall seek you the *1st* free hour—Want to hear about your Father—about everything[.] Ever yr.

                                                        H. James

   1. See letter 44, note 2.
   2. Henry Montagu Butler was the master of Trinity College; see letter 27, note 2.

46 / MS Duke   34 De Vere Gardens W.
                                                        June 29th 1888

Private
My dear Gosse—
   I am greatly obliged to you for your invitation to the great dinner of the 25th—about which however, I have no more knowledge than what I am helped to by an inference drawn from a paragraph which I saw in some newspaper yesterday—a paragraph to the effect that the Society of authors was to dine certain Americans in acknowledgment of their efforts in behalf of international copyright. *Is* this the origin & purpose of the banquet?[1] If so, alas, I am afraid I can't have anything to do with it. Really, please don't think me ungracious or unsympathetic if I say, thus crudely, that it will be *impossible* to me [to] attend. My reasons are numerous & for myself peremptory. I have in the first place an absolute & immitigable aversion to public dinners, with a chairman, speeches, reports & all the paraphernalia & have taken a most holy vow never again [in] my life knowingly to be caught at one. I think they are great mistakes—a part of the

odious newspaperism of our age—& do more harm than good,
encourage all kinds of humbug and cant. (I speak of the custom in
general, in its multitudinous *usual* applications.) In this particular
case—if I understand it rightly, in the absence of any information
given me on the subject—the mistake strikes me as flagrant & even
practically cruel—prompted tho' it be by extreme good will & hospitality. To give American authors a dinner when the copyright Bill is
not passed—mon cher ami, y-pensez-vous? It would be *torture* for me
to assist at it—it would almost be torture even if the *bad* Bill actually
in process of consideration—though from week to week nothing
appears to come of it—*were* passed. Let me say brutally, & for your
private ear, that I don't see how we—the "American authors"—can
accept the generous & ill-judged invitation without making fools of
ourselves. For me, at any rate, it would be a simply intolerable
ordeal—I am not cut out for such adventures. The thing to do, it
seems to me, is for us to thank the society, in confusion & *pro*fusion,
& scramble away in discretion & humility. My dear Gosse, if such a
manifestation takes place *now*, what would be left for the day our
national shame *is* quenched?—[2]

There are other cogent reasons why I can't be present—first
among which I rank this: that I feel strongly that in the present state
of Anglo-American relations all international *festive* manifestations,
all speechifying & palaver, all effusions & intercompliments in the
heat of the moment, are most short-sighted & dangerous—provoca-
tive of inevitable reaction—later-coming irony & acrimony. Such
things will never make the least difference—the least real difference—when a strain comes up; whereas other things—the quiet
work & the quiet forbearance of individuals—may & does. All that
sort of thing seems to me good only for advertising American
Exchanges & international newspapers & cables & telephones &
other unliterary enterprises.

The sweet flower of esteem between country & country can only
be crushed by such ponderous machinery. Moreover we men of letters are the people in the world who have least need of it; for we have
each of us a far more effective instrument of our own for working
exquisite & magical results. We have only to go about our business
with tact & taste writing better & better books for perusal *de part &*
d'autre, & the trick is played. *That*, it seems to me, will be the only
good way, the only way not vulgar & small, of celebrating the estab-

lishment of international copyright when it *does* come. The dearest wish of my heart—it is really what, as a literary man, I live for—is the coming to pass of such relations between the two countries as that the copyright matter shall be but a drop in the deep bucket of their harmony. This is one of the things that will make most in the world for civilization, & the whole programme of my existence (I think I sufficiently show it) is to contribute my mite to such a consummation. I work only for that—as one must work only to work well—in the long run. Nothing at this hour would give me more pleasure than if an intelligent stranger, deigning to cast a glance on my productions, should say that he was mystified—couldn't tell whether they are the work of an American writing about England or of an Englishman writing about America. I think that even *now* such a stranger might be a little mystified & I believe he will be still more so in the future. *That* I should regard as a practical contribution—as success! Therefore I am not afraid if it be said of me that if for instance I am not present at the dinner of the 25*th* I don't care for what it represents. I simply am conscious that I care with passion—to a tune which many a person saying that would perhaps have little power to conceive. But excuse my long-winded rigmarole. I address you both as the friend (don't wrestle with me, if you love me—*don't*!) & as the member of the committee of invitations. In this capacity please inform the Society that I am most cordially grateful for the honour they have done me in inviting me, but that to my *extreme* regret, & with every appreciation of the intention & hospitality of their project, circumstances over which I have no control render it completely impossible to me to engage to be present on the 25*th*. Ever yours, my dear Gosse,

Henry James

1. The dinner proposed by the Society of Authors and urged upon James by Gosse and subsequently by Walter Besant (1836–1901), one of the founders of the society, was indeed in "acknowledgment" of the efforts of "certain Americans . . . in behalf of international copyright." James Russell Lowell in particular was also sought out. The dinner is an important topic in letters 47–49.

2. James did not attend the dinner, as he wrote Stevenson a month later: "The incorporated society of authors (I belong to it, and so do you, I think, but I don't know what it is) gave a dinner the other night to American literati to thank them for praying for international copyright. I carefully forbore to go, thinking the gratulation premature" (*LHJ*, I, 138). James was right, for legislation concerning international copyright was not passed in America until 1891.

47 / MS Leeds   34 De Vere Gardens W.
                                                         July *6th* [1888][1]

My dear Gosse

Greatly do I commiserate your situation & that of your poor wife. There is nothing to do with our great hard natural debts but to pay them to the last penny—& economise afterwards. But hold on—it always pays, afterwards, to have held on—& simplifications *do* arrive—suddenly—& everything stops & there is relief & a retroactive piety which makes us glad for everything we didn't fail to do. Your father appears to be a veritable Ravager of Life—a sort of domestic Attila or Devonshire Hun! But though he makes a desolation where he passes, the flowers will grow again, quickly on the blighted spots—& he will do little hurt if you don't let him really kill patience—much as he may bruise & bleed it.[2]

I am glad you are not "mad" as they say *là bas*—at my non participation in the dinner. Further reflection has only confirmed my reluctance—& evidence suggested to me even that the banquet may languish & die. Since I wrote to you I have seen Lowell to whom it was primarily offered & who, I gather, is very shy about it—not at all wishing to be publicly thanked for having, as yet, achieved nothing at all. He mentioned to me yesterday that he is to see Besant in a day or two & lay before him the most deprecatory pleas; which I was glad to hear, as I couldn't understand his pure acceptance of the affair—it seemed to me a thing calculated to injure him with the *general* public of the 2 countries—a tumbling into a (however well intentioned) trap for fatuity.[3] I have no objections at all to your showing my letter to Besant—if you think it purged of every scorn. Endless sympathy to your wife. Ever yr.

Henry James

1. This letter is included in *SR*, 574–75.
2. For Philip Henry Gosse, see letter 44, note 1.
3. For Walter Besant and James Russell Lowell, see letter 46, note 1. Lowell attended the banquet and spoke in behalf of international copyright. See letter 49, note 1.

48 / MS Leeds   34 De Vere Gardens W.
July 12*th* [1888][1]

Private
Dear Gosse
Dear Walter Besant
   I feel that I shall perhaps excite on your part a mixture of surprise
& resentment—but in answer to your note just received I *must* again
most respectfully & regretfully plead complete inability. I really *can't*
be present at the dinner on the 25*th* & I am afraid no exhibition of
reasons can make my refusal less ungracious—especially when the
first I put forth is necessarily my fixed rule of never assisting at a
public dinner. I dislike them so much (& the better I love any cause
the more I dislike its connection with them) that I ask myself by
what means I can best do something to discourage them. The only
means open to me I inevitably take. Moreover let me candidly &
confidentially say that I now even less understand the why & the
wherefore & the general *raison d'etre* of the banquet in question.
What is one doing?—what is one in for? I ask myself—not you.
Why, at this particular hour, *should* a dinner be given by the English
authors to the American? I see no reason apart from the extrava-
gantly hospitable impulse of the former body,—& that impulse
seems to me to be exercised at a moment to the awkwardnesses of
which they are blinded by their generosity.[2] I thank you both for giving me a chance to repent; but verily I *can't*! Please believe in the
validity of the reasons that govern my apparent perversity & leave me
to the inglorious enjoyment of it. Most faithfully yours
                                                              Henry James

   1. This letter is included in *SL*, 87–88.
   2. James remains consistent in his objections to the "general *raison d'etre* of the
banquet." See letters 46 and 47.

49 / MS Leeds   34 De Vere Gardens W.
July 14*th* [1888]

My dear Gosse.
   I grieve to say that *am* going out of town tomorrow—from 4 o'clk
till night. But I will come in the 1*st* possible moment next week—I
have things hanging over me, so that I can't say definitely now. But I
will let you know promptly. It won't be the 18*th* or the 20*th*.

I am very sorry the project of the dinner is dropped (as I gather from your note) for those to whom it really commended itself. As for Lowell's action I can't pretend to judge it; but of this I am sure, that he took the only course that he believed to be open to him—I have spoken to him on the matter but once, & then he regarded himself, I know, as "cornered"—under pressure which did him great honour, but which he had not sought, but tried to avoid, as he thought the occasion injudicious. One gets out of such a tangle as one can![1] Ever yours

Henry James

1. The dinner was held on July 25, and Gosse spoke and proposed a toast to "American authors and authoresses" (*EG*, 313). For Lowell's remarks, see the *Times*, July 26, p. 6.

50 / MS Leeds   34 D.V.G.W.
                                               Aug. 1st [1888]

My dear Gosse—

I have waited to thank you for the beautiful big *Congreve* till I had read it—that I might do so the more advisedly. I have now perused it from beginning to end, so that my appreciation of your act is indissolubly commingled with my admiration of your talent. The latter shows in the charming volume to the greatest advantage, and your ability shines in a production which you have made so interesting & so entertaining, with so little material—comparatively speaking—to help you. It is a capital book, full of knowledge, taste, literature & the art of leading on the reader. I miss in it certain things which I shld., perhaps in your position, have tried to say; but I find in it many others which I couldn't possibly have said & which are of the essence of good biography & good criticism. Do more, do more, like this; with your Raleigh, the Congreve ought to constitute for you a brilliant speciality.[1]

I was at your door 'tother night but you were dining out, as usual. I shall awaken the echoes soon again, over your slumbering stream— I am very much localised here. Ever gratefully yours

Henry James

1. *Life of William Congreve* (London, 1888). *Raleigh* had appeared in 1886. Concurrently, James was writing Stevenson: "Edmund Gosse has sent me his clever little life of Congreve, just out, and I have read it—but it isn't so good as his Raleigh. But no more was the insufferable subject" (*LHJ*, I, 138).

51 / MS Leeds   34 De Vere Gdns W.
                                                   Aug. 22d [1888]

My dear Gosse—

I am very sorry to learn that you are again *en pleine crise* & I take
the liberty of devoutly praying, on your behalf, that it may be for the
last time. How terrible to be such a trampled, ensanguined battle-
ground (of life & death,) as your poor father must be—the victim of
so grim & interminable a tussle. His 96 hours' fast is like the doings
of the "early gods," & there is apparently something primitive &
Titanic in his composition. For a strictly human son I can well imagine how discomfortable this may be. I hope before long to hear from
you that he is at rest—& that you & your wife are too—He is not,
after all, an American fasting-man. Your picture of him as Julius II is
very striking. Let me know what further befalls.[1]

Sarrazin befell last night & is tolerably dreadful: a terribly intense,
demonstrative and analytic little 3d rate homme de lettres who would
almost make one like Rider Haggard & take Lang seriously.[2] However, he is intelligent (in France even the 3d rate are,) superabundant
& arch-communicative, & tho' I loathed him at the end of an hour I
almost liked him at the end of three—for he ceased only on the midnight—without pain (to me.) I am staying on & on & on in town—so
I shall be here when you come back. Every assurance to your wife.

                                                   Ever yours
                                                   Henry James

1. Philip Henry Gosse died the next day. For his last hours, see *EG*, 314–16.
2. Gabriel Sarrazin (b. 1853), the author of *Les Poètes modernes d'Angleterre* (1885).
H. Rider Haggard (1856–1925), British author of popular fiction, had already written *King Solomon's Mines* (1886) and *She* (1887). Andrew Lang (1844–1912), Scottish
folklorist, poet, translator, and journalist, had previously translated Homer and
Theocritus, published four or five books of poems, written some fiction—*The Mark
of Cain* (1886), for example—and contributed to many English periodicals. James had
known Lang since the 1870s.

52 / MS Leeds   34 De Vere Gdns. W.
                                                   Aug. 26th [1888]

My dear Gosse—

I can't help participating in your relief—for great it must be. I
hope your father's last hours were not distressing to himself or a tribulation to you.[1] I send you but this word—for you must be full of

immediate cares. When they are over & you are free—unless the saint bequeathes you but another charge, which heaven forbid!—let me hear of it, & if you return—or when you return—to town let me see you. Send me a line & I will come in the evening. I am ever in London.

If you have time or thought for it, look, at your opportunity, into the September *Scribner* for such a pretty, pretty paper of R.L.S.'s on the *Artist*, which, tho' it likens the Man of letters to a Male Bawd, is full of his better felicity, with some things charmingly felt & said—& others *off the mark as usual*.[2]

Requiescat—& requiescas!

Ever yrs
Henry James

1. For James's other remarks on Philip Henry Gosse, see letters 44, 47, and 51.
2. Robert Louis Stevenson, "A Letter to a Young Gentleman Who Proposes to Embrace the Career of Art," *Scribner's Magazine*, IV (September, 1888), 377–81.

53 / MS Leeds   34 D.V.G.W.
                                               Aug. 27*th* [1888]

My dear Gosse.

Thanks for your letter & the portrait of your father, which is very interesting—such a striking stern—such a fine *hard*-type. He looks like a theological male sybil offering the world its choice of heaven or hell, with strong probabilities of hell, in that important volume. How sensible must be the removal of so immitigable a presence. You must indeed have much occupation.[1] But let it, on your return, include the business of finding me. Ever, in haste, yours

Henry James

1. During the period of Philip Henry Gosse's final illness, James is consistently critical of him and sympathetic toward Edmund Gosse and his family. See letter 51, particularly.

54 / MS Leeds   34 De Vere Gdns. W.
                                               Sunday a.m. [December 23? 1888][1]

My dear Gosse—

Could you by any miracle—& if you are not afraid of a very modest dinner, come & break bread with me tonight at the primitive hour of *seven*? I am alone—& there is a solitary fowl. But she shall be dressed with intellectual sauce. I was at your door yesterday at 5.30, but missed you, & alas, Mrs. Gosse. I haven't seen you for months—by my own fault—no doubt. Raison de plus to make it up—for life slips from our grasp. If you can't come to night—come on Tuesday or Thursday at 7—*do*. Then I will give you a better dinner. But tonight is nearer. I am famished for a little literary conversation.[2] In this city of 5000000 souls, but not, alas, brains, I find *none*.

Ever yours
H. James

1. This letter presumably may be dated by the fact that Sunday occurred on December 23 in 1888 and that James had just returned from a two-month trip to the Continent.

2. "Literary conversation" is a vital element in the long friendship between James and Gosse. One can only regret that the two writers lived so near each other that talk and eventually the telephone frequently supplanted correspondence.

55 / MS Leeds   34 D.V.G.W.

Jan. *29th* [1889]

My dear Gosse.

I have waited to thank you for your goodly volume till I should have been able to spend a couple of hours with it in peace and plenty.[1] There has been less plenty than I could have desired, because there has been less peace, but I have the book constantly under my hand & am perpetually dipping into it. It is essentially entertaining & occupying. How pleasantly you write, how well you *say*, &, above all, how much you know! Don't, oh don't, cut up people in the *Saturday Review*; but leave the contemporary feeble utterly alone & produce more of this sort of thing. I shall read every word before I have done. I have perused your very interesting acct. of Ibsen, as I always peruse you when I find you.[2] You must tell me more about I. That is not in this case, female-American for *me*. Long live Mr. Baker!

Ever yours
Henry James

1. The reference presumably is to Gosse's *A History of Eighteenth-Century Literature (1660–1780)* (London, 1889).

2. For the account of Ibsen, see Edmund Gosse, "Ibsen's Social Dramas," *Fortnightly Review*, LI (January, 1889), 107–21.

56 / MS Cambridge   34, De Vere Gardens. W.
                                                         June 23*d* 1889.

Dear Mrs. Gosse.

Your kind & graceful note makes me ashamed to be able to make no better response to it than the gross dull statement that I am engaged. But such is the incongruous fact. On Tuesday 2*d* I am solemnly bound to go down into the country with a friend who is staying with me—E. L. Godkin, of New York—an adventure from which I return, if I survive it, only on the Wednesday a.m.[1] These are hideous truths—but a more pleasing, though not a less melancholy one is that I should have been delighted to dine with you had I been free. Please give my love to Gosse & convert him to this belief. My life is a fitful fever just now, but as soon as it is over, if you will have patience with me, I shall knock, ghostlike, at your door & we will again foregather & talk of the dangers we have escaped & the strange things we have seen. Tell Gosse I expect wondrous tales from *him* & I am, dear Mrs. Gosse, with a blessing on your house, yours most truly

Henry James

1. Edwin Lawrence Godkin (1831–1902), editor of the *Nation* and the New York *Evening Post*, and James had known each other since the late 1860s, when James began contributing to the *Nation*. For references to this visit of 1889, see James's letter to Godwin of September 20 [1889] in *HJL*, III, 258–60.

57 / MS Library of Congress   Hotel de Hollande
                                                         rue de la Paix [Paris]
                                                         Nov. 18*th* [1889][1]

My dear Gosse.

I got your note editorial yesterday, & am considerably bewildered &, I confess, also disconcerted by it. I wrote my tale for Grove several months ago—when the New Review was only a project & its material form was still invisible (my story was originally to have begun to appear in the 1*st* no.) Later, when I had seen the form & dimensions of the magazine I judged it folly to attempt to put serial fiction into the snippets imposed by such limits of space & requested Grove to kindly give me back my MS. that I might publish it in fairer conditions. He flatteringly insisted on retaining it with the assurance that I shld. have nothing to complain of in the condition when it shld. at last appear, & that every deference shld. be paid to

the particular dread, which had more & more taken possession of
me, that the 1st & most ineffective chapter of *The Solution* should find
itself condemned to stand alone as a first instalment, waiting over a
month for its sequel & justification. After that, I never ceased to intimate [to] him that I should be very glad to get back my story nor he
to make the deaf ear. Ten or twelve days ago, sending me proof, he
wrote to me that he saw, fully, for himself what a bad figure the
thing would make with the 1st chapter standing alone, & what a bad
thing it would be for the Review to begin the new feature of fiction
in so inadequate a manner: according to which, though my 2 first
chapters would take a great lot of space, it was absolutely settled they
should go in together, & universal justice shld. be done. I wrote him
back that I was only too sensible of the common prudence of his
course & delighted to rest peacefully in his promise. This promise he
renewed to me on his arrival here. He came into my room day before
yesterday, at 6 p.m., the moment your letter was about leaving London, & talked of the matter further, rejoicing with me afresh in the
fact that it had been so comfortably & favourably determined. Yesterday I breakfasted with him an hour after receiving your note (he is
staying in this hotel,) and on my communicating to him its contents,
he said he would write to you, or I believe, telegraph you, on the
subject. I don't know what he may have done, for I shall not see him
again—he leaves, I believe, today; but I hope some way out of the
difficulty may be found. The "difficulty" (which of course, you may
say, is a graver matter to me than it need be to others,) is that if my
1st chapter goes in alone I shall regard myself as a deeply injured
man. I could have published my tale 5 months ago in two equal parts
& would have asked nothing better than to be free to do so. The division I made for Grove after I saw what the Review was to be (I had
done another thing for his 1st no. & had measured his page,) I made
perfunctorily, sceptically & provisionally.[2] Excuse me, my dear
Gosse, for deluging you with this historical retrospect; but grief is
wild & verbose. When Grove told me you were to edit in his
absence, I aboundingly rejoiced for you, for I thought it would
amuse you & I hoped it would enrich you. Little did I know how
much it might amuse you (for I believed the question of the *Solution*
quite at rest,) at my expense, nor how soon I should be beguiled into
the reflection that it must be dreadful to be an editor. I shall lend, on
my return, a most sympathetic ear to your confidences on this point.

That return is to take place on one of the first days of next month. You must come & dine with me soon after & I will be as anecdoctical [*sic*] & impressionistic as I can about Paris. By way of preparing myself I am going this instant to breakfast with Coppée.[3] It is already time—hence the incoherent haste of my letter. I shall send this to your official residence; but let it carry soft messages to Delamere Terrace.

Tout à vous, my dear Gosse,

Henry James

1. The text of this letter is printed in *SR*, 575–76.
2. For "The Solution," see the *New Review*, I (December, 1889), 666–90, and II (January–February, 1890), 76–90, 161–71. T. N. Archibald Grove (d. 1922) was editor of the *New Review*.
3. François Coppée (1842–1908), French poet and dramatist, had recently published *À Brizeux* (1888) and *À l'Empereur Fréderic III* (1888).

58 / MS Leeds   January 24*th* [1890][1]
Dear Gosse

Tante grazie for your little illustration of the misplaced vigilance of B.M.'s.[2] It reminds me (I don't really know why) of an anecdote I just heard of an answer made by the irrepressible Whistler to a lady who asked him (àpropos of his late idiotic public squabble with Oscar Wilde,) why he couldn't "let sleeping Oscars lie."—"Ah, he won't sleep & he *will* lie!"—[3]

À bientôt
Ever yours
Henry James

1. There is no address given for this letter. Reform Club stationery is used, but the club's name is crossed out.
2. This may be a reference to Brander Matthews (1852–1929), American author, critic, and teacher who had known Gosse since the early 1880s; the British Museum is a less likely possibility.
3. The "irrepressible Whistler" is, of course, James A. M. Whistler (1834–1903), the American expatriate painter and etcher. For the "squabble" with Wilde, see H. Montgomery Hyde, *Oscar Wilde: A Biography* (New York, 1975), 130–31.

59 / MS Leeds   34, De Vere Gardens, W.
                                             August 20*th* [1890]
My dear Gosse.

I have been back some days, & have been intensely meaning to

communicate with you. Before I could turn round a friend who had
rendered me hospitalities in Florence arrived to *stay* (observe the
fierce italics) with me, is with me still & the end is not yet. This has
taken me up much—but it is the least—my hands have been full of
domestic & personal complications which have kept me from D.T.
[Delamere Terrace]—I don't mean *delirium tremens* (I *have* almost had
them) but Delightful Terrace.[1] And now, to finish, I have to go
tomorrow to *Yarmouth*, on mysterious business (I'm speculating in
bloaters,) & proceed then, all across England, on Saturday, to Liverpool, to meet the *Etruria*, freighted with a female friend. I shall have
to take some ten-hour Sunday train back to town, & Friday with you
therefore, is a forbidden fruit. But the very 1*st* hours of next week I
shall communicate with you—I want awfully to hear your news. Forgive my want of amiable catchability—my spirit is with you. Count
on me for the 1*st* possible day. Ever yours

Henry James

1. James had recently returned from a trip to Europe (mostly Italy) begun in
May. In Florence, he had visited Dr. W. W. Baldwin, an American expatriate and
friend, and upon James's return to England, Baldwin visited him in London. The
"personal complications" refer to James's sister Alice's illness. She had summoned
him from Italy, and he was making arrangements for examinations by physicians
and for her removal from Leamington Spa to London. See *HJ*, III, 285–86.

60 / MS Leeds   34 D.V.G,W.
Sept. 20*th* [1890]

My dear Gosse.

Many thanks for the pink international volume (very neatly translated,) with the felicitous preface & the citation from one on whom
not even the most delicate attention is lost. I hope the whole series
will continue to bloom rosily.[1] I pray you may be doing the same, &
have left behind you every memory of every *malaise*. I enclose a note,
lest you haven't heard. How we shall pump the young Lloyd![2] You
must, if possible, dine with him here. I have even offered to "put him
up"—which I consider magnanimous. All to you & to yours

Henry James

1. The preface, apparently, is to Eleanor Marx-Aveling's translation of Ibsen's *The
Lady from the Sea* (1890). See *EG*, 341.
2. For Lloyd Osbourne, Stevenson's stepson, see letter 26, note 2.

61 / MS Leeds   34, De Vere Gardens, W.
                                             Sept. 24*th* [1890]

My dear Gosse.

Your genial letter from St. Ives gave me some bad moments of
envy & *Sehnsucht*.[1] But I am able to congratulate you disinterestedly
on those it represented on your own part. I make an eager note of so
happy a refuge—but I wish we could have got, or could get, a
romantic walk or two there together. How little one catches, or con-
verts to one's purpose or pleasure, as it passes of this horribly *limited*
Life: it all seems made up of mere missings & losings—fleeting con-
ceptions of possibilities already defeated & opportunities already
flown!

I had just sent you a word to thank you for your robust god-child
of a book, & to mention to you, *via* S.C., the scrap of definite news
about Louis S., which I suppose, in the effulgence of the sunfaced
Lloyd, will widen to a larger day.[2] I send this into the country of the
Delameres, where let it greet you both tonight with a welcome. In an
hour or two I go for 2 days to *Sheffield* for 2 Rehearsals! We have a
devil of a life, in *my* profession: but we don't speak of it, except to
you.[3] I shall come one of these very next nights to see you—but I
would rather you come, if you don't dread the quasi-solitude of it [,]
to dine with me, at 7.30, either Tuesday, Wednesday, Thursday or
Friday? Ever yours

                                             Henry James

1. The Gosses were visiting the Leslie Stephens at St. Ives. See *EG*, 334.
2. S. C. is Sidney Colvin, one of Stevenson's closest friends. See letter 17, note
2. Lloyd Osbourne is Stevenson's stepson. For the "robust god-child of a book," see
letter 60, note 1.
3. The reference is to the theater and to the rehearsals of James's *The American*, a
play scheduled to open in Southport on January 3, 1891. James is now well into what
Edel has called "the dramatic years," 1890–1894, and he was frequently of two minds
about the theater, as, for example, is suggested in the ironic underscoring in "*my*
profession."

62 / MS Leeds   34 De Vere Gardens W.
                                             Sept. 27*th* [1890?]

My dear Gosse.

It will give me great pleasure to dine with you on Tuesday 4*th* at 7.
o'clk.[1]

I enclose a letter I have just got from R.L.S. which doesn't tell as

happy a tale as one could wish & as was promised till just before
they arrived. Colvin got a letter written while they were still at sea,
singing triumph in spite of loathsome discomfort—but his cold was
taken after that.[2] I wish they could put to sea again & sail for a year.
Would you return the wild & vivid pencilling to yours ever

Henry James?

1. Since the reference in James's next sentence to the Stevenson letter indicates in
all likelihood that the year is 1890, there is some confusion about James's mention of
"Tuesday 4*th*." In 1890 October 4 occurred on Saturday. November 4, on the other
hand, did occur on Tuesday. James may, of course, have confused the October day
or date or both.

2. The letter from Stevenson is dated August, 1890, and printed in Smith (ed.),
James and Stevenson, 190–92. For Colvin, see letter 17, note 2.

63 / MS Leeds   The Reform Club
                                          October 2*d* [1890]

My dear Gosse.

I am glad you are struck with Hennequin, in spite of his detestable
style.[1] It *is* most objectionable—but is kept from being absolutely
insufferable by the fact that its clumsiness is produced by a real
quantity of thought & not by a simulation of it—like the awful prose
manner of Swinburne, say. He is very strong & full & deep—I
think—& it is a wonder, the pitch to which he carries or tries to
carry characterization,—*does* carry it, in the paper on Tolstoi. But I
doubt if it be a pity he died—think what such a style seemed on the
way to become! But how the whole scope of his effort makes one
blush for *our* "critical school!"

I hear nothing of the young Lloyd.[2]

Ever yours
Henry James

1. Émile Hennequin (1858–1888), French critic and author of *Études de critique sci-
entifique* (1889), in which Leo Tolstoi is discussed.

2. Lloyd Osbourne, Stevenson's stepson, finally appeared later in the month. See
letter 64.

64 / MS Leeds   34, De Vere Gardens, W.
                                      Oct. 17*th* [1890]

My dear Gosse

I have waited to thank you for the beautiful blue biography till I should have had time to master its contents. I finished it this morning & lose no time in expressing what I owe you & how skilful & resourceful you strike me as having been in your rendering of all the quotations of verse.[1] Some of them read like Browning—I mean *du meilleur*. How I wish there had been more of these, especially from Brand & P. Gynt. Isn't the author's account of the latter surely quite exasperatingly inadequate? It is indeed no account at all—only a vague descant, without illustration, on the character of the mystic Peer. The book is interesting & earnest; but provoking throughout by its general ill-distributedness. But how respectably translated. And how provincial all those poor dear Norsefolk, including the Colossus himself. They all affect me like intensely domestic fowl clucking behind a hedge—the big bristling hedge of *Germany*.

I hope you found Lloyd Osborne—I saw him but an hour here; he was leaving for N.B. that evening, & my response to you had much guesswork.[2]

I applaud you for the note struck last night in the St. James's.[3] I am in a perfect panic lest all the vulgarity you refer to shld. simply undermine our getting *any* returns at all. But our race is Doomed for disinterested art. The very sense of it is dead & the handwriting is on the wall. I am coming to see you ces-jours-ci. Ever yours

Henry James

1. Gosse translated the quotations from Ibsen in Henrik Jaeger's *Life of Henrik Ibsen* (London, 1890). See *EG*, 341.
2. For Lloyd Osbourne, see letters 61 and 63. The name is frequently spelled "Osborne."
3. For Gosse's comment, see *St. James's Gazette*, October 16, 1890.

65 / MS Leeds   34, De Vere Gardens, W.
                                    Oct. 30*th* [1890?]

My dear Gosse,

The said little Jonathan Sturges says he will dine with me tomorrow, *Friday*, at 7.45—strictly unclad.[1] Is there any miraculous chance that combining inclination with liberty, you will kindly come? There may be another or two—but even if there isn't little Brother Jonathan has his share of the national genius. Therefore make *any* sacrifice. I shall tell my messenger to wait for a word.

Ever

yours   *H.J.*

P.S. Do you happen to possess *H. Harland's* address?[2] I would try to get *him*.

1. Jonathan Sturges (1864–1909), an American expatriate, lived in London and eventually became an intimate friend of James. Some of James's letters to him are included in *LHJ*, I, and *HJL*, III and IV. One reason for dating this letter 1890 is that Thursday did occur on October 30 that year.

2. Henry Harland (1861–1905), American novelist, would become editor of the *Yellow Book* in 1894 and invite James to contribute some of his best nouvelles of the period. Gosse had met Harland in 1889 (*EG*, 355).

66 / MS Leeds   Prince of Wales Hotel
                                                   Southport.
                                                   Jan. 3*d* [1891][1]

My dear Gosse,

I am touched by your *petit mot*. De gros mots seem to me to be so much more applicable to my fallen state. The only thing that can be said for it is that it is not so low as it may perhaps be tomorrow— after the vulgar ordeal of tonight.[2] Let me therefore profit by the few remaining hours of a recognizable *status* to pretend to an affectionate reciprocity. I am yours & your wife's while yet I *may* be. After 11 o'clk. tonight I *may* be the world's—you know—& I may be the undertaker's. I count upon you both to spend this evening in fasting, silence & supplication. I will send you a word in the morning—wire you if I can—if there is anything at all to boast of.[3] My hopes rest solely on intrinsic charms—the adventitious graces of art are not "in it." I am so nervous that I miswrite & misspell. Pity your infatuated but not presumptuous friend

Henry James

P.S. It would have been delightful—& terrible—if you had been able to come. I believe Archer is to loom.[4]
P.P.S. I don't return straight to London—don't get there till Tuesday or Wednesday. I shall have to wait & telegraph you which evening I can come in.[5]

1. The text of this letter is included in *HJL*, III, 316–17.
2. The "vulgar ordeal" is the opening night of *The American* in Southport.
3. James wired Gosse on the following morning: "Complete and delightful success universal congratulation to which I venture to add yours and your wife's" (Leeds).
4. William Archer (1856–1924), British dramatic critic and early advocate of Ibsen

in England, was soon to write a slashing attack on Gosse as a translator of Ibsen in the *Pall Mall Gazette*, January 23, 1891. The breach, however, was later healed, and Gosse and Archer worked together on a translation of Ibsen's *The Master Builder* (copyright reading, December 7, 1892). See *EG*, 339–46. For Archer's plan to attend the play, see James's letter to him of December 27, 1890 (*HJL*, III, 309–10).

5. James subsequently reported his return to London in a letter of January 8 and accepted an invitation from Gosse for Saturday, January 10, "at 9" (Leeds).

67 / MS Leeds   Hotel Westminster
                                                          Rue de la Paix. Paris.
                                                          Feb. 24*th* [1891]

My dear Gosse.

I'm sorry to be so far from the joys you hospitably whisk at me. I came here last week—to stay three or four. It wasn't so much to come here as to get, for a month, at a moment that happened to be propitious, away from London—whence I expect to make no further absence, to speak of, till late next autumn. Paris is bright, soft, mild, "empty," & tinted with all manner of pleasant suggestions. But lots of people are away, & the theatres are in the minor key. Bourget is in Sicily, Coppée at Algiers & Daudet (moribund) barely visible.[1] Few of my little group of friends here are in town. But I like it—I am working—& I don't go out till 4 o'clock. I will, however, try to get some impressions to bring back to you. If I hadn't been battling with the hours till up to the moment of my departure I wd. have come to press your hand in farewell. The *vitrines des librairs* are a desolation— there's nothing of any one. I send you 2 Figaros, one with a stinging but most deserved animadversion on E. de Goncourt's preface to his new volume (2*d* of the 2*ièm* série of his *Journal*,) in which he defends his ignoble caddishness in regard to Renan; the other containing, by Millaud, a very amusing little supposititious prayer of the said Renan.[2] But you probably have seen them both. I have scribbled all the morning—I can't come here save on some organized pot-boiling basis—& am going out (it's 3.50) to sniff the Lutetian air. I wish you could sniff it with me. I will transmit you anything that may seem to vous toucher—as a man of letters—de près. I have read, with the greatest pleasure, your Life of your Father.[3] It is an admirable skilful delightful piece of work. You ought to biographise more. But what a "rum" gentleman! Love to your wife. Ever yours

Henry James

1. For Bourget, see letter 10, note 1; and for Coppée, see letter 57, note 3. James had known Alphonse Daudet (1840–1897), French novelist, for many years and had translated *Port Tarascon* in 1890.

2. James had known Edmond de Goncourt (1822–1896), French novelist and critic, since the mid-seventies, and he had reviewed the first series of the journal in the *Fortnightly Review* in October, 1888. "Le Cas de M. de Goncourt," by Robert de Bonnières, appeared in *Le Figaro*, February 22, 1891, p. 1, and Albert Millaud's "Oraison de Renan," February 23, pp. 1–2. Since his own youth, James had admired Ernest Renan (1823–1892), French philologist and historian. See *HJL*, II, 26.

3. *The Life of Philip Henry Gosse, F.R.S.* (1890) had recently appeared. A month earlier, on January 12, 1891, James had characterized this book to Stevenson as a "singularly clever, skilful, vivid, well-done biography" (*HJL*, III, 326); later it served as a basis for Gosse's autobiographical *Father and Son* (1907). See letter 235.

68 / MS Cambridge   H. Westminster [Paris]
                                        March 26*th* [1891]

Dear Mrs. Gosse.

Your most benevolent & charming letter deserves a better answer than I can give it in these last hours of hurry & flurry—for I return to London either tomorrow or Saturday. I will come in and thank you for it, & all its interesting & inscrutable allusions on one of the first evenings of next week. Tuesday or Wednesday, probably—if either of them suit you? I find it an effort to leave this intenser city at the moment of the year when it is about to become most charming. But I have had some 6 weeks of it; & they have been refreshing, in spite of much vile weather & also, like our *éprouvé* Edmund, to whom pray give my friendliest greetings, a perpetual throat. The earthquake in Drangard is an impenetrable mystery to me (I hear of it for the 1st time;) but, whatever the elements, I go it blind for Balestier, as one always should for one's friends.[1] I shall bring you back all the impressions I can of Paris—but they will not be, for others than myself, very rich; for I have been intensely quiet & working hard, with little vision of *les sommités*. I am very sorry to miss the opportunity of showing Mrs. Williams the attention I shld. have been glad to bestow.[2] It is *you* who will have rich & rare things to tell me, I see; & I am impatient for the same. Tell Gosse to get them in order & to lay down his pen for a talk. I shall try & renew his beam while reducing his orbit. While I write to you I find I *am* homesick—which was what was to be demonstrated. With every invocation on your house, believe me, dear Mrs. Gosse, yours most truly
                                        Henry James

1. Wolcott Balestier (1861–1891), a young American whom James had met in 1890 and who would briefly become James's agent before his premature death from typhoid fever in Dresden in December, 1891. See James to Howells, May 17 [1890], in *HJL*, III, 284, for James's plans for Balestier.

2. Mrs. Emily Epps Williams was Mrs. Gosse's sister and a widow.

69 / MS Leeds   34, De Vere Gardens, W.
                                                                Apr: 28*th* [1891?][1]

My dear Gosse

I return the Ibsenite volume with many thanks—especially for the opportunity to read your charming preface which is really *en somme* & between ourselves (I wdn't. say it to Lang,) more interesting than Ibsen himself.[2] That is I think you make him out a richer phenomenon than he is. The perusal of the dreary *Rosmerholm* [*sic*] & even the reperusal of *Ghosts* has been rather a shock to me—they have let me down, down. Surely the former isn't *good?*—any more than the tedious *Lady from the Sea* is? *Must* I think these things works of skill? If I must I will—save to you alone: to whom I confide that they seem to be of a grey mediocrity—in the case of "Rosmersholm" *jusqu'à en être bête*. They don't seem to me dramatic, or dramas at all—but (I am speaking of these 2 particularly,) moral tales in dialogue—without the objectivity, the visibility of the drama. They suggest curious reflections as to the Scandinavian stage & audience. Of course they have a serious—a terribly serious, "feeling for life," & always an idea—but they come off as little, in general, as plays; & I can't think that a man who is at odds with his form is ever a first-rate man. But I may be grossly blind, & at any rate don't *tell* it of yours tremulously[3]

                                                                Henry James

1. This letter has previously appeared in *HJL*, III, 339–40.

2. James's opinion of Ibsen, ironically, began to change at about this time after he had seen some of Ibsen's plays and particularly Elizabeth Robins in *Hedda Gabler* in the spring of 1891. The change is evident in his article on that play in the *New Review* for June, 1891. See *HJL*, III, 344*n*. Gosse had championed Ibsen since 1870. The preface mentioned by James appeared in Volume I of the Lovell's Series of Foreign Literature edition of Ibsen's works (1890).

3. On the flap of the envelope attached, James commented on the preface again: "Your preface perfect, granting premises."

70 / MS Leeds   34, De Vere Gardens, W.
                                                                [May 2, 1891?]

A cheering word about one's "art," my dear Gosse, always waters a little the roots of things, & I feel quite gratefully irrigated. Such words never come amiss, for one always feels like such a fearful failure—at least *I* do. If it isn't log-rolling may I say—under my breath—that I think you are very pleasant & learned & interesting in the Same Number?[1] (Destroy this please—lest we be found out.)

It is very likely I shall come in & see you on Tuesday about 9. If I can't I will notify you.

I have been 3 times to see your century-enders. I really *raffole* of the play—which merely muddled & mystified me at *1st*. The young women's doing of it with their extra mouth, etc.—will have been a very honourable episode. I shall put that of your private-viewers into a tale—

Ever yours
H. J.

1. James is presumably referring to the May, 1891, issue of the *New Review*, in which both writers discoursed on "The Science of Criticism."

71 / MS Leeds   34, De Vere Gardens, W.
                                   May 13*th* [1891]

To night, *abimi*, it would be impossible—I am too engaged. But I will look you up the day you return from France. It was very good of you, among all the details of your life, to find time for the Lemaître—Ibsen detail. The little Jules is pleasant—but I have written for A. Grove a few tardy reflections (June,) which are so much better![1]

Bon voyage—bonne santé—bon gite—bon appêtit. Ever your sendentary [*sic*]

H. J.

1. James's "tardy reflections" are expressed in "On the Occasion of *Hedda Gabler*," *New Review*, IV (June, 1891), 519–30. The "Lemaître-Ibsen detail," apparently, refers to the comments of Jules Lemaître (1853–1914) on Ibsen in his *Impressions de théâtre* (1890). Archibald Grove was editor of the *New Review*.

72 / MS Leeds   34, De Vere Gardens, W.
                                   June 5*th* [1891]

My dear Gosse.

I had retained, in these bewildered days, no memory whatever of having passed my word to you for last night—& learn with horror that you vainly awaited me. But what in fact not only awaited, but received me was my bed—into which I was obliged to tumble prematurely with an overwhelming attack of lumbago, with which I returned on Wednesday afternoon from the country & which at the present moment agonizes me to such a degree that I can barely sit up to form these incoherent words.[1] Believe that I was bad—& that I still am, when I tell you that I am glad I had so failed to note my appointment with you—so much the baffled state wd. have added to my torment. I find these few weeks too utterly & loathsomely fatal to peace & work & friendship, & have so many things on my broken back that I will just wait a turn of the tide before taking an evening with you. At the 1st subsidence I am yours. I hope, however, to come in *Wednesday*—much.[2] The enclosed from Queen Square will strike you as characteristic. Will you return it? Ever yrs

Henry James

1. James was to continue to have occasional trouble with lumbago (see his remark in letter 313), and in 1893 he began to have intermittent attacks of gout.
2. For James's failure to visit Delamere Terrace on Wednesday (June 10), see letter 73.

73 / MS Leeds   34, De Vere Gardens, W.
                                               June 11*th* [1891]

My dear Gosse.

I did my best to reach you last night at a practicable—a decent—hour; but it was impossible.[1] I dined at an interminable big banquet of 30 people, at the American Minister's—at which we were invited for 8.15, didn't sit down till 8.30, & were still at table at 10.40.[2] I didn't get away till 11.15, & reasoning, then, that I shouldn't compass the long drive to Delamere Terrace in less than ½ an hour, judged that to turn up chez vous at a quarter to midnight would be a really presumptuous act. I find it almost always a delusive attempt, in London, to try to rush from dinner to *early* things. You abandon more or less rudely the first company & miss the 2d. They have dispersed while one is driving. But this is not an essay on nocturnal London. I will seek a quiet hour with you au 1er jour & renew to you & to your wife the assurance of the keen regrets of yours most truly

Henry James

1. For James's plan to come in Wednesday (June 10), see letter 72. He managed, however, to see the Gosses before the end of the month.
2. The "American Minister" at this time was Robert T. Lincoln (1843–1926), son

of Abraham Lincoln. Lincoln appreciated James enough to attend the opening night of *The American* in London on September 26, 1891. See *HJ*, III, 297.

74 / MS Leeds   Marine Hotel,
                                                      Kingstown, Ireland
                                                      July 24*th* [1891]

My dear Philomel.

Your liquid note—infinite passion, infinite pain!—reaches me on this disaffected shore. I pottered away from London shortly after last seeing you, &, after spending 3 or 4 days at Oxford—in delightful long vac—emptiness & greenery, which, however, I found "lowering"—I made my way hither, mainly because it is far from the metropolis, with which I which I [*sic*] wished to get out of touch.[1] I have succeeded, thank heaven, completely. But I have collapsed—I don't mean with illness—on the very spot on which I landed a fortnight since, lacking time & means for travel. This place is too suburban, but a very pretty coast & sea, & I have had lovely weather and have driven the pen, which was what I wished—& also have found, what I think one doesn't always find here, convenient meat & drink. Therefore I stay 4 or 5 days more. The moment of my return to town will depend on whether I then find it feasible or not to make a little journey—of about a week—round a portion of the edge of Erin. Without it I shall go home with scarcely any Irish impressions at all—not however, I judge, that they are indispensable to life. Yet this is a really charming shore. I will hie me to your immortalized terrace (poor Miss Browning!) from the very station of my return. When I do come it will be to stick fast—my travels are over. I hope *you* won't have spitefully fled. We must hang over the portico together: Ever yours

Henry James

1. For James's travels at the end of June, see *HJ*, III, 294.

75 / MS Leeds   Marine Hotel,
                                                      Kingstown
                                                      Aug. 6*th* 1889 [1891][1]

Dear diminutive Edmund.

I am touched & charmed by your sympathetic letter, & blush only not painfully because I *am* in an alienated isle. If I were any nearer, my cheek would the very atmosphere incarnadine. These things are good & make life seem much less of a beargarden. It is in the *effect* that I rejoice—I mean the feeling—yours—of going further: The cause, to my sense, is fit only to make me drop my eyes & do the proper thing—or determine more and more to do it.[2] I come back the beginning of next week—or early in it—& then we will talk of it & be delightfully serio-literary. I will look at Dowden—though I find him usually; that is, *did* find his Shelley—of such an inadequate spirit.[3] But I owe him thanks, & you, repeating it, for that admirable luminosity of Grimm's.[4] It is de première force—or at any rate very beautiful. I haven't stirred from this, as you see—it has sufficed to my needs & I have felt too poor to voyage. I can only voyage home. I'm extremely glad Wolcott B. struck you with any brightness—but oh that he *could* go far & stay long.[5] I see the future dark else. Oh, too, for a sight of your Devonshire Mill—on the castled crag—or under it. You must paint it to me wordily.[6]

Yes, how that voice does make one want him to cease from Kipling.[7] It is in his books too—2 of which I have just read over, with wonder at the *mixture*. The talent enormous, but the brutality even deeper-seated. It comes out so abnormally in the *Light That Failed*. And then the talent has sometimes failed. My dear Gosse, you have made me feel very big, & it is your fault if I am very importantly as well as faithfully yours

Henry James

1. The text of this letter is printed in *SR*, 576–77. James gives the date as 1889, but it is clear from the location and from internal evidence (especially the reference to *The Light That Failed*, 1890–1891) that 1891 is the correct year.

2. Gosse's "sympathetic letter" may have praised "The Marriages," a story by James that had just appeared in the *Atlantic Monthly* for August, 1891.

3. Edward Dowden (1843–1913), professor of English literature at Trinity College, Dublin, and author of a life of Shelley (1886).

4. Hermann Friedrich Grimm (1828–1901), professor of art history at the University of Berlin, corresponded with Emerson and wrote on Voltaire and Goethe.

5. For Wolcott Balestier, see letter 68, note 1.

6. Gosse was staying at the Mill in Dunster at this time. See letter 76. The Mill, by the way, was in Somerset, not Devonshire.

7. For Gosse's concurrent view of Kipling, see his letter of June 4, 1891, to Richard Watson Gilder, editor of the *Century*, in *TD*, 221–22, and his article "Rudyard Kipling," *Century*, XLII (October, 1891), 901–10.

76 / MS Leeds   34 D.V.G.W.
                            Monday [August 24, 1891?][1]

My dear Gosse.

Your note is an enchantment & Dunster is clearly the *pays bleu*.
Therefore it is hideous for me to have to say anything so prosaic as
that next Saturday will be impossible for me. I have absolutely
promised W. Balestier that I will go down to Blackgang for 4 or 5
days on Thursday; & it will be an act of common humanity to stick
to this, as his remaining away for the week will be fostered by it.[2]
(He is there now.) The only way to keep him there is to go & see
him. I will do my utmost to think of Dunster, to see it vividly, as
possible for *next* week or some early subsequent day. I shouldn't be
able to give more than a couple of days to it; but days of bliss are not
vulgarly numbered. How admirable the picture in your letter. Se
non è vero è ben trovato! What *is* vero at any rate, & charming, are
your delightful hospitable expressions, to which I beg both of you to
trust me to respond at the earliest possible day.

                                Ever faithfully
                                Henry James

1. This date is written in pencil on the letter. Since Monday occurred on August
24 in 1891, the Gosses were in Dunster at the time (see letters 75 and 77), and James
had returned to London on August 11 (*HJL*, III, 352), it seems reasonable to accept
the ascription.
2. For Wolcott Balestier, see letter 68, note 1, and letter 75.

77 / MS Leeds   34, De Vere Gardens, W.
                            August 26*th* [1891]

My dear Gosse.

I found your letter last night in coming in from a day at Oxford.[1] I
greatly grieve to say that I *can't* fix Wednesday for coming down—I
have a pressure of occupation here next week which makes the last
days of it sadly inconvenient for an absence. If you are to be here
from the last of them I shall see you & make my infirmities & regrets
very clear to you. Are you not to be at Dunster (after your few days
in town,) for 2 or 3 weeks more & can't we then fix upon a later
date[?][2] It breaks my heart not to be able to respond instantly to
your charming invocations. Please believe in my impossibility. I
delight to think that, saving this, all else is well with you—& all else

is really *all*. Let me know as soon as you come to town & distribute my greetings on your house. Ever unworthily yours

Henry James

1. James may have been visiting Constance Fenimore Woolson (1840–1894), an American novelist and old friend who was living in Oxford at this time. See Clare Benedict (ed.), *Constance Fenimore Woolson* (London [1930]), 369ff.

2. Because of the distance to Dunster, the mortal illness of his sister Alice (she died the following March), and the pressure of rehearsals for the staging of *The American* in London late in September, James apparently was never able to visit Gosse there.

78 / MS Leeds   34, De Vere Gardens, W.

Sunday [September 27, 1891][1]

My dear Gosse.

It is awfully late & I am awfully tired & jaded with sleepless nights & diurnal worry—but the strain is over—& the Rubicon crossed. I have had all the air of a success—even a great one. The papers, I believe, are very restrictive—very stingy, I call it—very stupid *you* must.[2] But the play goes—it went last night in an indisputable fashion. I don't forecast the future, but it was—I am assured—a remarkably good *l'ère*. Compton had a very great personal success—& he is so charming, so delightful that I can't doubt he will keep & prolong & repercute [*sic*] it.[3] I passed through hells of nervousness—but am in comparatively quiet waters now. I am, however, weary & sleepy exceedingly—& have 30 notes to answer. I will tell you all the rest & am ever yours & your wife's

Henry James

1. The date of this letter is based upon the reference to the opening night of *The American* in London on September 26, 1891 ("the strain is over—& the Rubicon crossed").

2. For the general critical reaction to the play, see *HJ*, III, 296–99. The London run totaled seventy nights.

3. Edward Compton (1854–1918), British actor-manager who urged James to write a dramatic version of *The American*, produced the play, and took the part of Christopher Newman.

79 / MS Leeds   34, De Vere Gardens, W.

October 2d [1891][1]

My dear Gosse.

Your good & charming letter should have been answered on the spot—but my days are abnormal & perpective [*sic*] & relation are blurred. I shall come & see you the moment you return, & then I shall be able to tell you more in five minutes than in fifteen of such hurried scrawls as this. Meanwhile many thanks for your sympathy & curiosity & suspense—*all* thanks, indeed—&, in return, all eagerness for your rentrée here. My own suspense has been & still is great—though the voices of the air, rightly heard, seem to whisper *prosperity*. The papers have been on the whole quite awful—but the audiences are altogether different.[2] The only thing is that these first 3 or 4 weeks *must* be up-hill; London is still empty, the whole enterprise is wholly new—the elements must assemble. The strain, the anxiety, the peculiar form & colour of such an ordeal (not to be divined in the least in advance) have sickened me *to death*—but I am getting better. I forecast nothing, however—I only wait. Come back & wait with me—it will be easier. Your picture of your existence & circumstance is like the flicker of the open door of heaven to those recumbent in the purgatory of yours not *yet* damned—ah, no!—

Henry James

1. Although this letter is included in *LHJ*, I, 185, and *HJL*, III, 356–57, my text is based upon the original and differs in several instances from the others.
2. For the general reaction to *The American*, see *HJ*, III, 296–99. Constance Fenimore Woolson (see letter 77, note 1) attended the opening night as James's guest and, a few weeks later, wrote a friend about the critical reaction: "The critics have, since then, written acres about the play. It has been warmly praised; attacked; abused; highly commended, etc." (Benedict [ed.], *Constance Fenimore Woolson*, 372).

80 / MS Leeds   34, De Vere Gardens, W.
                                                  November 17*th* 1891

My dear Gosse.

Please have patience with me a little longer. I am very susceptible to the friendliness of your note, but I have been not only infinitely occupied, but moody, misanthropic, melancholy, morbid, morose, & utterly unfit for human converse or genial scenes. I continue, frankly speaking, painfully & perversely unsociable—& shall, as the phrase is, never be the same man again.[1] When a relative light breaks it will guide me to your door; but in the meanwhile I must grope in solitude & blush (for my involuntary rigours,) in seclusion. I must throw myself on your charity, which I know to be liberal, & on your wife's, in which I have a still larger confidence, & I am, my dear Gosse, with every appreciation of your sympathy, yours, with every

impulse of conciliation but every instinct of retirement, most faithfully

Henry James

1. Throughout this period James is constantly concerned about his two
"invalids"—his play and his sister Alice, who is dying of cancer. See, for example,
his letter of October 10 to his brother William in *HJL*, III, 358–59.

81 / MS Library of Congress

Europaeischer
Hof.
Dresden.
Thursday [December 10, 1891][1]

My dear Gosse.

I delay as little as possible to tell you où nous en sommes. We
arrived at 9.0 last (Wednesday) night after a deadly, dreary journey &
a miserable delay on Monday night at Dover. The funeral, most happily—if I may use so strange a word—had been successfully delayed
till this a.m., when it took place most conveniently & even pictur-
esquely according to arrangements already made by the excellent
Heinemann ladies & the American consul Mr. Knoop. The English
chaplain read the service with sufficient yet not effusive sonority and
the arrangements were of an admirable, decorously grave German
kind which gives one really, a higher idea of German civilization.
The 3 ladies came, insistently, to the grave—the others were Heinemann, his mother & I, & the excellent Mr. Knoop.[2] The little cemetery is suburbanly dreary, but I have seen worse. The Mother &
sister are altogether wonderful, & so absolutely composed—that is
Mrs. B. & Josephine—that there is scarcely any *visible* tragedy in it.
By far the most interesting is poor little concentrated, passionate Carrie, with whom I came back from the cemetery alone in one of the
big black & silver coaches, with its black & silver footman perched
behind, (she wanted to talk to me,) & who is remarkable in her force,
acuteness, capacity & courage—& in the intense—almost manly—
nature of her emotion. She is a worthy sister of poor dear big-
spirited, only-by-death-quenchable Wolcott, & if we judged her—in
speaking of a certain matter lately—"unattractive," her little, vivid,
clear-talking, clear-*seeing* black-robed image today (& last evening)
considerably—in a certain way—to my vision, modifies that judgment. What is clear, at any rate, is that she can do & face, & more
than face & do, for all 3 of them, anything & everything that they

will have to meet now.[3] They are going home (to the U.S.) as soon as they can—& they are going to London 1st: I suppose about a week hence. One thing, I believe, the poor girl could *not* meet—but God grant (& the complexity of "genius" grant,) that she may not have to meet it—as there is no reason to suppose that she will.[4] What this tribulation is—or would be, rather, I can indicate better when I see you. Please tell your wife that gladly & piously I carried her box of English flowers to the poor women—and Josephine had them in her hand during all the service this morning. When the clergyman had said his last words at the grave—they were the first flowers dropped into the horrid abyss—poor Josephine tottered to the edge and let them fall. Strange enough it seemed to stand there & perform these monstrous rites for the poor yesterday-so-much-living boy—in this far-away, alien city. Even after them, & at this hour, it all seems like some deadly clever game or invention—to beat Tauchnitz of his own.[5] I stay 3 or 4 days and rest—see the Museum, &c.—& then I go back, the same way—by Cologne, Brussels, &c.—but not so fatiguingly fast. There seems little appearance that I shall travel with them—or wait for them—the 3 women: they are now perfectly capable themselves. They will probably write your wife their plans. They have plenty of present money. I am very tired—auf wiedersehen to both of you. Yours always—

Henry James

1. This letter is dated by the description of Wolcott Balestier's funeral in Dresden. The letter is included in *HJL*, III, 364–65, but my text is based upon the original and differs in several instances. Balestier had died of typhoid fever in Dresden on December 6, 1891. For other references to Balestier, see letters 68, 75, and 76.
2. William Heinemann (1863–1920), the British publisher. From this period on, Heinemann was a good friend to both James and Gosse and published many of their books.
3. Caroline Starr Balestier (1865–1939) married Rudyard Kipling on January 18, 1892, less than six weeks after the death of her brother. James gave the bride away. See his letter of January 18 to W. Morton Fullerton (1865–1952), an American journalist who worked for the *Times* in Paris and who was soon to become one of James's best young friends (*HJL*, III, 370–71). See also Gosse's letter of January 18, 1892, to R. W. Gilder in *TD*, 224. Both James and Gosse were subsequently to have mixed feelings about Carrie Kipling.
4. This is possibly a veiled reference to Kipling.
5. In partnership with Heinemann, Balestier, according to Edel, had "organized a new soft-cover publishing house to compete with the continental Tauchnitz editions" (*HJL*, III, 365).

82 / MS Leeds   34 De Vere Gardens W.
                                                    March 7*th* [1892]

My dear Gosse

I will come in some evening *next* week. I had yesterday the great
sorrow of the death of my sister.[1] It makes a great & sad difference in
my life. I thank you & I thank your wife in advance heartily for all
sympathy, & I am most faithfully yours

Henry James

1. Alice James died Sunday, March 6, 1892, and was cremated March 9. Her
ashes were eventually buried in Cambridge in the family plot. For her reaction to
her impending death and James's response to her last days, see *HJ*, III, 299–303. On
Thursday, March 10, James acknowledged notes of sympathy from the Gosses and
promised to "knock at your door . . . on Saturday evening, next" (Leeds).

83 / MS Leeds   34, De Vere Gardens, W.
                                                    March 17*th* [1892]

My dear Gosse.

A deadly occupied day yesterday (I went to Oxford early and
didn't get back till midnight,) rendered me guilty of keeping over
your paper on W.B., which I restore you herewith & which I should
at any rate have sent back today.[1] I have read it with interest & appreciation, and, knowing Wolcott so well, I know what you mean, as it
were, by most of it. That is, to my enlightened eye it recalls much of
the poor boy's personality. I am not so sure that it will do this in
equal proportion for those who didn't know him—that is in a way
absolutely just. But of those who didn't know him comparatively few
will pay much heed—they will have no association with his name. I
confess there are *three* passages in the sketch that I am sorry you left
just so—the one about his personal appearance, the one about his
"secretiveness" (particularly,) which I think, under the circumstances, ungracious—and the enumeration of his early books—
though, as to this last point, you may reply that it would have been
unfair to be silent. But to the young, the early dead, the baffled, the
defeated, I don't think we can be tender enough.

I am a little alarmed, too, at your allusion to my undertaking a
"biographical" work about him—almost as much alarmed as when
Heinemann wrote to me about "The Life of Wolcott." I wrote but a
few intensely summary & general pages, with *no* details—my sketch
(a mere "impression,") is shorter than yours.[2] Many thanks for the

thought of sending me yours in advance—much of which—*all* of which save the passages I allude to, strikes me as very happily & vividly expressed.

Ever yours
Henry James

1. Gosse's "Wolcott Balestier" appeared in *Century*, XLIII (April, 1892), 923–26.
2. For James's "sketch," see "Wolcott Balestier," *Cosmopolitan*, XIII (May, 1892), 43–47. This essay was reprinted as a preface to Balestier's *The Average Woman: A Common Story; Reffey; Captain, My Captain!* (London, 1892), vii–xxviii. In regard to the "early dead," James elaborates on the idea of being generous to those who "had not had time" and who "had only begun."

84 / MS Leeds   34, De Vere Gardens, W.
                                                  April 11*th* [1892]

My dear Gosse.

Thanks for votre pensée si gracieuse to have sent me the painful proof of poor Loti's woeful tendency to stray as soon as he ceases to treat—more or less—de ce que vous davez. All taste & wisdom seem to have deserted him here—it is deplorably feeble, frantically flippant & of an egotism that sets the very teeth of one's compassion for him on edge. How Zola scores in the little correspondence reported in today's *Times*—great big dear dirty Zola, who has got a little of everything—even of taste.[1] How the French keep performing the most interesting little dramas in the world—having in their big lighted Paris proscenium a succession of little personal scenes! Exit Loti this time—& Zola called before the curtain. How one feels here merely out in the street, looking at the affiche! Ever yours

Henry James

[P.S.] Excuse this blot on my character.[2]

1. For the disagreement between Pierre Loti (1850–1923) and Émile Zola (1840–1902), see "Pierre Loti and M. Zola" (datelined Paris, April 10) in the *Times*, April 11, 1892, p. 5.
2. James here refers to an ink blot on the stationery.

85 / MS Leeds   34 De Vere Gardens W.
                                                  May 31*st* [1892]

My dear Gosse.

I am very glad to receive your news—I think you have done the right thing. I am pleased to hear also that Lady Wolseley thinks so.[1]

Il ne tiendra qu'à vous, now, to sail in by the other door.

I couldn't after all & in spite of straining every nerve, reach D.T. [Delamere Terrace] on Sunday—to my great regret. I didn't get out till late, & I *had* to pay two or three calls, where against my cunning computation, I found the people at home. But I met Lady Wolseley later—& had a ¼ of an hour's talk with her. Vale. Yours ever

Henry James

1. Both James and Gosse were friends of the Wolseleys and corresponded with them. Lady Louisa Erskine Wolseley was the wife of Viscount Garnet Wolseley (1833–1913), later the commander-in-chief of the British armies.

86 / MS Leeds

34 De Vere Gardens, W.
H. Metropole
Brighton
Sept. *1st* [1892]

My dear Gosse.

I am covered with shame as with a garment & with contrition as with a leprosy. I haven't had the courage—these 24 hours—to tell you that yesterday, in a crisis of confusion, I managed to *lose* the paper containing your beautiful address on Shelley—so that I have been in anguish ever since & shall continue so until I hear that it was not the *only* copy of the journal that you had been able to put your hand on.[1] I yesterday changed my room—moved from one quarter of this monstrous caravanserai (the best hotel in England, by the way,) to another and remote one—& preparing my things to be transferred, went out to let the removal be made in my absence. I placed your paper, among two or three others, alongside my luggage, taking for granted they would be shifted with it—but they were carried off as rubbish(!!) by the porter or chambermaid & have disappeared in the vortex of this huge establishment. I am unable to get any trace of the precious sheet—& I curse my want of due solicitude. Please forgive me, & tell me *where* to write that I may forthwith enter into arrangements with the Sussex journal to have the loss made up to you. I forget the whereabouts & the exact title. I thought your speech singularly happy & charming—& it gives me great pleasure to applaud it after my rather reserved attitude about the little tale.[2] The Shelley is the sort of thing you do admirably. I feel as if you had much to forgive me. There is a horrid universal storm here, & it is such a sort of expensive lonely exposure that I shall probably return to town in a day or two. I hope Dunster is milder, humaner & cheaper!

Always yours
Henry James

1. Gosse's "Address at the Shelley Centenary" appeared in the *Author* for October, 1892. Apparently it was published first in the "Sussex journal" James mentions in this letter. As "Shelley in 1892. Centenary address delivered at Horsham August 11, 1892," it was reprinted in Gosse's *Questions at Issue* (London, 1893), 201–15.

2. The "little tale" may be Gosse's only novel published in book form, *The Secret of Narcisse* (1892).

87 / MS Leeds   34 D.V.G.W.
[September 3, 1892]

My dear Gosse.

I found here your letter, on coming back last evening from the too inclement Brighton. Meanwhile my second one—of Thursday—or was it Wednesday?—will have reached you, &, I fear, embittered you utterly against me.[1] I will perform any act of penance that you prescribe—any act of retractation [*sic*]—even to coming (I was *going* to say,) down to the pluvial Dunster.[2] But even the pluviality of Dunster can scarcely be regarded—*te consule*—as a mortification—so I leave that ambiguous speech unmade. To tell the truth, while this horrid condition continues I find that even my dreams root themselves by the domestic hearth. If the sun should come out I may summon my retinue. It is very good of you to bow your head so gracefully to my reserves about the historical anecdote. They were based wholly upon a (possibly morbid but intensely friendly) desire to keep you up to a tremendous standard of literary *responsibility*.[3] Any attempt in a new line is an exposure so long as one hasn't retired to the desert to pray; & it is not enough for a man of your talent to do something that some one else might have done. That is all—to which you may reply that even a man of your talent has a right to his little amusements. No doubt—no doubt, as Pater wd. say![4] I have no answer to that.

No, the manner of the *Soeurs Vatard* is *not* my ideal.[5] I hear you reply "What the hell *is* it, then?" & feel dreadfully cornered. Write me a few words not too *crowy*, & above all lay no more traps for the deplorable priggishness of yours ever

Henry James

P.S. I congratulate Philip on his glorious wound—so essentially in *front*.[6] I hope that at Haylebury [*sic*] they will all be *there*!

1. See letter 86, written on a Thursday.
2. For Gosse's previous efforts to get James to visit him in Dunster, see letters 76 and 77, note 2.
3. As their friendship matures, James consistently seeks to keep Gosse "up to a tremendous standard of literary *responsibility*." He was aware of Gosse's "genius for inaccuracy," as he had remarked in a letter to Stevenson on February 18, 1891 (*HJL*, III, 338.
4. Walter Pater (1839–1894), a fellow of Brasenose College, Oxford, and the author of *Marius the Epicurean* (1885) and *Appreciations* (1889), among other books. Both James and Gosse knew Pater, and Gosse would subsequently write about him.
5. *Les Soeurs Vatard* (1879) is a novel by Joris-Karl Huysmans (1848–1907).
6. Philip Henry George Gosse (1879–1959), Gosse's only son, was in school at Haileybury (*EG*, 366).

88 / MS Leeds   34, De Vere Gardens. W.
                                                              Jan. 7*th* [1893][1]

My dear Gosse.

It was very kind of you yesterday, to supply—or rather to remedy—the injury of fate by bringing me those marvellous outpourings. I had at the B. of T. a lurking suspicion that you *were* within, but my natural modesty—though strangely impaired since yesterday p.m.!—made me shy of too grossly insisting.[2] I was evidently avenged upon the erring janitor—but don't give him the sack (as I believe you fellows say,) for then *I* shall have to support him!

J.A.S. is truly, I gather, a candid and consistent creature, & the exhibition is infinitely remarkable.[3] It's, on the whole, I think, a queer place to plant the standard of duty, but he does it with extraordinary gallantry. If he has, or gathers, a band of the emulous, we may look for some capital sport. But I don't wonder that some of his friends and relations are haunted with a vague malaise. I think one ought to wish him more *humour*—it is really *the* saving salt. But the great reformers never have it—& he is the Gladstone of the affair. That perhaps is a reason the more for convoying him back to you one of these next days. I will drop in with him and defy the *consigne*. I am very very melancholy with the 1*st* attack of gout—in my left big toe-joint—that I have ever had in my life. I feel it's the beginning of the end. But I shall hobble to Whitehall. Yours, & if I may safely say so! *ever*

                                                              H. J.

1. This letter was printed by Edel in *Times Literary Supplement*, June 17, 1965, p. 523, and is also included in *HJL*, III, 398, but my text follows the original.

2. Gosse was a translator at the Board of Trade from 1875 to 1904.

3. According to Edel, "Gosse had loaned James [John Addington] Symonds's 'A Problem in Modern Ethics,'" his privately printed pamphlet on homosexuality (*HJL*, III, 398*n*). For more on Symonds, see letter 8, note 3.

89 / MS Duke   34, De Vere Gardens. W.
                                              March 14*th* 1893.

My dear Gosse.

I am infinitely disconcerted & distressed at the tenor of your wife's note, just received—for the liberality of which I thank her on a separate sheet. It is ill news that you have been having to have "operations" on your hand—& all so surreptitiously & unsociably. I am much tormented, my dear Gosse, at not knowing what nor how much you have suffered. Mrs. Nellie gives me no details—but it is kind of her to have given me the mere tragic outline & I make her no reproach. I hope with all my heart that it hasn't been a grave affection—as it seems to have been so sudden a one. I go to morrow only to Paris—& probably after all not to Italy at all, which will bring me back the sooner. Long before that however I hope your valiant hand will have recovered its cunning—& be able to give me evidence of the same. Meanwhile may the country & the simple kindness of kinsfolk have lightend [*sic*] your burden.[1] The last time I saw you this seemed to me—from the wretched things I learned from you—quite heavy enough. And now my heart is heavier still to know that on top of all that you have been maimed & disqualified. It is however but the worry of a moment & probably one of those fine old human comforts known to us as blessings in disguise. You have rested & rusticated willynilly, & that is so much to the good. But I wanted to talk with you more of the situation you told me about 2 or 3 weeks ago—it was in particular *that* I had in mind in writing to you on Sunday. Now I should like still better to hear more—& even say more on the whole chapter. But I am too late. I wish I had known of your trouble sooner. How delighted I shall be when it has passed! It will pass quickly—to make room for others: that's what I say, by way of comfort, in all life's outrages. But I take better comfort in the thought that your intrepid spirit is even now brandishing its left-handed steel. I shall see you again in a month or two. But I shall write to you before that & appeal to Mrs. Gosse for more news.[2] Soignez-vous, reposez-vous, calmez-vous. Yours always, my dear Gosse,

Henry James

1. Gosse was staying at the Grove, Great Stanmore, the country home of his stepmother's wealthy sister-in-law, Eliza Brightwen.
2. For more news about Gosse's trouble with his hand, see letter 90.

90 / MS Cambridge

Hotel Westminster
r. de la Paix.
March 21st [1893][1]

Dear Mrs. Gosse:

Many thanks for your better news—& especially for the good news that Gosse is coming to Paris. I shall be very glad to see him & shall rejoice to take him gently by that injured—but I trust soon to be reanimated, member.[2] Please express this to him, with all my sympathy and impatience. Won't he—or won't you (though indeed I shall cull the precious date from Harland,) give me a hint, in advance, of the particular moment at which one may look for him?[3] Please tell him confidently to expect that Paris will create within him afresh all the finest pulses of life. It is mild, sunny, splendid—blond & fair, all set in order for his approach. I allude of course to the specious allurements of its exterior. The state is obviously rotten—but everything else is charming. And then, it's such a blessing, after long grief & pain, to find the arms of a *climate* around us once again! Hasten, my dear Edmund, to be healed.

Thank heaven, my allusion to my own manual distress was mainly a florid figure. My hand *is* infirm—but I am not yet thinking of the knife.[4] Mille choses to the Terrace. Yours & Gosse's always

Henry James

1. This letter is included in *LHJ*, I, 201–202, but my text follows the original and differs in several details.
2. For Gosse's injured hand, see letter 89.
3. Gosse would visit the Henry Harlands in Paris in April. For Harland, see letter 65, note 2.
4. An allusion to the operations on Gosse's hand is in letter 89.

91 / MS Leeds

H. Westminster [Paris]
April 20th [1893]

My dear Gosse.

Pressing occupations have prevented me from thanking you for

your note, which brought me less perfect news of you than I could
have wished—a circumstance adding only greater lustre to your
geniality in writing. It sounds wretched that you went home only to
be ill again.[1] Be assured of my tenderest sympathy. Paris glows with
vernal fires—it is scorching hot and nature seems in a rage—a kind of
white heat of passion—at your abandonment. I am glad of your good
thoughts of us—but you were an apparition too intensely brief. I
wish I had more foregatherings to remember. We must talk them
over in the groves of Delamere—& that will make them *seem* more. I
return to the auditorium from the stage (which always seems to me
what the transit back to London from here is like,) as early next
month as I can. My parentes y sont toutes—30 petticoats. I took
them all to Versailles yesterday, & the [*sic*] was like the great historic
rustle described by St. Simon—the rush of the courtiers after somebody's death. I have scarcely seen Harland—but I did so (& his
wife,) 3 evenings ago. They seemed a little depressed—& he not at
all well. But I think it's only superficial. He is pathetic, poor fellow—with his intensity without a form, or an effect.[2] I lunched
today with Jusserand—in the open air. He & it—were charming.
Read for pure irresistible *beauty* Loti's *Matelot*—a mere empty *pleur-
nicherie* in reality but strangely charming for its exquisite manner.[3]
Vale—& may better days now avail for you. I shall make scarcely
more than a bound from Victoria to your door.

Always your
Henry James

1. Gosse had just returned to England from Paris. For his previous illness, see
letter 89.
2. For Harland, see letter 65, note 2.
3. James also refers to Pierre Loti's *Matelot* (1893) in letter 93.

92 / MS Leeds   Hotel Westminster [Paris]
                                    Friday [April 21, 1893][1]

My dear Gosse.

I am very glad of the emotion that led you to write to me immediately about the sudden—the so brutal & tragic extinction, as it
comes to one, of poor forevermore silent J.A.S.[2] I had never even
(clearly,) seen him—but somehow I too can't help feeling the news as
a pang—& with a personal emotion. It always seemed as if I *might*
know him—& of few men whom I didn't know has the image so
much come home to me. Poor much-living, much-doing, pas-

sionately out-giving man! Various things, however, seem to me to have made—to have contributed to make—his death—in the conditions—fortunate & noble. The superabundant achieved work—I mean, the achieved maturity—with age & possibly aberration (repetition & feverish overproduction) what was mainly still to come; and now, *instead*, the full life stopped and rounded, as it were, by a kind of heroic maximum—and under the adored Roman sky. I hope he will be buried there—in the angle of the wondrous wall, where the Englishmen lie—& not in his terrible Davos. He must have been very interesting—& you must read me some of his letters. We shall talk of him. *Requiescat*! I hope it isn't to the same "roundedness"— heaven save the mark!—that R.L.S. is coming home, if is [*sic*] his return be not again merely one of the lies in the dense cloud of mendacity in which *on se débat*—in these days.[3] I wrote to you yesterday. The *heat* here is simply fierce! Do let me know of any *circumstance* about Symonds—or about his death—that may be interesting.

Yours always
Henry James

1. This letter is printed in *HJL*, III, 409–10, but my text is taken from the original and differs in several particulars.

2. John Addington Symonds died in Rome on April 19, 1893. For other references to Symonds, see letters 8, note 3, and 88, note 3.

3. For other references to rumors in the press about Robert Louis Stevenson, see Gosse's letter to Stevenson of November 13, 1893, in *LL*, 228–30.

93 / LHJ[1]

Hotel Westminster,
Paris
Monday [May 1, 1893]

My dear Gosse,

I have delayed too long to thank you for your genial last: which please attribute to the misery of my Boulevard-baffled aspirations. Paris n'est plus possible—from any point of view—and I leave it tomorrow or next day, when my address will become: Hotel National, Lucerne. I join my brother there for a short time. This place continues to *rengorger* with sunshine and sauces,—not to mention other appeals to the senses and pitfalls to the pocket. I am not alluding in particular to the Queen of Golconda![2]

I have read *Matelot* more or less over again, for the extreme penury of the *idea* in Loti, and the almost puerile thinness of this particular donnée, wean me not a jot from the irresistible charm the rascal's very limitations have for me. I drink him down as he *is*—like a philtre or a *baiser*, and the collection of his *moindre mots* has a peculiar magic for me. Read *aloud* to yourself the passage ending section XXXV— the upper part of p. 165, and perhaps you will find in it something of the same strange *eloquence* of suggestion and rhythm as I do, which is what literature gives when it is most exquisite, and which constitutes its sovereign value and its resistance to devouring time, and yet what *niaiseries*![3] Paris continues gorgeous and rainless, but less torrid. I have become inured to fear as careless of penalties. There are no new books but old papiers de famille d'arrière boutique dished-up.

Poor Harland came and spent two or three hours with me the other afternoon—at a café-front and on chairs in the Champs Elysées. He looked better than the time previous, but not well; and I am afraid things are not too well *with* him. One would like to help him, and I try to, in talk: but he is not too helpable, for there is a chasm too deep to bridge, I fear, in the pitfall of his literary longings unaccompanied by the *faculty*.[4] Apropos of such things, I am very glad to see *your* faculty is reflowering. I shall return to England for the volume.[5] Are you writing about Symonds? Vale—especially in the manual part. And valeat your *dame compagne*.

Yours, my dear Gosse,
always,
Henry James

1. I have collated the text of this letter printed in *LHJ*, I, 202–203, with a typed copy of the manuscript at Duke University. In accordance with James's usual epistolary style, I have made some minor changes in Lubbock's text, though I have not been able to locate the manuscript itself.
2. For James's experience with the "Queen of Golconda" (a lady of the Latin Quarter), see Gosse's letter of April 6, 1893, to William Heinemann in *LL*, 225. See also *EG*, 355.
3. James also refers to *Matelot* in letter 91. The passage on p. 165 is reprinted in *LHJ*, I, 202.
4. For Harland, see letter 91 and letter 65, note 2. See also *EG*, 355.
5. Possibly a reference to *Questions at Issue* (1893), Gosse's next volume of essays.

94 / MS Leeds   Granville Hotel
                                   Ramsgate
                                   Friday [June 23, 1893]

My dear Gosse.

I owe you thanks for two notes, and an answer to a question. I shall be glad to become a subscriber to the catalogue of your books—though I feel that in doing so I thrust myself into the society of bibliophiles.[1] I have no such curious lore & I hate catalogues with a personal hatred. Nevertheless I shall doubtless end by cherishing yours. You don't tell me if the money is to be to you or to some one else. But in the doubt I enclose a cheque.

I am very sorry to say that I don't know when I shall see you. I bolted from London yesterday to save my life—that is my literary life—from the interruptions & embroilments of this horrible time. My days were being wrecked & my reason tottered on its throne. Having no cherubic Dartmoor (is your happiness there to have *no* fundament?) I have fled (wishing the sea & to be nearish to town,) to vulgar Ramsgate. But Ramsgate is *all* backside (ne laissez pas traîner ceci!) & I must again take up my pilgrim's wallet.[2] This place—which I didn't know—is fearful! Later, when the plot thins a little, I shall knock at your door. I mean to keep out of town till August; but shall probably spend that month with the chimney-pots. You then, of course, will be rolling in the heather. So I shan't see you till the late autumn! Eheu! So I can't say à bientôt. But till whenever. Yours always

Henry James

1. R. J. Lister, *A Catalogue of a Portion of the Library of Edmund Gosse* (London, 1893).

2. James, nevertheless, spent six weeks at Ramsgate, returning to London in early August. See his letter to Robert Louis Stevenson of August 5, 1893, in *HJL*, III, 428.

95 / MS Leeds   34, De Vere Gardens, W.
Monday [December 4, 1893]

My dear Gosse.

Your invitation for Xmas is most kind—but it finds me, to my regret, in a very hindered state.[1] I have an immemorial Xmas habit—consecrated by friendly tradition—a pledge renewed each year for the following year & dating from the first of those that I spent in London. I dine on Xmas with the Smalleys—who, on Saturday, freshly reminded me of my engagement to them.[2] Please believe, & ask your wife & children to believe, that I should have been delighted to be free to sit at your board and mingle in your mirth. It is very humane of you to have thought of me. You shall see me sooner—on a footing less pompous but quite as intimate. I hope then to find Mrs. Nelly quite hearty again.[3] Believe me yours & hers & the rest of the merry mummers' always

Henry James

1. During the 1890s and thereafter, the Gosses frequently invited James for Christmas or the new year. He occasionally accepted invitations for Christmas, and he frequently attended the celebrations for greeting the new year, though he grumbled about the games and activities of the occasion, especially in letters to W. E. Norris (1847–1925), the English novelist and a good friend to both James and Gosse. See also *EG*, 381.

2. The George W. Smalleys were Americans. Smalley (1833–1916), a well-known journalist, represented the New York *Tribune* in Europe from 1866 to 1895 and then served as U.S. correspondent of the London *Times* until 1905.

3. This is the first time in the correspondence that James refers to Mrs. Gosse as "Mrs. Nelly." The Gosses spelled her name "Nellie," but James frequently spells it "Nelly."

---

96 / MS Leeds   34, De Vere Gardens. W.
                                                    January 30*th* [1894][1]

My dear Gosse.

I told you I wd. tell you if I didn't go abroad. I haven't gone—& since I saw you has come the dreadful, the unspeakable news that you will have seen.[2] I have as yet had no word from Venice (in spite of many telegrams, received & sent, on the question of arrangements, funeral &c,) which throws any light on so unmitigated a tragedy; & till I do, the event remains impenetrably obscure to me save on the hypothesis of a sudden access of insanity. She is to be buried in Rome tomorrow afternoon—in that exquisite Protestant cemetery. Everything has been adequately & authoritatively done. But what an overwhelming, haunting horror—& intolerable obsession of the ghastly, pitiful *fact*!

Yours ever
Henry James

1. Printed in *SR*, 577–78.

2. The "unspeakable news" James refers to is the death of Constance Fenimore Woolson in Venice on January 24. In the delirium accompanying influenza, Miss Woolson had fallen or thrown herself from the window of an upper story of her apartment there. James had prepared to go to the funeral in Rome until he learned on January 27 that she may have committed suicide. See his letter of January 28 to John Hay, a mutual friend, in George Monteiro, *Henry James and John Hay: The Record of a Friendship* (Providence, 1965), 110–12. Many contemporaries, including James, believed that Miss Woolson's death was suicide. Recent scholarship is divided on the

issue. Leon Edel accepted the suicide theory in *HJ*, III, but in *HJL*, III, 524, he commented that Woolson "jumped or fell out of an upper window," a view earlier maintained by John D. Kern, *Constance Fenimore Woolson, Literary Pioneer* (Philadelphia, 1934) and me in *Constance Fenimore Woolson* (New York, 1963). James subsequently went to Venice in March to help Miss Woolson's sister and niece, Mrs. Clara Benedict and Miss Clare Benedict, to settle her affairs. For other comments on Miss Woolson's death and the closing of her estate in Venice, see letter 97 and *HJL*, III, 457–71, 475–77.

---

97 / MS Leeds   34, De Vere Gardens. W.
                                               Saturday [February 3, 1894]

My dear Gosse.

The crimson booklet is at hand—& I will come & thank you for it properly some evening next week. By properly I mean acquaintedly & in fuller possession. By that time (would Thursday or Friday suit you?) I shall have read it; & having already dashed into it and found it singularly alluring—all fragrant & scented with your distillations.[1]

Thanks also for your note of yesterday. There is much that is tragically obscure in that horror of last week—and I feel as if I were living in the shadow of it. But thus much is clear; viz. that she was very ill—much more ill than I supposed at first—& wholly delirious & irresponsible. It is all unspeakably pathetic.[2]

                                        Yours always
                                          Henry James

1. This volume may be Edmund Gosse, *The Jacobean Poets* (London, 1894), the work referred to in letter 98.
2. James is still distressed over Constance Woolson's death. See letter 96.

---

98 / MS Leeds   34, De Vere Gardens. W.
                                               March 2d '94

My dear Gosse.

A press of occupations had led me to put off from day to day the graceful ceremony of thanking you for the pleasure long since derived from the perusal of your *Jacobeans*—though the impulse welled up within me repeatedly during the charmed hours in which I had the book in my hand.[1] (I hung over it so often that I had time afterwards to make up.) They were charmed indeed by the vividness & colour, the life & movement of your criticism. For my envious wonder at your much reading a stronger word is necessary—it leaves me (the phenomenon itself) too sick & too sorry for myself. The book, at all counts, is charming, beguiling, *entraînant* & without a dull sentence. Let nothing divert you from writing—& you will always divert *me*, at least, from everything. I hope your harness, however, is not galling you. I am going abroad about the *20th*—or even sooner, & must see you, some evening, before. I shall presently propose one. Vale. Do have something strange & sweet—or even bitter—to tell me. Yours ever

Henry James

1. See letter 97, note 1.

99 / MS Leeds   34, De Vere Gardens. W.
                                             Wednesday [March 7, 1894]

My dear Gosse.

On Saturday, alas, I dine out.

But *Sunday* wd. suit me if you are free—& your usual afternoon party doesn't militate against the sweet boon of privacy as late as 9 or 9.30.[1]

I go abroad (I fear & hope,) later in the week—& am at a loss at present to name another night.

Yours ever
Henry James

P.S. Ulysses of the lecture-hall—red rose of Lancaster! (or was it t'other way?) Excuse my brevity (not on this occasion the soul of wit;) for I have been these 48 hours ill. But I pretend I'm better—though I'm "real sick."—Don't worry—I dine out, if I can drag myself, tonight. The grimness of the London dinner to the conscientious invalid!

1. The Gosses usually were "at home" on Sunday afternoons and then invited a few choice souls to supper afterwards. James would often arrive at the "immemorial" 9:00 P.M., as he later referred to his usual visiting time, and wait in a parlor for Gosse to come for a chat. See *EG*, 325–26.

100 / MS Leeds   Hotel de Gênes, Genoa.
                                            March *28th* [1894]

My dear Gosse.

Your genial communication overtakes me among the oranges & the

olives.[1] I left London many days ago—last Sunday week—making a
resolute dash for it in order to get off at all. I was rather grossly
unwell—as well as direfully busy—for many days before leaving &
just managed to squeeze off. Under the healing hand of Italy, I hasten to add, I have almost insolently revived. Of course I haven't seen
the friendly review, but I thank you for it with every confidence. It
is very good of you at this time of day to find *any* words to overplas-
ter a production now so seamed & cracked with antiquity. But your
notice will have been to the invalid work even as the breath of Italy to
its author. How I wish you could inhale with me this effluvium
divine. I must soon, somehow, somewhere, introduce you to it. It's
absurd your not coming here—it reconciles one again to an onerous
existence. I mean the Touch of Italy does! I am on my way to
Venice, where I hope, having lots of work in hand, to settle down to
2 or 3 months of quiet labour.[2] Please don't wholly neglect me while
I'm away—make me thrill, I beg you, from time to time, with the
passionate pulse of London. 34 D.V.G. will always promptly reach
me. I hope your days at the gabled mansion so charmingly represented on your letter-paper have done you various good. Still more
do I hope that Mrs. Nelly has been fortified & refreshed. Please tell
her with what joy I shall hear that she is better. I wish you could feel
with me the flood of sunwarmed air that pours in through my open
window, with the chattering sounds & voices of the market-place
leaping about in it like fishes in a net. You would never bow in the
house of Rimmon again but only stand forever erect under the silken
tent of heaven. If I hire a palace in Venice (with the proceeds of the
"sale" you will have started,) you must all come out & stay with me
in it. If I only hire a *Camera mobiliata* you must at least yourself
come. Yours evermore

Henry James

1. James has gone to Italy to help Constance Woolson's sister and niece settle her
affairs. See letter 96, note 2.

2. James was due to arrive in Venice on April 1. See his letter of March 20, 1894,
to Katherine De Kay Bronson in *HJL*, III, 467–68. He was scheduled to meet Mrs.
Benedict and Clare upon their arrival in Genoa on March 29. See his letter of March
24 to William James in *HJL*, III, 469.

Front entrance, Lamb House, Rye, showing projection of Garden
Room on left *Courtesy John S. R. James and H. Montgomery Hyde, with
the permission of the National Trust*

Lamb House from the garden   *Courtesy John S. R. James and H. Montgomery Hyde,*
with the permission of the National Trust

Henry James, 1894, detail of the painting by Sir Philip Burne-Jones in Lamb House   *Courtesy H. Montgomery Hyde, with the permission of the National Trust*

Hanover Terrace, including number 17   *Photograph by Shirley Turner, courtesy Shirley Turner and Ann Thwaite*

Edmund Gosse, 1886, portrait by John Singer Sargent   *Trustees of the National Portrait Gallery*

Edmund Gosse, 1928, portrait by William Rothenstein *Trustees of the National Portrait Gallery*

Henry James, 1913, painting by John Singer Sargent *Trustees of the National Portrait Gallery*

101 / MS Duke   Casa Biondetti.
                                                   San Vio, 715
                                                   Venice.
                                                   April 15*th* [1894]

My dear Gosse.

   This is mainly a very vague & helpless echo of the wish, the
regret, touchingly expressed in your letter of the other day. Would to
heaven indeed that the gross, the painful anomaly of your not knowing this classic land were promptly terminable; would to heaven I
could set, actually, in motion such divine-mechanical influences as
would transport you to the sometimes malodorous, the generally
ambiguous, the eternally romantic waters that I overhang. The
Grand Canal would be grander still when echoing to your expressions of innocent curiosity! We must manage it somehow—the whole
thing is a failure unless we ultimately do.[1] Do you remember the
lusty gondolier who propelled us—2 years ago—at Venice-on-
Thames? I hadn't been here 36 hours before he was in my apartment—sueing for every favour. So fast, in this tell-tale air, does every
reverberation travel. But I can't write about Venice: there is too
much to say—and I am too old a Venetian—I have said it all too
often before.[2] I have even said before that I have perhaps been here
too often. It is at any rate a little early yet; the weather is splendid,
but with the dry white glitter that comes from a long drouth, so that
the aspect is hard yet and without the rosy glow that will come later
& which is the real reconciling Venice. I have got a quaint little lodg-
ing, and I am bent on work; but there are already too many people,
the hotels *regorgent* and those who have nothing to do are always in a
conspiracy to destroy those who have much.[3] I hope you are not
finding a deadly force in this truism by the banks of *your* canal.[4] I
hear that London is tropically hot, but I trust that rank, luxuriant
life doesn't overgrow you. Mrs. Rudyard has written me *their*
arrival—& I am really very sorry to miss them, as I have written very
cordially to assure her. But I fear I shan't see them—unless they stay
all summer; and they must be interesting to observe. If I suspected
you of any leisure I wd. beg you to let me have a few of your notes
on them. And also, by the way, on the launch of the Yellow Book—
its apparent prospects or possibilities. Does Harland droop?—or
swoop?[5] I didn't know Robertson Smith—beyond having seen him at
Cambridge [t]hat time you regaled me at Trinity.[6] I had too little talk

with him—but if you have lost a good friend in him your state is so much the less gracious. They are the things we can least lose.

I'm afraid I haven't even heard of the Stickit Minister—& a fortiori of his *vates*.[7] I trust they may both prove treasures. They evidently indeed have already proved so to each other. You make me tremble for the general accuracy of him whom we ought now, I suppose, to write Wolselay [*sic*].[8] But I shall read his book, vowels and all. Don't forget, if you have 10 minutes for it, the psychology & sociology of the Kiplings—& what he seems to you [to] have—for the future—still *dans le ventre*. This will be my address for some time to come. Pazienza—you shall also some day have something like it. I hope your wife is well now, & greet her on it.

Yours, my dear Gosse, ever
Henry James

1. Gosse managed to go to Italy, the first of several trips there, in the summer of 1896. See letter 138.
2. See, for example, letter 183, note 4.
3. James is staying in Constance Woolson's old apartment and helping the Benedicts settle her affairs. See letter 96, note 2.
4. Delamere Terrace, where Gosse lived, overlooked Regent's Park Canal. See *EG*, 165.
5. The *Yellow Book* began publication in 1894. For Henry Harland, its editor, see letter 65, note 2, and *EG*, 355.
6. W. Robertson Smith (1846–1894), theologian and Semitic scholar at Cambridge, had died March 31, 1894.
7. S. R. Crockett's *The Stickit Minister* had appeared in 1893 and was dedicated to Robert Louis Stevenson.
8. Sir Garnet Wolseley, an old friend to both James and Gosse, had just become Viscount Wolseley. During this period he was commander-in-chief of British forces in Ireland. His book was *The Life of John Churchill, Duke of Marlborough, to the Accession of Queen Anne* (2 vols.; London, 1894). Henry James visited the Wolseleys in Ireland in 1895. See his letter of March 28, 1895, to William James in *HJL*, IV, 5–7. See also letter 117.

102 / MS Library of Congress   [Casa Biondetti]
S. Vio, 715 Venice.
April 23*d* 1894

My dear Gosse.

I make a long arm in a very short note & hold my hand to your couch of pain. It makes me toss in my own bed to hear that you have been so dedicated to yours. It would be heavy news were I not so mindful of your magnificent vitality—and of your still more magnificent wife—to say nothing of the ministering daughters. I see Mrs. Gosse and Tessa arching over you till their devotion meets and unites in a sheltering *soffito*, as we say here—a fair, curved vault—painted with the faces of angels. *I* am afraid to be ill—all uncovered and unfrescoed; but for you it's a recreation like another. However, I trust that by this time you have had enough even of so good a thing; & that Somersetshire and idleness are letting you up ever so gently. This is the sign of sympathy that I wanted to make you: please feel it very distinctly made. I quitted England mainly to get on with a task—but I find that absence promotes my correspondence more than my work.[1] Being away is a questionable boon when it is, in general, mainly filled with *explaining* that one's away. What fact ought more to dispense with a demonstration? Let me not then more elaborately poison your rural rest. All thanks for the pretty news about the Yellow Book. I hear today from Harland that it's in a *2d* edition: the only way—almost—that I have managed to attain even a fraction of an out-of-printedness.[2] There is one *corvee*, I confess, that I almost don't blush to lay upon you: if you could *me toucher un mot* about the air that Sargent's great lunette and arch have, in time, at the Academy—I hear they are going to be shown there.[3] Convalesce utterly, my dear Gosse—& be purged altogether. I insist on good news of you, & kiss my hand, in our gay Venetian way, as I dash past (on *your* canal—on a coal-barge) to Delamere Terrace.

Yours always
Henry James.

1. James had gone to work in Venice and to help Constance Woolson's sister and niece settle her affairs there. See letter 96, note 2.
2. The first number of the *Yellow Book*, the issue containing James's "The Death of the Lion," appeared in April, 1894. Henry Harland edited the magazine.
3. John Singer Sargent had begun studies for the murals of the Boston Public Library in 1890 and by the spring of 1894 had sent the north-wall decorations to the Royal Academy in London. See Ratcliff, *John Singer Sargent*, 141. The "great lunette and arch" may refer to Sargent's *Children of Israel Beneath the Yoke of Their Oppressors*.

103 / MS Leeds   Rome (Grand Hotel.)
                                                   May 30*th* [1894]

My dear Gosse.

I have just written to Mr. Holland Day—the most conciliatorily & appreciatively in the world—to tell him it is utterly impossible.[1] It simply is, believe me; & if I weren't afraid of sounding ungracious I would add that "that's all there is about it." It isn't, perhaps; inasmuch as I applaud, I subscribe, & I even weep. Basta. I am no more in question than if I were not in life; & this for reasons which it would be a weariness all round to inflict on you. Just as a specimen, however, one of them—perhaps even the very least—is that, like somebody or other in *Hedda Gabler*, I "don't do such things." Ask me, my dear Gosse, for your "pleasure," to do one of those I do do. Then you'll see. Otherwise it would be considering you as one of the ancient Roman blood-thirsty (with whose ghosts, in Colosseums &c., I here commune,) seeing before you the gladiator lie. This gladiator *can't* lie even to be called Massoo.

A thousand thanks, all the same, for holding out your hand to help me to be so honourably, so splendidly treated.

I haven't heard from you for many months—but I hope it is all because you have been busy being infinitely better than you were—being perfectly well indeed—and as happy as may be compatible with that state.[2] I am here for 6 days, & then go to Florence for 7; after which back to Venice for June. I shall scarcely be in England, alas, before August. I trust I may catch you on some midsummer eve before you go to grass. I wd. strain every nerve to do so. Don't, yourself, meanwhile, strain too many. Do write me how you are & your wife is. Let it be the truth, but let it also gratify yours most truly

Henry James

1. Fred Holland Day (1864–1933), wealthy American aesthete, pioneer photographer, partner in the publishing firm of Copeland and Day, and collector of John Keats's works, may have asked James to contribute in some active way to an American memorial to Keats that he and Louise Imogen Guiney (1861–1920), American poet and his friend, were establishing in Hampstead parish. See Ellen Foritz Clattenberg's introduction to *The Photographic Work of F. Holland Day* (Wellesley, Mass., 1945), 10.

2. James's memory betrays him here. His letter of April 23, 1894 (letter 102) is obviously in response to one from Gosse.

104 / MS Adeline R. Tintner¹   Casa Biondetti,
                                                   Venice.
                                                   June 25*th* 94

My dear Gosse.

Not another day shall your touching letter of the 13*th* go

unanswered. It should have had before this the glorious meed of a
response—but I have been both absent (in movement,) & unwell,—
that is I had the other day in Florence an attack—a lively little
brush—of influenza (bed, horrid fever &c,) which blighted one's
ideals and made me for a while even more incapable than usual of
legible penmanship. Fortunately I was in the house of a friend, &
that friend a doctor—even of genius; so no misfortune could have
been more fortunate.[2] And now I am as right as the scirocco will
allow. The blaze of summer is upon us and I shall presently edge
away from the fire. I leave this place July 1st & return to England by
the 25th. I hope this will be in time to put a little salt on your tail
before you fly away. No offence meant—it is the way we talk to a
singing-bird, as Torwald Ibsen would say. And to dispose immediately of a further important question—may I ask of you very
kindly & no matter how briefly, to transmit to me any notice or
inkling in your power of the movements—the return to London, date
of being there &c, of the unspeakable Howells? His bare card, & his
daughter's, have come to me from De Vere Gardens—but your letter
seems to denote that you saw him. I don't trust him for any communication—but *please* let me trust *you*. I would certainly come back earlier to catch him. But I hope he is to remain on into August.[3]

For the rest, your letter gave me both joy & anguish—the anguish
perhaps most colouring. I mean because, frankly, I suffer *with* you in
all that I see you must (I should think well nigh intolerably) suffer
from in your harassed, hunted, *accablant* London life. The London of
April—July was killing *me* when, some years ago, I took the death-
less resolve of an annual synchronous flight; & my exposures & burdens were in many ways as feathers compared to yours. You're
unwell because your life is insanely arranged, but keep alive till I can
come back & talk to you. Even at this distance the mere exhalation of
your fever (excuse my ambiguous images,) causes my own temperature to rise. Hang on this once & we will go to the root of things.
The curse of our lives "in this our troubled day" is indeed the huge
incubus of "people." One doesn't escape them here—on the contrary
the whole of my present effort toward 3 months of fruitful isolation,
independence & command of one's time, has been a fatal frustration,
a sacrifice constantly renewed to every sort of demand & interrup-
tion. One is cursed by knowing so many *unoccupied* people—people
who have nothing in life to do but conspire with a hideous amiability

& an infamous good conscience against one's own concentration. But enough of this—I am only trying, by devious ways, to give you patience. You gave me much by speaking so charmingly of my poor playbook—that's the pleasure your letter conferred.[4] One shouldn't perhaps publish one's exercises—& these things are exercises in the devilish little art of *structure*. They have[,] I make bold to say, great— even rare! merit in that line (in proportion I mean to the hideously mean 2 hours & ½ rule of the London stage. Pailleron, Sardou, Dumas, &c, have easily 3 hours & ½–4 hours![5] That's an abyss of difference.) But no one in London has a *grain* of the special gumption for appreciating this particular ability—no one but you. An amiable friend hasn't of course failed to advise me (from London) that *Pall Malls* & things have been "scathing".[6] But oh, I'm far away!

I'm going to *Asolo* in an hour or two to spend 48 with a friend (quand je vous le disais!) & have 36 things to do meanwhile. There- fore I press your hand in farewell. Kipling writes me from Wilts. a wail of despair or detestation over their wet, cold English summer— they apparently feel bitterly sold as well as cold—& announce their rush back to Vermont early in August. How strange are the revela- tions, or at least the exhibitions, of the revolving years. Let no man be pronounced unexpected till he has—married an American![7] He sends me too his jungle book which I have read with extreme admira- tion. But *how* it closes his doors & sets his limit! The rise to "higher types" that one hoped for—I mean the care for life in a finer way—is the rise to the mongoose & the care for the wolf. The *violence* of it all, the almost exclusive preoccupation with fighting & killing, is also singularly characteristic. But we will gossip—if Lord de Tabley will let me.[8] I greet your wife and all your house. Yours evermore

Henry James

1. The text of this letter is based upon a photoduplication of the original kindly sent me by Ms. Tintner, the owner, which I have collated with a typed copy at Duke University.
2. The friend is Dr. W. W. Baldwin. See letter 59, note 1.
3. Although James returned to London July 12, he presumably did not see Howells.
4. The reference is apparently to *Theatricals*, which had appeared earlier in the month. See *BHJ*, 97–98.
5. Edouard Pailleron (1834–1899), Victorien Sardou (1831–1908), and Alexandré Dumas fils (1824–1895) were contemporary French playwrights.
6. The reference is to the *Pall Mall Gazette*, a periodical that James may have sati- rized in "The Death of the Lion" (see letter 102, note 2).

7. Kipling had married Caroline Balestier in 1892 (see letter 81, note 3). *The Jungle Book* had recently appeared.

8. John Byrne Leicester Warren, baron de Tabley (1835–1895), was a good friend to Gosse, and after his death in 1895, Gosse wrote an essay on him for the *Contemporary Review*. See letter 129, note 1.

105 / MS Leeds   715 S. Vio. Venice
                                              July 1st '94.

My dear Gosse.

   I pray it be in your power to very kindly—& at cost of an el-eemosynary stamp—forward the enclosed to Howells.[1] I have no inkling of any address that may reach him, & he writes me no word. But I am offering to go to him in Paris if there is any danger of his not returning to London. This, his non-return, wd. be a sorry business. I am staying on here from day to day till the 10th—long enough to hear from him if my note reaches him through your beneficence. Your little letter telling me you go to Switzerland in July &c just comes to me. I rejoice in Alpine pastures for you—& only wish I could browse by your side. May they do you high heaps of good. I shall be back in time—July 20th—25th—to see you repeatedly.[2] It is very hot here, but *encore tenable*. Yours in great fury, as we say
                                              Henry James

   1. See letter 104, note 3.
   2. James, in fact, returned to London on July 12. See *HJ*, III, 379.

106 / MS Leeds   34 De Vere Gdns. W.
                                              Friday [August 10, 1894][1]

My dear Gosse.

   You were very happily inspired in writing me about Pater's inter-ment—&, in particular, in writing so charmingly.[2] Your letter makes me much regret that, having, as I had, fifty minds to go to his funeral, I didn't have the fifty first which might have carried me there. If I had known you would go I would have joined you—very possibly. But I was deterred by considerations—that of my very lim-ited acquaintance with Pater, my non-communication with him for so long, & above all by (what I supposed would be) the compact Oxfordism of it all; in which I seemed to feel myself to have no place. And now I feel, still more, that I should have liked to *faire acte de présence.* Meanwhile you are very vivid & interesting about it. It was not to be dreamed of, however, I think, that the event should have been more "noticed". What is more delicate than the extinction of delicacy—& what note more in place than that of "discretion"—in respect to the treatment of anything that might have happened to Pater—even the last thing that *could* happen? It presents itself to me—so far as I know it—as one of the successful, felicitous, lives and the time & manner of the death a part of the success. But you must tell me more. I don't cease to regret that being last February (I think,) at Oxford, and Herbert Warren taking me on the Sunday afternoon to see him, took me to the spare little house where Miss P. only was drearily visible, instead of to Brasen nose [*sic*], where I learned with a pang, that evening, from the curious Bussell[,] W.H.P. had been "disappointed" at my non-arrival.[3] Yes, the President of Magdalen is incurably young: I forgive him the youth only on acct. of the incurableness. I have been dividing my time between Rudyard Kipling and Hugues Le Roux; & if I stay in town all through next week (I leave it tomorrow till Tuesday,) I will come & see you of a night.[4] Thanks, thanks again for your letter.

Yours always
Henry James

1. This letter is included in *HJL*, III, 483–84, but my text is from the original and differs in several details.
2. Walter Pater died July 30 and was buried in Oxford. For other references to Pater, see letter 110.
3. Thomas Herbert Warren (1853–1930) was president of Magdalen College, Oxford; the "curious Bussell" was the Reverend Dr. F. W. Bussell, Pater's friend and later vice-president of Brasenose College. Pater had been a fellow of Brasenose College.
4. Hugues Le Roux (1860–1925), a French journalist, was a friend of Paul Bourget's.

107 / MS Virginia   Tregenna C.[astle] Hotel.
                                             St. Ives.
                                             August 22*d* [1894][1]

My dear Gosse.

I should have been very glad to hear from you yesterday if only for the sweet opportunity it gives me of crying out that I told you so! It gives me more than this—and I *didn't* tell you so; but I wanted to awfully—and I only smothered my wisdom under my waist-coat.

Tell Arthur Benson that I wanted to tell *him* so too—that guileless morning at Victoria: I knew so well, both then & at Delamere Terrace, with my ½ century of experience, straight into what a purgatory you were *all* rushing. The high Swiss mountain inn, the crowd, the cold, the heat, the rain, the Germans, the scramble, the impossible rooms and still more impossible anything else—the hope deferred, the money misspent, the weather accurst: these things I saw written on your azure brows even while I perfidiously prattled with your prattle. The only thing was to let you do it—for one can no more come between a lady and her Swiss hotel than between a gentleman & his wife.[2] Meanwhile I sit here looking out at *my* nice, domestic, inexpensive English rain, in *my* nice but stuffy insular inn, and thanking God that I am not as Gosses and Bensons are. I am pretty bad, I recognise—but I am not as bad as you. I am so bad that I am fleeing in a day or two—as I hope you will have been doing if your ineluctable fate doesn't spare you. I stopped on my way down here to spend 3 days with W. E. Norris, which were rendered charming by the urbanity of my host and the peerless beauty of Torquay, with which I fell quite in love.[3] Here I go out for long walks on wet moors with the silent Stephen, the almost speechless Leslie.[4] In the morning I improve the alas not shining hour, in a little black sitting room which looks out into the strange area—like unto that of the London milkman—with which this ci-devant castle is encompassed & which sends up strange scullery odours into my nose. I am very sorry to hear of any friends of yours suffering by the *Saturday Review*, but I know nothing whatever of the cataclysm.[5] It's a journal which (in spite of the lustre you add to it,) I haven't so much as seen for 15 years, and no echoes of its fortunes ever reach me.

23*d.* I broke off yesterday to take a long walk over bogs and brambles, & this morning my windows are lashed by a wet hurricane. It makes me wish I could settle down to a luxurious irresponsible day with the *Lourdes* of your approbation, which lies there on my table still uncut.[6] But my "holiday" is no holiday & I must drive the mechanic pen. Moreover I have vowed not to open *Lourdes* till I shall have closed with a final furious bang the unspeakable *Lord Ormont*, which I have been reading at the maximum rate of 10 pages—ten insufferable & unprofitable pages, a day.[7] It fills me with a critical rage, an artistic fury, utterly blighting in me the indispensable principle of *respect*. I have finished, at this rate, but the first volume—

whereof I am moved to declare that I doubt if any equal quantity of extravagant verbiage, of airs & graces, of phrases & attitudes, of obscurities and alembications ever *started* less their subject, ever contributed less of a statement—told the reader less of what the reader needs to know. All elaborate predicates of exposition without the ghost of a nominative to hook themselves to; & not a difficulty met, not a figure presented, not a scene constituted—not a dim shadow condensing once either into audible or into visible reality—making you hear for an instant the tap of its feet on the earth. Of course there are pretty things, but for what they are they come so much too dear; & so many of the profundities and tortuosities prove when threshed out, to be only pretentious statements of the very simplest propositions. Enough, and forgive me. Above all don't send this to the P.M.G. [*Pall Mall Gazette*]. There is another side, of course, which one will utter another day. I have a dictated letter from R.L.S., sent me through Colvin, who is at Schwalbach with the horsey Duchess of Montrose, a disappointing letter in which the too apt pupil of Meredith tells me nothing that I want to know—nothing save that his spirits are low (which I wd. fain ignore,) & that he has been [on] an excursion on an English man of war.[8] The devilish letter is wholly about the man-of-war, not a word else; and at the end he says "I *decline* to tell you any more about it!" as if I had prescribed the usurping subject.[9] You shall see the rather melancholy pages when you return—I must keep them to answer them. Bourget & his wife are in England again—at Oxford; with Prévost at Buxton; H. Le Roux at Wimbledon &c, it is the Norman conquest beginning afresh. What will be the end, or the effect, of it? P.B. has sent me some of the sheets (100 pp.) of his *Outremer*, which are singularly agreeable & lively. It will be much the prettiest (& I shld. judge kindest,) socio-psychological book written about the U.S. That is saying little. It is very living & interesting. Prévost's fetid étude (on the little girls,) represents a perfect bound, from his earlier things in the way of hard, firm, knowing ability.[10] So clever—& so common; no ability to imagine his "queenly" girl, made to dominate the world, do anything finally by way of illustrating her superiority, but become a professional cocotte, like a *fille de portier*. Pity's akin to love so I send that to Mrs. Nellie & Tessa & to A. Benson.

Yours ever
Henry James

1. This letter has appeared previously in *LHJ*, I, 217–20, and *HJL*, III, 484–87.
2. Gosse and his family had gone to Switzerland for a holiday with Arthur C. Benson (1862–1925), an old friend and a master at Eton.
3. Norris, a friend both to James and Gosse, lived at Torquay. See letter 95, note 1.
4. Although he was staying at a hotel, James was visiting the Leslie Stephen family.
5. The *Saturday Review* had recently been bought by Frank Harris (1856–1931), an American who had edited the *Fortnightly Review*, and many contributors, according to Gosse, had been driven "out into the street with cuffs and kicks" (*LL*, 239). Gosse, nevertheless, continued to write for the *Saturday Review*.
6. Zola's novel (1894), the first in his trilogy *Les Trois Villes*.
7. *Lord Ormont and His Aminta* (1894), by George Meredith.
8. The *Curacoa*, according to Stevenson, was "the model war-ship of Great Britain." See Smith (ed.), *James and Stevenson*, 243. The letter from Stevenson to James is dated July 7, 1894. For Sidney Colvin, see letter 17, note 2.
9. James is misquoting Stevenson, who instead said, "And I decline any longer to give you examples of how not to write" (246).
10. For Bourget, see letter 10, note 1. Marcel Prévost (1862–1940) had just published *Les Demi-Vierges*, the "fetid étude" James mentions. Bourget's *Outremer* appeared before the end of the year. H. Le Roux is mentioned in letter 106, note 4.

108 / MS Leeds
                                                                    15 Beaumont St.
                                                                    Oxford[1]
                                                                    Sept. 8*th* [1894]

I rejoice with you[,] my dear Gosse[,] over the happiness that has been crowning your efforts. The Lake of Lucerne, of a fine summer day, is indeed one of the noblest of pleasures—& there isn't a balcony there—at Lucerne, I mean, scarcely—over which I haven't at one time or another hung, nor a walk that I haven't at one time or another taken. *Don't* I know Stans & Stansstadt—& Alpnacht & Zug & all the little sturdy, stodgy, stony & withal most delectable Swiss townlets! I saw them almost all, afresh, 14 months ago. In short I am most glad that things have gone well with you. This is but a line to say so—& that we will talk them over. I quitted my Cornish retreat some days ago & have been here these several—in conditions I have found excellent both for industry and for conversation. My conversation (Oxford is as empty as your pocket will be when you get home,) has been exclusively with the Paul Bourgets, who are near me here, at the inn—but who depart on the 10*th*—12*th*, straight for Paris.[2] Oxford itself is comfortable in its stillness & lovely in its manifold gardens. I stay on, probably till the 17*th*—scarcely, I think, longer.

On my return I will very promptly knock at your door. Keep the romance of travel from leaking till I come—that I may tap it and enjoy the gush. I hope you have all been well set up—have renewed your youth like the eagles. Not a scrap of news that I know of has been born. Your return will be the *1st*—& have all the honours. Vale—valete. I hope you brought me a Swiss cottage in a box—or at least an Edelweiss—in a pot. It's really a relief to know you [*sic*] on your way—for I have been expecting every day to read in the Times that you had perished in attempting the ascent of some horn or other—without guides or at least with none but Mrs. Gosse & Tessa. Please don't tell anyone I don't like G. Meredith—what wd. become of my social position? I have finished the infamous book without seeing any reason to moderate my asperity.[3] But I indulge it only in secret.

Yours impatiently
Henry James

1. James is staying at Constance Woolson's old address in Oxford.
2. For Paul Bourget, see letter 10, note 1.
3. For Meredith's *Lord Ormont and His Aminta*, see letter 107. For other comments on Meredith, see letters 283 and 284.

---

109 / MS Leeds   34, De Vere Gardens. W.
                                              Nov. *9th* 1894.[1]

My dear Gosse.

Many thanks for the study of the roaring Norseman which I read attentively last night—without having time, claimed by more *intimes* perusals, for reading his lusty fable.[2] Björneson [*sic*] has always been, I frankly confess, an untended prejudice—a hostile one—of mine, & the effect of your lively and interesting monograph has been, I fear, to validate the hardly more than instinctive mistrust. I don't think you justify him, *rank* him enough—hardly quite enough for the attention you give him. At any rate he sounds in your picture—to say nothing of looking, in his own!—like the sort of literary fountain from which I am ever least eager to drink: the big, splashing, blundering genius of the hit-or-miss, the *à peu près*, family—without perfection, or the effort toward it, without the exquisite, the love of selection: a big superabundant & promiscuous democrat. On the other hand the impossibly-named *Novelle* wd. perhaps win me over.

But the human subject-matter in these fellows is so rébarbatif—
"Mrs. Bang & Tande!" what a Romeo & Juliet![3]

Have you seen Maurice Barrès's last volume—"Du Sang, de la
Volupté & de la Mort"?[4] That *is* exquisite in its fearfully intelligent
impertinence & its diabolical Renanisation. We will talk of these
things—all thanks meanwhile for the book.

Yours ever
Henry James

P.S. I think your preface singularly vivid & readable.

1. Previously printed in *LHJ*, I, 220–21.
2. Gosse's "study," an essay on the writings of Björnstjerne Björnson, served as a
preface to an English translation by Julie Sutter (London, 1895) of Björnson's *Synnove
Solbakken* (1857).
3. Characters in Björnson's novel *Magahild* (1877).
4. Barrès (1862–1923), French writer and politician, and author of *Du Sang* (1894),
would subsequently become a personal friend of Gosse's.

110 / MS Library of Congress   34, De Vere Gardens, W.
                                               Thursday [December 13, 1894][1]

My dear Gosse.

I return with much appreciation the vivid pages on Pater.[2] They
fill up substantially the void of one's ignorance of his personal history, & they are of a manner graceful & luminous; though I should
perhaps have relished a little more insistence on—a little more of an
inside view of—the nature of his mind itself. Much as they tell, however, how curiously negative & faintly-grey he, after all telling,
remains! I think he has had—will have had—the most exquisite literary fortune: i.e. to have taken it out all, wholly, exclusively, with the
pen (the style, the genius,) & absolutely not at all with the person.
He is the mask without the face, & there isn't in his total superficies
a tiny point of vantage for the newspaper to flap its wings on. You
have been lively about him—but about whom *wouldn't* you be lively?
I think you'd be lively about *me*![3]

Well, faint, pale, embarrassed, exquisite Pater! He reminds me, in
the disturbed midnight of our actual literature, of one of those lucent
matchboxes which you place, on going to bed, near the candle, to
show you, in the darkness, where you can strike a light: he shines in
the uneasy gloom—vaguely, and has a phosphorescence, not a flame.

But I quite agree with you that he is not of the little day—but of the longer time.

Will you kindly ask Tessa if I may *still* come, on Saturday? My visit to the country has been put off by a death—& if there is a little corner for me I'll appear. If there isn't—so late—no matter. I dare say I ought to write to Miss Wetton. Or will Tessa aimiably inquire?[4]

Yours always
Henry James

1. Printed in *LHJ*, I, 221–22, in *SL*, 141–42, and in *HJL*, III, 492.
2. Edmund Gosse, "Walter Pater: A Portrait," *Contemporary Review*, LXVI (December, 1894), 795–810. Reprinted in Gosse, *Critical Kit-Kats* (London, 1896), 239–71.
3. After James's death, Gosse had an opportunity to be "lively" about his friend. See his essay on James in the *London Mercury*, I (April, 1920), 673–84, and II (May, 1920), 29–41.
4. As Edel has pointed out, James occasionally spells *amiably* with a French touch, though neither Lubbock's nor Edel's text includes the initial *i* in this instance.

111 / MS British Library   34, De Vere Gardens. W.
                                              Dec. 17*th* 1894[1]

My dear Gosse.

I meant to write you to-night on another matter—but of what can one think, or utter or dream, save of this ghastly extinction of the beloved R.L.S.?[2] It is too miserable for cold words—it's an absolute desolation. It makes me cold & sick—& with the absolute, almost alarmed sense, of the visible material quenching of an indispensable light. That he's silent forever will be a fact hard, for a long time, to live with. Today, at any rate, it's a cruel, wringing emotion. One feels how one cared for him—what a place he took; & as if suddenly *into* that place there had descended a great avalanche of ice. I'm not sure that it's not for *him* a great & happy fate; but for us the loss of charm, of suspense, of "fun" is unutterable. And how confusedly & pityingly one's thought turns [to] those far-away stricken women, with their whole principle of existence suddenly quenched & yet all the monstrosity of the rest of their situation left on their hands! I saw poor Colvin to-day—he is overwhelmed, he is touching.[3] But I can't write of this—we must talk of it. Yet these words have been a relief.

And I can't write, either, of the matter I had intended to—viz. that you are to rest secure about the question of June 5*th*—I will do every-

thing for you.[4] *That* business becomes for the hour tawdry & heartless to me.

Yours always
Henry James

1. Included in *LHJ*, I, 223–24, and in *HJL*, III, 495.
2. Robert Louis Stevenson had died in Samoa on December 3; James apparently
has just heard about it.
3. The women referred to are Stevenson's wife and mother. For Colvin, Stevenson's intimate friend and future editor, see letter 17, note 2. For further expressions
of James's grief, see his letter to Fanny Stevenson in *HJL*, III, 497–501.
4. The date is a slip of the pen for January 5, the night of the opening in London
of *Guy Domville*. Gosse was to be James's guest for the first night of the play. See letter 113.

112 / MS Library of Congress   34 De Vere Gardens W.
                                                  Saturday [December 22, 1894]

My dear Gosse,

I have been too damnably occupied to reply to your cry of bewil-
derment till this moment. I can only say that *I* am bewildered too.
My pessimism makes me believe the worst—it being the only safe &
far the most *easy* thing to do. *Yet*, so long as the successive days go by
without bringing *any* news to *any* one, there remains just that flicker
of hope. Lest you shldn't. have seen the letter in today's *Chronicle*, I
cut it out & send it.[1] But [it] is too probably only a vain torment—
making one quite sick with the perverse confusion, the anxious
hauntings of it. Added to the demoralizing & exhausting & incongruous ordeal I am daily going through at the theatre—& which
from Monday on will be doubled—rehearsals by night as well as
day—it makes me miserably nervous.[2] But poor *really* tried Colvin—
I think almost only of *him*.[3] One waits, in all ways, for light. Excuse
my brutal haste.

Ever yours
Henry James

Letters this a.m. from Howells & from Mrs. Balestier.[4]

1. Apparently a letter casting doubt on Stevenson's demise. I have not been able
to examine a copy of the *Chronicle* for December 22, 1894, but a similar reference to
a letter in the *Pall Mall Gazette* for December 20 (possibly the same one in the *Chronicle*) suggests the content. See James's letter to Colvin in *LHJ*, I, 224–25.
2. *Guy Domville* was scheduled to open January 5, 1895.
3. For Colvin, see note 1, above, and letter 17, note 2.
4. For Anna Smith Balestier, the mother of Wolcott Balestier and Carrie Balestier

Kipling, see letter 81 and Charles Carrington, *Rudyard Kipling: His Life and Work*
(London, 1955), 176.

113 / MS Leeds   34 D.V.G., W.
                                                       Dec. 27*th* '94.[1]

My dear Gosse.

It will be all right—& I will take care. None of the seats can have
been sent out yet: they will go in a day or two. Those you will
receive are not to be paid for—they are direct from the author. I shall
be delighted if Norris can go with you—though appalled at his making that midwinter journey to such an end.[2] The responsibility of it!

Yes, I should like much to talk with you. The ghost of poor
R.L.S. waves its great dusky wings between me & all occupations—
& I am haunted for another reason that I will tell you.[3] I am unable
to say whether Friday or Saturday will be free evenings for me—the
damnable theatre is now given over to nocturnal as well as diurnal
rehearsals. But I shall probably know to-night. I have been reading
with the liveliest—an almost painful—interest the 2 volumes on the
extraordinary Symonds.[4] They give me an extraordinary impression
of his "gifts"—yet I don't know what keeps them from being tragic.

                                                       Yours ever
                                                       Henry James

1. Printed in *HJL*, III, 502.
2. The tickets are for the first performance of *Guy Domville* on January 5, 1895.
W. E. Norris was a mutual friend and would be coming to London from Torquay.
See letter 95, note 1.
3. The reference to Stevenson suggests that the other reason James may have felt
"haunted" by his friend's "ghost" is his refusal to serve as an executor of Stevenson's
estate. See James's letters to Colvin (*LHJ*, I, 224–25) and to Mrs. Stevenson (*HJL*,
III, 497–501).
4. Horatio Brown (1854–1926), a British historian and acquaintance of James's,
had written this biography of Symonds.

114 / MS Cambridge   34, De Vere Gardens, W.
                                                  Jan. 1*st* 1894. [1895][1]

Dear Mrs. Gosse.

Would Friday of this week—or Thursday either—suit your little
group for a visit to the Olympian show & a sociable supper at 34

D.V.G.W., afterward—?[2] I am of course hoping earnestly that little Edmund will have been a good enough boy in the interim to be permitted also to come. If this week doesn't agree with your other combinations, would not some early day next week—that is, Tuesday or Wednesday? There are 2 performances daily—one at 12 (noon) the other at 6.[3] I think you will agree with me in preferring the romantic night-effects to those of the garish morn. Better too, surely, for little E. Whatever day meets your approval, I shall be delighted. I wish everything to every-one! Yours always

Henry James

P.S. I will arrange with you afterwards—after hearing from you— our meeting & every detail.

1. James has forgotten momentarily that 1894 has been succeeded by 1895.
2. James is planning a small theater party after the performance of *Guy Domville*, but in the next letter, he changes the time and includes the Henry Harlands.
3. The performance actually begins at 8:00 P.M.

115 / MS Cambridge   34 De Vere Gardens. W.
                                                  Tuesday [January 1, 1895]

Dear Mrs. Gosse.

Will you kindly call it next Tuesday, *9th*? I have asked the 2 Harlands to be with us and have given them the margin of time involved in the later day, as I can't hear from them till tomorrow.[1] I am greatly obliged for the punctual, liberal, luminous response. I find that it's only the side-shows &c. of the place that are open at 6; & that the *performance* begins at 8.[2] So much the better—as I think you will agree. Therefore do kindly all come & have a nice stodgy infant-tea with me here at (say) *6.15*, before the affair instead of after. This is really an indispensable part of the business—don't, oh don't, despoil the occasion of it's [*sic*] choicest, its most intimate feature. I shall count on you for 6.15; & I have imposed the same stern necessity on the Harlands. Keep little Edmund, please, up—or rather down—to the mark! Yours most truly

Henry James

1. James is planning a theater party with the Gosses and Harlands as his guests. See letter 114. He is wrong about Tuesday's date; it was January 8.
2. James earlier thought that the performance would begin at 6:00 P.M. For James's plans to use Gosse as a reporter on the reception of the play during its first performance, see his letter of January 3, 1895, in *HJL*, III, 504–505. James attended

a performance of Wilde's *An Ideal Husband* and then went to check for himself the reception of his own play. For a full account of the fiasco that followed, see Edel's edition of *Guy Domville*, 96ff.

116 / MS Leeds   34, De Vere Gardens. W.
                                                   January 13*th* 1895

My dear Gosse.

All thanks for your graceful & humorous defense of Poesy, or of Comedy (it comes to the same thing.)[1] It would do much for the case, if the thing had not been, from the first, mortally wounded. I am none the less grateful for your wit & eloquence. This I shall express to you better some evening soon—I will come in. I have had a very tired & tiring week. Is there any night on which Mrs. Gosse wd. accept a box for the comedy & take Tessa & Silvia & even the young Athlete: or stalls, if she prefers?[2] Could she kindly name a couple of evenings? Yours and hers always

Henry James

1. This piece presumably appeared in the *Realm*, but I have not been able to examine all relevant issues for January, 1895.
2. The "comedy" is *Guy Domville*. See letters 111, 112, and 113. The invitation to the Gosses to attend the play a second time (they had been present on opening night) confirms a point James subsequently made to William and Alice James on February 2, 1895: "What appears largely to have enabled *G. D.* to go on even a month is the fact that almost every one who has been to see it at all appears to have been two or three times" (*HJL*, III, 515).

117 / MS Leeds   34, De Vere Gardens. W.
                                                   Thursday. [March 28, 1895?][1]

My dear Gosse.

I found here last night your little recital of your troubles & projects. I greatly grieve you have been so ill & also that I have to wait till Saturday* to come & sit by your couch. We will then talk of your plan for Dunster—which alas, charming as it is, finds me sadly embarrassed & empêché.[2] Just returned as I am from nearly 3 weeks (3 weeks Saturday,) of profligate & expensive absence, the vision of fresh excesses leaves me virtuously cold; & I never "do" anything at Easter but sit close & profit by the tranquillity of the empty town. But I will prattle of Dunster with you as platonically as you like. Above all I hope to find you better after your sorry, your accursed

month. You have all my sympathy. Ireland was very kind to me—
that is the sweet Wolseleys were: for my 6 days at the castle were,
like those of everyone else there (including poor Norris,) a simply
unmitigated hell. His Excellency is insane—simply.[3] But I will tell
you all. Pazienza.

> Yours & your wife's
> constantly
> *Henry James*

* I have for night an engagement unfortunately insoluble.

1. Although James provides "Thursday" only as a reference to date, we may
assume this letter was written March 28, 1895 (a Thursday), since several matters
discussed herein are also mentioned in a letter of that date to William and Alice
James (*HJL*, IV, 5–7).
2. During this period Gosse often spent holidays in Dunster, Somerset, to which
he often invited James, but James seldom availed himself of these invitations. See,
for example, letters 75–77.
3. James had visited Lord Houghton, Lord Lieutenant of Ireland ("His Excellency") and, subsequently, the "sweet Wolseleys," his and Gosse's old friends (see
letter 101, note 8). For W. E. Norris, another old friend, see letter 95, note 1.

118 / MS Leeds   Monday [April 8, 1895][1]
My dear Gosse.

Yes, I will come with pleasure tomorrow, Tuesday. Yes, too, it has
been, it is, hideously, atrociously dramatic & really interesting— so
far as one can say that of a thing of which the interest is qualified by
such a sickening horribility.[2] It is the squalid gratuitousness of it
all—of the mere exposure—that blurs the spectacle. But the *fall*—
from nearly 20 years of a really unique kind of "brilliant" conspicuity
(wit, "art," conversation—"one of our 2 or 3 dramatists &c.,") to that
sordid prison-cell & this gulf of obscenity over which the ghoulish
public hangs & gloats—it is beyond any utterance of irony or any
pang of compassion! He was never in the smallest degree interesting
to me—but this hideous human history has made him so—in a manner. À demain—Yours ever

> *Henry James*

[P.S.] Quel Dommage—mais quel Bonheur—que J.A.S. ne soit plus
de ce monde![3]

1. Printed in *SL*, 142–43, and reprinted in *HJL*, IV, 9–10. The envelope is postmarked April 8, 1895.
2. Oscar Wilde had been charged on April 6 with "committing indecent acts"

and arrested on the same day. His unsuccessful prosecution of the Marquess of Queensbury for libel had ended on April 5. For a full account of the Wilde trials, see Hyde, *Oscar Wilde*, 222 ff.

3. This sentence is not designated a postscript, but is instead written on the flap of the envelope. The allusion is to John Addington Symonds. See letter 8, note 3.

119 / MS Leeds   34, De Vere Gardens. W.
                                                Sunday. [April 28, 1895][1]

My dear Gosse.

Thanks—of a troubled kind, for your defense of my modesty in the *Realm*.[2] The article is brilliantly clever—but I have almost the same anguish (that is, my modesty has,) when defended as when violated. You have, however, doubtless done it great good, which I hereby formally recognise. These are days in which one's modesty is, in every direction, much exposed, & one should be thankful for every veil that one can hastily snatch up or that a friendly hand precipately [*sic*] muffles one withal. It is strictly congruous with these remarks that I should mention that there go to you tomorrow a.m. in 2 registered envelopes, at 1 Whitehall, the fond outpourings of poor J.A.S.[3] I put them into 2 because I haven't 1 big enough to hold all— & it so happens that of that size I have only registered ones. I'm afraid I shan't see you—so preoccupied do the evenings seem—till the formidable *9th*.[4] Our guest (you might have mentioned it in the *Realm*,) has a malady of the bladder which makes him desire strange precautions—& I see—I foresee singular complications—the flow of something more than either soul or champagne at dinner.[5]

Did you see in last evening's ½ d. papers that the wretched O.W. seems to have a gleam of light before him (if it really counts for that!) in the fearful exposure of his (of the prosecution's) little beasts of witnesses?[6] What a nest of almost infant blackmailers!

                                                Yours ever
                                                Henry James

1. Printed in *HJL*, IV, 12.

2. According to Edel, Gosse's article "dealt with Alphonse Daudet's impending visit" and was later included in *French Profiles* (1904). See *HJL*, IV, 12*n*.

3. John Addington Symonds. See letters 8, note 3, and 113, note 4.

4. James was planning a dinner party at the Reform Club in honor of Daudet on May 9. He also refers to it in a letter of June 1, 1895, to William James (*HJL*, IV, 16).

5. The reference is to Daudet's kidney trouble. Daudet had earlier contracted a venereal disease that affected his kidneys.

6. These witnesses, many of whom Wilde had admitted knowing, had been used by the defense in his first trial and were now being used by the prosecution in his second (Hyde, *Oscar Wilde*, 259ff.).

120 / MS Leeds   34, De Vere Gardens. W
                                                               Friday [May 10, 1895]

My dear Gosse.

All thanks for your graceful tribute—the model of the letter addressed on the melancholy morrow to Feeder by Fed. I am delighted that you have no worse indigestion. I flew to the *Times* this a.m. in spite of slightly drooping wings. I think your letter exactly the right one, & the portion of your speech that you cite not only very blameless & bland, but altogether felicitous—remarkably well & wittily said.[1] From the moment that "unbridled greed" isn't in it—as it doesn't seem to be—their action (the Society's,) is singularly silly. It was apparently those imputed words that angered the robust & virtuous Besantry. I think the ventilation of the whole matter ought to do good—though it still leaves more to be said—I mean in the sense of the plea for a little simple silence about the too-iterated money-question. That's all one wants—for *in* it (in the silence) some little sound may at last get a chance to be heard on some *other* aspect of authorship, which is no more mentioned, mostly than if it didn't exist. The fact is that authorship is guilty of a great mistake, a gross want of tact, in formulating & publishing its claim to be a "profession." Let other trades call it so—& let it take no notice. That's enough. It ought to have of the professions only a professional thoroughness. But *never* to have that, & to cry on the housetops instead that it *is* the grocer & the shoemaker is to bring on itself a ridicule of which it will simply die.

Please thank Mrs. Gosse, for me, for her card for Sunday & beg her to suffer me to leave the question open—. I fear I shall be, by that hour, rather *essoufflé*. Yours & hers ever

                                                               Henry James

1. Gosse had made a speech to the booksellers' dinner that had aroused the opposition of the Society of Authors, an organization that he had supported in the past. (See letters 46–49.) He had urged authors not to be "greedy," especially "popular novelists" who pressured their publishers for larger royalties and thus created a cycle of increased demands by publishers from booksellers and by booksellers from the public. The society had "censured" Gosse, and he, accordingly, wrote a letter to the *Times* on May 10, 1895, explaining, defending, and justifying his position in the matter (11). Walter Besant was also associated with the society. Its position, as described

by W. M. Conway in the *Times* on May 13, was that the author, publisher, and book-seller should each try to get the greatest share possible of the selling price and that there should be a "fair insistence upon justice" (11). Both Gosse and James were members of the society.

121 / MS Leeds   Osborne Hotel
                                                    Torquay.
                                                    Aug. *9th* [1895]

My dear Gosse.

Here's to your happy departure & your still happier return with all my heart. The mere wind of your pen-stroke is the stiffest breeze that has stirred my clustering tresses for a month. This still blue backwater has quite engulfed me. London had become execrable to me when I fled from it, & I have had a much-needed bath of solitude & quill-driving. I grieve to say I am obliged to go up to town on Monday or Tuesday; but only, I hope, for a week or two (missing you, alas, by just a day;) but I pray the gods to let me come back for September. I like the empty—utterly empty, soundless, scentless place, where the waves as they drowsily break on the curbstone of Hesketh Crescent are in the ambient air—almost as loud as the gong that summons me to dinner. You have a fevered tone & air which makes me hope the Alpine snow will reduce your temperature. I give you all 3—all 4 with sweet A.B.—my earnest invocations; but it isn't impotent spite that makes me glad I'm not going to double up in a Swiss caravansery under the pure breath of the glacier.[1] My heart's in the lowlands—but my imagination so long as you [are] gone, will be at the post-office. Do give it something, there, to preserve it from snubs. I haven't spoken to a cat for a month—for dear Norris has nothing feline.[2] I have seen him (he departed this a.m. for 3 weeks at Buxton,) most evenings in the week, after dinner (our day-habits utterly fail to coincide,) and am more than ever impressed with his loveable nature. On the other hand conversation with him fearfully flags—from his extreme simplicity & his want of intellectual life. One really doesn't see the solution, save in so far as it resides in just persistently liking him. His daughter has been rather gravely ill—& for 2 or 3 days he was very anxious. But she is better; & they are both to be purged & healed—or whatever it is Buxton undertakes. No echo of London has reached me, save yours—& a letter from the Kiplings which represents them as on the point of returning to the

U.S. If they have not yet done so I shall probably see Rogue Rudyard. Read, if you haven't done so, Huysmans' *En Route*.[3] It is strange & vile & perverse, but of an extraordinary *facture* & an interesting sincerity. But you have probably both read & reviewed it. I know your mother is in these parages & should ask her leave to come & see her if she were not in the condition you describe.[4] I dread also a little the vortex she may whirl me into. How ingeniously you have got rid of your children—you almost rival *me*. Seriously it is very graceful & symmetrical. Philip will perhaps colonise while Sylvia keeps an eye on the stately homes of England & Tessa learns to jodel. Yes Osterley is deeply desirable: exactly my idea of a sweet suburban home.[5] And the people the salt of the earth. Do prod me—while away—with your Alpenstock—& while you are about it *walk over the Simplon if only to Domo D'ossolo for just the bare sense of Italy the divine*. It is so easy, so lovely & so cheap.

Yours all always
Henry James

1. The Gosses—Edmund, Nellie, and Tessa—together with Arthur Benson, were leaving for Switzerland on August 12. For Benson, see letter 107, note 2.
2. W. E. Norris lived in Torquay. For other references to Norris, see letter 95, note 1.
3. Joris-Karl Huysmans, *En Route* (Paris, 1895).
4. Eliza Brightwen Gosse (1813–1900), Gosse's stepmother, lived at Sandhurst, St. Marychurch, Devon, near Torquay.
5. The reference to Osterley is presumably to Osterley Park, the home of Lord and Lady Jersey near London. See *HJ*, III, 163; *HJL*, III, 123.

122 / MS Duke   34, De Vere Gardens. W.
Aug. 22*d* 1895

My dear Gosse.

I shall be brief with you, for I am weary & worn with much writing & with the intolerable thunderous torrid stuffiness of this utterly irrelevant city. Tiresome things detain me here some days longer, but I hope to return to Devonshire soon as the charmed returns to the charmer. I go to Folkestone for 3 days tomorrow.[1] But though brief I shall also be expressive: expressive I mean of my appreciation of your vivid & graceful letter. Well, I'm glad you're in a great place—I suppose that's always so much to the good, but somehow—it's the old story—the Swiss Caravanserai in August is a thing—to me—of depressing promiscuities.[2] However, I rejoice to reflect that *your* promiscuities are mainly with the sublime objects that surround you. Don't go too far all the same, even with these—like poor, tragic, miserable Mr. Eyre.[3] What a bad business to be so close to. It must have jeté un froid—! Your sleeplessness has all my sympathy. For me such heights are prohibitive—I don't close the eye. There is not a creature in town save the crowds—a few millions—at the Indian exhibition where I dined last night. It's touching to see how the non-conformist conscience takes to beer-garden & café life as soon as the rain intermits. We should all be French but for the umbrella-merchants. I have a letter from poor Norris at Buxton—miserable with hatred of the place yet exemplary even in his despair.[4] His health gets worse there, but not his hand: nor, fortunately, his sweet nature—if anything so far from bad can be talked of as badder. I have no literature for you, & no life—save indeed that I spent Sunday at the Humphrey [*sic*] Wards where I was naturally up to my neck both in fleshpots & inkstands.[5] She is incorrigbly [*sic*] wise & good, & has a moral nature as Patti has a voice or Tessa a *chevelure*; but, somehow I don't, especially when talking art & letters, *communicate* with her worth a damn. All the same she's a dear—& has offered me her hill-side cottage for October. I haven't accepted—I dread the evenings. Don't be too long away—but go it while you are. May the spirit of the Lord descend upon you. Dear Mrs. Gosse of Devonshire—or for that matter, of the other place too![6] I *must* go to a tea with her qui d'annonce si bien. I have Arthur Benson's note—please tell him; or call it a letter, if he looks wounded, & am only crouching for my spring.[7] Meantime it makes me think of him—which I like. I think of you all, & like that too, & am ever, my dear Gosse, Yours constantly

Henry James

1. See letter 123. James's visit to Folkestone was to his old friend George Du Maurier.

2. Gosse was staying at the Hotel Bel-Alp in Valais.

3. Mr. Eyre is A. W. Eyre, the guest found " horribly smashed, on rocks almost within sight" (*LL*, 248). See also *EG*, 376, and letter 123.

4. For Norris, see letter 95, note 1.

5. Mrs. Humphry Ward (Mary Augusta Ward, 1851–1920) was the granddaughter of Thomas Arnold of Rugby and a well-known Christian novelist of the period.

6. The reference is to Gosse's stepmother; see letter 121, note 4.

7. For Arthur Benson, see letter 107, note 2.

123 / TC Duke   34, De Vere Gardens, W.
                                               August 27*th* [1895]

My dear Gosse,

Why, I feel as if I had done nothing but write to you! I answered immediately your first from the Bel Alp, & here I am at it again.[1] If I have a modesty about being at it every day it is that it seems a poor thing to show you that while you are wallowing in the eternal snows & flirting with princes of the church, I am only hanging about these empty courts & riding on the tops of penny-busses. But I *have* had an adventure—I have spent three days at Folkestone, from which I have just returned—going there to say How d'ye do to my melancholy old friend Du Maurier, melancholy in spite of the chink—what say I, the "chink"?—the deafening roar of sordid gold flowing in to him from the *intarissable Trilby* (the play is a 2*d*. gold mine) & preparing to flow in from its completed successor.[2] He was just arranging that question. I came back feeling an even worse failure than usual, & your luxurious letter only deepens my blush. You seem to announce your descent from là-haut, but you don't tell me where this graceful flutter alights. Not in Delamere Terrace, I opine—I don't dare to assume you return hither so soon, & fear there is no chance of my drinking in your reminiscences before I leave town again—till November 1st—in all probability on September 5*th*.[3] The humility of my situation leaves me absolutely nothing to tell you save that I admire equally your vivid letters & your pedestrian piety. Very beautiful & brave your monument to poor Eyre.[4] May you not however interweave with it any of your own bones. Wonderful your description of the sister & her brilliant grief—and strange to have to hang that way over the vertiginous gulf. I'm glad for the rest that you have the chatter of the Gaul about you rather than the expectoration of his victors. You make me long for a gossip with your noctambulist Viscountess. Àpropos of that order of the noblesse I do indeed feel it as delightful as ever of the Wolseleys to continue to give us in this prosaic world the spectacle of their 'romantic evolution'.[5] They are the best "circus" one knows, & they go round & round the ring. What wonderful Alpine rose Lady Dorothy—she'll come back with a collection of cow-bells.

I had four days ago a very interesting visit from Graham Balfour— just from San Francisco & from Fanny Stevenson—with probably effective powers to deal with the delirious Baxter. He was very lean

& brown and excellent, & said that the three at San Francisco are settled there on a good basis for six months to come.[6] Also that Baxter would probably prove more amenable henceforth. He himself spends the winter in England & it's a blessing.

I deplore more than I can say Mrs. Gosse's sprain—& if I were there would give her an arm or beguile her imprisoned hours. May she however have already yielded—that is may her ankle—to her rich vitality. I *think* I am writing to C.B. by this post—but he will be able to tell you better than[7]

Yours, my dear Gosse, always,
Henry James.

1. See letter 122, note 2.
2. *Trilby*, the novel, appeared in 1894; the play was produced in 1895.
3. James had gone to Torquay in late July, but his stay was interrupted by a three-week sojourn in London in August and September. See letter 124.
4. See letter 122, note 3.
5. For the Wolseleys, see letter 101, note 8.
6. Graham Balfour, Robert Louis Stevenson's cousin, subsequently wrote a biography of Stevenson (1901); Charles Baxter was Stevenson's literary executor; and the "three at San Francisco" are presumably Stevenson's wife, mother, and stepson.
7. Although the typescript has "C.B.," the reference is to Arthur Benson, Gosse's companion on the holiday. See letter 122.

124 / MS Library of Congress   Osborne Hotel, Torquay.
                                        Thursday [September 12, 1895]
Alas, my dear child, I shall not be there—I *am* not there—to welcome you. I left London again but the other day (I was confined to the torrid town from Aug. 12*th* to September 5*th*,) & my present idea is to be absent till November 1*st*. I am very sorry to miss all the freshness of your outpourings & all the bloom of your beauty. I can't ask you on the one hand to keep yourself bottled two months longer or on the other to unbottle through the funnel of letter-paper—so I suffer, I feel, a permanent privation. Pity me somehow, relieve & recreate me. Shan't you be coming down to have tea with your stepmother?[1] I *may* have to go up toward the end of the month for 2 or 3 days to see that they don't mispaper, mispaint & miselectrify my apartment (all the devils of hell are let loose in it!) but even if I do I shouldn't be able to sleep or stay there, so I hope to be saved the bother. Only if I do I shall of course notify you & ask for talk &

Traffistine. I hope you all return full of life & lustihood. You will make out that you are more interesting *than* you are, on purpose to torment me; but still, even allowing for that, you must be very interesting. Do a little Terburg & Teniers for me. I find myself so fond of this plain place that I shall probably (though not certainly—for I *may* go to Cornwall,) spend the whole of the rest of my absence in it. The Paul Bourgets—ubiquitous pair—are here; & we dine together tonight with the good & sad Norris, who has just come back from a month at Buxton, bursting with quickened disease.[2] He & his daughter, both seem to me pretty poorly. He is the gentlest & sweetest of men & one quite loves him—so that it almost makes up for that utter absence of anything to talk about with him which renders contact terribly difficult after the 1st quarter of an hour. However, I see him for a quarter of an hour every day or two—& love him all day long the rest of the time. Mrs. Benson writes me that Arthur Christopher escaped, in Switzerland, from the jaws of death—but gives me no details for which I palpitate.[3] Did *you* escape too? Tell me all about it. Say to Mrs. Nellie that I know *she* will reserve me her choicest eloquence & that I am hers & yours most yearningly

Henry James

P.S. How is the Newfoundland Pup?

1. Gosse has just returned from a holiday in Switzerland, and since his stepmother lives less than two miles from Torquay, James suggests the possibility of a visit.

2. For Paul Bourget, see letter 10. For Norris, see letter 95, note 1.

3. Benson narrowly escaped serious injury in a fall down a crevasse. See *EG*, 376.

125 / MS Leeds

Osborne Hotel.
Torquay.
Sept. 30*th* 95.

My dear Gosse.

I think I *have* persuaded her that my facial spasm was a mere heat-wave of the torrid air, which blurred & misrepresented my features—distorting, to her eyes merely, their absolutely classic calm: in short a purely subjective phenomenon. At any rate, I went, 3 days ago, wreathed in smiles, to call upon her; & am thinking seriously—or rather, most hilariously—of doing so again today.[1] This will depend on the relation of the temperature to my latent—you know what.

Perhaps indeed you *don't* know—& it sounds like something worse than I mean. I only mean perspiration. I made the acquaintance, among her lawns & flowers, of your venerable stepdaughter [*sic*], who gave me a very graceful welcome. As for Mrs. Nelly, nothing could exceed her artful geniality unless it was her still more artful bedizenment. She was most charming & most dressy. She told me of your entertainment of Nordau, & of his entertainment of you. He has got the formula of evil—didn't you say? But has he got the formula of Heinemann? I don't mean to intimate that they are identical.[2] But Heinemann is remarkable—to have caught the great Detective. The Weather, here, is beyond a joke. It is as if the summer, battering vainly at the door of Autumn, had at last lit a great fire in the porch to burn him out. I make you a present of that simile for your History of Eng. Lit.[3] How is it coming on? It is at least standing still (the Lit. itself) for you to mount! Write me something stirring.

Yours always
H.J.

1. James has called upon Eliza Gosse, Gosse's stepmother, at Sandhurst, St. Marychurch. "Mrs. Nelly," mentioned later in this letter, is Gosse's wife.

2. On his holiday, Gosse met Max Nordau (1849–1923), the well-known author of *Degeneration* (2 vols., 1892–93), published by Heinemann in 1895. At the same time (September 25, 1895), Gosse wrote Sir Alfred Bateman that Nordau was a "kind (really) of brilliant humbug" (*LL*, 249).

3. Gosse's *A Short History of Modern English Literature* was published by Heinemann in 1897.

126 / MS Leeds   34, De Vere Gardens. W.
                                     November 9*th* 1895

My dear Gosse.

I have waited to thank you for your very kind admonition until after the event: which was happy—very—though the elements were, apart from Brandes, rather meagre. But Lang was pleasanter than I have *ever* seen him—quite human & gracious & easy—& left me to undisturbed communion with the sympathetic little Dane.[1] I talked much & long with the latter & found him of a very bright & large intercourse—a really fine & general critical mind. We got on beautifully & I took him afterwards to the Savile & gave him lemon-squashes, & kept him up till one o'clk. He did me good—great good; it is such a joy to encounter a fine free foreign mind. But it's a peril—

it spoils one fearfully for some of one's other contacts. We will talk of him—à bientôt. Yours in fierce haste

Henry James

1. Georg Morris Cohen Brandes (1842–1927) was a well-known Danish critic and friend of Gosse's. For Andrew Lang, see letter 51, note 2.

127 / MS Cambridge   34, De Vere Gardens, W.
                                     Tuesday [December 17, 1895]

Dear Mrs. Gosse,

Alas, I am encompassed by obstacles. I have, for a number of years, dined regularly on New Year's eve with the George Lewis's & the other day, for old sake's sake, I again accepted, from Lady L., an invitation to do so.[1] It is a multitudinous & overwhelming affair—but it clutches me by so many the more hands. So, I'm sorry to say I can't be of your merry romp. Please believe in my regrets. I should have so liked (with your permission,) to whirl you in the dance & to catch Edmund under the mistletoe. Please say to him that I *will* catch him—in his coy corner—on *Saturday p.m. next at nine* if he doesn't meanwhile shriek & stamp me away.[2] If I hear nothing I shall rush it. Yours, dear Mrs. Gosse, many times

Henry James

1. James had known the Lewises for some years. Sir George (1833–1911) was a well-known solicitor. For one of James's letters to Lady Elizabeth Lewis, see HJL, III, 496.
2. James frequently visited the Gosses on Saturday or Sunday "at 9." See letter 128.

128 / MS Leeds   34, De Vere Gardens. W.
                                     Dec: 19*th* 1895

My dear Gosse.

On Saturday, at 9, then, very faithfully.[1] This new Hideousness is indeed abysmal[.] But it will not come to pass—simply Not. We shall see *how*—but it won't. The crudity of Cleveland's stand & the crudity of the 1*st* newspaper, &c. jingoism are the inevitable *first* things, là bas to rise to the surface. Behind them, below them, is the deeply-latent English consciousness of that great English-speaking, English-reading, English-imagining race. It will realize—& it will feel—& it will utter. This is what I believe. But we will talk of it, &

meanwhile there will be more light. Meanwhile I cling, too, to the solidity of one's sense—of the universal sense that absolute crimson Shame will prevent our giving to the world—& to derisive disgusted Europe in particular—the big brutal, cynical military powers—the spectacle of our fighting about *that*—we the 2 great pretendedly moral, pacific, powers. Read in Smalley's despatch to this a.m.'s *Times* (excuse this disfigured sheet,) the *admirable* extract from yesterday's N.Y. *World*.[2]

Yours ever
Henry James

1. See letter 127.
2. James is concerned about Anglo-American diplomatic difficulties on the question of the Venezuelan frontier with British Guiana. George W. Smalley, an old American friend, filed an article with the *Times*, December 19, in which he printed an extract from the New York *World*, December 18, that sought to deal with the situation calmly and rationally. See also *HJ*, IV, 153–55.

129 / MS Leeds   34, De Vere Gardens, W.
                                     Jan: 24*th* [1896]

My dear Gosse

I read today your article on Lord de Tabley & I can't forbear to express to you my lively appreciation of it.[1] It is very vivid, very brilliant, very successful in suggesting the elusive distinction of your subject. You do this admirably—& so acute a piece of portraiture & of style ought to do you great good. With *whom*? you will ask—who *is* there—in the whole aching void—to be done good with? Well, at all events, let me say more defensibly, if much less inspiringly, it does it with *me*. What a rare strange, picturesque subject you had— & how you *possess* it! You make me regret I never met him. Why did you never—in all those years—since '75—never show him to me? You *have*, indeed, at last—& perhaps in the best way. It *is* the best way. Art is Greater than Life! I am moved at any rate to say to you that you ought to find a real refuge from Torquay Treacheries (as it were,) in the sense that you can write so well & so valuably.[2] Don't suffer from those little rubs, rude though they be, when you have a talent to triumph withal. Cultivate the talent—give it every chance. It will see you through. How nice, how characteristically refined the lines you quote from A.C.B.[3] Ever, & very gratefully yours

Henry James

1. Edmund Gosse, "Lord de Tabley: A Portrait," *Contemporary Review*, LXIX (January, 1896), 84–99.
2. Apparently a reference to Gosse's sensitivity about gifts of money he received from his stepmother.
3. Gosse ends his article with some lines from their mutual friend, Arthur C. Benson, a master at Eton.

130 / MS Leeds   34, De Vere Gardens, W.
                                                  Feb: 2d *1896*.

My dear Gosse.

I've been endlessly prevented from thanking you for your charming letter, or from naming a night for a symposium. In fact it was the hope from day to day postponed, of being able to seize the night that stayed my pen from hour to hour. And I *couldn't* seize it—it has been a bad, a very bad, week. They have sent me an invitation to Leighton's funeral—& I shall of course go—in spite of having been at old Alexr. Macmillan's last week—; & I shall, in this case, perhaps see you there—for a talk & even (westward) a walk.[1] Look out for me—& come & *lunch* with me somewhere. What levities to project, however, over that stately grave. I had never known a man so long & so little. But I much admired him;—he was very fine. How characteristic, however, of the ugly, snobby side of the Academy, that he should be to have but *one* artist for pall-bearer![2] I shld. have thought such a man shld. be borne to his tomb by his comrades & fellow-fighters: with the equerries & historians & other figureheads *following*—subordinately—as much as they liked. But to elbow out the Academicians & reduce them to *one*: frankly I *must* come (on *Tuesday* at 9?) to tell you how hideous I think it. Look out for me, to answer, tomorrow.

                                                  Ever yours
                                                  Henry James

P.S. When I am borne it must be by you & Norris & Arthur B. & Mrs. Burnett: with the P. of W. well back.[3]

1. Frederick, Lord Leighton (1830–1896), had been president of the Royal Academy. His funeral took place on February 3. See *Times*, February 3, 1896, p. 7. For further comment by James, see his letter of February 4 to W. E. Norris in *HJL*, IV, 27, and his article in *Harper's Weekly*, February 20, 1896, p. 183. Alexander Macmillan was a senior partner in Macmillan and Company.
2. Sir John E. Millais (1829–1896), well-known painter of portraits and genre scenes.
3. For W. E. Norris and Arthur Benson, see, respectively, letters 95, note 1, and 129, note 3. Frances Hodgson Burnett (1849–1924), the author of *Little Lord Fauntleroy* (1886), among many other books, was a friend to both James and Gosse. The P. of W. is the Prince of Wales, the future King Edward VII.

131 / MS Leeds   34, De Vere Gardens, W.
                                              March 18*th* [1896?]

My dear Gosse.

Your vanity is amply justified by your vivid & brilliant little picture.[1] It shows a light & charming hand & no one could have done it
better. It is most droll & pretty—as droll of the reality & much prettier; & is most happily benignant in its sarcasm. It is in short all
right. And it brings back the dear old Queen. What can have become
of those substantial charms? She is perhaps now a Queen-Consort—
even a Queen-mother. She was really meant for the family circle. I
return the *ravissante page* with thanks. For heaven's sake do some
more. "Great showy publications" bring you bonheur. I will come in
next week some night—the remaining days, or nights, of this one are
not very convenient. I will in a few days propose you an evening.
Are you, by chance, to dine with the Om. Khayyam Club on the
27*th*? I accepted—for a reason—& now I've a horror & terror of it.[2]
Do come. That is the Friday. Ever your Enrico.

1. This "brilliant little picture" of the "dear old Queen" may be an early draft, in
anticipation of the jubilee celebration in 1897, of Gosse's later anonymously published essay, "The Character of Queen Victoria," *Quarterly Review*, CXCIII (April,
1901), 301–37. The De Vere Gardens address and the reference to the Omar
Khayyam Club dinner on March 27, 1896, suggest a date of 1896 rather than 1901.

2. James had been invited to the dinner by Clement K. Shorter, editor of the
Illustrated London News and president of the club. See James's letter of February 26,
1896, to Shorter in *HJL*, IV, 31. In an article in the *Sketch* entitled "The Omar
Khayyam Club," James is listed as one of three "chief guests." Gosse is mentioned as
tendering "the usual tribute of the Club to the memory of Fitzgerald" (April 1, 1896,
p. 410).

132 / MS Leeds   Point Hill.
                                              Playden.
                                              Sussex.
                                              Sunday. [May 17, 1896]

My dear Gosse—

I am very, very sorry for your news; & particularly for that part of
it which concerns your wife's illness. What a cloud on your house!—
out of which, however, doubtless shoot the forked (& spooned) light-
nings, or auburn sun-rays of Tessa & Silvia. Please let the sufferer
not doubt of my tender interest & sympathy & of my prostrate
prayers for her rapid amendment. I rage that she is in pain. I rage

also that you just escape me in town. But you *shan't* altogether escape
me, ingeniously as you may try. I shall be there, I fear, *over* the *31st*:
to the *1st* June; on which latter night I have an engagement. I want
extremely that you shld. take a favourable view of coming down to
me here for the *1st* Saturday to Monday you can spare—June *7th?*—
14th?[1] I'm afraid you will be cold to it—after a considerable absence;
but I shall try to heat you up. Meantime you've all my sympathy in
your troubles—which will thin out—as troubles do—to leave a margin for the next. I deplore what you say of the dear little Doctor's
Life—the more that it was what I feared: the haste seeming to me
almost indecent.[2] There was the making of a very pretty book about
him. You & I ought to write all the books ourselves! I feel as if I were
looking through poor Wolcott's horrified eyes at the events of
B[r]attleborough![3] What acts in the drama—what a curious & interesting play. Quelle pièce bien faite! Yes, I *have* read A.L. in the last
Cosmopolis.[4] He is literally *imitating* himself. Ever condolingly & con-
solingly yours

Henry James

1. June 7 and 14 occurred on Sundays in 1896.
2. This possibly is a reference to John T. Morse's *Life and Letters of Oliver Wendell
Holmes* (1896). Holmes had died October 7, 1894.
3. The reference is to Wolcott Balestier (now dead; see letters 81 and 83). The
"events of B[r]attleborough" refer to his sister Caroline and her husband, Rudyard
Kipling, who lived in Brattleborough from 1892 to 1896.
4. Andrew Lang, "Literary Chronicle," *Cosmopolis*, II (May, 1896), 371–91. In this
consideration of "new and interesting books of the spring season," Lang character-
izes Gosse's *Critical Kit-Kats* as "not important, only beguiling" (384).

133 / MS Duke   Point Hill
                                                         Playden.
                                                         Sussex
                                                         June 16 [1896][1]

My dear Gosse.

I am delighted with your news of Philip's definite attachment; &
congratulate heartily both you & his mother. Great things, I am sure,
open out before him—I mean sound, sane, large, educative, not
banal or second-rate things. All the omens are genial almost exces-
sively—but let us not tremble where *he* won't. It's a good chance & a
good boy—& now you must let them shake down together.[2]

Your London news comes to me as the breath of hot rooms and the prattle—almost—of strange tongues. I don't allude either to *your* room or your tongue—but as regards the one, to Mrs. Dugdale's, & as regards the other to the *macabre* Barbey's. "Je ne peux souffrir que les Vierges ou les femmes stériles": he said that (I think) to Sargent, who repeated it to me.[3] But I dined with him once in Paris—with one other person only—& he scared & depressed me. He was *falot*— & he *was* macabre. He had probably been a rare talker—but he was grotesquely self-conscious, & invraisemblablement figged out. I pity you for having to write of him—he was a *pen* & praeteria nihil. I wd. like to contend with you—had I time (àpropos of these things) over the manner—the way you I thought *took*, as it were, your last *Cosmopolis* causerie.[4] But there is too much to say—& I can't. It is more—much—of a chance for you than your preliminary remarks expressed—it is a great chance, & I wish you would see it more as one. But I am not saying what I mean—& as you wouldn't do what I mean, it doesn't matter. Only excuse this rudely imperfect beginning—&—ending. May the Countesses prove honest! But there is no class that requires more looking after.[5] *When* will you come for a Sunday? It is really very nice—though hot, alas; & I want you with a rigour which your marked evasion of the question doesn't at all discountenance. Will the *27th* suit you? I don't want to bore or bully you—but may I have a sole wee word to say *whether* you could manage that: as I have only one spare room. Harland was here two days since—very pleasantly indeed—to me.[6] There is a good 4.30 from Charing Cross to Rye: reaching Rye at 6.45.[7] I am 10 minutes from Rye Station. Be you, on your side, not too far from yours ever

Henry James

1. The envelope clipped to the original of this letter is dated June 16, 1896. The letter is printed in *TD*, 236–37.

2. James's letter is in response to Gosse's of June 14 (printed in *TD*, 235–36), in which he announces that Philip "is now definitely attached to Edw. Fitzgerald's expedition" to the Andes. James had written in support of Philip's application for the expedition.

3. Gosse delivered six lectures on Matthew Arnold at the house of Mrs. Stratford Dugdale. The "*macabre* Barbey" is Jules Amédée Barbey d'Aurevilly (1808–1889), French novelist and critic. Sargent is John Singer Sargent, the painter, a friend both to James and Gosse.

4. Edmund Gosse, "Current French Literature," *Cosmopolis*, VI (June, 1896), 637–54.

5. Gosse had mentioned in his letter (see note 2, above) that "some of the smartest ladies in London" were attending his lectures.

6. For Henry Harland, see letters 102, note 2, and 114, note 2. June 27 actually

fell on Saturday.

7. Both here and subsequently, James, ever the thoughtful host, offers useful information on the best trains to Rye.

134 / MS Leeds   Point Hill
                                                                            Playden.
                                                                            Sussex
                                                                            Thursday. [June 18, 1896]

My dear Gosse.

I am delighted you can come on Saturday 11*th* July—& shall look for you then with intense blandness. I will write you every instruction—concerning what your'e [*sic*] not to bring, &c—in due time. And we will, then causer causerie as much as you will tolerate.[1] I can scarcely bear it in the meantime—to postpone the day of reckoning for ces Messieurs—but am sustained by the hope that you will inspire me to inspire you—goad me to goad you—to make it complete when it comes. Charing Cross to Rye*: *4.30 p.m*. But you shall have every detail. Tout à vous.

                                                                            Henry James
* from which station I am 10 minutes afoot.

1. The immediate reference is to letter 133, note 4, but James and Gosse enjoyed a good chat about the current literary situation (see, for example, letter 137). In the last decade or so of his life, James in particular came to rely on Gosse for his impressions gleaned from travel and socializing among the literati.

135 / MS Leeds   Point Hill
                                                                            Playden.
                                                                            Rye. Sussex
                                                                            Wednesday [July 8, 1896][1]

My dear Gosse.

I hope I shan't be the last straw on your too busy back if I mention to you that—unless you execrate the idea & can't really manage it—I hope you will be able to act on your soft avowal of some time ago that Saturday next, 11*th*, will be a possible day for you to come down here.[2] I don't know whether they are the morbid visions of a rustic, but it seems to be borne in upon me that you must be in these days overdone, overwhelmed, overheated, overcharged. If you can't comfortably work me in, don't hesitate to chuck me—*but* I shall be delighted to see you, & I can't help thinking that you'll be rather glad when you *get* here—even if you do curse me all the way down. My little perch has really—for the troubled soul—a sovereign balm, & I can promise you to squeeze out every drop of the same for your use.[3] My tenure of it draws to a close, alas; only the 19*th* & the 26*th* (in the way of Sundays) further remain to me—& for them & my one spare room, I have a guest apiece. Therefore come. You shall be overfed & not overwalked; & shall be so talked to that no talk will need to issue from your congested person. And you shall see all the Kingdoms of the earth. Above all you'll quite like it. To this end you have simply to take the *4.30* p.m. from Charing Cross for *Rye*, & change at 6.15 (without *any* delay) at Ashford. At 6.45 I tenderly assist you to alight at Rye Station, & then as tenderly sustain you up a gentle eminence—during some 10 minutes or so—to my door. There you are. If you can't come, at least won't Mrs. Gosse? I wish you would both. Ever your

Henry James

P.S. N.B. Don't deliriate that I dress for dinner!

1. Printed in *SR*, 578–79. The envelope attached to this letter in the Brotherton Collection is postmarked July 8, 1896.
2. See letter 134. Although Gosse had planned to come on July 11, he was apparently not feeling well at the time of this letter. In the end, however, he paid the visit. See letter 136.
3. It is from this period that James dated his interest in Rye and "hopelessly coveted" Lamb House, which, at the time, was not available. A year later, however, he was able to lease it for twenty-one years and two years thereafter to purchase it, "an indispensable retreat from May to October" (James to Arthur Christopher Benson, *LHJ*, I, 262).

---

136 / TC Duke   Point Hill,
                                                    Playden,
                                                    Sussex.
                                                    Saturday [July 25, 1896][1]

My dear Gosse,

Overwhelmed with obligations to you, I've not had time, since incurring them, to thank you for any of them—for the genial visit to begin with, which leads off the list, & for the almost equally genial *Aphrodite*, which did its best to console me for your departure, & which, more completely veiled than her poet ever represents her, I return, at last, postally, with much discretion, to Whitehall.[2]

How very genial *Aphrodite* is, & what an interesting document I

won't say on the manners of Alexandria, but on those of more neighbouring localities. Everything is interesting, I think, that illustrates
the French genius, & this volume does that, in certain directions, in
a rare way. (Excuse my squalidly finding, on turning over this sheet,
that I had already used it—or begun to—& forgive my untidy
scratchings). That they should *want* to illustrate it in that way so
much as they do & in the face of the (if you like, so much stupider,
world) that indeed is an endless mystery. But life & literature would
be awfully dull if there weren't such & other mysteries. Where
would either be without the French? & where would the French be
without Aphrodite? Without Goncourt, however, they are for the
moment more interesting even than with him.[3]

All thanks for your scrap from the Figaro or whatever it was. I
enclose some things—newspaperisms sent me from Paris which you
haven't perhaps seen. They are all curious. Read the Bergerat [*sic*]—
the désofilant Bergerat—on Flaubert's genius.[4] I'm a great admirer of
the talent of Bergerat. It looks as if a rather pretty little drama—or
row—or fresh illustration of the Aphroditic genius, in some way,
were to produce itself round his tomb, his bibelots, his will, his academy, his friends the Daudets—round everything but his books.

I liked, in its way, Zola's speech—it was frank & brave homme—as
Zola seems to be more & more becoming.[5]

Rome is of a *lourdeur*—as I read it here at the rate of ten pages a
day—under which even my little rock-built terrace groans. I leap
from its Tarpeian eminence—the terrace's, alas,—the prosy Vicarage
receives me.[6] But I rejoice to have *any* immediate refuge. I'm afraid
London has been deadly these last days. But this place has been
deadly too, & I scarcely stir off the terrace.

Give me a sign before you leave & believe me

Always your
Henry James.

1. Although the text in *HJL*, IV, 32–33, is based upon the copy at Duke, I have
used the copy itself because it includes a sentence omitted in Edel's text.
2. Since *Aphrodite* (1896), a novel by Pierre Louÿs (1870–1925), was considered
rather scandalous by some English readers, James spoofs such a reaction by returning the volume discreetly to Gosse's office at the Board of Trade. For Gosse's visit,
see letters 134 and 135.
3. For Edmond de Goncourt, who had just died, see letter 67, note 2.
4. Lucien Bergeret, a character in Anatole France's *L'Histoire contemporaine* (1896–
1901). James consistently spells the name "Bergerat."
5. Apparently a reference to Zola's interest in current political and social affairs,

which would eventually lead to his involvement in the Dreyfus affair. *Rome*, his latest novel, had just appeared.

6. James had to move fron Point Hill to the Vicarage in Rye.

137 / MS Harvard

The Vicarage
Rye.
Aug. 28*th* [1896][1]

My dear Edmund.

Don't think me a finished brute or a heartless fiend or a soulless ass, or any other unhappy thing with a happy name. I have pressed your letter to my bosom again & again, & if I've not sooner expressed to you how I've prized it, the reason has simply been that for the last month there has been no congruity between my nature & my manners—between my affections & my lame right hand.[2] A crisis overtook me some three weeks ago from which I emerge only to hurl myself on this sheet of paper & consecrate it to you. I will reserve details—suffice it that in an evil hour I began to pay the penalty of having arranged to let a current serial begin when I was too little ahead of it, & when it proved a much slower & more difficult job than I expected.[3] The printers & illustrators overtook & denounced me, the fear of breaking down paralysed me, the combination of rheumatism & fatigue rendered my hand & arm a torture—& the total situation made my existence a nightmare, in which I answered not a single note, letting correspondence go to smash in order barely to save my honour. I've finished (day before yesterday,) but I fear my honour—with *you*—lies buried in the ruins of all the rest. You will soon be coming home, & this will meet or reach you God only knows where. Let it take you the assurance that the most lurid thing in my dreams has been the glitter of your sarcastic spectacles. It was charming of you to write to me from dear little old devastated Vevey—as to which indeed you made me feel, in a few vivid touches, a faint nostalgic pang. I don't want to think of you as still in your horrid ice-world (for it is cold even here & I scribble by a morning fire;) & yet it's in my interest to suppose you still feeling so all abroad that these embarrassed lines will have for you some of the charm of the bloated English post. That makes me, at the same time, doubly conscious that I've nothing to tell you that you will most languish for—news of the world & the devil—no throbs nor thrills from the great beating heart of the thick of things. I went up to town for a week on the 15*th* to be nearer the devouring maw into which I had to pour belated copy; but I spent the whole time shut up in De Vere Gardens with an ink-pot & a charwoman. The only thing that befell me was that I dined one night at the Savoy with F. Ortmans & the P. Bourgets, & that the said Bourgets—but 2 days in London—dined with me one night at the Grosvenor club.[4] But these occasions were not as rich in incident & emotion as poetic justice demanded—& your veal-fed table d'hôte will have nourished your intelligence quite as much. The only other thing I did was to read in the *Rev. de Paris* of the 15*th* Aug. the wonderful article of A. Daudet on Goncourt's death—a little miracle of art, adroitness, demoniac tact & skill, & of taste so abysmal, judged by *our* fishlike sense, that there is no getting along-side of it at all. But I grieve to say I can't send you the magazine—I saw it only at a club. Doubtless you will have come across it. I have this ugly house till the end of September & don't expect to move from Rye even for a day till then. The date of your return is vague to me—but if shld. be early in the month I wonder if you couldn't come down for another Sunday. I fear you will be too blasé: much. For comfort my vicarage is distinctly superior to my eagle's nest—but, alas, beauty isn't *in* it.[5] The peace & prettiness of the whole land, here, however, has been good to me, & I stay on with unabated relish. But I stay in solitude. I don't see a creature. That, too, dreadful to relate, I like. You will have been living in a crowd, & I expect you to return all garlanded & odorous with anecdote & reminiscence. Mrs. Nelly's will all bear, I trust, on miraculous healings & feelings. I feel far from all access to the French volume you recommend. Are you crawling over the Dorn, or only standing at the bottom to catch Philip & Lady Edmund as they drop?[6] Pardon my poverty & my paucity. It is your absence that makes them. Yours, my dear Edmund, not inconstantly

Henry James

1. The text of this letter has appeared in *LHJ*, I, 246–48, and in *HJL*, IV, 33–35. My text is based upon the original and differs in details from both.

2. James, presumably, is responding to Gosse's praise of "The Old Things" (later *The Spoils of Poynton*), which had begun to appear in the *Atlantic Monthly* in April, 1896. See *LHJ*, I, 246.

3. *The Other House*, a play that James had written for Edward Compton in 1894 and was now turning into a serial for Clement Shorter of the *Illustrated London News* (July 4 to September 26, 1896). For James's correspondence with Shorter on this serial, see *HJL*, 30–31.

4. For Fernand Ortmans, editor of *Cosmopolis* and a mutual acquaintance, see let-

ter 157; for Bourget, see letter 10, note 1.

5. James's house, Point Hill, Playden, had a wonderful view that the Vicarage could not match.

6. Mrs. Nelly and Lady Edmund are one and the same; Philip is Gosse's only son. James had been referring to Ellen Gosse as "Mrs. Nelly" (the family spelled the name "Nellie") in his letters since 1893 (see letter 95).

138 / MS Duke   The Vicarage
                                                               Rye
                                                               Sept. 2*d* 1896[1]

Ben' caro amico.

Your cry of ecstasy from Orta comes in to me this minute and excites me to that pitch with its arousal of every ineffaceable memory of the land so loved & so lost, that I break off the most pressing occupations to *howl* back in answer—to screech an unspeakable congratulation. I rejoice with you more than I can say that you've *done* it— that you've been able at last just (if only) to break the seal of the most precious message on earth. There is none other like it—there is none other to compare to it, & your whole life (let me so comfort you!) will henceforth be poisoned with this one little nibble of the tree of knowledge. *You will never be the same again*! Your peace is gone. But the torment is worth all the dungeon-darkness of the innocent past— & new worlds have opened up to you.[2] I wish to God you might have pushed on as far as Milan—for there is Italy indeed—if only for 24 hours. But it wouldn't have done for the ladies. The last time I saw the Lago d'Orta was some nine long years agone, when, in broiling dust, I *drove* over to it with Mrs. Kemble from L. Maggiore.[3] We spent a kind of shimmering, sweating, lunching day there. But I want all *your* (& Tessa's & Lady G.'s) details, even to the last drop of perspiration. Meanwhile I repeat my joy that the bright, blank name of Italy has lighted for you, like a long, long, lifelong pipe, at the glowing coal of your August day. Now smoke away—it will never go out. But I hope you hate your Germanic glaciers adequately on your return. Everything else is ugly & Protestant afterwards. This is all I've time for—I wrote to you some days ago, but had lost your address—so could only direct to 1 Whitehall. I then explained the turpitude of my silence & craved forgiveness. Even now I am vague—but I shall risk Saas-Fie. No, on re-reading your letter I won't. I shall send again, at peril of delay, to the B. of T. [Board of Trade] I hope this will *meet* you somewhere—for if you reach town by the *11th* I fear you will have quitted your cleric lyric. Do give me some sign of return. I hope your wife is quite frozen-well.[4]

> Yours, my dear Gosse,
> always,
>> *Henry James.*

1. Printed in *SR*, 579–80.
2. James had for years urged Gosse to visit Italy (see, for example, letter 101, note 1).
3. For Frances Anne Kemble, the well-known Shakespearean actress, see letter 37, note 2.
4. The manuscript ends here, but a typescript attached includes the farewell greeting that follows. It is also possible, of course, that a page of the manuscript is missing.

139 / MS Leeds   34, De Vere Gardens, W.
                                          Friday. [October 2, 1896]

My dear Gosse.

I shall be charmed to receive from you the other volumes of the pretty Johnson (the great lexicographer made "pretty"!) of which I gratefully, some months ago, recd to [from] you the *1st* (*not* the *2d* too.) So I welcome the coming gift.[1]

On your side, tell me this. Heinemann has just published for me a small story (in 2 densive vols.) which I desire you to have with my name in it.[2] *But* I seem to gather that Heinemann's books come to you by a law of graceful gravitation—& if this one does seem to follow that law I will stay my hand. In other words let me know (only) if you *haven't* the book—that is if it doesn't come. Then *I* will send it to you. I go for Sunday to Sir G. Tressady's—but shall see you thereafter.[3] All thanks.

> Yours toujours
>> *Henry James*

1. Presumably a reference to Arthur Waugh's edition of Samuel Johnson's *Lives of the English Poets* (6 vols.; London, 1896). See letter 140.
2. *The Other House.* See letter 137, note 3. William Heinemann had published the book on October 1. See *BHJ*, 105–106.
3. This apparently is an indirect reference to Mrs. Humphry Ward, the author of *Sir George Tressady* (1896). See letter 140.

140 / MS Duke   34, De Vere Gardens, W.
                                          Tuesday. [October 6, 1896][1]

My dear Gosse.

I have both your charming note & your charming present; & such is my tender sensibility that I'm not sure I am not more affected by the first than even by the second. I am touched by your word about the tale. You see what it is—a little thrifty pot-boiling turning-to-acct. of the scheme of a chucked-away 3 act play—an old relinquished scenario turned into a little story on exactly the same scenic lines.[2] If it holds the attention, so much the better; but I am doing much better things. The Tale Heinemann is to publish 3 mos. hence is better.[3] I spent Sunday in the lap of Marcella herself—i.e. at Mrs. H.W.'s with scarcely any one else. I told her with a good conscience that her book is very, very beautiful. It isn't written, alas; *but* it is very finely thought & felt, & has, I think, great charm & pleasantness. I got on with it better than with anything of hers yet. But what a "selling", what a British public *instinct*—the happy mixture of high life & earnestness—edification with £ 30 000 a year. But it is a very graceful & even honourable achievement.[4]

The little row of the so well turned-out Lives is a delightful possession.[5] It enriches a conspicuous bookshelf. I shall arrive one of these near evenings—but with harbinger & herald. I hope the young mountaineer holds firm.[6] I shall immediately buy the *Spectator*.

I seem to blush even here for the genuflexions of France. But the Bon Dieu isn't genuflexing, is he?—par un temps pareil! À bientôt.

Ever your
Henry James

1. The envelope attached to the manuscript of this letter is postmarked October 6, 1896, and Tuesday occurred on this date in 1896.
2. James is referring to *The Other House*. See letters 137 and 139.
3. Heinemann brought out *The Spoils of Poynton* in February, 1897. See *BHJ*, 108.
4. For Mrs. Humphry Ward, see letter 139, note 3. James obviously is of two minds about Mrs. Ward's success.
5. Apparently a reference to Johnson's *Lives of the English Poets*, edited by Arthur Waugh, Gosse's kinsman. See letter 139.
6. Philip Gosse was about to leave with a British scientific expedition to Aconcagua in the Andes. See letter 133, note 2. See also *EG*, 367–68.

141 / MS Leeds   34, De Vere Gardens, W.
                                    Wednesday [October 14, 1896][1]

Dear St. Edmund.

I am greatly flattered, honored & touched. Vous êtes magnifique; & I will generously except you when I do "the Nights, the Fights, the Plights & the Blights of *our* Notorious Contemporaries." And meanwhile you shall share the proceeds of the boom you will have created.[2] Dear G.D.M. yesterday had decorous—dignified—& picturesque interment in that fine old Hampstead churchyard. Even Phil May was there.[3] Ever your

Henry James

[On back of envelope] Faites-vous, par hasard, the pilgrimage of Canterbury? Je désire bien que vous y alliez—pour me—pour *nous*—le reconter[4]

1. George Du Maurier died on October 8, was cremated, and subsequently was buried in the cemetery at Hampstead Parish Church on Tuesday, October 13. The envelope is postmarked October 14, 1896. For Du Maurier's death and funeral, see Leonee Ormond, *George Du Maurier* (Pittsburgh, 1969), 496–98.
2. For James's reaction to Gosse's opinion of *The Other House*, see letter 140.
3. Phil May (1864–1903) was one of Du Maurier's colleagues on *Punch*.
4. Edward White Benson, the archbishop of Canterbury and a friend both to James and Gosse, had died on October 11 and was buried on October 15, the day after James's letter. Arthur C. Benson, another mutual friend, was his son.

142 / MS Leeds   34 De Vere Gardens, W.
                    Thursday [October 15? 1896?][1]

My dear Gosse.

You have all my sympathy. But remember that at best one is always giving one's self away: therefore at worst! H [G?] is a desperately queer creature—& he seems to me exactly, on the whole, *as* queer today, with silvered locks & a ¼ of a century of lore & lucre, as he was in the perverse puerility of his phenomenal youth.[2] It was told me the other day that he is of *gypsy* strain—positively: can that have anything to do with it? Write you a new rhymed version of M.A.'s "Gypsy-Scholar." (I put it 'tother way round as more expressive!) He was very genial to me two days since—dona ferens; but perhaps *I* shall have to write to the *Times*! Calmez-vous & cultivate divine philosophy & yours, also, ever

Henry James

1. *Thursday* is written in pencil on the manuscript, and the letter is included with others of October, 1896, at Leeds. The date could be another Thursday in October.
2. Not identified.

143 / MS Leeds   34, De Vere Gardens, W.
                                              Sunday [October 18, 1896]

My dear Gosse.

This is to thank you for your note anent Philip's last throes—or your own; & to tell you that I posted you back the French satiric volume.[1] I think you were liberal of praise to it—to be very plain I didn't find it very amusing—it in fact rather bored me. Doubtless you can easily refute this—but it doesn't matter. I daresay I didn't persist enough. I will, with pleasure, come in again soon—if possible by the end of the week. But I will name my day. I hope that relief & rest—a *détente* & a holy calm have descended by this time on your house. I sing you a sympathic [*sic*] lullaby. And àpropos of such things, how can one wish them enough to those stricken ones of Addington—perked up from the *1st* hour of their blow in such a public pomp of bereavement.[2] They must feel as if they had been seated in a row in some great undertaker's—Mr. Jay's—big plate glass shop-window—& the empty Addington will make them howl with the balm of its privacy.

I had little Karageorgevitch to dine me with him—alone—& wanted to ask you: but was precisely deterred by its being, that night, Philip's last.[3] Little K. moreover was tired & slack. He is a sweet little nature—but not a bit of a personality, an individual— only a well-directed little faintly-perfumed spray of fluid, of distilled, amenity. That's something—in this football age. Till—Saturday, perhaps. But I will wire. Ever yours

H.J.

1. Philip Gosse was leaving on a scientific expedition under the direction of Edward Fitzgerald. See letter 140, note 6.
2. Addington was one of the homes of the late archbishop of Canterbury. See letter 141, note 4.
3. Prince Bojador Karageorgevitch, of Servia, had visited Gosse a week earlier, on October 11. For a brief account of this visit, see Philip Gosse's introduction to *A Catalogue of the Gosse Correspondence in the Brotherton Collection* (Leeds, 1950), xii.

144 / MS Leeds   34, De Vere Gardens, W.
                                              October 28*th* 1896

My dear Edmund.

I shall be delighted, now, if you will let me send—as I will, taking your consent for granted—one of these very next days for the bivoluminous Lang-Lockhart, which you will perhaps kindly give orders for the surrender of to my messenger.[1] I today arranged with Bain for the resumption of the copy he supplied; & I am free to leap at your liberality.[2] Let me not neglect, either, to appreciate your pointed & accomplished article in the St. James's.[3]

I had yesterday a visit from the gifted Andrew—strange & discomfortable being.[4] But I will tell you of it—& I am, with this & other intentions, constantly yours

Henry James

P.S. I hope Mrs. Nelly has overthrown the enemy. Please give her love & sympathy.

1. Andrew Lang's biography of John Gibson Lockhart had recently appeared.
2. James Bain, the well-known London bookseller, had apparently loaned James a copy.
3. "Mr. Lang's Lockhart," a review of the biography, appeared in the *St. James's Gazette* on October 28, 1896, the day of James's letter.
4. James had known Andrew Lang (1844–1912) since the 1870s.

145 / MS Leeds

34, De Vere Gardens, W.
Sunday p.m. [November 8? 1896][1]

My dear Gosse.

All thanks for the little grey, pretty Pater, of which I have tasted fully the faint, feeble sweetness.[2] Of course it's casual work, but it gives one that odd, peculiar sense that reading him always gives— that kind of little illusion that some refined, pathetic object or presence is *in the room* with you—materially—& stays there while you read. He has too little point, & a kind of wilful weakness; but he's divinely uncommon. I went, by the way, yesterday to see his sisters, my neighbours; & found them in a state of subdued flourish & chaste symmetry which I hope means all manner of solid comfort. But why do I speak of the chaste, the weak & the feminine while I am still prostrate beneath the impression of *Rudyard's* supreme deviltry? As Du Maurier once said in a note, "The little beast is Titanic." The talent, the art, the hellish cunning of this last volume (& all exercised in its amazing limitations, which only makes the phenomenon more rare,) have *quite* bowed me down with admiration.[3] I ween they have you too. We must talk of him soon. And Norris—strange collocation!—will tell us of him.[4]

Ever your
Henry James

1. The date of November 9, 1896, is written in pencil on the manuscript, but in

1896 Sunday occurred on November 8. James, of course, may have written this letter after midnight, or the postmark on a now-lost envelope may have indicated November 9. Since "Sunday p.m." is all that is given, I am conjecturing November 8 as the date.

2. Walter Pater had died in July. *Gaston de Latour: An Unfinished Romance* appeared after his death.

3. Kipling's most recent collection of verse, *The Seven Seas*, had appeared in October, the month Du Maurier died. See letter 141.

4. W. E. Norris, a mutual friend, knew Kipling rather well.

146 / MS Leeds   34, De Vere Gardens, W.
                                        Thursday [November 26, 1896]

My dear Gosse.

On *Monday* next, please, at 9. I will then pour forth a flood of explanations & documents. There has been a fierce outbreak of *dinners*, which have blighted all my nights. But we will make it up. Monday is the *1st*, alas, free night.

A note this a.m.—very charming—from Josephine Balestier—telling me of her engagement to Theodore Dunham (whom I don't know,) & of her coming out, married, in the spring.[1] The most interesting thing that has happened to me is the perusal of G. Sand's letters to A. de Musset & Ste. Beuve in the 2 last *Rev. de Paris*.[2] Astounding Female!—or rather, astounding Females! Nous en causerons—& d'autres choses encore. Tout à vous!

Henry James

1. Josephine Balestier was the sister of the late Wolcott Balestier and of Caroline Balestier Kipling. See letter 81.

2. George Sand, "Lettres à Alfred De Musset," *La Revue de Paris*, November 1, 1896, pp. 1–48, and "Lettres à Sainte-Beuve," *La Revue de Paris*, November 15, 1896, pp. 277–301, December 1, 1896, pp. 559–88.

147 / TLS Leeds   34, De Vere Gardens, W.
                                        5th February, 1897

[Dictated]
My dear Gosse,

Your note and your wife's bloody dream only as yet have terrified me, but they will doubtless, if we give them time, do all the rest. My compassion is all for her: her accident is much the worst. The only one I have had was that the hansom I stopped from your doorstep on

Tuesday night, and which pulled up a little way off, proved to have a lady in it. I was filled with confusion and she with indignation; but she didn't tear my right eye out. Meanwhile I go softly, and I hope your wife doesn't dream so hard. I saw the two Kipling's yesterday at an hotel close to this, and in town but for 24 hours.[1] He struck me as magnificent, and

>I am,
>ever yours,
>*Henry James*—

reduced to this—forevermore—by general complications, foremost of which is a Scotch amanuensis—a desperate dodge to catch up with Crockett & Co.[2]

1. Caroline Balestier Kipling and Rudyard Kipling.
2. James had hired William McAlpine, a Scottish amanuensis, at this time because he had a severe case of writer's cramp. See also *HJL*, IV, 42*n*. The passage after James's signature is in his own hand. "Crockett & Co." may refer to S. R. Crockett (1860–1914), a popular Scottish novelist of the day. See letter 101, note 7.

148 / TLS Duke   34 De Vere Gardens, W.
                                                   12th February, 1897.[1]

[Dictated]
My dear Redmond,*

I owe you apologies for not restoring to you sooner, with the supreme commendation it deserves, the brilliant *Contemporary*. Your picture of Patmore is a real Sargent-portrait—altogether in the Sargent manner; with, to make the resemblance complete, just a trifle of a tendency to give away a little your sitter.[2] But you have made him wonderfully alive and individual—in this sort of thing decidedly *il n'y a que vous*. The thing is better even than your posthumous Pater—doubtless partly because the model is, as a model, better.[3] The only criticism I should make of it is one that explains my remark about Patmore's enjoying at your hands an objectivity almost, as it were, too great. That comes from your describing and defining him so exclusively as a person, and so almost not at all as a poet. For the latter, of course, you didn't try; but one's neglecting that—I have felt, myself, in similar cases—tends to the effect of one's presenting only one blade of the scissors and showing thereby an instrument of too singular form. All I mean is that the mere inclusion of three or four short citations from him—three or four more important than the

quotations you have given—would have carried off or lifted up the so
peculiar personality and made us feel more what the personality
was—so to speak—all *about*. But this I will hint at better when I see
you—so far as it is worth hinting at all. You have put more life into
the man in your twenty pages than all his own—for the multitudinous uninitiated—in all the years they followed each other. And
no one else, in this paradise of criticism, does, remotely, anything of
the sort. But outlive me not. Only outlive a few others—for the particular advantage of

> Yours, my dear
> Redmond, ever
> *Henry James*

* an artless *bèane* [?] of my amanuensis—left, by me, to beguile &
mislead him. I didn't want him to know how ill I think of you.[4]

1. This letter has been printed in *SR*, 580–81.
2. Edmund Gosse, "Coventry Patmore: A Portrait," *Contemporary Review*, LXXI
(February, 1897), 184–204.
3. See letter 110, note 2.
4. This note is in James's hand.

149 / MS Leeds   34, De Vere Gardens, W.
                                          Feb. 18*th* [1897?]

My dear Edmund.

   I could bear with fortitude, I believe, the extremity (absit omen.)
of misfortune. But under such strokes of its opposite as your bene-
diction from the Leeds express I am prostrate—I lie down flat, with
my hands crossed as an image's on a tomb-stone—I close my overflowing eyes & let the golden hours brush me in their flight. You
speak very handsomely—too handsomely—of my simple (but I *won't*
affectedly say artless) little tale. Fort de votre confiance, I shall
henceforth do only bigger & better things. The *Spoils* are only a last,
loose old thread, of the far-off past (I *began* it, & laid it aside long
ago,) tucked in.[1] À bientôt. I hope Leeds was lavish. I wish I lived in
the provinces. Ever your [*sic*] Let me come soon.

> Yours very constantly
> *Henry James*

1. *The Spoils of Poynton* was published in February, 1897, by Heinemann. James
recorded the germ of the novel in his notebooks on December 24, 1893. See *N*, 136–
38.

150 / TLS Leeds   34, De Vere Gardens, W.
                                               May 5, 1897

[Dictated]
My dear Edmund,

I am very, very sorry that my Thursday and Friday are taken. But
let us cherish Saturday—on which occasion you shall know all. I
shall expect an eye for an eye and a lie for a lie—and, on that, even to
have the best of the bargain. What a *nouveau frisson* is this Paris unut-
terability![1] Yours always,

Henry James

1. Apparently, this is a reference to the Dreyfus affair, which attracted headlines
again when new evidence implicating Major Esterhazy was brought forward in
Paris, and the question of Dreyfus' guilt was reopened.

151 / TLS Leeds   Dunwich, Saxmundham,
                                               SUFFOLK.
                                               11th, August, 1897.[1]

[Dictated]
My dear Gosse,

Bourget's address is Drummuie House, Golspie, Sutherland.[2] I
hope your flight from town is near at hand. Your post mark reminds
me that you are still there, and my own rusticity is now so complete
as to make me feel quite superior. Yes, I feel superior even at the
Dunwich that you so luridly pictured. I toy with the dead men's
bones—and with no such desperation, as yet, as might usher in a
surrender of my own. I quite adore the little place and the lowly,
lovely, latent scenery. It is all delicious—if there were only a cuisine.
Still, a cuisine would be no use without other things; and it's the
other things precisely, I admit, that just don't over flow. But that is
only our grossness. Dunwich itself is divine, and I am yours always,

Henry James

1. James had arrived in Dunwich on August 6 to visit his Emmet cousins. See his
letter of August 7, 1897, to William James (*HJL*, IV, 53–54).
2. For Bourget, see letter 10, note 1.

152 / TLS Leeds   Dunwich, Saxmundham,
                                                     SUFFOLK.
                                                     August 15th, 1897.

[Dictated]
My dear Gosse,

Thanks for the *Saturday* and the gem of its number.[1] Your vision
has great entrain and is very successfully droll—causing me to launch
a merry peal over the rude, and dead, forefathers of the hamlet; over
the promiscuous waters, that is, in which so much of Dunwich life is
more or less represented. But I can't help being just a trifle sorry that
by this same vis comica ce monsieur should practically find himself
crowned afresh with a public and voluminous wreath. I am dying for
some treatment of him which shall exactly *not* advertise him: yours,
though so Aristophanesque, is still too amiable, too much of an
expansion and diffusion of the horrid creature—too much of a sounding board. But we must talk of these things later, when we are gathered together again—the time of the autumn lamp and fire that I am
already almost impatient for. I'm glad you've been kind to Bourget;
but more flattered than convinced by your mention of the effect on
him of a nameless one.[2] All this takes for granted that you are not yet
Bundorenized [*sic*].[3] In this lovely weather and lovely land I could
wish you were, even to my own loss. Dunwich continues most Swin-
burnian—it is only our landlady that hasn't the afflatus. I am sitting
down to a most pedestrian lunch, and mustn't be too redundantly
even yours

Henry James

1. Gosse reviewed Vallery C.O. Greard's *Meissonier: His Life and Art* (1897) in the
Saturday Review, August 14, 1897, pp. 170–71.
2. Bourget's opinion of James was as well known to Gosse as it was to James.
3. Gosse was planning a visit to Bundoran, a town on Donegal Bay in northern
Ireland.

153 / TLS Library of Congress   Dunwich, Saxmundham,
                                                     SUFFOLK.
                                                     September 1st, 1897.

[Dictated]
I am very sorry, my dear Gosse, that, contradicting the pastoral picture impressed upon the paper of your charming letter, you describe
yourself as engaged in pursuits to which my solicitude would greatly

prefer for you some of the milder forms of sport and peril. It is delightful of you, at any rate, to have launched toward *me* your swan-song before partaking of the fate of sailor Shelley. I promise more-over to be your Byron and conduct your remains, as B. would have done in this improved age, to some more organised crematorium. You sound meanwhile very brave and wild and, with your lugger, your comrade, and the Italian eyes of your desperadoes, as Stevenso-nian and Ebb-Tidish as possible. And if it doesn't kill you, your account of it seems to give me to understand that it's curing you apace—I mean of Delamere Terrace and Whitehall—and t'other Hall too; him whom I needn't more jealously name. What yarns I expect you to bring back!

But I shall bring back none. Nothing whatever has happened to me here—not even, as yet, to depart in despair; not even to perish of not having done so. I quite like it, liking as I always do the minor key. This is the very minimum. But all the land is sweet, and almost all the weather sweeter. I live mainly on buns and jam, but find them just the right diet I have all my life looked for. In fact your so happy description of Bundoren [*sic*] really seems to me to fit *à merveille* all that surrounds me here—the absence of any natural features except the sea and the landlady, combined with the curious poetry of the universal void.[1] I have no peaty lakes to walk by—but only, as the goal of excursions, inn-parlours, in all directions to which I vulgarly bicycle and where I partake of more buns and more jam. Sweeter than any jam, and more filling than any bun, let me not delay to assure you, is the charming extract you give me from Bourget; with whom I congratulate you—on every ground but the obvious, if obvious be the word—on being in correspondence.[2] What he so gen-erously says of me is not the least characteristic expression of his gen-eral, systematic amenity. Don't think me rebarbative if I still persist that it still more illustrates the said amenity than the said influence.

I shall probably be in town, at least in passing, before you are, if you are staying on and on. Do stay on, even to my loss, as long as Mrs. Nelly continues to bloom. We shall have plenty of time to grumble together at the worst. I feel my own summer draw to an end, and begin to hunger for better conditions of work and evenings less furiously social. But give me a sign again when you have doubled your Cape. I wish I could have a paddle with Tessa and Sylvia—I like to think of our bare legs all fraternally in a row. The great thing, however, will be for them to bring us all safely together again. You must prepare for me—à propos of bare legs—a full and authentic account of the sufferings of Sarah at being accused of showing *hers* as much as the naughty Émile![3] Don't fail, please, to get up this subject thoroughly. Yours thoroughly, for an example,

Henry James

1. For Bundoran, see letter 152, note 3.
2. See also letter 152, note 2. James had seen the Bourgets during the past summer. See *HJL*, IV, 69.
3. Tessa and Sylvia were Gosse's daughters. Sarah and Émile apparently were Bundoran locals mentioned by Gosse.

154 / *TLS Leeds*   34, De Vere Gardens, W.
20th September, 1897.

[Dictated]
My dear Edmund,

Returning late last night from an absence, I found your interesting news: which reminded me afresh that I had, at some time of each day that had since elapsed, meant to make you some response to your signal about Philip.[1] If I didn't it was because, also from day to day, I was craning my neck for a glimpse of the hour at which I might arrange with you for a nearer view. Please let that hour be next Thursday or Friday p.m.: whichever best suits you. Tonight I must not stir abroad, tomorrow I shall be much taken up, and on Wednesday I go, for twenty-four hours or so, into the country again. We had better take Friday, if Friday is the same to you. I take up with great intensity what you say about Philip and enter deeply into it. I shall rejoice much to see him and will then arrange with him for an interview properly convivial and of a nature to make it worth his while. Please tell him that meanwhile I embrace him. Count upon me definitely for Friday. I am sorry to have to wait even till then. Oh yes, I know about the Samoans—dona ferentes—and also about Scudder, who does not, however, I believe, spend his time here, but in the more credible Italy.[2] But I have as yet seen neither. I jubilate over what you tell me of your wife's acquisition of the Irish temperament—I mean to the extent of being proof against,—well, everything. Always yours,

Henry James

1. Philip Gosse had returned from a scientific expedition to South America. He

was now concerned about what to do for a living and wished to consult James. He subsequently became a physician, a practicing naturalist, and a fellow of the Royal Society of Literature (*EG*, 368).

2. The Samoans are Fanny Stevenson, the widow of Robert Louis Stevenson, and her son, Lloyd Osbourne. Horace E. Scudder (1838–1902), an editor with Houghton, Mifflin & Co. for many years, was editor of the *Atlantic Monthly* from 1890 to 1898.

155 / MS Yale   34, De Vere Gardens, W.
Friday a.m. [December 31, 1897]

My dear Gosse.

Here, for a small Etrenne, is the somewhat time-stained little Procter-Carlyle pamphlet.[1] The back is dirty—& that is why I send it to you this a.m. rather than court the embarrassment of incurring your rebuke coram publico (should I bring it in my hand) this evening. Receive it at any rate with all the prayers that may assuage for you (all) the bleak 1898.[2] We will put some more up together tonight; à ce soir, then, & yours always

Henry James

1. *Letters Addressed to Mrs. Basil Montagu and B.W. Procter by Mr. Thomas Carlyle*, printed for private circulation [by Anne Benson Procter, London, March, 1881]. In 1907 the pamphlet was issued under a slightly different title—*Letters of Thomas Carlyle to Mrs. Basil Montagu and B.W. Procter*—with an introduction by Gosse. See Isaac Watson Dyer, *A Bibliography of Thomas Carlyle's Writings and Ana* (1928, rpr., New York, 1968), 134–35.

2. James has accepted an invitation for another New Year's Eve party at the Gosses.

156 / MS Huntington   Welcombe,
Stratford on Avon.
Friday [April 15, 1898]

Dear Mrs. Nellie.

My heart is broken by the same foul blow as your most lamentable collar-bone; which I *just* hear of from Edward—there are people talking in the room & I mean Edmund!—to a tune that makes me quite sick & faint. What a woeful, weary business—what a pack of troubles to be sure. But it comes of being born a heroine—the great celestial Aristophanes must keep winding you up to enliven his boredom at other matters—& making you do your tricks. I do hope with all my heart that you are well through the worst of it—that it doesn't hurt *very* much. Yet it can't have been soothing while the equestrian statue actually *was* employing you as its pedestal.[1] Dear lady, what you've been through! I feel quite abashed to be frivolising here with the nephew of Macaulay & the speaker of the H. of Commons— when I ought to be holding your hand or fanning your brow. I return to London Monday & shall rush to the Terrace for news. I trust Thornycroft is doing the group—& working Tessa well in.[2] It's lovely here—& awfully Shakespearian—every step seems, somehow, on William's grave & every word a quotation.[3] And the beauty of this primrosy day! I go tonight—in state—to Antony & Cleo. & the Benson Company.[4] I will tell you more, tell you all at the 1st approach to your sofa. Do, dear Mrs. Nellie, grace it but for an hour—*we* all want your courage more than you do yourself, & no one wants your hospitality so much as your affectionate old friend

Henry James

1. One of Hamo Thornycroft's statues apparently had fallen on Mrs. Gosse and broken her collarbone. Thornycroft, the well-known sculptor, was one of Gosse's most intimate friends. He was elected to the Royal Academy in 1888. See letter 6, note 1.

2. Thornycroft was presumably using Tessa (b. 1877), the eldest child of the Gosses, as a model.

3. On a subsequent visit to Welcombe in 1901, James obtained from Lady Trevelyan—the wife of Sir George Otto Trevelyan (1838–1928), the historian and "nephew of Macaulay"—the germ for "The Birthplace." See *N*, 306–307.

4. For James's comment on the productions he saw, see his letter to William James of April 20, 1898 (*HJL*, IV, 73).

---

157 / MS Leeds   Welcombe,
                                                      Stratford On Avon.
                                                      Friday [April 15, 1898]

My dear Gosse,

Your news fills me with horror & replenishes all my sympathy. I have just written to the most unhappy & heroic lady—& this is only a p.s. to say that I will come in to see you the 1st moment after *Monday* next that I can. I don't return till Monday—a most unprecedented—for me—exploit. *Wednesday*, I fear, is my 1st clearest time though I *could* try Tuesday if your Wednesday is taken.[1] You must be bowing beneath the burden of fate. I much want details. Courage mon ami. This is George Trevelyan's—& the divine William's. I will fill up the picture.[2]

Ortmans has forked out![3]

Tout à vous.
Henry James

P.S. Bravo bike!

1. See letter 158.
2. See letter 156.
3. James and Gosse both had been contributing to Ortmans' magazine, *Cosmopolis*.

158 / MS Leeds   34, De Vere Gardens, W.
                                        Monday [April 18, 1898]

My dear Gosse.

I return to town to find your letter & be much & very sympathetically moved by it. It adds much, positively, to my desire for
Wednesday p.m. —little potency as I attach to any special remedy
that the likes of me has to offer for the complaint you suffer from.[1]
Still, I have *this* remedy: "Sit close & see *me* as often as possible." I
will develop it better on Wednesday. Meanwhile hold on tight. It
always pays to have done that—it sees things through. I rejoice your
wife is better—but *what* a superfluity would her *not* being be—![2]
Yours ever

Henry James

1. See letter 157.
2. See letter 156.

159 / MS Duke   Lamb House, Rye.
                                        Sept. 14, 1898.

My dear Gosse.

I am mortally ashamed of my loathsome, my infamous delay in
thanking you for your noble pamphlet & your graceful note. I am
afraid it will considerably qualify your esteem for the Master's House
that the mastery of manners should appear to be least what it teaches
its occupant. But it has had, alas, since you were here, to teach me a
good deal rather the sterner, or higher, virtues of patience & perse-
verance, of faith, hope & charity: by which I mean that complications considerable followed on your departure—in the form of fresh
"series" of visitors bringing with them very high thermometers &
almost no watches. They recommence on Saturday, & meanwhile I

seize this moment. I seized one this afternoon to roll Ixion-like over to Tenterden—with MacA., who might with a finger have stayed me, but who unerringly used that member to kindly show me the way.[1] I will show it to you when *you* next come—I yearn & burn to do so—& the really grand old bravely British village—transporting almost to your Fielding's moment & medium. Àpropos of whom we went also last week over to Rolvenden to call, at Maytham Hall, one of the lordliest seats of the county, on his fair disciple & our old friend Fluffy Burnett, gorged with the fruits of editions & dispensing those of 3 magnificent old walled gardens.[2] (Such a basket of peaches & grapes as I've had from her since! Hurry to come & call *with* me!)

Your so handsomely printed (but with the words, on some lines, systematically too *crowded*, I think,) Preface has the great vividness & interest of everything you do—but I trust you won't think me fantastic if I say I rather miss in it a critical *Idea*, don't find it quite as intimately literary as I shld. have liked to see it.[3] I would have said to you: "Neglect all biographical facts, since you can't go *into* them; your space is precious—give it all to some really critical presentation or picture of the nature of the man's imagination & of the world—the image of life—that *ressort* from his volumes." You will say doubtless that this would have taken you too far—but I don't think the thing as it stands (for a handsome New Edition general preface,) takes you quite far enough. On the other hand not 3 persons among the English-reading millions, I hasten to admit, care 3 straws for any attempt to get *at* any literary subject whatever—& A. Constable & Co. would probably never have forgiven you. I shall guard of course the privacy of your communication closely.

I perspire with poor Philip & I palpitate with all of you. Only I feel rather far away. But we must build, & hold, a bridge. Valete omnes.

Yours always
Henry James

1. Presumably McAlpine, his amanuensis. See letter 147, note 2. Tenterden was the home of Ellen Terry, for whom James had written "Summersoft" in 1895. See *N*, 184–87, and *HJL*, IV, 11.

2. Frances Hodgson Burnett. See letter 130, note 3.

3. The preface is the "noble pamphlet" mentioned at the beginning of the letter. Gosse had written a preface for a new edition of Henry Fielding published by Constable, and had a few copies privately printed. See *LL*, 510.

160 / MS Duke   Lamb House, Rye.
                                             Wednesday p.m. [October 12, 1898][1]

My dear Gosse.

You make me cry—you make me cry bitterly. You have done it before, but it is worse this time. I thank you very sincerely—I am awfully pleased.

But oh, I can do—I shall do still—so unspeakably better than that: which is only cleverness & ingenuity. To think of the good old Addington Archbishop (by a vague fragment of a tale he ineffectually tried to tell me) having given me the germ of anything so odious & hideous! I hope his family won't mind—I wrote, when the thing was serialized, to Arthur.[2]

The difficulty, the problem was of course to add, organically, the element of beauty to a thing so foully ugly—& the success is in *that* if I *have* done it. But I despise bogies, any way. The other thing has of course, like *The Other House*, its base origin smeared all over it: being as it systematically shows itself but a one-act comedy completely worked-out & finished, but never acted; reclaimed a little for literature—& for my pocket—by being simply turned, on the absolute same Scenic lines, into narrative.[3] And now if somebody will only *buy* them!

You must come down here again: the autumn sun & feeling are as charming here as everything else & I shall remain late—on into December probably. It is admirable cycling weather, & I did 22 miles to-day with my irrepressible Scot between luncheon & (a late) tea.[4] Name your day & join us. I shall be in town, of course, for a group of days (next month) before coming up to stay; if, even I *do* that at all. If I let D.V.G.[,] I shall be an exile.[5] I hope your house is safe & your burden adjusted; & I am, my dear Gosse, very gratefully yours,

                                             Henry James

P.S. I like more than I can tell you the things you say about the things—in the T. of the S.—that you *felt*. I believe they *are* all there.

1. Printed in *HJL*, IV, 81–82. The date is derived from the postmark on the attached envelope, October 13, 1898. James had signed a lease on Lamb House in 1897 but had not moved there until the following summer.
2. James had heard Edward White Benson, the archbishop of Canterbury and father of Arthur C. Benson, tell a ghost story at Addington on January 10, 1895 (*N*, 178–79). He used it as the germ of "The Turn of the Screw," which had just appeared in book form (*BHJ*, 113).
3. The "other thing" is "Covering End," a narrative version of "Summersoft" (see

letter 159, note 1). It was published together with "The Turn of the Screw" in a volume called *The Two Magics*. For *The Other House*, see letter 137, note 3.

4. The "irrepressible Scot" is William McAlpine (see letter 147, note 2).

5. James eventually gave up 34 De Vere Gardens and in 1901 took a room at the Reform Club as his London base.

161 / MS Leeds   Lamb House, Rye.
                                          Tuesday night [February 28, 1899][1]

All thanks, my dear Gosse, for your note. No thank heaven, I've escaped by a narrow squeak—but I've escaped: with only 2 rooms partially, very partially damaged—& only "structurally"—not as to furniture, & not—rare fate—at all by supererogatory water—as so easily might have been.[2] By the "finger of providence" I was sitting up to a very undue, (& for me) unusual hour—2 a.m.—meaning at last, at last, to have "gone abroad" today, as ever is—& thereby lingering late by my *foyer* to write a great many procrastinated letters that I knew I shouldn't have time for on the morrow. *That* saved me—I sniffed the danger much sooner than if I had been with my head under the bedclothes; & could quickly summon the brave pumpers, who arrived promptly & showed most laudable tact, sanity & competence—above all in not nervously & prematurely flooding me. They pumped most subtly—& in short save for a scare & an absolutely too strained & sleepless—*debout*—night—with the temporary loss of the use of two rooms (insured completely,) I am not the worse; & I am on the other hand cheaply *warned*—old houses have insidious structural traps; old recklessness & barbarities of fire-place-building & infamous juxtapositions of *beams* & chimnies. It is all to be made again better & saner & safer than it *ever* was—& I wait here a week longer to see reparations started. Then I do at last go away for 10 weeks. Influenza, proofs, other things—above all the longing to wait for spring—to really meet it—have kept me till now. I was for a fortnight more or less down with the beastly blight—but am erect & purged again. Only I don't *want* even *now* to go: this house is so sustained a fit.

Don't you palpitate & gasp with poor great little Rudyard—?[3] I pray for him tenderly, though with consistent pessimism. Good-bye & all thanks again. I seem to have innumerable letters to write. We shall gather ourselves together on my return. Love to your house. Ever your

                                          H.J.

1. Printed in *HJL*, IV, 99–100. Although the typed copy of the original at Leeds gives the date as March 1, 1899, the actual date of Tuesday is February 28 in 1899. It is true, of course, as James notes in this letter, that when he "sniffed" the fire, he was writing letters at "2 a.m." The present text differs in several ways from the previously printed text.

2. The fire had occurred on the night of Sunday, February 26 (actually in the early hours of February 27). See James's telegram of February 27 to Edward Warren in *HJL*, IV, 98–99.

3. Kipling was seriously ill in New York with inflammation of the lungs (presumably pneumonia), and bulletins were issued to the press daily from February 22 on. A crisis came on February 28, the date of James's letter, but by March 4 he was out of danger. On March 6 his eldest child, Josephine (b. 1892), died of the same illness. James wrote on March 6 to congratulate Kipling on his victory, but after hearing about Josephine's death, he wrote Carrie Balestier Kipling on March 8 to apologize for his "mistimed jubilation" and to express his grief over the loss of "dear little delightful vanished Josephine, dear little surrendered, sacrificed soul!" See Carrington, *Rudyard Kipling*, 287–91.

162 / MS Duke   Lamb House, Rye.
                                                          Aug. 19*th* 1899.

My dear Edmund.

Very delightful your letter & deserving of publicity & renown—also exactly qualified to make me howl with envy of all the far-awayness & unexpectedness of your field of vision—so unlike the extreme banality—by familiarity—of everything that constitutes *my* few changes of scene & pursuits of impression. But how answer it with *any* proportionate pomp of circumstance whatever? how converse with you at all at this vertiginous pictorial pitch? The balsam of pines & plash of fiords & remote thunder of Sagas are exhaled from your pages, & the most uncompromising (though not perhaps most uncompromised) heroines of our dear old Henrik [Ibsen] seem to sit at your elbow.[1] (This embodies, I beseech her to believe, no allusion whatever to Mrs. Edmund.) I had, oddly enough, on your arrival, a young Norwegian (tho' Americanized) staying with me—a young Roman sculptor (Hans Christian Andersen, by name!) of whom, out of the frenzy of my poverty I had bought, 2 months ago, a charming terra-cotta bust, & I took the liberty of reading him your most vivid passages, which he enjoyed in spite of an evident relief that the over-trousered & over-crinolined race had not remained his immediate inspiration.[2] When I show you a photog. of one of his groups you will appreciate his altogether alternative vision. I congratulate you with all my heart on the intensity of your "change," as my servants always write me when I am away. *My* changes are quite over—my very smallest is quite spent. Rye is hot & heavyish, but I find it good to be back here.[3] My little old house hugs me almost too tight & my garden blooms with the expensive insolence begotten of a new lawn-sprinkler. We are having a wonderful luminous summer; as fine-weathery, it would seem, as last, but not so continuously hot. I've got back, thank heaven to what the "creatures invariably speak of as their 'work'," as I remember to have read somewhere in the trenchant Birrell; & heaven knows it was high time.[4] I must stick to it tight till the New Year—& then stick tighter. I've had no visitors but Hans—though I'm putting up tonight two golfing men—Bernard Mallet & young Grenfell—who come down to play tomorrow. [The] Godkins & Dan Curtises loom for later on—but all brief.[5] My brother W*m* has been obliged to come out to Nauheim, & I am to have him & his wife thereafter—a lively expectation to me, though I hate his having had to throw himself invalidically on that particular place. However, it is doing him extreme good. For the rest I live, I confess, in the great shadow of Dreyfus.[6] I hope it isn't projected across the cool blue fiord. The *Times* (reporter) is very good & sane about it—&, somehow, it keeps my heart in my mouth. The proceedings are passing strange—& Picquart apparently a man of rare ability—to speak of *that* alone. The wretched Alfred is, to one's haunting apprehension, *condemned*—a victim inexorably appointed; for even if he be acquitted (& the Ct. Martial will *perish* 1st!) he will be assassinated the next moment. And our friend Clam-Patty isn't produced, & Esterhazy is, at a distance, positively *choyé*. It's a dark, dark business—it isn't pretty for France. It *poisons* the gentle summer. But why should I talk to you of this if you have the good fortune to be out of it? I am void of other news. I shall have none till you bring it on your return. I'm delighted Mrs. Edmund has found her real combination. Again I seem accidentally ambiguous—my phrase but personifys the climatic genius of Scandinavia. Give her very affectionate remembrance. Let yourself go—by which I mean coagulate in the immobility of rest. But while you're resting, *do* it! I mean write it, immortalise it. Àpropos of immortality I just remember that Lewis Hind & Clarence Rook come over to see me from Winchelsea tomorrow—after correspondence.[7] I feel as if there were more in it than meets the eye—for I know neither. But it's 5 p.m. & I must put in an hour of the open. Come & tell me all the rest when you return. Ever constantly yours

Henry James

P.S. How beautiful—& how *literary*—R.L.S.'s principal letter to you in the Aug. Scribner—the one on "happiness" &c, &c. I saw Fanny S. in town 10 days ago—& must tell you about her.[8] It's too long here.

1. The Gosses are holidaying in Kristiania, Norway.
2. James often referred to Hendrik Christian Andersen (1872–1940) as Hans. Andersen, though born in Norway, had grown up in America. He had set up a studio in Rome and thus established, to James, his "Roman" character.
3. James had gone to France and Italy in the spring after his house had been partially burned and had returned to Rye early in July. See letter 161.
4. Augustine Birrell (1850–1933), British author of *Obiter Dicta* (1884, 1887).
5. Bernard Mallet (1859–1932) was commissioner of inland revenue (1897–1909); "young Grenfell" may be Cecil A. Grenfell (d. 1924), the brother-in-law of the ninth duke of Marlborough; Edwin L. Godkin, editor of the *Nation*, had known James for over thirty years (see letter 56); and the Dan Curtises James had known for years and had often visited in Venice. Gosse would subsequently visit the Curtises in 1901. See letters 184 and 185.
6. The Dreyfus affair occasioned a number of lead articles in the *Times* of July and August. On August 17 and 18, for example, the articles reported Major Esterhazy's admissions concerning his part in the forgeries, and on August 19, the day of James's letter, Lieutenant-Colonel Armand DuPaty de Clam, though called earlier as a witness, was absent from court.
7. Charles Lewis Hind (1862–1927) was editor of the *Academy* from 1896 to 1903 and author of *The Enchanted Stone: A Romance* (1898); Clarence Rook (d. 1915), author of the best-selling *Hooligan Nights* (1899), was also a contributor to the *English Illustrated News*.
8. Sidney Colvin's edition of "The Letters of Robert Louis Stevenson" ran in *Scribner's Magazine* from December, 1898, to November, 1899. For the August, 1899, number, see XXVI, 338–50. Fanny S. was Stevenson's widow.

163 / MS Duke   Lamb House, Rye.
                                         Wednesday. (Thursday)[1]
                                         [October, 1899]

My dear Gosse,

Your responsive note of the other day was very handsome—too handsome to have deserved this delay of *riposte*. But we seem destined to treat of a point not yet actual & pressing enough. I fear the 18*th will* be the 1*st* favourable day—but, Colvin or no Colvin (he is as yet ambiguous,) I confess I should so much rather see you alone—for free converse's sake—that I am tending to propose to you, for that consummation, the still remoter 25*th*, unfriendly as such a relegation seems. If Colvin *doesn't* (& I shall soon know,) decide for the 18*th*, I shall then instantly wire to you on the hope you may still have it free. I am miserably *sous le coup* of this wretched South A.[frican] news.[2] It keeps one's heart in one's mouth. What tension for the next days & weeks. What a heartening for the Boers—& how canny they be! *Not* canny, not canny *enough*, ever, especially at first, these Islanders. But at last—! Only, *before* that—? But I can't bear midnight fears: therefore, as it's 12.30 p.m. [*sic*], enough.

I've just been reading over, together & continuously, the whole 2 vols. of R.L.S. *Letters*, which S.C. has kindly sent me.[3] I find the impression mixed, but on the whole very great; & beauty & oddity & genius & intense originality, & prevailing melancholy, galore. Some of the best—*the* best, perhaps, on the whole, save one long & supreme one, at (nearly,) the end, to R.A.M.S.—are to you; & the final one, to you, quite divinely fair.[4] But I get again the sense of what a strange mixture he was of parts of high, rare beauty & odd juxtaposed gaps & lapses. But the total 2 vols. are what the *Vailima Letters* were not [—] exceedingly distinguished. Bring me down some talk.

Ever your most nocturnal
Henry James

1. This letter is difficult to date precisely. It was apparently written in October, 1899, at about the same time James wrote Sidney Colvin (see *LHJ*, I, 330–32), and it also refers to Colvin's proposed visit on "the 18*th*." Since that date falls on a Wednesday in October and on a Saturday in November, the latter month seems indicated for the visit (see letter 164). James's listing of both Wednesday and Thursday as dates for this letter is explained by his reference to the time: "12.30 p.m." [*sic*]. See also letter 164, note 2.
2. James frequently mentions the difficulties with the Boers during this period. See, for example, letters 164 and 166. The Transvaal and the Orange Free State declared war on Great Britain on October 12.
3. Sidney Colvin (ed.), *The Letters of Robert Louis Stevenson to His Family and Friends* (2 vols.; New York, 1899). This edition had been appearing in installments in *Scribner's Magazine* (see letter 162, note 8), but had just come out in book form in October, 1899.
4. Robert A. M. Stevenson, the cousin of R. L. Stevenson. For the "supreme" letter, see Colvin (ed.), *Letters of Stevenson*, II, 423–30.

164 / MS Leeds   Lamb House, Rye.
                                                          Oct. 24*th* 1899.

My dear Gosse.

All thanks for your sympathy. I left my brother rather better than when he first came up to town (or than when I saw you last;) but in consequence of having, practically, given up almost everything for the present & *consented* to be really ill. The best London specialist (Beseley [*sic*] Thorne,) has him in charge, & has begun by (among other things,) practically putting him to bed—or almost—for 2 or 3 weeks—or more: after which, & after other things, one will be able better to judge of what further may be done for him.[1] But it all makes him a graver & more precarious case than I had dreamed of his being; & his condition is a worry that I can't yet throw off. But there are, thank heaven, better possibilities—& everything that can best be done *is* being attempted. I will let you know more.

The peace & softness & stillness & sunshine of this little place continues to be a boon. Can't you come down for some Sunday next month? The difficulty is, I admit, even while I urge it on you, that for various reasons (mainly of such extreme pressure of occupation as make solitude for the next 2 or 3 weeks imperative to me,) the 19*th* is my 1*st free* Sunday. That is not only remote, but on it *Colvin* may also be here![2] I met him, as it happens, (at Bain's) after I last saw you, & he was (after symptoms I had read otherwise,) so completely, all cordiality & communication, that an old plan of his coming down here came up again, & I think his advent on that day possible. It would be less likely on the following Saturday 25*th*—if the fact makes a difference to you—; only that is still more duskily remote. However, do settle for *either*, won't you? I shall be very glad of whichever decision. I hope you are quite firm on your feet.

What a gloom this African slaughter of brave men, & how difficult the Joy of Battle![3] This place & weather are shamelessly pacific, & I am ever so nervously yours

Henry James

1. For William James's illness (he had recently suffered a heart attack), see letter 162 and Henry James's letter to Charles Eliot Norton of November 24, 1899, in *HJL*, IV, 121–22, 126. Dr. Beasley Thorne was indeed a well-known heart specialist.

2. James's concern over his brother's health apparently led him to forget that he had already invited Gosse for November 18 or 25 (see letter 163). Colvin had also been mentioned earlier as a possible visitor.

3. For the Boer War, see letter 163, note 2.

165 / MS British Library   Lamb House, Rye
                                                              Nov: 5. 1899
My dear Gosse.

I am delighted you can come on the 18*th*; & as to the presence of the Y.M.C.B. I guarantee you complete immunity.[1] I am sorry he afflicts you—mais je comprends tous les points de vue. I'm afraid he rather exaggerates his devotion—as to "flying down," he spent a Sunday here a month ago—& another last (I think,) January; but these have been the limits of his benevolence—& there is at any rate no present question of his coming back. Therefore *rassurez-vous*. If I'm not wholly alone it will be that possibly my young friend Jonathan Sturges will be here—but even that is very doubtful.[2] Arrivez donc de confiance.

I am much taken up with the immediate & pressing—but your Donne insists on getting himself regarded, at moments, in that light, & when I open him again, snatches, each time, the bread from my lips.[3] What a beautiful literary man—what a poet & what a prosator: with almost as much style as R.L.S.! But what, above all, a literary man *you* to have managed so big & complex a job so quietly & in such mere marginal time as you must have been able to give to it. It's wonderful, admirable, & you are prodigious. I hope the book is doing you, in one way & another, a great lot of good. It's so awfully *interesting*.

For the rest, I've drunk deep (over Colvin's loan of the consecutive sheets) of the handsome book-continuity of R.L.S.[4] This, however, I believe I've told you. It is a charming personal joy—I come back to it; though with such a wretched renewed sense of the horridest thing that has publicly, as it were, (if not privately) happened to us, in all these later years, being this excision of the beautiful creature from our lives—with nothing but the bloody hole & socket left. He was so much too precious for us to have lost for a while longer—& the clumsy tragedy of it all as one pieces it backward, as a whole, together! But arrivez donc. Yours always

Henry James

1. "Y.M.C.B." may refer to Charles Baxter (1848–1919), Stevenson's cousin and executor. Gosse had accepted James's invitation to visit. See letters 163 and 164.
2. James had known Sturges (1864–1909), a young American expatriate, for almost a decade. For his letters to Sturges, see *HJL*, III, 435, and IV, 40.
3. Edmund Gosse, *The Life and Letters of John Donne Dean of St. Paul's* (2 vols.; London, 1899).
4. See letter 163, note 3.

166 / MS Leeds   Lamb House, Rye.
                                   Sunday [November 12, 1899][1]
My dear Gosse.
    I wholly agree with you as to any motion toward the preposterous

& unseemly deportation from their noble resting-place of those illustrious & helpless ashes.[2] I find myself, somehow, unable to think of Louis in these days (much more to speak of him,) without an emotion akin to tears; & such blatant busybody ineptitude causes the cup to overflow & sickens as well as enrage[s]. But nothing but cheap newspaperism will come of it—it has in it the power, fortunately, to drop, utterly & abysmally, if not *touched*—if decently ignored. Don't write a protest—don't write *anything*: simply *hush*! The *lurid* asininity of the hour!

All thanks for your reference to your devil of a Donne: Donne Giovanni, in very truth, as to his ravage of the bare-breasted muses.[3] I read the Vol II passage with bated breath. I will write you about your best train Saturday—which heaven speed! It will probably be the *3.23* from Charing Cross—better, really, than the (new) *5.15* from *St. Paul's*. I find S. Africa a nightmare & need cheering—Arrive therefore primed for that office.[4] Ever yours

Henry James

1. Printed in part in *LHJ*, I, 332, and in *SR*, 581–82. My text follows the original and restores two sentences excised by Lubbock.
2. The suggestion had been made that Stevenson's body should be removed from above Vailima and brought home to Britain.
3. For Gosse's *Donne*, see letter 165, note 3.
4. For James's comments on the Boer War, see letters 163 and 164.

167 / MS Leeds   Lamb House, Rye.
Friday p.m. [November 17, 1899]

My dear Gosse.

This is a word to say that if you *can* take the *3.23* from Charing X tomorrow afternoon (due here 5.27) it will be, I think, the rightest thing.[1] There is a *4.28* from Charing X & a *5.15* from St. Paul's (Chat. & Dover line;) but they get in *late* in reality, though not nominally (the 5.15 *due* here 7.9,) & the other thing brings you to tea & a little talk before dinner. If you *can't* manage the 3.23 the *5.15* is next best—from St. Paul's (close to Blackfriar's Bridge,) *without* a change at Ashford. But I shall attend at the station here for the 3.23 if I hear nothing from you adverse. I've been, I'm sorry to say, shut up for 3 days with sciatica, but am better & shall be able to face gently tomorrow & very firmly indeed, I think, Sunday. I am utterly solus—& don't encumber yourself with the articles of dress.[2] Please look in your A.B.C. & assure yourself about the *2d 3* of the 3.23. I haven't one here—nor a Bradshaw. But the train exists—some friends came to me by it a fortnight ago. If it's not 3.23, it's 3.27. Bon voyage! It will be a joy to claver with you. Love to your Home.

Ever yours
Henry James

1. For other references to this visit, see letters 163–166.
2. James frequently advises Gosse not to bother about bringing dress clothes. See, for example, letter 182.

168 / LHJ[1]   Lamb House, Rye.
January *1st*, 1900

My dear Gosse,

I much welcome your note & feel the need of exonerations—as to my own notelessness. It was very good of you, staggering on this gruesome threshold & meeting only new burdens, I fear (of correspondence,) as its most immediate demonstration, to find a moment to waggle me so much as a little finger. I was painfully conscious of my long silence—after a charming book from you, never properly acknowledged, &c.; but I have been living with very few odd moments or off-hours of leisure, & my neglect of every one & everything is now past reparation. The presence with me of my brother, sister-in-law and little niece has, with a particular pressure of work, walled me in and condemned my communications.[2] My brother, for whom this snug and secure little nook appears to have been soothing and sustaining, is better than when he came, & I am proportionately less depressed; but I still go on tiptoe & live from day to day. However, that way one does go on. They go, probably, by the middle of the month, to the South of France—& a right climate, a *real* one, has presumably much to give him. . . .

I never thanked you—en connaissance de cause—for M. Hewlett's Italian *Novelle*: of so brilliant a cleverness & so much more developed a one than his former book.[3] They are wonderful for "go" & grace & general ability, & would almost make me like the *genre*, if anything could. But I so hunger and thirst, in this deluge of cheap romanticism & chromolithographic archaics (babyish, puppyish, as evocation, all, it seems to me,) for a note, a gleam of reflection of the life *we* live, of artistic or plastic intelligence of it, something one can say yes or no to, as discrimination, perception, observation, rendering—

that I am really not a judge of the particular commodity at all: I am out of patience with it & have it *par-dessus les oreilles*. What I don't doubt of is the agility with which Hewlett does it. But oh Italy—the Italy *of* Italy! Basta!

May the glowering year clear its dark face for all of us before it has done with us! . . . Vale. Good-night.

Yours always,
Henry James

1. Since I have not found the manuscript of the letter, my text is based upon *LHJ*, I, 344–46. I have made a few changes according to James's usual stylistic practice (as concerns ampersands and *etc.*).

2. William James and part of his family had been with Henry James off and on for several months, and during this period William had been ill from heart trouble. See letters 162 and 164, and letter 164, note 1. Later in January he will go to Hyères for the climate. See letter 169.

3. Apparently Maurice Hewlett's *Little Novels of Italy* (1899). Hewlett (1861–1923) was also the author of historical romances, and was one of Gosse's friends and followers at the National Club. See *LL*, 206.

169 / MS Leeds

Lamb House, Rye.
January 16 1900

My dear Gosse,

I take your letter to me—your observations on my N.A.R article—as a very kind thing.[1] If it does seem at all "fresh," so much the better: it was miraculously hard, in all the circumstances, to make it & keep it so. And the kind of things I wanted most to say—the kind that the subject, at every turn, gave me from the standpoint of my own literary & craftsmanly sense, judgment, discrimination &c, opportunity and pretext for, I didn't say *at all*. 1st, there was no space, & 2d I didn't wish too much to discriminate. Your appreciation is highly liberal—Eliza's surely is not less so.[2] It fails but by a step that you "chassez-de race." The rift within the lute at Sandhurst must be by this time indeed a cold crevasse! What a supererogation—or whatever they call such things!—such a job surely must have become! Scarce longer to be borne. But patience. The stop will be short when it comes. That *I* should say such things! My brother (all thanks!) has just reached *Hyères* with much appearance of being able to hope something good from a kind of healing climatic air-bath there.[3] Heaven forward it. It's his great—his one—chance. He will stay, if possible, 3 months. I miss him here, much—as you may think. It's cold & dark & contracted in these weeks here—but I am worrying through it. *What* weeks, what days these, of quite too horrid tension![4] I can't say what I fear. I fear too much. Du calme! Ever your

H.J.

1. Henry James, "The Letters of Robert Louis Stevenson," *North American Review*, CLXX (January, 1900), 61–77. This is actually a review of Colvin's edition of Stevenson's letters to his family and friends. See letter 163, note 3.
2. A reference to Gosse's stepmother. James had met her in 1895 when he spent some time near Torquay. See letter 125.
3. William James had been in poor health for many months and had been advised to go to Hyères for the climate. James mentions this plan in a postscript to a letter to Charles Eliot Norton dated January 13, 1900 (*HJL*, IV, 126).
4. In addition to his concern for his brother, James was worried about the Boer War.

---

170 / MS Leeds   Lamb House, Rye.
                                          Feb. 28*th* 1900

My dear Gosse.

I have so many things to talk to you of—it would seem—of which my appreciation of your kindness in sending me your Russian vol. is the fine flower—that there seems nothing for it but to come up to town & take you by the beard.[1] I will postpone everything—thanks, questions, exclamations, lamentations, jubilations, till then! Only this can't be, alas, till the 10*th*. Shall you be, by any chance, at home on Monday 12*th* p.m.?—or on Tuesday or Wednesday? Kindly let me know *which* evening, & I will keep it pure & undefiled. A single word will suffice. There seem, don't there? great accumulations of historic & other matter. I breathe, *ces-jours-ci*, more freely—but they are ill days for trade. The courage of your Waliszeuskiism!—or whatever your wild flight may be called.[2] Let us have a good grumble. Only, please, fix the date. I hope your house is whole & your life holy. My benison on it all. Yours always

Henry James

P.S. I've been looking over your Russ—whose history-books are so clever. But how cleverer he seems in French! He strikes me here as slightly common; but what do I know? Good luck to him.

1. Presumably Kozimierz Waliszewski's *A History of Russian Literature* (London, 1900), a volume edited by Gosse in the series entitled "Short Histories of the Literatures of the World."
2. Another reference (continued in the postscript) to Waliszewski (1849–1935),

several of whose earlier books had been in French. The present history is in English.

171 / MS Duke   Lamb House, Rye.
                                                                  April 3*d* 1900

My dear Gosse.

I have owed you a letter ever since you sent me Arthur Symonds's book—ever since I saw you, in town, so unwell & so accompanied with unwellness—ever since, in particular, some rumour reached me that your interests might be compromised by the failure of the Appletons![1] And yet all these things have but left me, or rather kept me, silent—by the very effect, I think, of their massive magnitude. I go up to town—for 24 hours—again (mainly, alas, to the Dentist!) & I may perhaps meet you at dinner: but on this I don't venture to count, & I dedicate you these poor lines as desperately as if no happier chance promised in any degree to relieve you, as the Italians say, of the inconvenience of them.

I needn't tell you what a hope I cherish that the Appleton cataclysm either *isn't* one, in a grave or practical sense, or that, if it is, you hadn't so many eggs in the basket as that any omelette of real tragedy has been made by the smash. Let me partake of it, in spirit, with you, sympathetically indeed—such as it is—consuming my slice in proportion to the total size. *Bain*, the omniscient, told me they would go on again better than ever—perhaps therefore only a new breeze has filled your sail.[2] For these things I pray, & for the reign in your house, of a more careless sanitary consciousness. I have been taking, heartlessly, for granted, that both you & your wife are essentially better—& it would abase me so to learn that you are not, that I'm sure you won't reduce me to any such humiliation. *Où en est* Philip?—has he got his exams. behind him? I don't mean to press you with questions—or any other indiscretions—these are mere dim rockets of interest, clearing the long night of the last three weeks. I staid on in town longer than I meant, but shorter than I liked, & have been a week at home. I got no moment for reading Symonds's book till my return. I've read it attentively. It is very intelligent & charming; & anything perceptive & liberal, in this desert of Boeotian bêtes, extremely appeals to one. I think him too solemn & Paternal, as it were, about his people—it's Pater's manner, awfully well reproduced, without Pater's subjects. I moreover, some how, constitutionally hate English writing on French subjects—& never so much as when it is my own. But that, I admit, we can't help, &, if we must have it, Symonds does it better than any one, &, if you get a chance, please tell him that I've read his book with great pleasure & profit. There are other things that I don't want him told; so I won't mix them up with this poor message. It is cold here & backward & harsh & I have no hope of any decent air till after Easter. On the first hint that it has really come I shall ask you to name some day. I want you to get, really, the happy impression.

And Eliza—sur ces entrefaites? Are you to spend a happy Easter with her?[3] I think of her with anxiety—she seems so capable of everything but one. Make me some sort of an inclusive sign. This one of mine is meant to be all-enfolding. It takes in everything that concerns you & leaves me still with my hands up. Yours, my dear Gosse, & your wife's always,

Henry James

1. The book by Arthur Symons (1865–1945) that James is apparently referring to is *The Symbolist Movement in Literature* (1899). James consistently misspells Symons' name in this letter. For the failure of the Appleton firm in New York, see Samuel C. Chew (ed.), *Fruit Among the Leaves: An Anniversary Anthology* (New York, 1950), 51–53. Gosse edited the "Short Histories of the Literatures of the World" for Appleton during this period (*TD*, 34). He may have lost some or all of his salary in 1900.

2. Presumably James S. Bain, the bookseller. The Appleton firm was reorganized in 1900 and continued business with a new president and a new capital structure. See Chew (ed.), *Fruit Among the Leaves*, 52.

3. Eliza Brightwen Gosse, Gosse's stepmother.

172 / MS Library of Congress   Lamb House, Rye.
                                                   May 14*th* 1900[1]

My dear Gosse

Your proposal in respect to Tolstoi, with the great honour it does me, greatly (I won't attempt to conceal from you,) embarrasses & complicates my soul. I should like *much* to oblige & serve your cause—how much I needn't say; but there are reasons why I am not in a position to produce at present, or within any *near* time, the needed 3,000 words about our friend. Rather there is *a* grave reason—nay, there are two! The first is I don't materially *know* any of Tolstoi's work but his 2 or 3 great novels (& one or two Kreutzer Sonatas &c.;) & that I see, of his later incarnation a list of 10 or 12 volumes reproduced on the fly-leaf of the issue of a single publisher.

(Beside which there is other fiction.) *Or*, it so happens that I haven't at present *time* to read all or any of this stuff; it's impossible to me— other matters press on me too hard. And yet no estimate of him can have any value which doesn't take full acct. of them. I don't really, in other words, *possess*, at all, my whole Tolstoi; & I am afraid I must ask you accordingly to let me off. It must—the job—be done by some one who *does* possess him.[2] This is a poor & scrambling scrawl—& I shall write you better—less scramblingly & more explicatively & personally (which I want greatly to do—& to arrange to see you,) in a day or two. Forgive my impracticability & incompetence. I feel a great jadedness in your note, & give it a still greater sympathy. Your life is a miracle to me; & it has the proportionate wonder & admiration of yours always

Henry James

1. Printed in *HJL*, IV, 189–90, but therein dated May 14, 1901. I have used the original, and I read the year as 1900. There is another substantive change in the text: *cause* for *case*.

2. Years later, ironically, Gosse himself declined in 1907 to write on Tolstoi for the *Atlantic Monthly*, though he subsequently published an essay on the Russian writer in the *Contemporary Review* for September, 1908.

173 / MS Duke Lamb House, Rye.
September 22*d* 1900.[1]

My dear Gosse.

I am very sorry you have had occasion to write me so sadly & sternly, & I will do every—any—penance you may impose upon [me] for having, by an endless close tissue of inevitabilities & fatalities, struck you as giving it.[2] I *have* been silent & signless, & I've been painfully & uncomfortably conscious of the same; but I find myself affected in very melancholy fashion by having at this time of day to write you that there has been no *intention* in my troubled case. I have had an extremely worried, disturbed, preoccupied, in a manner overwhelmed summer—out of which my issue has only been to sit as tight as possible & keep my complications down, to escape without disaster. I've in other words, for the last 4 or 5 months, since just after I saw you, had an endless assault, as it were, of family history playing over me in uninterrupted episodes, which would have condemned me to a surrender pure & simple to the same—i.e. to an anxious economy of time, nerves, communications & other matter—, even had it had any gaps & interaction. But it has in fact had none: I've had relations more worried than myself & the anxious problems of relations, installed with me in permanence, & have been doomed to make no signs, outward, at all. I go to morrow with my sister-in-law to Dover, to see her off to the Continent rejoining my brother, & on my return on Monday shall be alone for the first time these many weeks.[3] In view of this I've been fully meaning, each day, to write to you & ask if you wouldn't come down & see me some near Saturday—the prospect of a Sunday *alone* holding such an attraction out that I've been only waiting for it. That I *haven't* written till today is a misfortune I much regret—it would [have] averted the piercing shaft of your letter. I am in truth, through a summer in which 9/10s of my time has gone, on the spot, to others, not to myself, in shocking *general* arrears with letters, & writing each day, under coercion, some several dreadfully *other* than those I promised myself on rising. *Then* I should have told you in a way more graceful than with this extorted air, that what has been really at the bottom of my constantly post-poning writing was the dislike I felt of writing at all *not* to ask you down here to see me, so far as you could come; & asking you, asking any one, was all these weeks impossible. Two or three persons prac-tically proposed themselves,—one or two in fact very directly, not long since: but they have been the only persons under my roof not consanguineous. I don't know how you come by your impression that I've been in town & dining—so strange an irony it is of the actual current of my days. I dined the night I last saw you—April?— & after that—end of June, I think, went up to spend one night with a friend & one other, the next, at Windsor. Save those occasions a day or two of sweltering hurried business, in the canicular between trains (12.30 & 5.15) are the only witchcraft I've used. If I say that I went a month ago to spend a Sunday at the Wolseleys—straight hence—my *plaidager* is complete.[4] But it's too long, & you must come down, now, at last, for a day of peace with me & talk everything over that the air has hummed with since we parted; in other words all things *but* these absurdities. Will Saturday *29th* suit you?—do try & make it![5] I would wire asking you for tomorrow were it not for my rig-orous absence. I can't get back from Dover till Monday—as it's a p.m. business. If not *29th*, how about the *6th* Oct? But what is near-est to this divine weather is best. I've been full of vain speculation about you all & shld. have been delighted to hear from you. I hope your wife & children bear up, & I send them much love—to Mrs. Nelly not least. But I hope all sorts of things that I will tell you better when we meet. Ever, my dear Gosse, yours

Henry James

1. The postmark of the envelope attached to the letter reads September 21. The context of the letter suggests that James may have confused Friday's and Saturday's dates. Friday occurred on September 21.
2. James wrote W. E. Norris September 26 that Gosse was coming to see him as a result of "such a letter as, had I been such another, would have, vulgarly speaking, put the fat on the fire," but, he concluded, "*I'm not* such another" and will "await him with the other cheek turned." This passage has been excised from the letter as printed in *LHJ*, I, 301–303, but is in the manuscript (Yale).
3. During much of the period James describes, he had been concerned about his brother William's health. During part of this time, William and his wife Alice had stayed with James at Lamb House.
4. For the Wolseleys, see letter 101, note 8.
5. For Gosse's visit, see James's letter to Mrs. William James, October 1, 1900 (*HJL*, IV, 168).

174 / MS Leeds   Lamb House, Rye.
                                                     Oct: 16: 1900.

My dear Gosse.

I see in to-day's *Times* that the bolt has fallen—too heavy an engine, surely, for so frail a victim; & I think with much sympathy of your immediate heritage of trouble & confusion.[1] I imagine you all—or your wife with you at least—gathered for the last offices in a place where you must feel it to be the End of so much—so much of your own past. May it not only also have proved the end of Everything Else! May you not find yourself face to face with a situation *too* bothering & boring. This is at any rate my word of extreme participation—which please communicate to your wife with all the kindness of yours always

Henry James

P.S. Don't *think*—immersed & overburdened & beset—of "answering" this. Only write me at some full subsequent leisure.

1. Eliza Brightwen Gosse, Gosse's stepmother, had died on October 14 at Sandhurst, St. Marychurch, Devon. Gosse, an only child, inherited her house and more than one-third of her estate, exceeding £16,000 after a few bequests had been made. See *EG*, 382–83.

175 / MS Leeds   Lamb House, Rye.
                                    Friday p.m. [October 19?, 1900][1]

My dear Gosse.

Wonderfully vivid & interesting your letter & marvellously blooming on the funereal yew! I make out *sans peine* all your quandaries &
troublements, & this is but a word to say that my sympathy moves
through the labyrinth at your side. I'm very sorry indeed you had to
travel down ill, & I trust you return to an altered scene. What a
happy, delightful, convenient evanishment! How kind *can* Nature be!
There's therefore the less excuse for her in general. I hope the bits
will fall together, kaleidoscopically, so as to make a pretty figure or
two—I hope this with all my heart. And I feel moved to say to you
with extreme emphasis, from my vantage-ground of these near 3
years of experience here, that I hope you won't undervalue the possession of a house in the country. *Cling* to it, believe in it; don't sacrifice or surrender it. *It is everything* to have one—a refuge out of
London. *Since* you have it, clutch it, even if it be not just where you
want it. *You won't get another*—& I find this asylum has been of
unspeakable worth to me. That is really the moral of this midnight
scrawl.[2] I could develop it to you face to face *à perte de view*. The difficulties are secondary—the *alternative of a fixed* & assured asylum out
of the London riot [&] everything.

                                    Ever yours
                                    Henry James

1. The typed copy of this letter at Leeds proposes in brackets a date of October
20, 1900, but Friday (James's heading) occurred on October 19 in 1900. Since James
is writing a "midnight scrawl," he may have considered that he was writing the letter
on Friday, and then posted it on Saturday, October 20. At any rate, the date must be
October 19 or possibly October 26, for James is following up his letter of October 16
(letter 174) with further comment on the death of Eliza Gosse.
2. Although Gosse considered James's proposal about Sandhurst, he sold the
place for about one-third of its value and apparently had few regrets. See *EG*, 383,
and letter 176.

176 / MS Leeds   Lamb House, Rye.
                                    November 18*th* 1900

My dear Gosse.

Many thanks for the portrait of my so benevolent friend (I'm
afraid I can scarcely say yours!)—which recalls her to me as I saw
her last (or *first*—I forget which!) interestingly panting & agitated by

the romantic ascent to my sittingroom in Hesketh Crescent, & requiring just the proper amount (for a lady who *had* done it!) of tender reassurance & jocose encouragement.[1] As I look over the catalogue of the other furniture of her life I can't help feeling a little glad that she found room just for that one small alien episode—of another texture & colour—though doubtless less cataloguable. It is interesting & suggestive that in the picture she looks just a little surcharged with remorse. It is even excessive. But she would like to think how badly I feel about the going "out of my life," of Sandhurst.[2] Could you only keep it, it would be a link. Still, I suppose I can hardly expect you (though I'm not sure *she* wouldn't) to keep it *for* that. So long as it might be yours—but I won't pursue the vanished (& slightly confused) possibilities! It's perhaps better for me that all should be over.

I'm sorry, seriously speaking, that for *you* it is so. My plea for the retention of the estate was doubtless a plea for impossible ideals. I can only hope, for you, then, that your sale may be decently productive. I suppose it can't be at best *very* fruitful. I trust you are, in respect to the whole episode, in the phase of subsidence—yet not of subsidence too utter. You must tell me, when I come to town, of these things. I stay here till Xmas (inclusive;) then I come for 3 or 4 months, having secured a small but sufficient perch. (My flat is still as interminably as luckily let.)[3] I quite yearn for Westbourne Grove, the 4 penny busses, & all the rest. I shall have been confined to this hamlet for two years & a 1/2 on end—save for 3 or 4 months abroad. You *must*, all, take me to *Mme* Tussaud's. With many anticipatory greetings all round, Yours always

Henry James

1. Gosse had sent James a picture of his late stepmother, Eliza Gosse, who had visited James in 1895 in Torquay. Mrs. Gosse was charmed by James, and subsequently, the two friends teased each other with the prospect of James becoming Gosse's stepfather. James had even alluded to the charade in a letter of February 26, 1899, to their mutual friend, W. E. Norris: "Of course I saw Gosse in town—twice—and had the latest news of his fond relative, the unreserved *victim* of my charms. Well, there are many things I should like to do for Gosse—But I'm not sure that becoming his stepfather figures in the list" (Yale). For Mrs. Gosse's death, see letter 174, note 1.

2. Gosse apparently has informed James that he does not intend to keep Sandhurst, his father's old home. See also letter 175, note 2. For a rather caustic comment on Gosse and the "spoils of 'Sandhurst,' " see James to W. E. Norris, December 23, 1900 (*HJL*, IV, 173). James, apparently, has not quite forgiven Gosse for the "piercing shaft" of his letter mentioned in James's letter of September 22 [21], 1900.

3. James had leased his flat in De Vere Gardens and arranged for a room in the Reform Club. At this time Gosse still lived at 29 Delamere Terrace in Westbourne Square. On several occasions James refers to the location as "Westbourne Grove."

177 / MS Leeds   Lamb House, Rye.
                                                                 Sunday
                                                                 [December 30?, 1900][1]

My dear Gosse.

I come up on Monday tomorrow again (I've been here a week,) but perversely, wretchedly I'm afraid I shall be unable to join in your midnight mirth. I've accepted an invitation from the George Lewis's—& that means midnight mirth *there*.[2] I shall escape thence at the earliest hour, but it can only be to convey my poor old bones to bed. I shall convey them to your door on the earliest other occasion. Don't meanwhile break yours, or any one's else, in your rush for the infant favours of the new century—but keep them sound, all of you, for the longest possible stretch of the same. Yours, all, always

Henry James

1. The date is fixed by James's reference to a week in Rye; Sunday occurred on December 30 in 1900. See also, for example, his reference to "this week here . . . as a picturesque parenthesis" in his letter of December 23, 1900, to W. E. Norris (*HJL*, IV, 172).

2. James had known Sir George (1833–1911), the prominent solicitor, and Lady Elizabeth Lewis for years and occasionally appeared at their revels on New Year's Eve. He had welcomed the new year at Gosse's parties in honor of 1897 and 1898, and would again from time to time (*EG*, 381).

178 / MS Leeds   105, Pall-Mall [London]
                                                          Tuesday [January 22, 1901]

My dear Gosse.

Most kind & most welcome your reassurance yesterday about Philip. I am delighted to hear the brave youth is not paying too heavy a penalty for his bravery. But it's enough, surely. Give him please my affectionate greeting & blessing. Grand that he came in 1*st*. He will always come in 1*st*.[1]

How weariful this tension of suspense & uncertainty for the poor ancient Lady—a kind of paralysing blight.[2] When the event *comes* there will be a kind of historic thrill that will, like all Events, even sad & bad ones, have its Excitement; but this grey situation—to be succeeded by a black one—doesn't stimulate. Requiescat!

Arthur Benson & I dined together last p.m. at the Grosvenor Club, & as he tells me he is to see you to-day he will give you pale news of your ever-flushed, but ever feeble[3]

H.J.

1. For more on Philip Gosse (1879–1959), see letters 234, note 3, and 317, note 8.
2. Queen Victoria died on January 22, the very date of James's letter. For Gosse's view of the queen, see "The Character of Queen Victoria," *Quarterly Review*, CXCIII (April, 1901), 301–37.
3. For Arthur C. Benson, see letter 107, note 2.

179 / MS Leeds   The Reform Club [London]
                                    Thursday p.m. [March 14? 1901][1]

My dear Gosse—

I am very sorry to say that it is impossible to me to lunch out— yielding to that temptation too gravely incommodes me. Kindly pardon therefore my not being able to join you on Wednesday next.

But shall you be at home on Saturday evening? If so I will come in with great joy at 9.

I am extremely shocked & disconcerted to hear of poor Philip's so hindered & hampered recovery.[2] I supposed—too superficially, but by what I had last gathered from you—that he was on his feet again & going quite straight. What a tedious, disappointing ordeal—& what a test of his virtue! I congratulate you & his mother heartily on the admirable quality of that element. I wish I had seen him, poor boy—& I wish I could assuage him. But you must tell me more. *Do* be at home Saturday—otherwise I fear I must wait till the week *after* the following—& that is hideous. Always your

H.J.

1. Although this letter is dated March 15, 1901, in pencil by another hand, Thursday occurred on March 14 in 1901. James may have written this letter, as was his habit, late at night, or the postmark may have been March 15 (no envelope is available with the manuscript). For a similar dating, see letter 180.
2. For more on Philip Gosse, see letters 234, note 3, and 317, note 8.

180 / MS Leeds   The Reform Club [London]
                                    Thursday night. [March 22? 1901?][1]

My dear Gosse.

Oh, but I *must* tell you the pleasure your news gives me; & I greatly appreciate your feeling sure I couldn't fail to vibrate, in this matter, in unison with you & his mother. He is now in the hands of his youth & his good sense, & he has such a quantity of both that everything may be looked for from them.[2] Dear gallant much-tried boy! — I think of him with benedictions & sympathies, — & only wish these could go to him in some more effective shape. But he'll now, like V. Emmanuel's Italy, *farà da se*: he will hobble alone.

I've been thinking also, quite upliftedly, of your Regent's Park house—which I'm sure will open a new era for you altogether.[3] My blessing too on that! Goodnight. Always your

H.J.

1. Thursday occurred on March 21 in 1901, but the letter is dated March 22, 1901, in pencil on the manuscript. See letter 179, note 1.
2. See letters 178 and 179.
3. Gosse had just purchased a seven-year lease on a house at 17 Hanover Terrace, overlooking Regent's Park, a place that was to be his home for the rest of his life. See *LL*, 270, 272, and *EG*, 409–10.

181 / MS Leeds   Lamb House, Rye.
                                                   July 2d 1901.

My dear Gosse.

I am delighted you can come, & I pray that all Nature smile upon it. The *4.28* from Charing X is the train that, for Saturday afternoon, I recommend. You change at Ashford, but the delay is inconsiderable, & at 6.40 (six-forty), you are due at this station, where I advance to meet you wreathed in smiles even if Nature, before-named, isn't.

I am greatly interested in Hanover Terrace & singularly impatient to see it.[1] May your last barriers fall & your drains be as mountain brooks (which, by the way, is not, I believe, what drains are wished to be. I mean may they tinkle like crystal-rills—or rather, I don't know *what* I mean save that I shall rejoice to find you *in* & to be in myself.) Your new frame will make you a new picture to hang, as it were, on the walls of friendship. If you miss the 4.28 there is a 5.15 from St. Paul's, which *doesn't* stop at Ashford; but though it's a very good train it gets here a little late & deprives us of the 1/2 hour in the garden before dinner. But *don't* miss the 4.28. Yours & Mrs. Nelly's & everyone's always

Henry James

1. Gosse's new home. See letter 180, note 3.

182 / MS Leeds   Lamb House, Rye.
                                                   July 3*d* 1901

My dear Gosse—

A hasty p.s. to my note of yesterday.

No dress-clothes: a simple tunic & loose girdle, with a few flowers in the hair or the bosom.[1]

I can't tell you how I rejoice that you can speak of your coming down as so *timed*: (timed—not timid!) It would be always timed—& also a little timid!—with *me*; but it's a long way to bring people for Spartan broth & all the rest. But most heartily do I pray that some refreshment may eventuate for you—from, however, the all-too-brief. You must stay as long as possible & come again as soon, & must also feel yourself an object of the tenderest & happiest preoccupation to yours very constantly

Henry James

1. For James's remarks concerning dress at Lamb House, see letter 167, note 2, for example.

183 / MS Library of Congress   Lamb House, Rye, Sussex.
                                                   Sept. 16 [1901][1]

My dear Gosse.

I hurl this after you, there, for good luck, like the outworn shoe of ancient usage. Even a very, very old shoe will take you properly over Venice. I wrote a week ago to Mrs. Curtis about you, & you will doubtless hear from her, beckoningly, in respect to the ever-so-amiable Barbaro; an impression well worth your having.[2] For the rest I commit you both, paternally, to Brown, to whose friendly memory I beg you to recall me.[3] I wish I cld. assist at some of your raptures. *Go to see the Tintoretto Crucifixion at San Cossiano*—or never more be officer of mine. And, àpropos of masterpieces, read a thing called *Venice* in a thing called *Portraits of Places* by a thing called H.J., if you can get the book: I'm not sure if it's in Tauchnitz, but Mrs. Curtis may have the same.[4] Brown certainly won't, though J.A.S., in the only communication I ever got from him, told me he thought it the best image of V. he had ever seen made.[5] This is the *1st* time in my life, I believe, by the way, I ever indulged in any such—in *any*—fat-

uous reference to a fruit of my pen. So there may be something in it.
Drink deep, both of you, & come home remorselessly intoxicated, &
reeking of the purple wine, to your poor old attached abstainer

Henry James

1. This letter has been printed in *LHJ*, I, 378, and in *SR*, 582–83, but the manuscript, which I have followed, differs in several particulars.
2. Mr. and Mrs. Daniel S. Curtis had often entertained James at the Barbaro in
Venice.
3. Horatio Brown, friend and biographer of John Addington Symonds (see letter
113, note 4), had offered to show Venice to the Gosses.
4. "Venice" had first appeared in *Century*, XXV (November, 1882), 3–23.
5. For John Addington Symonds, see letter 8, note 3.

184 / MS Duke   Lamb House, Rye, Sussex.
                                    September 29*th* 1901.

My dear Gosse.

It was delightful to crouch with you & Mrs. Gosse in the shadow
of your felze, or your tenda, or your bridge, or of all three together,
while the rain came down on the canal the other day & you couldn't,
as it were, see the lagoon for the water. But I do hope that nothing
more has been blurred for you since then, & nothing blotted out but
the possibility of anything but pleasure. Go it as hard as you can, &
pile up the ecstasy—then roll out for me your Persian carpets, &
fling round your Tyrian dyes, on some nearly-ensuing evening at No
17.[1] Heaven grant, in short, that your "purple" have [*sic*] *not* been too
diluted. Venice in rain at all continuous is indeed a bad joke. It isn't,
really, sour grapes, but we *have*, really, been having even here the
most golden, glorious days, a week—a month—of intensely, inef-
fably Indian summer, with a great (as I write) Hunt & Roskell silver-
moon of "presentation plate," that shines into my garden at such a
rate that you wd. fairly think it was Bond St. For the rest, I am sorry
to say, however, it has all been domestic upheaval & tidal wave—my
fate having at last overtaken me in a whirl-wind determining the violent elimination from my life, in the course of 48 hours, of the pair of
old servants, man & wife, whom you know & who had been with
me—the mainstay, with qualifications & titubations, of my existence—for 16 years.[2] It was very cataclysmal & tragic, &, with the
passages leading up to it, destructive of precious time & of better
engagements; but I now see, though I sit among the irreparable ruins

of my mere material comfort, for how long their fatal aberrations had weighed on my anxious mind. Bacchus & Ariadne, quoi! So paints the Titian of our British doom! Pardon my sordid, my squalid confidence. Shake it off & go & toy à la Ruskin, with the breakers of the Lido shore. I rejoice that you know the Barbaro, & I await your reminiscences of the conversation (*quâ* a plumpudding of *mots*) of D. S. Curtis.[3] But you know him too late. The pudding remains, but the plums are gone. However, my spirit abides in that delightful old 2-storey drawingroom. Heinemann has asked me to do Balzac *vice* the impudent G. Moore; but it has been vital to me to say, as I said to *you*: "Impossible, utterly, *now*; but boldly place him last & *then* tant que vous voudrez: & any others too! — There I am.["][4] But it's, as usual, 1 a.m. & the scandalised moon fairly knocks at my window. Keep up your notes, for if once they get ahead of you I'm lost. Tanti Saluti to Brown, &, for me, please, again, very, very cordially, to the Curtises, should you see them further.[5] A thousand things above all to her who palpitates at your side, from your distant but perfect palpitator in sympathy

Henry James

1. The Gosses are visiting Venice, and James is looking forward to their return to their new home at 17 Hanover Terrace.
2. For a full account of the "tragedy of the Doom of the Smiths," see James's letter of September 26, 1901, to Mrs. William James in *HJL*, IV, 204–207. The Smiths left James's employ on September 23.
3. For the Curtises and the Barbaro, see letter 183, note 2.
4. Gosse was editing a series for William Heinemann entitled "A Century of French Romance." James eventually agreed to write an introduction to Balzac's *The Two Young Brides* (1902).
5. For Brown, see letter 183, note 3.

185 / MS Library of Congress   Lamb House, Rye, Sussex
                                                  Friday Night.
                                                  [October 18, 1901][1]

My dear Gosse.

I have waited till tonight to write to you for fear of missing you at the Barbaro, though my immediate impulse on learning you to be there was to outpour to you, in congratulation, on the spot.[2] You mentioned the 20*th* as your day of arrival home, though without saying your day of leaving, nor what stops, at Milan, or elsewhere, you might be making on the way. My own hope is that you may have made none, leaving them all for another time; but have clung to the divine Barbaro, noblest of human habitations, as I always feel it to the last possible hour. Thus, in short, I've *kept* my welcome to you, for security. I rejoice exceedingly that you were able to put in those several days in that painted (& gilded,) paradise; & that you hit it off so well with the rare & racy Curtises, whose hospitality to you gives me almost as much pleasure as if I myself had been able to offer it. Your letter thence, in short, was particularly delightful to me—only making me *too* impatient for your reports & revelations. For some instalment of these at the earliest day I earnestly pray, & for some prompt arrangement as to the same. May your home-journey meanwhile have been a proper wrench, though without prejudice to smoothness & swiftness. The winds & waves have been of the highest, hereabouts, these last days, but I note with joy tonight their apparent subsidence. So float you gently, & bump you softly, & alight you majestically, toward against & on, the Dover dock. The deuce is that after so much absence & such other bribes to it, you will be awfully averse to having the question of 36 hours down here put to you, & will disgustedly push it from you—for heaven knows what gestures both of depreciation & of its opposite, you may not, with so many sensations, have picked up. *But you must come*—You went, to come—so, à fortiori, you came back to come. That is the meaning of it all. Besides, you will *need* to see me, absolutely require to, to know what you *have* seen & felt. I will tell you. I will make it plain; & you won't really have been to Venice, in short, till you have had it from me *that* you have. Therefore, please, an early date—*any* near Sunday; & I thus shamelessly press you in spite of the fact that, as I think I mentioned to you in last writing, my household arrangements are in ruins, & my servants are in dissolution & exile.[3] I haven't yet got a cook, & I can only give you plain & wholesome fare. No matter; you must swallow it. My cook is, in fine, still my charwoman, but she can roast a fowl & fry a sole, & we will depend on the famous "flow" of the latter. All this constitutes, I needn't say, a welcome as intimate & an invocation as pressing in respect to Mrs. Nelly to whom I send tanti saluti affetuosi.

I hope your house is whole & none of your children mis-allied or otherwise compromised in your absence. But come & tell me of that too. Yours uncontrollably

Henry James

1. In 1901, October 18 occurred on Friday. The date of October 19, however, is written by another hand on the first page of the manuscript. This is possibly the date of the postmark, though the envelope is no longer available for verification.

2. For the Barbaro and the Curtises, see letter 183, note 2.

3. James had recently dismissed two servants of sixteen years' service. See letter 184, note 2.

186 / MS Leeds   Lamb House, Rye, Sussex.
                                   Saturday [October 26, 1901][1]

My dear Gosse.

I could only in a delayed & baffled way dictate for you a day or two ago what I had wished to say ever since your last note. I've been most discomfortably ill, from a mere poisonous accident, but am better & can be again as illegible as usual. Your acceptance of the *intempestif* idea of coming down here has given me compunctions, & I feel (as fully I felt, also, in proposing it,) that it's not a further hole you can really find it profitable to punch in your time. If, freely & frankly, you *can* come, without effort, I shall be enchanted; but if effort is the least in the case I will do what I can to ease you off. I would come up myself on *Saturday*—I will, if you say it, for the day (having an urgency in relation to Friday p.m., that is, which I can meet by coming up on the Friday afternoon[)]. I could *lunch* with you on Saturday & give you all the p.m. you could endure—catching my evening train back here. Let me know if you wd. prefer that. It's frankly offered & wd. be stoutly sustained.[2] Pardon my rude brevity. Your speech of "*disaster*" in connection with your return worries me[.] I hope it's not—it wasn't—a loss of luggage, gold, health or reputation![3] But it's ill fooling, & I am your sickish & solemn, ever,

Henry James

P.S. No—it's *well* fooling; for even as I write comes in to me your small white book, tossed like a rose from a window, & of which I've inhaled enough to see that it is merry & mocking (oh, merriment!) & that it must be, well—the only word *can* be divine.[4] It shall be my *livre de chevet tonight*. But from what hoard in an old stocking do you steal your hours? I've read *Kim*; but I starve (mildly) for Graham B.[5]

1. In 1901, though Saturday occurred on October 26, October 27 is written in pencil in another hand. See letter 185, note 1.

2. James had urgently invited the Gosses for a weekend at Lamb House (letter 185), but now seems to be expressing second thoughts.

3. The "*disaster*," apparently, is Gosse's illness; see letter 187.

4. Edmund Gosse, *Hypolympia; or, The Gods in the Island: An Ironic Fantasy* (London, 1901).

5. *Kim* had appeared at the end of 1900 (Carrington, *Rudyard Kipling*, 360). For James's opinion of it, see his letter to Kipling of October 30, 1901 (*HJL*, IV, 209–12). Graham Balfour's two-volume *Life of Robert Louis Stevenson* was published in October, 1901, and James wrote Balfour (1858–1929) on November 15, 1901 (*HJL*, IV, 212–14).

187 / MS Leeds   Lamb House, Rye, Sussex.
                                       Thursday p.m. [October 31, 1901][1]

My dear Gosse—

I ought before this to have amplified my telegram to you; but the great thing was, after all, to have made you sure about Saturday. I, as soon as I got your letter, infinitely preferred it—I mean your coming down, since come you can.[2] It will do you good, if you've been ill—the air here is admirable now, & will be generally much cosier & more *intîme*. Besides, there will be more of it. I hope complete recovery is now your portion. I am all right—but I had a strange & poisonous week. I meet you on Saturday on the arrival of the aforesaid *4.28* from Charing X—due here, after its little change at Ashford, 6.40. I venture to hint to you that I shall, for the sake not only of Romance but of Reality, probably decree our dinner, like Kubla Khan, at the Mermaid. I am cookless still—& till the 11*th*. As among three or four conventionalized golfers there, accordingly, you will perhaps be glad of a dress-jacket.[3] Basta.

I have found a charming charm in your polytheistic fantasy—which is full of wit & wisdom, "quaintness," style & wandering airs, or, as it were, fragrances; to say nothing of the lovely lyric at p. 132.[4] The blank verses, on the whole, in spite of some very "clever" lines, I like less. It's a peril I think to deal again, however tricksily with the gods of Greece in disponibility—this always, & in the nature of the case: I don't know why, but even in our time, from *la Belle Hélène* on, they seem to have been so *done*, & the burlesque smutch is on them. But you have, with your literary indiarubber, quite rubbed it off & kept yours distinguished. At the same time, at a time of life, there's a horrid sort of responsibility about what one does—it's dismal, but it's there—& I'm not sure your little affair wholly meets *that*—which is, ever, as a pair of great public goggles *bracqués* upon us. However, be the goggles wholly satisfied or not, my private eyes have been beguiled.

I've only just got by purchase, on credit, of Bain, G. Balfour's 2 volumes, & have had no time but to glance at them.[5] I find I feel all the reserves that hang over the question of such a book—lumbering up in the rear—at all, but I find I also feel that, in the produced *presence* of Louis again, as ever, everything breaks down—it may be as it will. He *was* a story. He *is* a story. He *will* be a story. So he's placed —the Puss in Boots or Hop o' my thumb, or whatever of Biographic Literature.[6] But we will talk of this, & of much else. I'm only afraid the glow of your Venice is chilled before I've had it warm.[7] But heat it up, & don't miss the train.

Yours always
Henry James

1. This letter is printed in *SR*, 583–84. Although it is dated November 1 by another hand, in 1901 Thursday occurred on October 31. Apparently the party who assigned the date of this letter (the hand is not Gosse's), as well as those of letters 185 and 186, was off by one day, unless he was referring to postmarks now unavailable.
2. Plans for the visit that James had written about in letters 185 and 186 are now being settled.
3. James is still without a cook (see letter 184, note 2), and for once he suggests that Gosse bring a "dress-jacket."
4. *Hypolympia* (see letter 186, note 4).
5. For Graham Balfour's biography of Stevenson, see letter 186, note 5.
6. James would write Balfour on November 20 that "you have made him—everything has made him—too *personally* celebrated for his literary legacy" (*HJL*, IV, 213).
7. Gosse had returned from Italy on October 20 (see letter 185).

188 / MS Duke   Lamb House, Rye, Sussex.
                                             November 20, 1901.[1]

My dear Gosse.

I have been very sorry to hear from you of renewed upsets on quitting these walls—the same fate having, I remember, overtaken you most of the other times you've been here.[2] I trust it isn't the infection of the walls themselves, nor of the *re*fection (so scant last time) enjoyed within them. Is it some baleful effluence of your host? He will try & exercise next time some potent countercharm—& meanwhile he rejoices that your devil is cast out.

All thanks for your so vivid news of the overflow of Henley's gall. Ça ne pouvait manquer—ça *devait* venir. I have sent for the article & will write you when I've read it.[3] I gather from you that it's really rather a striking & lurid—& so far interesting case—of long discomfortable jealousy & ranklement turned at last to posthumous (as it were!) malignity, & making the man do, *coram publico*, his ugly act, risking the dishonour for the assuagement. That *is*, on the part of a favourite of the press &c, a remarkable "psychologic" incident—or perhaps I'm talking in the air, from not having read the thing. I daresay moreover, at all events, that H. *did* very seriously—I mean sincerely—deplore all the graces that had crept into Louis's writing—all the more that they had helped it so to be loved: he honestly thinks that L. shld. have written like—well, like who but Henley's self? But the whole business illustrates how life takes upon itself to give us more true & consistent examples of human unpleasantness than expectation could suggest—makes a given man, I mean, live up to his ugliness. This one's whole attitude in respect to these recent amiable commemorations of Louis—the having (I, "self-conscious & alone,") nothing to do with them, contained singularly the promise of some positive aggression. I have, however, this a.m., a letter from Graham Balfour (in answer to one I had written him on reading his book,) in which, speaking of Henley's paper, he says it's less bad than he expected.[4] He apparently feared more. It's since you were here, by the way, that I've read his record, in which, as to its *2d* volume, I found a good deal of fresh interest & charm. It seems to me, the whole thing, very neatly & tastefully done for an amateur, & non-expert. *But*, I see now that a really curious thing has happened, a "cosi" occurred much more interesting than the *cas* Henley. Insistent publicity, so to speak, has done its work (I only knew it was *doing* it, but G.B.'s book's a settler,) & Louis *quā* artist à now, definitely the victim thereof. That is, he has *superseded*, personally, his books, & this last re-placement of himself so *en scène* (so largely by his own aid, too,) has *killed* the literary baggage. Out of no mystery now do they issue, the creations in question—& they couldn't afford to lose it. Louis himself never understood that; he too publicly caressed & accounted for them—but I needn't insist on what I mean. As I *see* it, at all events, it's a strange little evolution, all taking place here, quite compactly, under one's nose.

I don't come up to town, alas, for more than a few necessary hours, till I've finished my book, & that will be when God pleases.[5] I pray for early in January. But then I shall stay as long as ever I can. All thanks for your news of Norris, to whom I shall write.[6] I envy your Venetian newses—but I myself have written for some. I rain good wishes on your house & am yours always

Henry James

P.S. *What* a world, verily—the one in which your Hoelsing-Shorter banquets &c *flourish* & in which, above all, they *mean* so much.[7] A world *pour rire* only I more & more feel it. And to have to *pretend* it's serious!

    1. Although printed in *LHJ*, I, 385–87, I have followed the original throughout and included a postscript that Lubbock omitted.
    2. Gosse had visited James earlier in the month. See letter 187.
    3. William Ernest Henley, "R.L.S.," *Pall Mall Magazine*, XXV (December, 1901), 505–14.
    4. For James's letter to Balfour, see *HJL*, IV, 212–14.
    5. *The Wings of the Dove*.
    6. For W. E. Norris, see letter 95, note 1.
    7. Clement K. Shorter (1857–1926) was editor of the *Illustrated London News* (1891–1900) and the *English Illustrated Magazine*, periodicals to which both James and Gosse had contributed. James had been invited by Shorter to a dinner in 1896 (see letter 131, note 2).

189 / MS UCLA   Lamb House, Rye, Sussex.
                                   January 25*th* [1902?]
                                   (Saturday night.)

My dear Gosse.

    I come up at last, after long delays, on Monday 27*th*—in other words, *tomorrow*, as I write you at near 1. a.m. May I not have a word from you—a kindly *early* one, however single—at Reform Club, Pall Mall, S.W., to say whether, by a miracle, you be free to receive me, breathless & blushing, either on Wednesday or on Friday p.m. next (or even on Saturday,) in which case the usual *nine* (the Muses, verily, I titter to say, will see me at your door.)[1] I pray, piously, I shall find you, find all, well. I seem to have been living of late in the liveliest air of your presence—so that the portents encourage yours always

Henry James

    1. For James's arrangements at the Reform Club, see letter 176, note 3.

190 / MS Leeds   Reform Club.
                                    Pall Mall. S.W.
                                    April 21*st* 1902

My dear Gosse.

    I don't know where this will find you or whither pursue you; in

some swift untroubled current of foreign experience I trust, & with
the laceration of your sense of a supererogatory flight quite smoothed
down by senses more gratified. I don't at any rate wait for your return to let you know that I shall be from May *1st* at Lamb House[,]
Rye—certainly till the *20th*, when I may be very briefly absent. So
that anything sent *there* will be well sent. I'm afraid you won't be
back before I depart. I always miss your *special* freshnesses, & Mrs.
Gosse's—though I fare so well on your general. *Valete!* Yours always

Henry James

P.S. Oh, as to Crewe, you needn't fear the weight of my hand save as
patting you on the back for your bewildering good intentions.[1] They
leave me, however, & ever always leave me, only so mystified & with
all real thanks to you, uninvolved, that I shall ask you to let me very
gently & gracefully—in connection with my poor self—drop him
forever & ever.

1. Presumably Robert Offley Ashburton Crewe-Milnes (1858–1945), earl of
Crewe and subsequently first marquess of Crewe. During this period Gosse noted
that Lord Crewe was "very chummy and merry" (*EG*, 407).

---

191 / MS Leeds

Lamb House, Rye.
May 13*th* 1902

My dear Gosse,

I wired you, feebly yesterday, in answer to your sympathetic note
of three days ago—feebly & reassuringly. Reassuringly because, I am
happy to say, I left town 3 weeks since under the shadow of nothing
worse than a torment (strangely prolonged & recurrent) of *gout* (in
both feet!)—with one of my feet in a bag, but no part of my person
in an ambulance.[1] Thank heaven I am normally shod now & the
nightmare, so to speak, is over. I call it a nightmare because, at *3
reprises*, it had imposed solitary confinement in a single bleak cham-
ber, & I couldn't face again that lone ordeal. So I hobbled away to a
wider horizon. Here I am in the throes of finishing—by a *date*, May
20th—a long & awfully retarded novel, which *must* be published by
July *1st*, & the final, terminal process of which (while ⅘'s, printed,
wait for the remainder,) leaves me not a little spent.[2] That's why I
"feebly" wired. I find myself, the daily battle of "art" waged & the
dose of quality distilled, sapless & inkless even for the smallest note:
But I near my term, & then I shall, for a number of days, react &

escape, hoping to see you on one of them. Four or five I spend in going to see my brother at Edinburgh (where he is lecturing) & staying there, briefly, with him. I hope, àpropos of such tensions, that your wild whirl through Auvergne came happily & beneficently off. I thought of you there anxiously, for I thought of you as freezing: it being here at the time, as it still is, infamously cold. May you both have returned mainly intact.

No Balzac proof has yet come; still less, all this time, any Flaubert, & anxiety begins to possess me.[3] May I not beseech you to keep in this particular a kind eye on my interests? Good night & many things *chez vous*. Yours scarce coherently—though still adhesively

Henry James

1. James's trouble with gout had begun in 1893, and it continued intermittently throughout the rest of his life.
2. *The Wings of the Dove* (1902).
3. James was writing introductions to translations of Balzac's *The Two Young Brides* and Flaubert's *Madame Bovary* for "A Century of French Romance," a series Gosse was editing for William Heinemann.

192 / MS Duke   Lamb House, Rye.
                                         Thursday p.m. [May 15, 1902][1]

My dear Gosse,

I *have* indeed been much disconcerted at finding that though I gave you my Flaubert in September last, 8 months ago, it is now printed without a proof having been sent me. I find it good enough, as I read it over, to think it might have been treated with that ordinary consideration. I find it a refinement of *torture*, always, to read a thing of which I have seen no proof—the things one *would* have amended & bettered are so pilloried there in an eternal publicity. There are in this thing no monstrosities of error, though there is a distressing misprint on p. 35, toward the bottom, *vivi*fy for verify (please correct it in any copy under your hand;) but to get off simply without *them* isn't what one bargains for, & there are many things I should have felt happier to have slightly altered.[2] What does Heinemann mean? I think he will have difficulty in saying. Please, I beseech you,—for I am nervous & anxious now—*insist* on my seeing a proof of the Balzac.[3] Now that this vol. is out of its order in time, do make any needful further postponement to render this certain. I sent you a very rough copy, you will remember, on your assurance that proof was what I shall have; & the thing needs it *more* than the Flaubert. Delayed as it has been, its frankly best place, now, would be to wind up the series. There it is out of all pretence to order, & yet *is* an important *finale*. Please think of this, & heal the gaping wound of yours ever

Henry James

1. Printed in *HJL*, IV, 230. The postmark on the envelope reads May 16 (Leeds).
2. James's essay on *Madame Bovary* had just appeared as an introduction to Volume 9 of "A Century of French Romance" (see letter 191, note 3). In letter 193, James acknowledges that he had received proofs in October and "dealt with them."
3. See letter 193 and note 3 of that letter.

193 / MS Leeds   Lamb House, Rye.
                                                Friday p.m. [May 16, 1902][1]

My dear Gosse.

I roll at your feet in the dust—crawl & grovel—an apologetic worm. My memory has remained all day a blank utter & complete, as to my having *had* Flaubert proofs, in October, & dealt with them: it's an extraordinary case of a perfect lapse & extinction (forgive this filthy paper!) of the impression made.[2] But from the moment Heinemann has the dated & recorded *facts* about it he *must* be right, & I deeply regret having challenged his fidelity. Please express this to him (There are some small stupidities in the published pages that I can't understand my not having amended.) But we live in darkness—& I've not been *willingly* black. For the bad quarter of an hour I've given you I will do any penance you impose—even to that—if you are ruthless—of foregoing the Balzac proof.[3] Only, as you are now strong, be merciful & not impose that extremity if you are not yourself cruelly forced to it.

Yours ruefully &
wretchedly
Henry James

1. Included in *HJL*, IV, 231.
2. See letter 192, note 2.
3. James's essay on Balzac appeared as an introduction to *The Two Young Brides* (1902), Volume 7 of "A Century of French Romance."

194 / MS British Library   Lamb House, Rye.
                                              June *26th* 1902

My dear Gosse.

I lose not an hour in responding to your request about Conrad—whom I had not in the least known to be in the state you mention. It horrifies me more than I can say, & I applaud to the echo your attempt to do something for him. Do let me know what may result from it. *May* my letter, enclosed, & which I've endeavoured to make warm yet discreet, weigh in the scale![1] It is at least wholly sincere. Heaven speed your work!

And what a drama; altogether—the circumjacent crash of things! It makes me want much to see you, & I'm sorry you're going abroad before it seems possible to you to come down here for a Sunday. Or may that still not be? I go up indeed to town about the 12*th*—for several days—& there are, alas, female relations here before that.

> Yours ever—with
> benedictions on your
> house,
>   *Henry James*

1. See letter 195.

195 / MS British Library   Lamb House, Rye.
                                              June *26th* 1902.[1]

My dear Gosse.

I have the highest opinion of the title Joseph Conrad would have, on literary grounds, to become one of your beneficiaries: all the more that in spite of his admirable work he is not so known to a wide & promiscuous public that his claims may speak wholly for themselves. He has been to me, the last few years, one of the most interesting & striking of the novelists of the new generation. His production (you know what it consists of,) has all been fine, rare & valid, of the sort greeted more by the expert & the critic than (as people say,) by the man in the street. His successive books have been real literature, of a distinguished sort, the record of his experience, in navigating years, of Eastern seas, strange climes & far countries, all presented in a form more artistic than has been given to *any* "tales of the sea" among English writers & that approximates more than anything we have to the truth & beauty of the French Pierre Loti. *The Nigger of the Nar-*

cissus is in my opinion the very finest & strongest picture of the sea &
sea-life that our language possesses—the master-piece in a whole
great class; & *Lord Jim* runs it very close. When I think moreover that
such completeness, such intensity of expression has been arrived at
by a man not born to our speech, but who took it up, with singular
courage, from necessity & sympathy, & has laboured at it heorically
[*sic*] & devotedly, I am equally impressed with the fine persistence &
the intrinsic success. Born a Pole & cast upon the waters, he has
worked out an English style that is more than correct, that has *quality* & ingenuity. The case seems to me unique & peculiarly worthy of
recognition. Unhappily, to be very serious & subtle isn't one of the
paths to fortune. Therefore I greatly hope the Royal Literary Fund
may be able to do something for him.[2] *Do* let me recommend him to
you in the name of his charming, conscientious, uncommon work. It
has truly a kind of disinterested independent nobleness. Believe me
yours always

Henry James

1. Printed in *HJL*, IV, 231–32.
2. Conrad received a grant of £300 from the Royal Literary Fund in the following
month. See letter 196. The Conrad grant is just one of a number of literary causes
Gosse had initiated or supported from the 1890s onward. See, especially, what James
says in letter 196 about Gosse's efforts to help others.

196 / MS Colby   Lamb House, Rye, Sussex.
                                              July 11*th* 1902[1]

My dear Gosse.
   I rejoice more than I can say in the news you give me about the
grant to J.C.—nor can I tell you, either, how I applaud, esteem, ven-
erate you for the noble energy with which you put these things
through.[2] It does me good. It will also do me good if you are by any
chance to be at home *Monday* night, next, 14*th*. Then would I come
in for a day or two. Forgive my confusion—I am not drunk, save perhaps with satisfaction. I mean come in at 9—being about to be in
town for a day or two. If you are not, 2 words on a postcard at
Reform Club would light the uncertain path of yours always

Henry James

1. Printed in *CLQ*, 163, but dated July 11, 1905, and with one or two other differences from the manuscript.
2. For the effort to get financial support for Joseph Conrad, see letters 194
and 195.

197 / MS Leeds   Lamb House, Rye, Sussex.
                                                              Sept 3*d* 1902

My dear Gosse—

Wonderfully vivid, interesting & welcome your more than outlandish, your Gothlandish, letter just received & not less admirable the heroism—*prowess* is weak—of parents & child alike exhibited in your wild quest & triumphant find.[1] I envy you, from the midst of the cold ashes of my senility, the power & the passion to do these things. What an impression & what an adventure! All my congratulations! I hunger & thirst for your filling-in of details & to this end, as well as to many others, beseech you to come down here, if possible (*make* it possible!) on Saturday 13*th* for the Sunday. I am sure of being alone then—& I would sooner so have you. I may have complications later. Kindly, when you can after the 7*th*, make me some simple sign. But if the 13*th* is impossible to you, come on the 20*th* or the 27*th*. I pray the Scandinavian gods, Thor, Odin & co, retroactively that they have given you, in the subjunctive, a kind back-voyage. But I await your little word & send much love & loud plaudits to Mesdames Nelly & Sylvia. I fear, however, you are spoiling the latter for more Regent's Park waters & for anything but the wild lot of a Viking's, nay a Berserker's, bride.[2] Yours in fond suspense

                                                              Henry James

   1. The Gosses and their youngest child, Sylvia, were in Sweden, where Gosse, after feeling that he was overworked and about "to break down altogether," was taking the "cure" at Saltsjöbaden on the Baltic. See *LL*, 283, and *EG*, 411.
   2. Sylvia Gosse was twenty-one at the time.

198 / MS Leeds   Lamb House, Rye, Sussex.
                                                              Sept. 23*d* 1902

My dear Gosse.

Your rashness was a happy rashness, which has given me pleasure, for which I thank you: nothing could be more amiable—& droll also—than the *Westminster* gentleman, whom I wholly fail to trace. It is "gentleman,["] I think, & not (as in these days mostly, when one comes to find out,) a lady. If you do find out you must remember him for me.

You will be glad to know then, in the interest of literature, immortality & all the rest, that I have been since you were here, quite definitely better & that I consider the tendency thereunto on which I was flattering myself to have undergone no real deflection at all. I ask nothing better, therefore, I assure you, than to live up to the glorious character you so handsomely offer me the chance of—so handsomely that I scarcely know how at once modestly & graciously to respond. Trust me, however, & I will provide you with a "literary treat" compared with which the poor flopping "Wings" will be as a Satyr to Hyperion.[1] Only take care of *your* insides to be at the fête too.

I've just had a charming & rather touching letter from Norris, who is beginning to break, actually, with Torquay.[2] He goes to Tasmania, but is not to be in London till November. Meanwhile his daughter has backed out of the convent "sell," & only wants to be a "paying guest" (of the Church.) So poor dear Norris must pay. But what a decidedly frivolous & futile young woman! Love to all the Berserker's égrèe. Yours very constantly

Henry James

1. *The Wings of the Dove* had been published by Constable on August 30; it had appeared in New York on August 21. The reference is to *Hamlet*, I, ii, 139–40.
2. W. E. Norris, a good friend to both James and Gosse, lived at Underbank in Torquay.

199 / MS Leeds   Lamb House, Rye, Sussex.
                                               Oct. 5, 1902

My dear Gosse.

I have been waiting to thank you for the Balzac till the Balzac, despatched on the 1st, according to your kind note, should have arrived.[1] But still he lingers—has had apparently an embarrassed start, & I continue to languish for him. Kindly give him an effective push; & I shall then be in a position to enthuse with you over the beauty of B. as portraiture transmits him. I only ask to meet you, on this, or any, ground. I walked this p.m., alone & purely self-supported, over to Winchelsea, to have tea with some bullying people, & in my absence the 2 Rudyards puffed up to my door in their own motor, *proprio moter*, from Burwash, where they have gone to live (an obscure locality in Sussex) leaving for me, on my return, but a black plume as a token—or rather a blackened card.[2] Otherwise I might have more history—not to say poetry, for you. But we miss our most precious opportunities. However, I am greatly hoping that this one will be renewed; & am looking Burwash, an obscure locality in Sussex, up on the map. (I didn't mean to repeat that formula—I meant to say I believe it to be near Tunbridge Wells. However, for all you care!) But a truce & goodnight. Ever your

Henry James

1. See letter 193, note 3. *The Two Young Brides* appeared September 30, 1902.
2. Caroline Balestier and Rudyard Kipling, old friends of James's. See letter 81. Burwash is about twenty miles from Rye.

200 / MS Leeds   Lamb House, Rye, Sussex.
                                    Dec: 14*th* 1902

Dear Mrs. Gosse.

It breaks my heart not to be with you on New Year's eve; but it is impossible to me to leave home.[1] I come up to town for a worthy stay very shortly after that, & with our weary winter train-service, a thing of torment, I have not prowess for the exploit of coming up only to return & start afresh. So the lonely hermit can but bless the glittering revels & all the merriest mummers. Will you tell Edmund that the lonely hermit, coming back here the other day, from London to atrocious cold & a house scarce fit, from it, for human habitation, hadn't the *cheek*, vulgarly speaking, to make him then any sign of hospitality—especially after a journey also most prolonged & hyperborean. And now, on the edge of the time for my being nearer you, I shall see him at home first. I hope meanwhile, very heartily (I affectionately assure him,) that he is less invalidated than a fortnight ago. And I am yours, all, with every seasonable much more than reasonable wish, very constantly

Henry James

1. For James's response to other invitations from the Gosses for New Year's Eve, see, for example, letters 177, 218, and 228.

201 / TC Rutgers[1]   Lamb House, Rye, Sussex.
                                     June 12*th*, 1903.

My dear Gosse.

I greatly appreciate the graceful present from you of the Brontë booklet, which undermines even my *malaise* in the presence of very tiny volumes.[2] This one is of a charming form which indeed is their general case. What is more to the point is that the matter seems to me of the happiest—the thing is a beautiful little *talk*, which is what it should be, & what your auditors could have had few (or none) but you to gaily give them—It was time the Fatal Sisters *should* have a smile play over them—sullen as I yet figure their "psychic" response. Thanks, truly, for the bibliographic pearl. Won't you come down some time (for some Sunday next month) & tell me where & what of wondrous you have been & seen: plucking it, I mean, from the deep heart of France. May I some day have a small word from you as to when you "leave town" for the final go?—so that I may make sure of you for a date well before that? Where is Sylvia, meanwhile—where is *she*? Tell her with my love that I haunt the station in the hope of her train, & that I have just "saved" out of an empty pocket a bit of the rococo here in order that Rye may [not?] be (what it tends so swiftly and horridly to become) unworthy of a maiden's faith or of an artist's brush.[3] I hope Mrs. Edmund travelled to her profit; I crowd myself on her remembrance & I am yours always

Henry James

P.S. How refreshing to an artist in a passionless pictureless age, the flare of the Byzantine Belgrade!

1. Although the typed copy is one of those apparently made by J. Alex Symington at Leeds, the manuscript is not at Leeds but at Rutgers. The letter was published by Rudolf Kirk in "Five Letters of Henry James," *Journal of the Rutgers University Library*, XII (June, 1949), 55–56. My text is based upon a collation of the printed and typed copies.

2. *The Challenge of the Brontës* (1903), originally an address delivered by Gosse before the Brontë Society on March 28, 1903, was subsequently printed for private distribution. See *LL*, 511.

3. Sylvia Gosse (1881–1968) was studying painting with Walter Sickert (1868–1942).

202 / MS Leeds   Lamb House, Rye, Sussex.
                                              July *1st* 1903

My dear Gosse—
    Your good letter of today, arriving at a moment when I was languishing almost beyond recovery under the sense of not having, in all decency, acknowledged a not less genial one of some days ago—well, adds to the intensity of my contrition! And the way I am obliged to meet your present appeal does nothing, I grieve to say, to make *any* part of my consciousness more tolerable. It is not in my power, alas, to come up to town on the 10*th*. The dear Curtises are only on my mind, & I go up to see them, on purpose to see them, on the 15*th*.[1]
    But there are reasons overwhelming why I must not go *before* that, & reasons more than overwhelming why I must dip as little as possi-

ble at all into the London maelstrom of these fell weeks, when there is a compatriot in every bush & a trap at every street crossing. It is through the affluence of the compatriot in fact that my days have been darkened (from one to the other,) in respect to proposing a date for your coming down. My Sundays have each been, at short notice, violently compromised & again on *this* (coming) one 2 American visitors present themselves. But could you come either on Saturday 11*th* or on Saturday 25*th*? I am obliged to leave out of account the 18*th*, as, going to London on the 15*th* & staying away hours enough to make a hole in a pressing occupation, I must so make up *all* the hours on that Saturday & Sunday that my attitude would be scarcely civil to a guest under my roof. On August 1*st* I go, damnably, away, but if you are up to your eyes, already, for the 11*th* & the 25*th* there remain all the other Sundays in August, when I shall be delighted to see you (since I seem to recall that your August *is* to be spent in town.) The 8*th*? or the 15*th*? There are 4 Saturdays to choose from. Choisessez. Your news & your negations of news are alike uplifting. I hadn't heard the *canard* about Meredith, and rejoice in the vanity of evil reports.[2] Still, *some* day they won't be a canard. But we shall see him before that. Somehow I kind of pity A. Hope.[3] Yours always

Henry James

1. For the Daniel S. Curtises, see letter 183, note 2.
2. For James's comments on George Meredith (1828–1909), the novelist and poet, see letters 283 and 284.
3. Anthony Hope Hawkins (1863–1933), the author of *The Prisoner of Zenda* (1894), wrote under the name of Anthony Hope.

203 / MS Yale   Lamb House, Rye, Sussex.
                                                   July 31: 1903.

My dear Gosse.

I sent the brilliant judge off to your symposium this a.m. in the best form, & doubt not that he graced it as perfectly as he graced here my more rustic boards, & beds. His grace—that is his abounding conversational presence—is part of the reason why I didn't more immediately acknowledge your good news about Sylvia.[1] Do tell that Academic maid that I immensely rejoice in her triumph & am weaving a garland to have ready for flinging over her neck here, on her arrival, & leading her, in the chain of flowers, up the cobbled little Via Sacra of my Capitoline hill. And I think I am *as* happy for you &

her mother—for these must be indeed the purest joys of parenthood. I often fancy I am gleeful at not having *bambini*; then I think how rich & mellow it must be to have them like yours, & I feel then that I have failed of the true life. But I've now my train to catch for London tonight & for, furthest, Shropshire tomorrow. It hangs before me as simply *ghastly*—such is my alienation from the social scene. May yours, tomorow, be less; a superfluous wish to you. The elements continue so to rage here that I almost envy you—with such an August possibly ahead—the cloistered charm of Hanoveria.[2] My blessing on each head! Ever yours

Henry James

1. Sylvia had just, according to Thwaite, "distinguished herself at the Royal Academy School" (*EG*, 424).
2. Hanover Terrace, Gosse's home.

---

204 / MS Duke   Lamb House, Rye, Sussex.
                                             [October 2, 1903][1]

My dear Gosse

My principal "last 6 weeks' news" is that my Story vols. (which I am glad you received) contain a horrid misprint somewhere, which I couldn't correct in your copy—a dreadful "causal" for "casual"; also that, through an accident, I had to send you a vol. 1*st* that I had cut (one I had kept for myself,) instead of a fresh one.[2] But these are details—as well as the fact that there are 2 or 3 provoking little misplacements & omissions of punctuation—perpetrated *after* my last proof had gone back right. But of such misères is the literary life composed. Find & correct the beastly "causal"—I only spied it & shuddered & closed the vol. in terror lest I shld. find another, & didn't dare to look at it again—so didn't heed where it is. *Basta*. Your so wantonly tantalizing post-cards told me of a "far cry" on your part—all of which I hope was the pure delirium of joy.[3] You must have seen charming places & things at a charming season, & I hope the charm will abide with you & again overflow when we meet. My own chronicle is all of very small beer—& in fact really (& to be a bit cynical) almost only of of [*sic*] the suckling of fools. I have had a most *invaded* summer—a positive superfluity & importunity of people, playing absolutely the devil with my time & preoccupations & preferences, &, as symptomatic of a lurid future & the breakdown of the desired privacy & quiet of this little place, I don't see how to view it or to face it again. But I am hoping the worst, for this season, is over—though the air, in truth, still bristles with threats.[4] Write me thereanent (if you are able at some moment amiably to write me at all,) soothingly rather than mockingly—as to which latter tone the nature of my wail would perhaps preferably tempt. It is a wail, alas, over *real* spilled milk. My "work" has been dismally blighted & my arrears are ugly to behold. But to what arrears must *you* return—& what a piper you must be in the act of paying! Attend only at your full convenience to *my* little bill. I shall perhaps be able to look in on you at Whitehall (No. 1,) for a quarter of an hour (if you have it to spare) on Wednesday (a.m.) [,] the only possible way of my putting in a scrap of you during an obligatory 24 hours in town. What a strange picture of muddle & misery are public affairs! I can't but think that the actual "administration" of them is preparing darkly to *sombrer*—but for what other administration I don't pretend to dream. The immorality of mere stonily-watching "Europe" is meanwhile too sickening—there has been nothing so publicly ugly in our lifetime & it poisons our declining years & the "dignity" of our age. But a truce to this mere ululation! Ever your

Henry James

1. James dates this letter 2.9.03, but the envelope is postmarked October 3, 1903. James, presumably, has absentmindedly retained September's number in his dating.
    2. Henry James, *William Wetmore Story and His Friends* (2 vols.; Edinburgh, 1903).
    3. Gosse was in France. See *EG*, 415.
    4. James was also complaining to others about his "*invaded* summer." See his letters of September 15 to Jocelyn Persse (*HJL*, IV, 284–85) and of September 17 to W. E. Norris (*LHJ*, I, 426–27).

205 / MS Library of Congress   Lamb House, Rye, Sussex.
                                        November 3*d* 1903

My dear Gosse.

How can I thank you, ever, for your beautiful, beautiful letter, which not only causes the tears to rise to my eyes but makes them roll down from the same in generous streams? One *doesn't* "thank" for such things, but one doesn't either—one can't—pocket them in silence. Better than anything else that I can say to you is the assurance that you assist, contribute & confirm—that really, yes, you materially help me by speaking to me as you do.[1] I seem to plod along mostly in deep darkness, so far as seeing any mark made by my passage is concerned & whistling to myself, hard, to keep up my courage. Suddenly then I hear *you* whistle *for* me, much better than I can do; whereupon the whole gloom lifts & it's as if it were all sunshine, lilacs & black birds. So I *must* thank you, after all. Your domestic items & annals move me scarce less & I am sorry indeed that a momentary cloud hangs over either, over any, of you. I pronounce it, on my full authority, momentary, & if I could only fill my lungs to blow it straight away—! These things make it all the more generous of you to have found freedom of heart & hand to write me so handsomely. Yes, some day or two during the autumn I shall spend in town & will then unfailingly make you a sign. But won't there be a Sunday sooner or later that you will be able to give me down here?

Poor Lady Spencer!—I didn't know her to speak of, but have slightly known him, & liked him enough to be very sorry for him.[2] It will either blight him for any conceivable "leadership"—or he will marry again! All my tender sympathy to Mrs. Nelly,—my earnest *voeux* for the house generally.

Yours all & always
Henry James

1. This, apparently, is a response to Gosse's comment on *The Ambassadors*, which had been appearing in installments since January in the *North American Review* and which had been published in book form on September 24.

2. Charlotte Frances Frederica, countess Spencer (1835–1903), wife of John Poyntz Spencer, fifth earl Spencer, had died on November 2.

206 / MS Harvard   Lamb House, Rye, Sussex.
                                         November 24*th* 1903

My dear Gosse.

Thanks for your word about Norris, whom, as it happens, I *shall* see, on Friday p.m.—that is if I can manage to reach town in season to do so, before leaving it, accursedly, again for Sunday.[1] (I return here, ruthlessly, Monday.) I rejoice extremely meanwhile to have such good news of him—better than of you, doomed to draughty Dukeries.

I am wondering too if you are finding—or to find time to look at our friend Wolseley's 2 vast & artless volumes, a most gallant forlorn hope of a book—yet which I, for the affection I bear him & to be able to write to him, have been regularly reading—with curious gallant pleasure too, & wonder at their characteristicality.[2] They are of a natural, & also of an interesting; though not always of a tact. But if one had *seen* the billionth part—! Good night! Ever yours

Henry James

1. For W. E. Norris, see letter 107, note 3.
2. *The Story of a Soldier's Life* (1903), by Viscount Garnet Wolseley, former commander-in-chief of the British army. For James's comment to the author himself, see *HJL*, IV, 297–98.

207 / MS Leeds   The Reform Club [London]
                                                     Feb. 25th '04

Dear Mrs. Gosse.

On Wednesday March 16*th*, at 8.15, with great pleasure. I feel a little nervous about invitations far ahead, having been falling a prey to renewed gout, alas—which a few days ago forced me to bolt from town & tumble into bed & domestic tendance at home. But I hobbled up again in time to go, mournfully, to dear Leslie Stephen's funeral yesterday, & I am better & shall strain every nerve to be right & punctual for your august—that is for your March—date.[1] My love, please to his Lordship.[2] I am told he is making delicious discoveries of infinite Nothing as he explores the smiling void of his Future. How ideal a reward of earnest inquiry!

Yours always
Henry James

1. For James's trouble with gout, see, for instance, letter 191. Leslie Stephen, editor of the *Cornhill Magazine* and of the *Dictionary of National Biography*, was cremated February 24, 1904.
2. This is James's arch way of alluding to Gosse's recent appointment (February 9) as librarian of the House of Lords.

208 / MS Leeds   Reform Club
                                                     Pall Mall. S.W. [London]
                                                     Tuesday [April 12, 1904][1]

My dear Gosse.

Let us then make it Saturday, please; when I will come, without fail, at 9.[2]

Yes—of course I hate "Jeremy Taylor"—how could I not? I haven't spoken to you of him mainly for lack of opportunity—I was keeping him till you should ask me, as you perjuredly said you would, to gape at your halls of State—when it was my plan to apply, by my praise, the finishing touch to your exaltation. I have greatly admired the book & your entrance into possession of your so bristling & *touffu* subject.[3] It is beautifully & cunningly done & it has ever so soothingly & painlessly fitted itself into the deep void of my ignorance; so that now I'm boldly allusive & unashamed. But I will tell you more on Saturday.

Yours ever
Henry James

1. Dated by James's letter of April 11, 1904, in which this proposed visit is discussed (Leeds).
2. James usually arrived at 9:00 P.M. and frequently referred to the hour as "my immemorial nine" (see letter 210).
3. Gosse's *Jeremy Taylor*, another volume in the English Men of Letters series, had just appeared.

209 / MS Leeds   Lamb House, Rye, Sussex.
                                               Monday p.m. [May 9, 1904?]

My dear Gosse.

Alas I am afar off—otherwise I would do it with pleasure. I fled days & days ago—on the 30*th* last—the formidable, fatal, *funeste* city. And, pressed as I am here with urgent duties, I don't know when I shall be able to venture back for longer than between two trains. If I *do* that, I will, with pleasure, ask you for a piece of gingerbread with whatever remains of the gilt. Many thanks for the charming Davray translation.[1] How the gilt thickens on our English gingerbread—or even fine sponge-cake—under the French transformation! Yours always

Henry James

1. Henry D. Davray (1873–1944) had previously translated some of Gosse's work into French. Presumably the item in question is *L'Influence de la France sur la poésie anglaise* (1904). Gosse had recently been honored by Davray and the Société des Conférences in Paris and had lectured in February on the influence of France on English poetry (*EG*, 415–16).

210 / MS Leeds   Lamb House, Rye, Sussex.
                                               Aug: 14*th* 1904

My dear Gosse,

This is most happy—that I am not too utterly to fail of catching you by the tip of your ear before we are borne such different ways.[1] I think, all things considered, that I had best name the after dinner-hour (9 sharp) on Saturday next, 20*th*, as my time for looking in. I seem to be condemned to try on clothes, of sorts, in the a.m. & *close* up till luncheon & to be liable to complications & accidents in the afternoon & till late. But the clock & my bell will simultaneously sound at my immemorial nine, & I am yours all ever

Henry James

1. James departed for America from Southampton August 24 on the *Kaiser Wilhelm II* and arrived in New York on August 30. See *HJ*, V, 232–34. This was his first trip to America since 1883. His impressions were to become the basis for *The American Scene* (1907).

211 / MS Library of Congress

The Mount
Lenox, Mass.
Oct: 27*th* 1904[1]

My dear Gosse,

The weeks have been many and crowded since I received, not very many days after my arrival, your incisive letter from the depths of the so different world (from this here,) but it's just because they have been so animated, peopled & pervaded, that they have rushed by like loud-puffing motor-cars, passing out of sight before I could step back out of the dust & the noise long enough to dash you off such a response as I could fling after them to be carried to you. And during my first 3 or 4 here my postbag was enormously, & appallingly, heavy: I almost turned tail & re-embarked at the sight of it. And then I wanted, above all, before writing you, to make myself a notion of how, & where, & even *what*, I was. I have turned round now a good many times, though still, for 2 months, only in this corner of a corner of a corner that is named New England; & the postbag has, happily, shrunken a good bit (though with liabilities, I fear, of re-expanding,) & this exquisite Indian summer day sleeps upon these really admirable little Massachusetts mountains, lakes & waves in a way that lulls my perpetual sense of precipitation. I have moved from my own fireside for long years so little (been abroad, till now, but once, for ten years previous) that the mere quantity of movement remains something of a terror & a paralysis to me—though I am getting to brave it, & to like it, as the sense of adventure, of holiday & romance, & above all of the great so visible & observable world that stretches before one more & more, comes through & makes the tone of one's days & the counterpoise of one's homesickness. I am, at the back of my head & at the bottom of my heart, transcendently homesick, & with a sustaining private reference, all the while (at every moment verily,) to the fact that I have a tight anchorage, a definite little downward burrow, in the ancient world—a secret consciousness that I chink in my pocket as if it were a fortune in a handful of silver. But, with this, I am having a most charming & interesting time & seeing, feeling, how agreeable it is, in the maturity of age, to revisit the long neglected & long unseen land of one's birth—especially when that land affects one as such a living & breathing & feeling & moving great monster as this one is. It is all very interesting & quite unexpectedly & almost uncannily delightful & sympathetic—partly, or largely, from my intense impression (all this glorious golden autumn, with weather like tinkling crystal & colours like molten jewels) of the sweetness of the country itself, this New England rural vastness, which is all that I've seen. I have been only in the country—shamelessly visiting, & almost only old friends & scattered relations—but have found it far more beautiful & amiable than I had ever dreamed, or than I ventured to remember. I had seen too little in fact, of old, *to* have anything, to speak of, to remember—so that seeing so many charming things for the 1st time I quite thrill with the romance of elderly & belated discovery. Of Boston I haven't even had a full day—of N.Y. but 3 hours, & I have seen nothing whatever, thank heaven, of the "littery" world. I have spent a few days at Cambridge, Mass. with my brother & have been greatly struck with the way that in the last 25 years Harvard has come to mass so much larger & to have gathered about her such a swarm of distinguished specialists & such a big organization of learning. This impression is increased this year by the crowd of foreign experts of sorts (mainly philosophic &c,) who have been at the St. Louis congress & who appear to be turning up, overwhelmingly under my brother's roof, but who will have vanished, I hope, when I go to spend the month of November with him—when I shall see something of the goodly Boston. The blot on my vision & the shadow on my path is that I have contracted to write a book of Notes—without which contraction I simply couldn't have come; and that the conditions of life, time, space, movement, &c. (really to *see*, to get one's material,) are such as to threaten utterly to frustrate for me any prospect of simultaneous work—which is the rock on which I may split altogether—wherefore my alarm is great & my project much disconcerted; for I have as yet scarce dipped into the great Basin at all.[2] Only a large measure of Time can help me—to do anything as decent as I want: wherefore pray for me constantly; & all the more that if I can only arrive at a means of application (for I see, already from here, my *Tone*), I shall do, verily, a lovely book. I am interested up to my eyes—at least I *think* I am! But you will fear, at this rate, that I am trying the book on you already. I *may* have to return to England only as a saturated sponge & wring myself out there. I hope meanwhile that your own saturations & Mrs. Nelly's prosper, & that the Pyrenian [*sic*], in particular, continued rich & ample.[3] If you are having the easy part of your year now, I hope you are finding in it the lordliest, or rather the *un*lordliest, liesure [*sic*]. I saw of course in Cambridge dear old C. E. Norton, very ancient & mellow now, àpropos of whose daughters & whose Dantean fame this undergraduate pleasantry may, though irrelevant, interest you.[4] The eldest of the 3 girls is much the prettiest, & they go declining; whereby they are known in College as Paradiso, Purgatorio & Inferno. (The 3*d.* is very plain). I commend you all to felicity & am, my dear Gosse,

Yours always
Henry James

1. Printed in *LHJ*, II, 19–22, and in *HJL*, IV, 331–33. My text is based upon the manuscript and differs in details from both printings. The Mount is Edith Wharton's home, and James is her guest.
2. This "book of Notes" would eventually become *The American Scene*.
3. The Gosses had spent some time on vacation in the Pyrenees.
4. Charles Eliot Norton (1827–1908), editor, art historian, teacher, and old friend of James's, had translated Dante's *Commedia* in 1891 and 1892.

212 / MS Library of Congress   The Breakers Hotel
                                                  Palm Beach: Florida
                                                  Feb. 16*th* 1905[1]

My dear Gosse,
    I seem to myself to be (under the disadvantage of this extraordinary process of "seeing" my native country,) to be [*sic*] perpetually writing letters: & yet I blush with the consciousness of not yet having got round to *you* again—since the arrival of your so genial New Year's greeting. I have been lately in constant, or at least in very frequent, motion, on this large comprehensive scale & the right hours of *recueillement* & meditation, of private communication, in short, are

very hard to seize. And when one does seize them, as you know, one is almost crushed by the sense of accumulated & congested matter. So I won't attempt to remount the stream of time save the most sketchily in the world. It was from Lenox, Mass., I think, in the far-away prehistoric autumn, that I last wrote you[2]—& I reverted thence to Boston, or rather, mainly, to my brother's kindly roof at Cambridge, hard by—where, alas, my 5 or 6 weeks were harrowed & ravaged by an appalling experience of American transcendent *Dentistry*—a deep dark abyss, a trap of anguish & expense, into which I sank unwarily (though, I now begin to see, to my great profit in the short human hereafter,) & of which I have even yet not touched the *fin fond*. (I mention it as accounting for treasures of wrecked *time*—I could do nothing else whatever, in the state into which I was put, while the long ordeal went on: & this has left me belated as to everything—"work," correspondence, impressions, progress through the land.) But I was (temporarily) liberated at last, & fled to New York, where I passed 3 or 4 appalled midwinter weeks (Dec. & early Jan.;) appalled, mainly, I mean, by the ferocious discomfort this season of unprecedented snow & ice puts on in that altogether unspeakable city—from which I fled in turn to Philadelphia & Washington. (I am going back to N.Y. for 3 or 4 weeks of developed spring—I haven't yet (in a manner) seen it or cowardly "done" it.) Things & places southward have been more manageable—save that I lately spent a week of all but polar rigour at the high-perched Biltmore, in North Carolina, the extraordinary colossal French château of George Vanderbilt in the said N.C. mountains—the house 2,500 feet in air, & a thing of the high Rothschild manner, but of a size to contain 2 or 3 Mentmores & Waddesdons—the *gageure* of an imperfectly aesthetic young billionaire.[3] Philadelphia & Washington would yield me a mild range of anecdote for you were we face to face—*will* yield it me then; but I can only glance & pass—glance (even at the extraordinary & rather personally-fascinating President—who was kind to me, as was dear J. Hay even more, & wondrous blooming, aspiring little Jusserand, all pleasant welcome & hospitality.)[4] But I liked poor dear queer flat comfortable Philadelphia almost ridiculously (for what it is—extraordinarily *cossu* & materially civilized,) & saw there a good deal of your friend—as I think she is—Agnes Repplier, whom I liked for her bravery & (almost) brilliancy.[5] (You'll be glad to hear that she is extraordinarily better, up to now, these 2 years, of the malady by which her future appeared then so compromised.) However I am tracing my progress on a scale, & the hours melt away—& my letter mustn't grow out of my control. I have worked down here, yearningly, & for all too short a stay—but ten days in all: but Florida, at this southernmost tip, or almost, does beguile & gratify me—giving me my first & last (evidently) sense of the tropics, or *à peu pres*, the subtropics, & revealing to me a blandness in nature of which I had no idea. This is an amazing winter-resort—the well-to-do in their tens, their hundreds, of thousands, from all over the land; the property of a single enlightened despot, the creator of 2 monster hotels, the extraordinary agrément of which (I mean of course the high pitch of mere monster-hotel amenity) marks for me [how] the rate at which, the way *in* which, things are done over here changes & changes. When I remember the hotels of 25 years ago even! It will give me brilliant chapters on hotel-civilization. Alas, however, with a perpetual movement & perpetual people & very few concrete objects of nature or art to make use of for orientation, my brilliant chapters don't yet get themselves written—so little can they be notes of current picturesque—like one's European notes. They can only be notes on a social order, of vast extent, & I see with a kind of despair that I shall be able to do here little more than get my saturation, soak my intellectual sponge—reserving the squeezing-out for the subsequent deep, ah, the so yearned-for peace of Lamb House. It's all interesting, but it isn't thrilling—though I gather every thing is more really curious & vivid in the west—to which & to California, & to Mexico, if I can, I presently proceed. Cuba lies off here at but 18 hours of steamer—& I am heartbroken at not having time for a snuff of that flamboyant flower.

Saint Augustine,
Feb. 18*th*

I had to break off day before yesterday, & I have completed, meanwhile, by having come thus far north, my sad sacrifice of an intenser exoticism. I am stopping for 2 or 3 days at the "oldest city in America"—2 or 3 being none too much to sit in wonderment at the success with which it has outlived its age. The paucity of the signs of the same has perhaps almost the pathos the signs themselves would have if there *were* any. There is rather a big & melancholy & "toned" (with a patina) old Spanish fort (of the 16*th* century,) but horrible little modernisms surround it. On the other hand this huge modern hotel

(Ponce de Leon) is in the style of the Alhambra & the principal church (Presbyterian) in that of the mosque of Cordova. So there are compensations—& a tiny old Spanish cathedral front ("earliest church built in America"—late 16th century,) which appeals with a yellow ancientry. But I must pull off—simply sticking in a memento (of a public development, on my desperate part,) which I have no time to explain.⁶ This refers to a past exploit, but the leap is taken, is being renewed; I repeat the horrid act at Chicago, Indianapolis, St. Louis, San Francisco, & later on in New York—*have* already done so at Philadelphia (always to private "literary" or Ladies' Clubs—at Philadelphia to a vast multitude with Miss Repplier as brilliant Introducer. At Bryn Mawr to 700 persons—by way of a *little* circle.) In fine I have waked up *conférencier*, & find, to my stupefication, that I can do it. The fee is large, of course—otherwise! Indianapolis offers £ 100 for 50 minutes!⁷ It pays in short travelling expenses, & the incidental circumstances & phenomena are full of illustration. I can't do it *often*—but for £ 30 a time I shld. easily be able to. Only that would be death. If I could come back here to abide I think I shld. really be able to abide in (relative) affluence: one can, on the spot, make so much more money—or at least I might. But I would rather live a beggar at Lamb House—& it's to that I shall return. Let my biographer, however, recall the solid sacrifices I shall have made. I have just read over your New Year's eve letter & it makes me so homesick that the bribe itself will largely seem to have been on the side of reversion—the bribe to one's finest sensibility. I have published a novel—"The Golden Bowl"—here (in 2 vols.) in advance (15 weeks ago) of the English issue—& the latter will be (I don't even know if it's yet out in London) in so comparatively mean & fine printed a London form that I have no heart to direct a few gift copies to be addressed. I shall convey to you somehow the handsome New York page—don't read it till then. The thing has "done" much less ill here than anything I have ever produced.⁸

But good-night, verily—with all love to all, & to Mrs. Nelly in particular. Yours always

Henry James

1. Printed heretofore in *LHJ*, II, 24–28, and in *HJL*, IV, 350–53. The present text is based on the manuscript and differs in a number of details from either printing.

2. See letter 211.

3. For other comments by James on the Biltmore, see his letter of February 8, 1905, to Edith Wharton in *HJL*, IV, 346–48. Mentmore and Waddesdon Manor were

English homes of the late Ferdinand de Rothschild (1839–1898).

4. Theodore Roosevelt (1858–1919) was president at the time, and John Hay (1838–1905), an old friend, was secretary of state. Jean Jules Jusserand (1855–1932), another old friend (see letter 38), was French ambassador to the United States. For James's earlier opinion of Roosevelt as a "dangerous and ominous Jingo," see his letter of September 19, 1901, to Jessie Allen (*HJL*, IV, 202).

5. Agnes Repplier (1855–1950), American essayist and author, had had cancer in 1896, but recovered and outlived the physician who treated her. See George S. Stokes, *Agnes Repplier, Lady of Letters* (Philadelphia, 1949), 127.

6. This memento, according to Edel, was a "card of admission to H.J.'s lecture, 'The Lesson of Balzac,' at Bryn Mawr College, 19 January 1905" (*HJL*, IV, 353*n*).

7. Approximately $500 in 1905.

8. *The Golden Bowl* was published in New York on November 10, 1904, and in London on February 10, 1905. The novel appeared in a second printing in the United States in 1905. See *BHJ*, 127–28.

213 / MS Leeds   Reform Club
                                                          Pall Mall. S.W. [London]
                                                          July 14*th* [1905]

My dear Gosse.

Hearty thanks for your so warm welcome. I got back but yesterday p.m. & I go down to Rye tomorrow afternoon but want *much* to see you & will seek you at the British Senate (as I assume you go there even Saturday a.m.) at *12.30* of the mid-noon; unless you shld. wire me that you are not to be there, or are to be elsewhere.[1] I don't know my way in to your penetralia—but will beg it, from door to door—I should urge you to make a point of receiving me in my freshness if I had any of that article left from my année terrible. Yet I find it comes back a little for the free toss, to Hanover Terrace, of all greetings of yours always

                                                          Henry James

1. James has just returned from almost a year in America. The "British Senate" refers to the House of Lords, where Gosse had begun to serve as librarian in 1904.

214 / MS Library of Congress   Lamb House, Rye, Sussex.
                                              August 31*st* 1905

My dear Gosse.

All thanks for your rather bad news—news, I mean, of your so immediate & sustained (beyond reach of my soon seeing you) absence. I have failed of seeing you through the need of absolutely sticking fast here & resuming stern duties. I came back from the

U.S. to formidable Arrears, & I have had to get into relation (intimate) with the question of working them off—which I *have* achieved, thank God, by stopping at home & not invoking the aid of the London August. And I came back too to a very disorganized household—the fruit of my absence, & have had to stop & watch over it & put it together again. I give you all good wishes over your journey, & envy you the sense, for so many weeks, of the unutterable Italy. But go to Baveno, on L.M. [Lago Maggiore], rather than Stresa—forgive my meddling. I never wrote a word, however, about either. I have left that for *you*—so now mind you do it. Go over from Stresa to Orta & thank me for making you.[1] We will talk it all over by an autumn fire—I shall be eager to put my teeth a little into London then. Go to Florence this time (not in September, though—make it late,) & give my love & blessing, please, to Mrs. Nellie & the Infantas.[2] It's past midnight, long—forgive my dull hand. Yours, my dear Gosse, ever

Henry James

1. For James's comments on Orta and Stresa, see letters 138 and 215, respectively.
2. See letter 215.

215 / *MS Leeds*   Lamb House, Rye, Sussex.
                                                    Sept: 20: 1905

My dear Gosse.

Your letter from Stresa is beautiful & admirable—you so *give* the whole too adulterated actuality. Yet you give—give *me*—the heart break of I know not what divine despair (of the nostalgic passion that *only* Italy can produce—a wholly ineffable thing;) so that I could lay me flat on the carpet & wildly weep. It's 6 or 7 years since I've been there at all—& I see no *near* possibility—& it's a very awful thing. But go on, & bring me back, to administer in some good hour of Hanover Terrace, a due dose of torture. That chain of cities is a rosary of fretted golden beads, & these also you must tell over to me while I squirm with anguish—not sparing me one. I'm not sure you *haven't* been to Florence—(last year?) but hope it, for the pleasure of thinking of you in the intensity of the initiation. *Don't* try to do other outside things—only sink deep into her yielding jewel-cup that the place all & only is. It's a perfect little treasure-house (in spite of *such* profanations;) but there is no use talking & you will see for yourselves.[1]

I sit fast here, having much *besogne*, of a humble sort, to put through—& a great coming & going of rather superfluous people (through Rye itself) to reckon with as an (invasionary) worriment & importunity. But we are having a restorative, an exquisite, *2d* half of September (so far,) after a vile *1st*. I went the other day up to Wimbledon on purpose to see poor Harland—whom I *fear* to be engaged in a last tragic *losing* fight. But the plan still holds, I believe, of moving him so precariously (& expensively!) back to San Remo—soon.[2] His wife is most gallant—& his mother is there. But heaven help them all! It makes one feel so coarsely, selfishly, *cruelly* well. But be you twain so, consistently, all the same. Make me a sign from H.T. [Hanover Terrace] & I will try to put in a late October evening there. *Tanti Saluti*; Tuscanissimi ones; to Mrs. Nelly. Yours & hers always

Henry James

1. The Gosses visited Florence in October, 1905. See *EG*, 423.
2. Henry Harland, an old friend to both James and Gosse, was seriously ill and would die the following December. See letter 220.

216 / MS Leeds   The Reform Club [London]
                                    Wednesday p.m. Oct. *18th* [1905]
My dear Gosse

Only a word to wish you both heartiest welcome back & to say that if I hear nothing from you to the contrary, I will come in on *Sunday, p.m.*, *22d*, at 9.[1] Yours ever

Henry James

P.S. Irving a "strange" figure—yes; but surely never so strange as when interred—the mummer & mountebank—in the Abbey. I admit there is the Garrick and Siddons precedent—but will there be the G. Alexander Sequel?[2]

1. The Gosses had just returned from Italy. See letter 215.
2. The remains of Henry Irving (1838–1905), the well-known British actor, were placed in Westminster Abbey on October 19, 1905. George Alexander, another British actor-manager, was not quite so well known as Irving, though he had starred in and produced James's *Guy Domville* in 1895. James, of course, is being ironic.

217 / MS Leeds   Lamb House, Rye, Sussex.
                                           Nov. 1st 1905.

My dear Gosse.

I thank you kindly for your pretty letter about my little lecture-book & your good news of poor Harland.[1] Ah, you should have been *at* the conférence!—as the Frenchman of anecdote, wondered at for the fresh exuberance of his grief over a lost wife, retorted with an "Ah, you should have seen me at the Grave!" At the grave (or is it—was it—the cradle?) I too was much more exuberant & irresistible. I rejoice at any rate in what you tell me of the exile of San Remo. Only, what grimness of exile he must at the best convalesce to! He can clearly never come back here. And how he will hate that!

Let me not omit to tell you that I found here duly, on my return, which was but 3 days ago, your consummate *Sir Thomas*—which, however, under extreme & inordinate pressure, I have not yet had, & shall not immediately have, a free mind or free time to read.[2] But I keep him for the ripe hour, & am yours always

                                           Henry James

P.S. I dream of the guarded massive majesty in which you sit![3]

1. James's "lecture-book" is *The Question of Our Speech*, a book composed of the two lectures he had delivered in America in 1904 and that were published on October 7, 1905, in Boston. See *BHJ*, 129. For "poor Harland," later referred to as "the exile of San Remo," see letter 215.

2. Edmund Gosse, *Sir Thomas Browne* (London, 1905), in the English Men of Letters series.

3. Gosse had become librarian of the House of Lords in 1904. Here and in subsequent letters, James twits Gosse about his position with "their Lordships."

218 / MS Leeds   Lamb House, Rye, Sussex.
                                           December 12*th* 1905

Dear Mrs. Nelly.

I will with great joy make a point of being in London for your New Year's night party, & of presenting myself punctually on that Monday Jan. 2*d*.[1]

Please ask Edmund to bear with my silence & gloom till then—when I shall be wreathed in irresistible smiles & vociferous as a cage of linnets. I am bowed over continuous work & glued to it, & can only be now, with breathless benedictions, yours all, & all round,

                                           Henry James

1. Monday in 1906 was January 1. James had only occasionally accepted New Year's party invitations from the Gosses in the past, but during this period he often attended such affairs. See letter 228, for example.

219 / MS Virginia   Lamb House, Rye, Sussex.
                                                          Dec. 16th 1905

My dear Gosse.

If I didn't fear to seem not to fall into line over your malicious blue eyes, the elevation of your tail & the grossness of your moustache, I should say, frankly, with a giggle: "How *do* they do these things in such a way? with such a completeness & consistency of manner, & such a sustention of tone?" However, it is doubtless easy to do them when one is genuinely inspired, as M. d'Avray evidently is, & with every reason to be.[1] How extraordinarily bien renseigné—in *general*, I mean, as well—& for *whom*, over there, are such *renseignements* a need? It is all a mystery—everything but your predestined apotheosis—with which the whole thing so perceptibly preflashes. And what a brilliant acct. of English criticism!—& poor we who had always thought it left a little to be desired! Even *we* are renseignés too! And the funny little lovely periodical, with its little lovely advertisements of "gratuitous libraries"! But it is all very interesting & I shall watch in the eastern sky, your premonitory pink deepen daily to scarlet! I don't send back the sheet. Ever

H.J.

1. Henri d'Avray (Henry Davray; see letter 209, note 1) wrote a column called "Lettres anglaises" in the *Mercure de France*. See *EG*, 415. Gosse has apparently sent James a column on English criticism.

220 / MS Leeds   Lamb House, Rye, Sussex.
                                                          Dec: 22: 1905

My dear Gosse.

All thanks for your melancholy word. The good Merrian had already wired me. It's a shock—& very grim at the best; I thought he was still holding a somewhat upward course again.[1] How little he wanted it! I have most difficultly written to the poor little woman. Yours ever

Henry James

1. Henry Harland had died in San Remo on December 20. See letter 215, note 2.

221 / MS Leeds   The Reform Club [London]
                                                       Feb: 11*th* 1906

My dear Gosse.

I am in town, since Tuesday last, & have been meaning each day
to make you some sign—but have been held under by many small
first things to do (I am staying, D.V., for some weeks.) You, on your
side, must be immensely immersed in public affairs—even if mainly
occupied in trembling for the continuance of their Lordships at all;
(whose knell, to my sense, *would* seem to have virtually rung.)[1] Yet is
there any evening on the stroke of nine—? I will come up if you will
give me some date. Would Wednesday or *Thursday* of this week do? It
will have to be otherwise next week—19*th*, 22*d*, or 23*d*? I greet you
all & am

                                                       Yours always
                                                       Henry James

   1. For other comments by James on the House of Lords, see letters 217 and 225,
for example. The present comment should be viewed in the light of letter 253,
note 1.

222 / MS Leeds   The Reform Club [London]
                                                       Monday p.m. [February 12, 1906]

My dear Gosse.

On Thursday night then, at 9, with great pleasure, but I will then
explain to you why & how I am condemned—cruelly—not to be able
to accept your tempting invitation to your picturesque mummery
(forgive the term) of tomorrow.[1] I miss the chance—only under
extreme pressure. Yours always

                                                       Henry James

   1. James may have been writing after midnight, as was frequently his habit, and
his reference to tomorrow may actually mean February 14, St. Valentine's Day.
Whether this is true or not, the "picturesque mummery" he refers to is obviously a
party to celebrate the occasion.

223 / MS Leeds   Lamb House, Rye, Sussex.
                                                       March 9*th* 1906.

Dear Mrs. Gosse.

I have wired you, for your more immediate convenience, about
Sunday, but this is the rest of my sorry tale. I was obliged, some

days ago, to flee (temporarily) the city of Dreadful Nights (by which I mean of too many dinners & other dire frustrations,) in order to proceed with pressing duties; & I don't return for another week; so that I shall be far off on the occasion of your Sunday feast. Please believe (though it looks like the beginning of *blease pelieve*) in my lamenting the loss of *any* opportunity of seeing you gathered together—& let me make it up at some calmer hour. I am getting redress here, & must stick to it till Friday or Saturday next. If you were at home on *Sunday 18th*, je ne dis pas—! But you probably won't be for the two "running"??[1] I will at any rate keep the 18*th*, & am yours & Edmund's & everyone's ever

Henry James

1. Since the Gosses had been "at home" on Sunday afternoons for many years (*EG*, 173) and James was quite aware of the custom, including the usual intimate supper following, he presumably had a reason for this question.

224 / MS Leeds   Lamb House, Rye, Sussex.
                                                  April 23*d* 1906

My dear Gosse.

   Mrs. Nelly, with Sylvia, & the two Tademas (Lady T. & Laurence,) came over & lunched with me yesterday, & when you see your members of the party they will explain to you a little why I've been such a poor correspondent (since getting your Irish letter.)[1] While I was about to put pen to paper descended this overwhelming California horror, & it paralysed & distracted me for the time, for my poor brother & his wife (as you will have learnt,) are there; not, thank God, at S.F., but at Leland Stanford 30 miles South—where the whole thing is in ruins but the loss of life almost nil.[2] *To day*, for the 1*st* time, come at last 2 telegraphed words from my sister, "Both uninjured." That is all, & the obsession of the vision of their frail fatigued misery in the general desolation & squalor doesn't leave me. More will come, since communication is now to that extent open—though as yet of course with appalling congestion. I floundered back to this place Saturday, but shall flounder back to London again: my 2*d* nephew is on the sea (having sailed the day of the Horrors—2 hours before the news reached Boston,) & I go to Liverpool at the end of the week to meet him.[3] I was very glad of the four so genial & braced-up ladies here yesterday—the day was lovely (though Polar) & they helped—very kindly—to soothe my unrest. I am nervous &

occupation, the fixing of my attention, is difficult. But everything passes, & we pass, thank heaven, de même. Your Irish letter reflected a wealth of impressions & I envy you these (or rather the youthful capacity for these) far & long adventure-visits, replete with people & scenes which have (too) utterly dropped out of my life, being incompatible with everything else that makes it. But I like to think there *are* great adventurers still. So keep it up—I shall see you some time & somehow, in town, before long & am yours always

Henry James

1. The two Tademas—the wife and daughter of Sir Lawrence Alma-Tadema (1836–1912), the well-known painter—were Mrs. Gosse's sister Laura and niece Laurence. Gosse's "Irish letter" apparently contained his impressions of a visit to Mountstewart, the marquess of Londonderry's Irish estate. See *EG*, 406, 450.

2. The earthquake in San Francisco occurred April 18, 1906.

3. William James (1882–1961), the second son of William and Alice James.

225 / MS Leeds   Lamb House, Rye, Sussex.
                                    July 20*th* 1906

My dear Gosse.

The weeks go by—*have* gone—without my seeing my title clear, or my conditions truly helpful, to asking you if you won't come down here for some week-end before you make (as I assume you likely to make for the autumn,) some grand dash for the steam boat & the railway, for the trains that shake mankind. And if there has been a great inevitability in it (what with Sundays of compatriots & cousins, Sundays of ardent work & Sundays, 2 or 3, spent away from home,) so too I've seemed to see you periodically junketting in parks & palaces from which it were an outrage to drag you; junketting with Lady Clara Vere de Vere at "the Hall"—at a Thousand Halls—from which the attempt to divert you would have been vain.[1] The coast is clearer even with *me* now—is it at all so with yourself, & is there any Saturday till Sept. 1*st* (inclusive—& with the exception of Aug. 4*th*) when you *can* come for a couple of days? (A Friday even would be better.) There isn't the faintest chance you're free for this coming 28*th*, I suppose—otherwise I should rejoice to see you. Would Aug. 11*th* be any more possible? Name to me, in short, however briefly, *some* date—if it's possible to you! Even a week-day wd. perfectly serve. It's a hundred years since we conversed & I feel as if accumulations were thick. I hope Peace—no, I won't say Peace, but some Violent form of

Plenty—flourishingly reigns with you—though I fear Tessa told me at Eton that her mother hadn't been well. I offer her every kind assurance—even to that of hoping Tessa almost imagined or invented. But goodnight! Yours, my dear Gosse, always

Henry James

1. During this period Gosse, as a result of his position in the House of Lords, associated socially with some members and their families (*EG*, 420–21, 422–23). James often taunted him about his "junketting in parks & palaces," but whenever he needed help from Gosse through his connections, he never hesitated to take advantage of his friend's position. The most obvious example of such privilege occurred in 1915, when James asked Gosse to intercede with his friend H. H. Asquith, prime minister, in the matter of James's application for British citizenship. See letter 312.

226 / MS Leeds   Lamb House, Rye, Sussex.
                                              October 28*th* [1906]

My dear Gosse.

I am obliged to go up to town on Friday & will stop over Sunday if I may count on finding you at home after dinner that evening (Sunday next, 4*th*).[1] May I in that case have an amiable word from you here? I greatly desire your news since those days of emotion here, & above all Mrs. Nelly's, who has, as you all have, the earnest greetings & hopes of yours ever

Henry James

1. Nellie Gosse wrote James that Sunday, November 4, would be convenient, and he answered on November 1 that he would "come on Sunday at 7.30 with greatest pleasure" (Leeds).

227 / MS Leeds   Lamb House, Rye, Sussex.
                                              November 18*th* 1906

My dear Gosse.

I am much obliged to you for your kind offer of Maitland's *L.S.* — but I already possess & have more or less read the so excellent & interesting—even I think rather charming, book—which, as also I think, I mentioned to you, is the cause of a little heartache for me over my very accidental failure to despatch to M. a couple of contributory & commemorative pages in *time*; small bricks for the monument—which is yet, however, substantial & shapely without them.[1] I am quite ashamed to appear so basely absent from it—& it was all a fatality!

I hope *your* monument (which I think makes a brave little weekly show,) hasn't any perverse air for you of proving your tomb![2] Yours always

Henry James

1. Frederic William Maitland, *The Life and Letters of Leslie Stephen* (London, 1906). Maitland (1850–1906) was a professor of civil law at Cambridge. James apparently did not send Maitland any of his correspondence with Stephen, and there are no letters from Stephen to James in Maitland's book. James also praised Maitland's study in his letter of December 21, 1906, to Anne Thackeray Ritchie in *HJL*, IV, 433–34.
2. This may be a reference to the weekly columns (some on Gosse) written by Henry Davray in the *Mercure de France*. See letter 219, note 1.

228/ MS Leeds   Lamb House, Rye, Sussex.
                                             Jan: 4*th* 1907

Dear Mrs. Nelly.

I got back here, belatedly, night before last, to find yours & Edmund's beautiful & graceful & desirable pot or jug—shining & shapely & infinitely elegant, so that it fills me with pride & joy. I rejoice in it to positive extravagance, & am deeply touched by the sentiment, on your part & on Edmund's, that I seem to feel it represents. It *represents* them indeed to extravagance—but I must try & live up to the picture. I hope your chairs & tables are reduced to order since that generous & charming New Year's eve agitation & that you have echos of Edmund's carouse in Paris that are not wholly unintelligible—or at any rate unacceptable.[1] I am here all this month, but shall be in town more or less after that & shall come & record afresh the gratitude & elation of yours both, most faithfully

Henry James

1. James has attended another New Year's party at the Gosses. He had also been present at the 1906 party. See letter 218, note 1.

229 /MS Leeds   Reform Club
                                             Pall-Mall S.W. [London]
                                             Feb: 2*d* 1907[1]

My dear Gosse.

I have just come up to town, & I gave myself this morning very promptly to the beatific perusal of your beautiful notice of *The American Scene* in the D.M.[2] It has given me extraordinary pleasure—more, I can emphatically say, than any Appreciation of any book of mine has *ever* given me. Therefore my eyes really fill with tears as I very devoutly thank you. I waited just for this before acknowledging your charming note. But now I acknowledge, up to the hilt, every bounty. And I must see you. I am here, just now, to the 12*th*, about; but should you be at home, nocturnally, on the 8*th* or 9*th* (this next Friday or Saturday?) or on Monday 10*th*??[3] On a sign as to any such free date I wd. gladly come. (I go out of town for 2 nights Wednesday.) Yours all & altogether

Henry James

1. Printed in *SR*, 584–85.
2. On February 1 Gosse had written more than a column for the *Daily Mail* on *The American Scene*, two days after it was published in London on January 30, 1907. In 1906 Gosse had agreed to edit for the *Daily Mail* a literary supplement called *Books* and to contribute articles and reviews both to the newspaper and to the supplement for extra pay (*EG*, 428–29).
3. As James's other dates suggest, Monday fell on February 11 in 1907.

230 / MS Leeds   Lamb House, Rye, Sussex.
                                                                  July 15*th* 1907

My dear Gosse.

I returned a week ago from 4 wild months beyond the sea (& eke the mountains—the 2 last in Italy,) but I come up to town for 2 or 3 days, 3 or 4 at most, next week. They seem in advance considerably compromised with special things to do, but I am clinging to the evening of *Thursday 25th* on the chance that with the drop of the hurly-burly you may perhaps then be at home & accessible. I wd. in that case very eagerly knock at your door at nine o'clock—& "book" the occasion (atrocious expression!) on a sign from you. It will have been my 1*st* approximation (1*st* access to London) for 6 or 7 months.[1] I count on your making me communications of an eloquence proportionate to such a chance on their part to accumulate, & richly to mature—& shall not myself be without travellers' tales to thrill you withal. But the great thing will be to find you all sound & serene, happy & good. On this I build—& on the said 25*th* p.m. if humanly possible. It *is* a time & I am yours & your wife's all constantly

Henry James

P.S. But I shall forbid you to speak of Ouida![2]

1. James actually had been in London in February and had visited the Gosses at the time. See letter 229.
2. Ouida (Marie Louise de la Ramée, 1839–1908), a prolific and popular novelist

of the day, is now remembered best for *Under Two Flags* (1867) and *A Dog of Flanders* (1872).

---

231 / MS Leeds   Lamb House, Rye, Sussex.
                                                    July 17*th* 1907
My dear Gosse.

This is delightful, & your bell-pull will on Thursday night next, 25*th*, vibrate to my touch even as the neighbouring minster steeple vibrates, as usual, to the stroke of nine. The prospect of a whole evening with dear proud Ouida attracts me beyond all things.[1] And tell Mrs. Nelly, please, with my love, that her conduct in refusing for my sake 40 invitations (from Dukes) makes her the very heroine of Ouida that I have always felt her—if she would but let herself *go*! Now that she has done so it is enchanting to yours & hers always

Henry James

1. See the postscript to letter 230. For Ouida as a "little terrible and finally pathetic grotesque" who "means nothing," see James's letter to Elizabeth Lee, February 10, 1913, in *HJL*, IV, 650–51.

---

232 / TC Harvard[1]   Lamb House, Rye.
                                                   August 7*th*. 1907.
My dear Gosse.

A very kind and welcome windfall your brave and interesting letter—which gives me the greatest pleasure. The breath of the Humanities blows little about me here (save as my own poor little pair of bellows strives to create it, too asthmatically,) and, charged with your references and honeyed stores, produces for me the balmiest stir. Your account of the gentle Carriére greatly appeals—*what* a Refined People the race that bore him!—and I shall try to put my hand upon him.[2] And yet there is so much too much all round to read—so that I almost dread to hear of anything new and appealing. The longer I live the more the act thereof (of reading) becomes to me the great anodyne and even the great ideal Experience—but with work and letters and people and servants and walks and the total Leakage of time the moments for it are gnawed all round. We can't *all* be Arthur Christophers—we *can't* all be ideally constituted and masters of our Fate—a mastery for which, and the example of which and the emoluments of which, and the motor-cars of which, I envy and revere and love A.C.!³ It is thus at any rate a positive joy to me (or almost,) that Bourget has now for long become of a *poncif* so abandoned that I absolutely find in him neither life nor style nor interest—without counting his extraordinary monomania of elegance and highlife and the haughty patriciate and all the rest of it. It relieves and simplifies that he has ceased thus to be an obsession—to constitute a demand on one's attention. To me, as a member of the romancing craft, his procedes[?] are almost pathetic in their naivete. But I will tell you when we next meet some interesting facts—as I find they are—that I gathered in Paris lately about the *nature* of his present very large and very paying public.⁴

When we meet—I fear it must be as early as possible in the autumn—I am so little *alone*—for free talk—now—with two nephews in the house and two Parisians (the Robt. d'Humières) presently to lunch, and an architect (not for building) tonight for 3 days etc. etc.—and a week in Scotland from about the 20th.⁵ This, however, will straighten out and I will then signal you. Since you are kept in London I congratulate you on the cold and haughty season—the *only* merit, however, that I see in it (that it relieves you of the London swelter in general and of the Parliamentary in particular.) Here it blows too many gales and engenders—or tries to—too many rheumatics. But I must haste me to the station to meet the Parisians—hark the Gaul is at the gates of

> Yours breathlessly,
> always,
> *Henry James*

1. This typed transcript was prepared for *LHJ* but was not used. It was called to my attention by Philip Horne, University College, London.

2. Eugène Carrière (1849–1906), French painter and lithographer, was often identified with the Impressionists.

3. For Arthur Christopher Benson, see letter 107, note 2, letter 235, note 2, and letter 236.

4. For Paul Bourget, see, for example, letter 10, note 1, and *HJL*, IV, 456–57.

5. Robert Vicomte d'Humières (1868–1915), French poet and translator of Kipling and Barrie; the d'Humières were friends of the Bourgets and Edith Wharton. See *HJL*, IV, 442, 454–56.

233 / MS Leeds   Lamb House, Rye, Sussex.
                                                    October 14*th* 1907.

My dear Gosse—my dear Mrs. Nelly!

I can't not greet you & above all felicitate you on your charming little Death's-Head & Crossbones taken from Rome. Like what bloody pirates you must indeed be enjoying yourselves! I'm so glad for you that I really lose myself in the vision of your Roman October, & I walk between you, each hand in one of yours, all up & down the Corso & all over the Palatine. Ain't it interesting? & in *these* weeks how yellow, how gold-coloured, how spacious & empty. I'm afraid the late Lady Edmund isn't there, but you can't have everything.[1] Take it as it comes, & prepare to tell me all. My sympathy with you is of that fine strain that I dash away the impulse to say to you that the old vanished Pio Nono Rome, *my* 1st old Rome of 1869, was the place—! No I *don't* say it, & if you'll come back here & tell me every-thing—you, Edmund, in particular, by coming down here for a Sunday on your return, or early in November, I won't say anything, but only, charm-struck, will listen, listen, listen! Try me & see. Yours both & always

                                                    Henry James

1. On occasion James refers to Mrs. Gosse as Lady Edmund (see letter 137, for example). Although the Gosses still are in Italy, they have apparently missed the old Rome.

234 / MS Leeds   Lamb House, Rye, Sussex.
                                                    [October 30, 1907][1]

My dear Gosse.

There came to me tonight the so handsome tribute & presence of your imposing & evidently most interesting Document, &, inscribed (or superscribed) in your hand, it gives me to think that you are probably restored to your nothern [*sic*] stronghold, after, I trust, a foray rich in spoils. I am greatly obliged to you for the goodly (that looks like *goody*, which I take to be a most inapplicable word,) book; which pressed with occupation, I shall not have time to read for a week or two—when I shall unfailingly surrender myself to its spell.[2] But this is, more even than to express my gratitude, designed to say: won't you come down to me for the 1st possible Saturday & before the flush of memory & the bloom of sensibility have faded from your late adventures (from which I hope you have both returned like young giants refreshed)? Will either the 9*th*, the 16*th* or the 23*d* not suit you? Let me urge you earnestly to choose the 16*th* only if the 9*th* is utterly unthinkable & the 23*d* only (if the 16*th*) is a derision. Each will be in its own discreet way a pleasure of a high order to yours all impatiently

Henry James

P.S. I hatefully *missed* the other day, to my deep disgust, a most miserably mysterious visit from Philip.[3]

    1. This date is apparently written in Gosse's hand, as are the last four words in the postscript.
    2. Gosse's *Ibsen* (1907) had just recently appeared, but the reference presumably is to *Father and Son*. See letter 235.
    3. Philip Gosse (1879–1959), Gosse's second child and only son, presumably was seeking advice or recommendations concerning his career. James's influence had been used in Philip's behalf when he wished to go on a South American expedition with Sir Edward Fitzgerald in 1896. See letter 133, note 2, and letter 140, note 6.

235 / TC Harvard[1]

Lamb House, Rye.
November 10*th*, 1907.

My dear Gosse.

I shall greatly rejoice to see you on Saturday next, 16th, by the 4.28 from Charing Cross—as I have these last days been so leaving you to infer. I have been reading you meanwhile with deep entrancement—spell-bound from cover to cover. *F. and S.* is extraordinarily vivid and interesting, beautifully done, remarkably *much* done and deserving to my sense to be called—which I hope you won't think a disparagement of your literary and historic, your critical achievement—the very best thing you have ever written.[2] It has immense and unfailing *life*, an extraordinary sort and degree, quite, of vivacity and intensity, and it *holds* and entertains from beginning to end—its *parti-pris* of absolute and utter frankness and objectivity being, it strikes me, brilliantly maintained—carried through with rare audacity. You have thus been in a position to write a book that must remain a document of the first importance—à consulter—about the pietistic passion and the religious rage; unique, surely as a detailed and ironic yet a so perfectly *possessing* portrayal of these things—from so very near. No one who has seen them from so very near has ever had your critical sense or your pictorial hand, and thus been able to write about them in any manner to be *called* writing: which is what your manner almost inordinately *is*! Your wonderful detachment will, I daresay, in its filial light, incur some animadversion—but this is to my mind the very value and condition of the book—though indeed there are perhaps a couple of cases—places—in which I feel it go [*sic*] too far: not too far, I mean, for truth, but too far for filiality, or at least for tenderness. On the *whole*, however, let me add, I think the tenderness of the book is, given the detachment, remarkable—as an intellectual, reflective thing: I can conceive the subject treated with so much more uneffaced a bitterness. I can conceive it treated too, on a side, I may further add, with a different shade of curiosity, a different kind of analysis—approached, as it were, at another angle—but at one that is a bit difficult to express—so that I must wait till I see you; when I shall have various other things to say about it—as well as to pressingly ask. Suffice it for the present that you have had, immediately, the advantage of a living, intimate subject, and that cela vous à porté bonheur and caused you to produce a real work of art: which the theological world (even not the more besotted) will moreover instinctively hate—to your great credit and advantage. Let me subjoin lastly that I think you have been of an excellent discretion, and produced a real effect of vivid candour, about your infant Self. But you break off at a point too interesting—I could have (literally) done beautifully with as much again. That "lastly" just now isn't my last, either: this is, rather, that, as a fact, your picture will have *this* to reckon with—that its whole evocation is somehow of visible *ugliness*: a very interesting and pathetic truth and value about the facts themselves, and quite a part of the importance of your record. But it colours your page, it becomes the note of your material—a study of the *consistently* ugly. (I speak of the suggested *visibilities*—the whole key of aspect and association.) The charming pages about the old Babbacombe seaside beauty (they are lovely) come in as a blessing. But I want awfully to *talk* of these things. Therefore fail me not. These last have been beautiful days here; I pray for something, a week hence, *like*. Good-night: *tanti saluti*!

Yours always
Henry James

1. This typed transcript was prepared for *LHJ* but was not used. It was called to my attention by Philip Horne, University College, London.

2. *Father and Son*, Gosse's masterpiece, had been published anonymously on October 25 (*EG*, 433), but many of Gosse's friends, A. C. Benson, George Moore, and James among them, knew about its authorship and considered it, as James maintains, the "very best thing [Gosse had] ever written."

236 MS Leeds   Lamb House, Rye, Sussex.
                                  Nov. 30th 1907.

My dear Gosse.

   The tears literally fill my eyes on perusal of your momentous letter, & I have to exert a practised skill (for I "cry" too easily) to prevent their making little channels down this page. I have by natural constitution too intense, too penetrating a perception, or imagination of the lives and situations & affairs of others—& of what it is to "be" others—& that is a bias often so productive of anguish that I've wished, on the whole, that I were less "sympathetically" formed. Then again I have rejoiced in being so—but really I think *never* so much as on the occasion of this beautiful drama of yours & your wife's.

   Beautiful, beautiful, beautiful! a great thick firm savoury slab of comfort that one can bite into! And I am almost as impatient as you can be yourselves for the full *psychological* evolution—the sight & sense of what such accretion will do with you & make of you![1] You— even you—can't know in advance—any more than your all rejoicing—all round—old friend

                                  Henry James

P.S. Do force me upon the luxurious languor of dear A.C.B.—I mean as the image of one always tenderly interested in him.[2] Do if necessary sacrifice me even—in (spiritual) honour or estate for any momentary effect or else unobtainable diversion. He has my very absolute & unreserved participation.

   1. Nellie Gosse was soon to inherit £46,000 (approximately $230,000) of a fortune made in cocoa and left by James Epps, her uncle. See *EG*, 384. For a more ironic, though covert, comment on this "beautiful drama," see James's letter of December 23, 1907, to W. E. Norris (*HJL*, IV, 483–84). References to the inheritance also appear in letter 237 and subsequent letters.
   2. For Arthur C. Benson, see letter 107, note 2.

237 / MS Leeds   Lamb House, Rye, Sussex.
                                  Dec: 6: 1907.

My dear Gosse.

   This is a mere irrepressible word. I should hate to say vain things—as to your affair, & be all horrified at the remotest danger of doing so; but I seem (to myself) to feel pretty well within the limits when I say that the reflections in your interesting letter from

Aldeburgh have the weight of your due discretion—as against any dip into a possible fool's paradise of fatuity; but don't to my sense invalidate at all what has *happened*. The adversary's solicitor must, I think, have *exhausted* every alternative before writing you that letter, & anything he waited to find to say or do before accepting the necessity—or advisability— of such a communication, & then gave up the hope of, is scarcely likely to occur to his depleted mind afterwards.[1] Mustn't he have written only under the extremity of exhaustion? That's all I presume to say, & this only because one hates as much to lash you into pessimism as into optimism[.] And every day gnaws away a little of the strain. So at at [*sic*] least I suffer you to say that I contend in order that you may reply "Oh *does* it?" Write to me daily, & even gnashingly, if *that* wears any of it away.

Your account of Arthur B. is almost a little sinister—& yet no: it's the state *preceding* the present one that was uncanny, & the present is (probably) a very natural & wholesome protest which will expend itself in a little while.[2] He will recover & delight fresh millions, & almost make them.

Yes, it's a really new & charming idea to find Germany of a sudden the Missionary & representative of a richer & wider grace to life![3] In what a very interesting age—all round—we live! Yours so gratefully for it

Henry James

1. See letter 236, note 1. The litigation over James Epps's will had gone on for years, and this may have been the last legal effort to delay a settlement.
2. Arthur Benson and Gosse, though intimate friends, were frequently at odds. See *EG*, 371–76, 423–27, 442–48, 492.
3. For various considerations of contemporary Germany, see the *Times*, December 5, 1907, p. 4, and December 6, 1907, p. 7.

238 / MS Leeds   Lamb House, Rye, Sussex.
                                                    December 19*th* 1907.

My dear Gosse.

You are more & more interesting, though I can easily understand that you are more & more worried; by which I mean more & more conscious of a nervous strain. But grin & bear it, you will see it through—for the sands in the hourglass *are* all the while running; & meanwhile a large bland patience is a just & proper homage indeed to the groping New Zealanders—who must so deeply appreciate it.[1]

Tell me more in due course—my appetite for more is insatiable. Now that the Campden Town Murder is over (which even in its squalor really does, or did, produce in me a certain intensity of wonder,) your affair occupies unchallenged the centre of my consciousness. Meanwhile your mature travel-passion, & its fine crescendo movement, excites my envy if not my emulation; *my* capacity for déplacement has so utterly died out that I have absolutely spurned even a remarkably engaging invitation to go to Paris for Xmas. Well, consume as large a slice of the Midi as you can cut, but don't gamble away your "expectations." I am afraid there is no possibility of my being in town for New Year's Eve.[2] I really don't hope for it, but shall probably see you shortly later. I hope the Book is handsomely circulating,[3] & am yours always

Henry James

1. This is a reference, apparently, to the settlement of James Epps's will. See letters 236, note 1, and 237, note 1.
2. James had been present at the parties for 1906 and 1907. See letters 218 and 228.
3. Presumably *Father and Son* (London, 1907).

239 / MS Leeds   Lamb House, Rye, Sussex.
                                            January 28*th* 1908

My dear Gosse.

Shall you by any miracle be at home either Saturday or Sunday night February 8*th* or 9*th*?? I fear that with your rallying to the throne tomorrow you will be more likely to be smothered at that & at almost any time in the folds of its ermine.[1] But I am to be in town on those days (& 2 or 3 before, but I have kept those free,) &, if I might have a word from you, wd. come at 9 on either of them. Your news *me manque* to an almost unbearable extent. I hope something definite—to put it colourlessly and mildly—fills that void for all of yourselves.[2] You must be hideously taken up—a bare bald postcard will do. All greetings! Yours always

Henry James

1. The reference to "the throne" is to the House of Lords, not to Buckingham Palace.
2. The news apparently concerns the Epps will, which was on the verge of settlement. See letters 236, note 1, 237, note 1, and 240.

Lamb House, Rye, Sussex.
                                                 February 22*d* 1908

My dear Gosse

Your news is of incomparable interest—as your whole story has
been from the first—when you originally presented it to me as a
mere unconsidered trifle. It "ends well," as *my* poor stories are
accused of not doing—if that can be called the end which is clearly,
for so many patient persons, the beginning—of so much new convenience & ease.[1] By the way, I hereby ask you, when you begin definitely to realise—or Mrs. Nelly at last credulously does—just to send
me by post a *sixpenny postal order* as a signal & emblem: then I shall
know where you are—& also doubtless a little *how*. I have a sixpenny
p.o. order that I sometime ago received from the Harpers as money
due to me for my annual *droit d'auteur* (on several books,) framed &
hung up as a token of the general appreciation of literary merit—& I
want to make yours a pendant to it—as illustrative of another form of
reward. But the *fairytale* quality of the Epps adventure is of pure
beauty, indefeasible, & showing so admirably that the f. t. [fairy tale]
still, on occasion, *is* of this world—when one happens to be loved of
the fairies. I really most unreservedly & pointedly congratulate your
wife on the immense happiness she will enjoy in being able to be
beneficial to her children &c. Therefore don't forget the sixpenny
token—I shall feel then, tell her, *like* one of her children.

Anatole's Jeanne d'Arc has but this a.m. reached me, & I promise
myself joy of it. Of course he is a Renanunculus—& a marvel; but I
can't *compare*; by reason of my really devout sentiment for dear old
Ernest—one [of] the blessings of my youth & idols of my prime &
influences, generally, of my life.[2] I feel him in his mass—& Anatole
is (though such a *product* &c) of a monstrous modernity. It breaks my
heart (àpropos of the genii) that you shld. be reading the *Spoils of P.* in
anything but the Edition—which has begun to appear, very handsomely, in the U.S., but is further delayed & temporarily checked
here, though only temporarily; so that in due course you shall have
to receive it all as a penalty of your not waiting.[3] Greedy! Yours,
with renewed participation always

                                                         Henry James

1. Mrs. Gosse received £46,000. See letter 236, note 1.
2. Anatole France's *Vie de Jeanne d'Arc* (1908) had recently appeared. For other references to Ernest Renan (1823–1892), see, especially, James's letter of February 8
[1876] to William James in *HJL*, II, 26.

3. James is referring to *The Spoils of Poynton* as it appeared in the New York Edition, Volume X, which Scribner's had begun to publish on December 14, 1907.

241 / MS Duke   Lamb House, Rye, Sussex.
                                                   Apr: 6: 1908.

My dear Gosse

It's a great relief to hear from you even though you have nothing very positive to tell me—for my imagination has all these last weeks been very busy with you & decked you out at moments rather with the rue than with the rose: so that it's really a blessing to gather that your roses are simply a little backward, a little belatedly flowering, & destined to break out & cluster about you, almost smother you, with blushing freshness & fragrance a little time only from now. That sixpenny bud will still be a thrilling sign to me; & meanwhile though you suffer from the law's delays you can't in the least, I am sure, from the insolence of office.[1] Continue just patiently to twiddle your thumbs & in the "larger day" this crepuscular moment will shrink to the mere memory of a luxurious sigh.

I appreciate however your having, in your inevitable tension; [*sic*] a troublesome shift of the telescope (Sister Anne's on the tower-top) to icy Edinburgh, where, on the 26*th* last, my little stage-play was "successfully" produced—so successfully as to diffuse for the evening a really quite large & genial glow.[2] It has all the air of being a very clear & charming little victory—& the dreary (though not all undiverted) business of rehearsing it at Manchester & at Edinburgh itself for some ten days previous (after preliminary rehearsals in town upwards of a month before) was more or less made up to one. Companies on "tour" can play one piece but 3 times a week at most, but I hear that it much flourished at Glasgow last week—[t]he "tour" ends the end of April. What was brought most home to me is that the little rot, such as it is—pure comedy-rot—is primarily addressed & adapted all to London, & that what fortune it has *en province* will be necessarily bettered here. It has been done solely for sordid coin—in the hope of the same—& I am therefore praying that arrangements may take effect for its production in town early in May. But there is a terrific *treacherous* side—or possibility—to any theatric matter—& I tremble even while I yearn. To London it will of course however come sooner or later—it's all in the lap of the gods—& meanwhile therefore consider me as in the same box as yourself—only me hanging on seven—&—ninepence, & you as seven-times-nine thousand.[3]

I read your vivid *Ibsen* at once, & at one breath, or almost, after you sent it me & found it exceedingly attaching.[4] But it roused in me the critical & commentative impulse—yet to which I can't now give voice. I will tell you later what I mean. I speak here as to the manner of the book—and also, after all, not less, as to the manner of the man & the genius. What sort of a queer "great man" & great artist & writer was this terrible unlovely gentleman at all, at all? We will talk of him—I shall be in town through May (I think). All greetings & backings! Ever yours

Henry James

1. The reference is to Mrs. Gosse's legacy and to James's request in letter 240 for a *"sixpenny postal order* as a signal & emblem" of when the settlement was cleared.
2. James's *The High Bid*, a "little stage-play" fashioned from "Covering End," which, in turn, was a long story based upon *Summersoft*, a one-act play James had written in 1895 for Ellen Terry. The play was produced by Johnston Forbes-Robertson (1853–1937), the well-known British actor, and featured Gertrude Elliott, his American wife, in the central role. For other comments by James on this play, see his letter of April 3, 1908, to Henry James, Jr., in *LHJ*, II, 96–98.
3. *The High Bid* appeared in London for matinee performances during the week of February 19–26, 1909. For a review and comment, see the *Times*, February 19, 1909, pp. 10, 12. See also letter 244.
4. Gosse's *Ibsen* had been published in 1907.

242 / MS Library of Congress   Lamb House, Rye, Sussex.
                                               Sept. 3. 1908.

"Adventure", my dear Gosse?

I've had no faintest shadow of one, thank the Powers—& my nearest approach to the same, ever, is just to hear of your own last—which seldom fails. *My* own last wholly exceptional capture of one was that frolic up to town to Philip's nuptials—the whole sequel to which, I hope, presents itself as graceful & comfortable.[1] I haven't otherwise stirred from here, to speak of—where I have had, & shall have for some time yet, superabundance of occupation & visitation: the latter will wane at least—but the former, I trust, not unduly shrink, which it promises little indeed to do. My brother has been with me much—& my sister-in-law & niece (abroad for the brief time, but presently returning to stay till they depart home about the *20th*.) This has been an intense interest & joy—especially as (till this last horrible tempestuous break,) the summer here fairly rioted in blandness & he (my brother) got 3 or 4 weeks of tranquil recuperative days (he had come to me unwell) largely in my garden—all to our great profit all round—while a pressure of labour that still continues with me could yet unmolestedly go on. And there have been invasions pure & simple, but they don't matter now. I sit tight from now indefinitely on. I've just walked back in a deluge from Lady Maude Warrender's (where I've hardly been since *our* funny day)—having tea with the dark-eyed Maguire's.[2] We talked of the Luard murder—& they made me sit up by the (London) rumour that *he* is more & more suspected of having done it. But that doesn't *fit*! Very welcome, but not wholly soothing your news of poor wakeful A.C.B.[3] I think of him ever so tenderly—but *see him* now, somehow, but through the grey mist of his own many words; the strangest effect of his literature. Oh how *I* hate either starting, going or arriving! Wherefore crouching here, I am

> Your marvelling, but
> abiding,
> *Henry James*

1. Philip had married a distant relative, Gertrude Hay, on July 14, 1908.
2. Lady Maude, James's "amiable neighbour," had invited James and Gosse in the summer of 1906 to lunch "to meet" the duke and duchess of Connaught. H.R.H., Arthur William Patrick Albert, the duke of Connaught (1850–1942), was the third son and seventh child of Queen Victoria. See James to W. E. Norris, December 23, 1906 (Yale). Although this letter has been printed in *LHJ*, II, 58–61, this passage was not included. This is frequently the case with other letters from James to Norris when Gosse is mentioned. Gosse himself, as literary advisor to Lubbock, is presumably responsible for these excisions.
3. For Arthur C. Benson, see letter 237, note 2. For James's letters to Benson, see *HJL*, IV, 57–59, 522–23.

243 / MS Leeds   Lamb House, Rye, Sussex.
                                                   [December 29, 1908][1]

My dear Edmund & Nelly (though—since this p.m.—a shade more Edmund *than* Nelly—"which", my dear Nelly, you shall see why!) This celebrated Season is notoriously overwhelming, but I— in my comparative obscurity & lack of obviousness—have never before so effectually found it so. While still gasping under the deposits of postal matter that have made my acknowledgment of your earlier bounty a damnably delayed thing,—though my life, since its arrival, had been one prolonged roll of—what you know—under my tongue—an appeal to my appreciation even more insidious has

heaped up the measure of my anguish, at once, & my joy. Your box
of chocolates affected me truly as having gathered in the rarest lyrics
& sonnets & madrigals into which the material could be wrought—
while now your beautiful letter, Edmund, seems all compact of the
chocolate-creams of criticism & homage. Each offering appeals in its
own irresistible way to my characteristic greed—so that in fine I feel
as if I had fifty mouths & the sweetest taste possible in all of them. If
I wasn't afraid of seeming to imitate your conception of the madri-
gal—that is of the bonbon—I would say that it really *takes* fifty to
degustate your delightful tribute. I extract extraordinary pleasure
from your letter, my dear Edmund—one of the very handsomest I
ever received. "One of" indeed, I say?—*the* most precious pearl
rather of my crown of recognition. None other, whatever, begins to
approach it in lustre or loveliness. The Edition has been a weary
grind (such a mass of obscure & unmeasurable labour,) but I feel all
you say as the most delightful consequence of it. So I am tenderly
grateful for your brave & generous words.[2] It bewilders *me* that in the
very act of uttering such as it were, you should—that is your second
self Nellie—be incommoded & undeservedly ailing. Please let my
appreciation medicate you both so far as possible. Failing this I shall
blush to mention that *I* am not otherwise burdened or stricken than
my great age & vast bulk render natural & even becoming. I have a
letter flushed with the rosiest health, clearly, & the dewiest morning
valour from [W. E.] Norris—il nous enterrera tous.[3] But we must
buck up—& indeed I am rosy enough with your letter. I heartily
hope Lyme Regis may be kind to you—but take plenty of hot-water
bottles (I hope Tessa & Sylvia have them) & believe me ever so constantly yours both

Henry James

1. Printed heretofore in *SR*, 585–86.
2. The English issue of the New York Edition began appearing in London on
September 29, 1908, and the remaining volumes were published in 1908 and 1909
(*BHJ*, 138).
3. For W. E. Norris, see letters 95, note 1, and 242, note 2.

244 / MS Duke   Reform Club
                                           Pall Mall. S.W. [London]
                                           Feb: 19*th* 1909.

My dear Gosse,
    All thanks for your so prompt & vivid gratulation. The little

ancient disinterred—after 14 years or so!—potboiling *plaisanterie* will doubtless "do" all the very moderately much I expected of it. I only wince a little at having it treated—vide this a.m.'s *Times*—as a fresh & contemporary effort of my genius & an offer (heaven help us!) of the wanton "exquisite!"[1] It has been *printed* these many years.[2] However, if it earns for me the nine & nine-pence ha'penny that every thing else seems determined *not* to earn, it will have amply expressed its character.[3] I thank affectionately dear gregarious, applausive Gosses all & am yours & theirs always & ever

Henry James

P.S. I am very precariously & briefly in town—but if I stay over a little will make you some other sign.

1. *The High Bid* was making its first appearance in London. See letter 241, notes 2 and 3.
2. The play had been published as a story, "Covering End," in *Two Magics* (1898).
3. The play was performed four afternoons from February 19 to February 26 and made little money. As Johnston Forbes-Robertson wrote Gosse on February 22, 1909, "Our dear friend's play is not a 'money maker,' but my wife & I love it very much" (Duke).

245 / MS Library of Congress

Reform Club,
Pall Mall. S.W. [London]
June 4*th* 1909.[1]

My dear Gosse.

I have read your Swinburne in the *Fortnightly* & find it admirable—delightfully done & very *interesting*; the best, on the whole, I think, of your portraits in that kind—& with the advantage of so excellent a subject.[2] I am sending you with this, àpropos of it, the *Times* Lit. Supp. of Thursday last, for the two long Stedman letters (*favoured* Edmund Clarence!) which you may have seen, but which I post on the chance. I find them quite charming—& deserving *that* particular description more than anything of C.A.S. that I can remember—certainly than any other morsel of his prose.[3]

Happy fugitives from a horror of black cold & wet—fires & overcoats & rivers of mud—to which we have fallen heirs since you left. You breathe of course a golden air & perspire in pearls & diamonds. I still hobble in a grandmother shoe—but am thankful to circulate even so. The Holbein Duchess has been saved—by a veiled lady who has bought her off for £40,000.[4] Can you lift the veil? I am afraid on second thought that you are not at *my* hotel, but wherever you are I

invoke all the local graces upon you & am yours all auspiciously,
Henry James

1. Printed in *TD*, 263–64.
2. Edmund Gosse, "Swinburne: Personal Recollections," *Fortnightly Review*, XCI (June, 1909), 1019–39.
3. Since June 4 occurred on Friday in 1909, James could be referring to the *Times Literary Supplement* of May 27 or June 3. Each issue contained two letters from Swinburne to Edmund Clarence Stedman (1833–1908), the American poet and critic. James, strangely enough, has inverted Swinburne's initials.
4. See the *Times*, June 4, 1909, p. 6. The reference to a "grandmother shoe" suggests that James is having another siege of gout. See letter 246.

246 / MS Leeds
Reform Club,
Pall Mall. S.W. [London]
[July 1?], 1909[1]

My dear Gosse.

I thank you very kindly for your renewed inquiry, & send this poor word—so charged with dreary references—off after you into high-breasted Tuscany where it will seem to you, when it reaches you, wretchedly irrelevant & inferior. I am better, thank you, & was able on Sunday to hobble down to some friends in Oxfordshire, whence I returned to-day, still hobbling & unable to wear a proper shoe, but with most of my torment of pain gone & only lumpishness & a slight residuum (of local anguish) remaining.[2] The lumpishness declines but slowly & takes patience. Such are my prosy little facts. Yours, by this time, must be all romantic & delightful; & I hope you are now up to your necks in the whole wondrous matter. Give my love to every old stone & my blessing to every old woman—as that of an older one still. Go to San Gimignano—& *drive* back in the late June p.m. It has been a lovely Whitsuntide—save for desperately wanted rain today—during which it has bravely & bountifully poured. I was motored 30 miles of Monday—through a beauty of country & *moment* that had nothing to envy even Tuscany.[3] Amusez-vous-bien. My bestest love to your comrades. Always your
H.J.

1. James has presumably misdated this letter as June 1; it should be July 1, for the postmark on the envelope attached reads July 2, 1909. Moreover, internal evidence supports this date. James's reference to a trip of thirty miles on Monday is to a drive he took with Edith Wharton, and since Wharton did not come to England until June 3, James could not have motored anywhere with her before this date. See R. W. B. Lewis, *Edith Wharton: A Biogtaphy* (New York, 1975), 258. The letter is printed with

the date of June 1 in *TD*, 262–63. My text is based upon the manuscript.

2. James had suggested his problem in letter 245.

3. Edith Wharton had driven him to Hurstbourne on Monday, June 28. See *HJ*, V, 415.

---

247 / MS Leeds   Lamb House, Rye, Sussex.
                                     July 16th 1909

My dear Gosse.

A couple of friends descended upon me here by motor 4 days ago & carried me off on a tour that would take no remonstrance—need I name the all-imperative Mrs. Wharton as one of the brilliant invaders?—from which I returned but last night to find a huge pile of letters, with your engaging note among them.[1] It makes me feel greatly in your debt—as I have before me two unacknowledged favours of your Siena time; your delightful record of your own motor-flight from the high nest & the elegant postcard commemorative of some similar occasion.[2] I wish indeed I could make my acknowledgments by immediately naming some near nights for Regent's Park; but London enfolds me no more—I quitted it long since, save for a single night a week ago when I (with that mere brevity) came back again.[3] I am in deep retreat now, embanked in urgent work, & with no distinguishable occasion or possibility of a present return to town, even for a day or two, open to me. But if that call *should* break upon my ear should I still find you accessible? I seem to see you more likely to sit quiet awhile after your long absence (& with such a summer—to say nothing of the Long Parliament) than to seek fresh adventures.[4] Therefore *all* possibility seems not to fail. And after a while, if London does remain your base, perhaps I shall be able to induce you to spend a Saturday-to-Monday with me. In fact I shall much aspire to propose you this at some sunnier hour.[5] I feel as if a mountain of circumstances & subjects calling for treatment only awaited our earliest convenience. I greet you all meanwhile fondly—Mrs. Nelly indeed demonstratively most so—& am all faithfully yours

                                     Henry James

1. The other friend was W. Morton Fullerton (1865–1952), with whom Edith Wharton was having an affair.

2. For Gosse's letter from Siena of June 11, 1909, see *TD*, 264–65.

3. Gosse now lived in Regent's Park.

4. Gosse was presently librarian of the House of Lords.
5. See letter 248, and Gosse's of August 27 in *TD*, 265–66.

248 / MS Leeds   Lamb House, Rye, Sussex.
                                                    July 28*th* 1909.

This is delightful, my dear Gosse—do, *do* come! There are reasons just now why the "week-ends" are rather more auspicious for *me* than other moments—though the 1*st* one, after your date of the 5*th*—Saturday 7*th* is in fact compromised by the expected presence of a friend, & I would infinitely rather have you to myself.[1] That, however, is the only engagement I have made, & the following Saturday, 14*th*, would be delightful to me—with the only abatement that it is a little remoter than I should wish. But the weeks simply melt in the hand at my age—of course they are more coagulated at yours; & at any rate if you will fix your eyes & your intentions on that 14*th* you won't be conscious of more time to await it than you will very patiently know what to do with. Therefore I then count on you, & on the vast totality of your budgets of news, before the prospect of which I sit *bouche béante*.

I am full of pleasure at your liking the article on H.J. in the Times Litt. Sup.—which is by young Percy Lubbock (an old pupil of Arthur Benson,) & I think really intelligent & superior; a difficult thing very ably done.[2]

Let me hear from you then that the Saturday I name will do for you, & that you are packing your store of anecdote. Place me at the feet of Mrs. Nelly—but with Tessa near to give me a hand up; & believe me yours always

Henry James

1. James frequently sounds this note, for he counts on Gosse to share his "budget" of literary news and anecdote. Gosse came as planned for the weekend of August 14. See his letter to James of August 27, 1909, in *TD*, 265–66.
2. Percy Lubbock (1879–1965), "The Novels of Mr. Henry James," *Times Literary Supplement*, July 8, 1909, pp. 249–50. For Arthur Benson, see letter 237, note 2.

249 / MS Library of Congress   Lamb House, Rye, Sussex.
                                                    Aug. 28*th*. [1909][1]

My dear Gosse.

All thanks for your letter—with its note of the wretched actual surmounted & overpast—so far as such wretched actualities may be;

which brings home to one that there is always an *after* to current events, however damnable *as* current, & that so long as one lives (by which I mean the longer,) this blest subsequence seems to *se faire de moins en moins attendre*. It is already with us at the acute moment, getting the acute moment behind it—though only, unfortunately, that particular one. It has, alas, itself, other acute moments up its sleeve. But, in short, let us go on taking them one by one. Which reflection indeed is better addressed, in its very imperfect ingenuity, to you than to your wife—to whom the blackness of a couple of weeks ago may have become a relative greyness—but a greyness that won't so soon in turn change colour. A very hard grim fact that of charming Laura Tadema's unmitigated absence & extinction, surely.[2] And you must still be under the projected shadow of that dreadful consciousness of your daughter-in-law's.[3] Poor Philip—who is so very *straight* under it! I quite unspeakably feel for them—& for Mrs. Nelly in this sore maternal connection too. Let her not dream of "writing" me a single syllable. What a horrible addition that to the other burdens of bereavement & anxiety!

I am extremely glad meanwhile that you were able to work through, in A.C.B.'s company, into another aspect of things; & particularly into another aspect of his condition, since you can definitely report it as ameliorated.[4] On which I definitely congratulate *you* almost more than anybody else—that is almost more than the suffering subject himself—in whom you must have done more than anybody else to bring the happier result about. Very interesting & charming your account of the classic Haworth, which I've watched, in my long life, *grow* classic, & yet never seen nor been within miles of, but which you make me want to see.[5] I don't despair of it yet, for I don't mind traveling (by which I am afraid, however, I but sneakingly mean motoring) in these islands.[6] On the mainland I more & more hate it. It is very tranquil here, for a wonder; in spite of motors—& very beautiful—& I am unsociably & inhospitably applying myself—in view of having to be away a part of next month. Today here has really been a ravishment. But good-night, & please speak afresh, at home, of the continued participation of yours ever

Henry James

1. Previously printed in *TD*, 266–67.
2. Laura Alma-Tadema was Nellie Gosse's sister. See letter 224, note 1.
3. Gertrude Hay Gosse, Philip's wife, in the late months of her pregnancy with

her first child, was concerned presumably with the safe arrival of relatives from Australia. See letter 254, note 2.

4. Gosse had reported on August 27 that Benson was "really and substantially better" (*TD*, 266).

5. Haworth was the home of the Brontës in Yorkshire. Gosse had found it a "surprise" and "much prettier" than he had expected (August 27, 1909, in *TD*, 266).

6. For James's interest in "motoring," see, for example, letters 246 and 247.

250 / MS Cambridge   Lamb House, Rye, Sussex.
                                               Sept. 1*st* 1909.

My dear Nelly Gosse.

How kind it was of you to write to me—burdened as you must have been with many letters! I do think of your Sister as a delightful presence all almost unbearably *misused*, to us, by gratuitous extinction.[1] There are times when life seems indeed too odious & too *bête*. But you have sorrows enough brought home to you, & I follow you to poor Philip's darkened hearth very tenderly—so tenderly indeed as to be very timidly.[2] A dismal, dreadful vision there must reign—but there too reign at the same time youth & life—things of miraculous power. Yet great must be your strain & sore your heart. I wish you rest afterwards—save that you'll never rest from the sharpness of affection—which is nothing *without* sharpness. I got a beautiful letter from Edmund in Yorkshire—it made me thankful for the Yorkshires—though I don't myself go to them.[3] But, you see, I lead the lives of my friends, & am thus all intimately yours

                                               Henry James

1. For Mrs. Gosse's tribulations, see letter 249.
2. See letter 249, note 3.
3. For Gosse's letter of August 27, see *TD*, 265–66.

251 / MS Library of Congress   Lamb House, Rye, Sussex.
                                               Nov: 11: 09

My dear Gosse.

I have been vainly intending these several days to write you a word on a trivial matter—but which I have at heart such as it is. I asked Heinemann some little time since to send you for me a copy of a lumpish & not intrinsically very successful (I fear) piece of catchpenny bookmaking entitled "English Hours"; when he replied to me that he had already of his own fond motion addressed one to Mrs. Nelly—& would that do?[1] I did think one in the family enough &

Mrs. N. can, as we used to say in mutual infancy, "let you pretend its [*sic*] yours"—if you are obstreperous that way. But I wanted to let you know that I did have the operative thought—& will even, if you like, inscribe the gift of Heinemann with words representing it as *my* gift; without a scruple. There is some little dingy verbiage in it about Siena any way.

I shall have to be in London at the end of the month (the beginning of next) for a small number of days; & shall, as that time approaches, write to ask you if you are to be at home one of those evenings; the 1*st*, second, third, or thereabouts. Or if you are to be so on Sunday 5*th*, I would hang on for *that*.

Norris was very briefly with me last week, & dazzled me by the youth & grace & lustre & general power & prowess of his ruddy autumn.[2] He beggars all calculations & defies all theories. I think of *you* as not so much in a ruddy as in a flushed & empurpled "fall," though with an atmosphere of power & prowess too hanging thick about you. Don't however, let our old nobility (for what should we be, & what would the Librarian of their lordships in particular perhaps—*as* a Librarian be, without them?) blaze too grandly with those attributes; for I rather feel with them and enter into their ease, & yet wouldn't have our present historical year known as the Year of the Great Fatuity.[3] Let it become rather the Year of the Great Librarian. Well, goodnight to that possibly worried warden—& *sleep* all you can anyhow. I greet Mrs. Nelly always tenderly—& have so wondered about the much-tried Philip.[4] Yours always all

Henry James

1. James's reference to *English Hours* (1905) is a slip of the pen for *Italian Hours*, a similar collection just published by Heinemann on October 28, 1909. See *BHJ*, 142–43.
2. For W. E. Norris, see letter 95, note 1.
3. Gosse was librarian of the House of Lords. James doesn't miss many opportunities to tease him about "their lordships."
4. For Philip Gosse's trials, see letters 249, note 3, and 254, note 2.

252 / MS Leeds   Reform Club,
                                                Pall Mall. S.W. [London]
                                                Nov: 30: 1909.

My dear Gosse.

I practically receive at once your two interesting notes—both having gone to Lamb House (& the earlier been inevitably delayed there a bit) before following me again hither. I rejoice with you heartily over the brave news which makes you grandparents—a very confirmed great-uncle (awful image!) can do that without suspicion of *malice*. I therefore hope that the event, with all my heart, is a transition to a new & brighter horizon altogether.[1]

And I shall be delighted to act (that is to figure—for I am in such cases no possible actor,) in the little body organizing the compliment (immensely cordial, surely on the part of all of us) to dear Austin D.[2] Kindly also count on me as a subscriber to the object up to the permitted amount.

Should you be miraculously at home on *Sunday* evening? I shall be here till Monday or Tuesday & wd. come in at 9 with the old punctuality. Yours all ever

Henry James

1. Philip's first child, Helen, had been born some weeks earlier.
2. Austin Dobson (1840–1921), poet and essayist, worked at the Board of Trade with Gosse and was his close friend for years.

---

253 / MS Leeds

Reform Club,
Pall Mall. S.W. [London]
Dec 1st 1909.

My dear Gosse.

Most interesting & liberal your letter, & to that degree intensifying my desire to see you (how I envy you your spectacular & other privileges!) that I will come in on *Saturday* at 9 instead of Sunday—availing myself of the so handsome choice you allow me. I find the Situation thrilling indeed—& long so to get nearer to it through your genial art.[1] But we shall see what we shall see. All thanks about Mrs. Freshfield.[2] I think I shall be able—& shall strain every nerve—to go to see her tomorrow. Tanti saluti a tutti!

Yours ever
Henry James

1. The House of Lords had just rejected the budget of 1909 on November 30, the day before James's letter. This was an important event in the struggle between the houses of Parliament that eventually led to the restriction of the authority of the Lords to reject legislation passed by the Commons. See J. A. Spencer, "H. H. Asquith," *Dictionary of National Biography, 1922–30,* 32. See also letter 251 and letter 260, note 3. In 1906 James had observed that the "knell" of the Lords "*would* seem to have virtually rung" (letter 221).
2. Augusta Charlotte Ritchie Freshfield (d. 1911) was the wife of Douglas William

Freshfield, chairman of the Society of Authors during 1908 and 1909. The Fresh-fields had been occasional guests at the Gosses' home since 1896.

254 / MS Leeds   Lamb House, Rye, Sussex.
                                                    Dec: 30: 1909.

My dear Gosse.

   This must be a scant & shabby greeting—so spent & voided is your poor old correspondent by a singularly prolonged & uninter-rupted outflow of epistolary ink. If that fluid were the red vital I should show every symptom of acute—yea, of fatal—anaemia. I had let a thousand obligations of that order—& my figure is literal—accu-mulate during months & years; I have been working these off hero-ically—but with the consequence that I can now but artlessly & emptily prattle, as a forecast of the sweet simplicity of my dotage. I have had, in these pursuits, the quietest possible Xmastide; a single rather love-lorn & stranded old friend shared it with me[1]—but he has departed, & I think absolutely nothing else has befallen me but that I went today, here—a day of miraculously exceptional beauty—to the funeral of a local worthy to whose memory I wished to pay the dreary compliment. Meanwhile you will have been adventurous—I feel it adventurous for *me* now to walk to the post-office—& if your bold campaign has come off must have affronted strange scenes, amid which the consonant thing was of course only to do strange things. You must give me every detail of them when we next meet—& then, whatever they may have been, I will tell you how more & more glad I am to have all my *déplacements* vicariously effected. I revel more & more in the practice of staying "put." This has the one defect for me of utterly depriving me of news to give you. What you tell me of Mrs. Philip's belated "realisations" is very dreadful, alas—& the more that you must have felt it to be at a given moment inevitable.[2] Yes, isn't it a grievous pity that the fortune my poor old Italian book might have made for me as pornographic has been dashed from my hands by the appearance that the soft impeachment was made by mistake. They declare it's perfectly proper—& again I am destitute.[3] The winter none the less rushes for me & I shall soon see a time in town at the end of the vista. There your house & its gentle inmates will loom again large & vivid to yours & theirs all faithfully

                                                    Henry James

   1. T. Bailey Saunders (1860–1928), a British journalist and author who had been

present at Lamb House in 1901 when James decided to fire his inebriated servants, the Smiths. See letter 184 and James's letter of September 26, 1901, to Mrs. William James (*HJL*, IV, 205).

2. Gertrude Hay Gosse's "belated 'realisations' " concern the presumed death of her mother and sister in the burning of the *Watarah* en route from Australia to England (Ann Thwaite to author, January 6, 1986).

3. This is a reference to a brief misunderstanding on the part of one of the libraries in the Circulating Libraries' Association about the acceptability of *Italian Hours* for circulation among its readers. When one of the libraries refused to supply a copy to a reader, this reader informed the *Times* that he was told the book did not meet the library's standards for "thoroughly wholesome literature" (December 15, 1909, p. 12). Two days later the secretary of the association wrote the *Times* that "some misapprehension must exist" concerning *Italian Hours*, and the matter had been speedily resolved by the time of James's letter to Gosse. On the more general matter of the efforts of the libraries to discourage the circulation of "improper books," see Gosse's letters to the *Times* of December 3, p. 11, and December 9, p. 6, opposing such action.

255 / MS Leeds   Lamb House Rye
                                                        Feb. 13*th* 1910.

My dear Gosse.

You will forgive these faltering accents & feeble signs when I tell you that I have been quite dismally & continually unwell (or, to put it plainly, quite drearily *ill*) since Jan. 1*st*, & passing through much tribulation.[1] I have had & am still having a difficult time—especially through a recent relapse or drop back of a disheartening sort, after I had begun to believe I was a bit steadily improving. However, I *am*, I believe, *un*steadily doing so—& the relapses are not absolute collapses, but it all takes much patience—rather endlessly much. A very bad & obstinate & rather obscure gastric, stomachic crisis—making food repulsive & nutrition proportionately difficult (damnably so at times—with consequent weakness, prostration, depression &c, as much as you like,) is what has ailed me, without other complications of of [*sic*] any sort. But the beastly thing has—so prolonged—in itself sufficed! However, I absolutely believe in my gradual redemption—it seems sometimes (before another drop) quite near: only round the corner. Then it gets further off—then I almost clutch it again: all of which has been a sorry 6 weeks' history; which I relate because I *must* account for my poor show to you—& also anticipate thus your & your wife's, certain sympathy. I have an excellent devoted doctor & nurse—& shall infallibly pull through. I have been a couple of days back in bed again—but now am sitting up—for this day's latter end (7 p.m.)

All that to preface my assurance, please, of how highly I appreciate, & how deeply I am touched by, the great honour & distinction you speak of as offered me (in pursuance of the so intensely interesting scheme,) & with what responsive gratitude I should accept it.[2] Let these poor shaky words suffice for the moment—you shall have better ones as soon as I can manage them. These have me a little spent, but I am yours, both, all round, all faithfully ever

Henry James

1. For other comments on his illness, see James's letters to Edith Wharton (February 2, 1910) and William James (February 8, 1910) in *HJL*, IV, 545–48. James apparently was in a state of depression. In March, Henry James, Jr., arrived at Lamb House to be with his uncle, and shortly thereafter, James was examined by Sir William Osler, the famous physician, who pronounced James "splendid for his age" and prescribed rest and relaxation (*HJL*, IV, 550). But James was still feeling "ill and afflicted" in June. See letter 258.

2. Presumably a reference to the establishment of "an Academic Committee of English Letters," an activity of the Royal Society of Literature to promote in its way aims similar to those of the French Academy. The original list of committee members included Conrad, Hardy, James, Pinero, Yeats, and Gosse himself. Kipling, Shaw, and Wells refused to accept membership (*EG*, 453).

256 / MS Leeds   Lamb House, Rye, Sussex.
                                                          Mar—9—1910.

Dictated.

My dear Gosse:

I am much touched by your note and have only awaited the return of my blessed nephew from town, where he had gone for the day, to dictate you this on the whole hopeful reply.[1] Please take it from me thus in very few words that, though I have been having a very bad and black and interminable time and am keeping, for these days again, very guardedly in bed, I feel that I have been through the worst and have begun a *movement ascencionnal* that can be kept up if only sufficient care is taken. One learns strange lessons in so long an illness and then comes a day when one feels that all the mistakes have been at last made, and that, as there are none left to make[,] the straight and safe course rather stares one in the face. I think I am really making good steps on it now, and shall be able before very long to report to you still better in that sense. Meanwhile I much appreciate your position and your wife's, and hope to be able, before long, to report to you in a rosier sense. I think of you meanwhile frequently and confidently as the very bulwark or *planche de salut* of their Lordships! How quick and how strong the pulse of life and of conversation must be beating for you! Truly, indeed, my opposite extreme seems to have its advantages.

> Yours always—
> *Henry James* [signed]

1. See letter 255, note 1. Theodora Bosanquet (1880–1961), who had become James's amanuensis in 1907, was not in Rye during James's illness.

257 / MS Leeds   Lamb House, Rye, Sussex.
                                                         April 12*th* 1910

My dear Gosse.

Forgive a very short report for my Nephew has gone, & though my brother William & his wife have just come to me (from là bas) they have so many letters of their own to write that I haven't yet impressed them into my service. The essential & happy fact at any rate is that I upwards of three weeks ago began to take a much more assured turn for the better (by an intense rest-cure process) than at all as yet—& that though I have (as I seem doomed to proceed inveterately by heart-breaking relapses) more lately had 3 or four bad days, yet from these too I am now emerging, & take it for really indicated that I am at last, after 14 dreary, weary unspeakable weeks on the right & straight path.[1] If this appearance holds, as God grant it shall, I shall probably be able to come up to town by the end of the month—for 2 or 3 weeks. Pardon this feeble picture & untidy scrawl & believe in the better prospects of your invincible old

> *Henry James*

1. See letters 255, 256, and 258. William James also was in delicate health and would die the following August. See letter 259.

258 / MS Library of Congress   Hotel Hohenzollern
                                                         Bad-Nauheim, Germany
                                                         June 13*th*, 1910.[1]

My dear Gosse,

Forgive a very ill and afflicted man, amid all his difficulties, more silence than he would fain be guilty of—for speech is *supremely* difficult to him. My blest sister-in-law brought me here 8 days ago to join my brother, himself very unwell & making a cure here. I can't be *alone*—it is of the last impossibility, & moreover, I had been hoping much from absolute change of conditions. This benefit has not yet been realized—on the contrary—my damnable nervous state, chronic, but breaking out too in acuter visitations—is a burden almost not to be borne. It has a definite physical basis—& that basis is nominally now of smaller extent—I have turned, in respect to strength, some part of the physical corner. I can *walk* a good deal, & that helps a little. But black depression—the blackness of darkness & the cruellest melancholia—are my chronic enemy & curse—& it is because of that—the wanting not to *write* just blackly—that, my weakness aiding, I lapse into silence & gloom. If I report a gleam of improvement it's all on me again—& then congratulations come as in bitter mockery. My fight is hard, believe me—but, with an immense patience, I expect to come out; the very devil as the bristling dragon of such a condition of nerves is. My brother & sister are angels to me—& I have asked *him* to write you also a brief account of me; which I am sure he will do in a rosier sense than I myself feel ground for.[2] But I leave you to his impression. Meanwhile the monstrous truth is that I go [to] America with them sometime in August—our date not yet fixed. I cling to them unspeakably: such is my terror of solitude, at once—& my unfitness for society. I shall try to let Lamb House for several months—the whole autumn & winter; & when I come back shall try & have some small flat or house (for the winter months, regularly, in town—no more of *them* at Rye,) instead of my contracted perch in Pall Mall. Such at least are my present vague poor plans.[3] I have thought of you much & yearningly in all the present & recent turmoil of your, & "our" history & am, my dear Gosse, always your & your wife's struggling & clinging though infinitely & equally afflicted & attached old friend

Henry James

1. Printed in *HJL*, IV, 556–57. The present text is based upon the manuscript and differs in a number of particulars. For James's illness, see letters 255–57.

2. William James wrote Gosse on June 14, 1910, that James was slowly recovering from a "nervous breakdown" (Leeds).

3. James eventually found a flat in Carlyle Mansions, Cheyne Walk, Chelsea, and moved there in January, 1913. In the meantime, he maintained his room in the Reform Club, Pall Mall.

259 / MS Duke   Chocorua N.H.
                                                   Sept. 10*th* 1910.

My dear Gosse.

   I welcome the affectionate fidelity of your letter & the tender participation of all of you—for we have been through great distress, & I feel that I still sit stricken & in darkness.[1] My beloved Brother's more rapid loss of ground dated from that ominous day on which I last saw you (the afternoon at Howells's, when I drove with you to Hanover Terrace.)[2] We took him down to Lamb House almost immediately afterwards, & there, under excellent care, he remained till the day before we sailed—we came up but to spend one night in town on our way to Liverpool. His suffering had rather a marked alleviation at the last (of the time he was at Rye,) & we embarked with a certain arrest of immediate anxiety, & our voyage to Quebec was extraordinarily fair & short. But he at once got worse again (at sea) in spite of it & we had, my sister-in-law & I, six very tormented & distressed days— so much had he *wanted* to sail & such a hope & possibility had there been that it might do him good. The one long day's journey from Quebec—a dreadful memory—greatly tried him, & he reached this little refuge of his 23 last summers, a real lodge in the wilderness, but of which he had always been fond, only to let us see him sink more & more swiftly. We had a most intelligent young doctor in- stalled in the house from the first, an excellent local man (from 8 miles away,) & a high authority hurried up from Boston—it's a wonder here what the ubiquitous telephone & the extraordinarily multiplied motor achieve. But he suffered too damnably—or rather *would* have, heartbreakingly, if it hadn't been so far as possible pre- vented, & succumbed exactly a week after our arrival.[3] His death means for me more than I can attempt to say—he has always played, from far-away dimmest childhood, so large and admirable a part of my life. He was not only my dearest of Brothers but my best & wisest of friends—& his beautiful genius & noble intellect & charac- ter were really, I felt, at their high consummation. However, of this unutterable pang I can't pretend to talk—I only feel stricken & old & ended. Let me add, for your reassurance, that against this I shall of course struggle, &, with time, react; & also that I am in spite of everything leaving more & more behind me my own miserable phys- ical & nervous state of so many months. (It will have been an atro- cious, a more than terrible year.) I cling to my sister-in-law & her children for the present, & they to me—we hang, we almost huddle, so closely together. We stay here—where his shade, amid a great deal of melancholy American beauty of mountain & lake & forest & through his fond dispersal of himself over his own so many, & other,

acres, seems in a manner to abide with us; & then I go to Cambridge
with them, to remain till the New Year. Beyond that I don't plan.[4]
Go on thinking of me kindly & faithfully, & believe me, my dear
Gosse, yours all responsively

Henry James

1. Printed in *SR*, 586–87. The motif of James's sitting "stricken & in darkness"
runs throughout his letters of this period. See, for example, his letters to Thomas
Sergeant Perry (September 2) and Edith Wharton (September 9) in *LHJ*, II, 167–68,
168–169. The letter to Perry is also printed in *HJL*, IV, 561.
2. Wednesday, July 13, 1910. See Gosse's letter to Howells, July 14, 1910, and
Howells' letter to Gosse of the same date in *TD*, 268–69.
3. William James died August 26, 1910.
4. James remained in the United States until July 30, 1911, when he sailed for
England on the *Mauretania*.

260 / MS Duke

Millden Lodge.
Edzell,
Forfarshire.
Sept. 19*th* 1911[1]

My dear Gosse,

Your good letter reaches me in this remote & contrasted clime—so
different a milieu, I mean, from sweet Savoy—& I cordially welcome
it & thank you for the welcome it contains—thank you both, that is,
all faithfully & impatiently [.] I am impatient to see you, after so
strangely & woefully long, & rejoice that there appears a good near
prospect of it. I came up hither on the 15th to spend a week with an
old American friend (who has occupied this grouse-moor every summer for many years,) & shall be here till toward the end of this week,
probably—by which time, or very shortly after it, I seem to make
out that No. 17 will enclose you again.[2] Then I shall knock at your
door—making sure of the case first; on my way back to Lamb
House, which I have occupied but few of these days since my return
to England. I fled at the end of the 1*st* 10 days from the hot glare &
the parched & stricken state of the South Coast, & have had something of a troubled & restless time since—so uncanny so many of the
conditions here, even after the great American uncanniness—which I
had but just barely out-weathered; & now I strain toward my too-
long forsaken hearthstone & the possible favours of an outraged &
abandoned Muse—whom I must use every art to appease. I stayed
my hand from writing to you—indeed writing to any one during the

torrid transatlantic time was out of the question; for I thought of you
as too worried & even tormented (over the crash of institutions, or at
least of every propriety, about you)—so that that [*sic*] superficial sig-
nals seemed a mockery & searching ones an indiscretion—or even an
anguish.[3] The legend of my having let off epistolary squibs in other
quarters, as I approached, I shall be able, I think, when I see you,
very effectually to dissipate. Everything went to pieces for me during
the awful weeks between May 1st & the end of July—I mean through
my constitutional intolerance of 98° in the shade—& all that order of
impressions, which were so far from being eased off on my arrival in
England. But they have been a little eased off since, & I am bearing
up as I can—with a strong sense of all there is to bear up *against*. I
am delighted to gather that you have all, on your sides, had a happy
frisk—it all sounds most rare & romantic. I hope to be able to try for
you either on the 25*th* or 26*th* p.m.[4]

Your "before the end of the month" would seem to consort with
the possibility of then finding you. But if I should fail I should look
to another pretty early though not immediate chance—for I must be
at home again not later than the 27*th*—at least for some little time.[5]
You'll have lots to tell me, of a hundred people & things—& I await it
all with a yearning ear. I really come back from very far off indeed. I
saw Howells in London early in the month, girding himself for
Spain even like another conquistador. His capacity to knock about
excites my liveliest envy—but clearly it assuages a restlessness in him
that makes it a sharp need: if it were all mere elderly fire & flame it
would be *too* humiliating—to one's self. But his stoutness & tough-
ness are yet wonderful enough. Clearly yours & Mrs. Nelly's compare with it bravely—only you & Mrs. Nelly are not elderly. I shall
send this of course to 17—& if it shld. extract from you the *beau geste*
of a sign of presence please address that sign to *Reform Club Chambers*,
105 Pall Mall S.W. I scarcely even send loves—I shall like so much
better delivering them in person—even in the ponderous person of
your all-faithful old

Henry James

1. This letter and Gosse's letter of September 11 (to which James's is in reply) have
been printed in *TD*, 283–84 and 281–82, respectively.
2. James had disembarked at Liverpool August 8 and returned to Lamb House
August 9. See his letter of August 16, 1911, to Hendrik C. Andersen in *HJL*, IV,
580. In Scotland he was apparently the guest of John Cadwalader of New York, an

old friend also of Edith Wharton (*HJL*, IV, 462, 465). Gosse was still living at 17 Hanover Terrace.

3. The House of Lords had passed the Parliament bill in August, 1911, in which it, in effect, gave up its veto over legislation and after which time it entered, according to Gosse, "the crepuscule des dieux" (*TD*, 282). See letter 253, note 1.

4. James returned to Rye September 26. See letter 261. For the Gosses' "happy frisk," see *TD*, 281–82.

5. See letter 261.

261 / MS Leeds   Lamb House, Rye, Sussex.
                                             September 27*th* 1911.

Dear Mrs. Nelly!

I wired you last night after getting home & finding your so good letter here along with Edmund's. A stupid fatality had attended them: the Reform Club is closed for cleaning, &, instead of being delivered straight as they should have been, they had gone on to the Devonshire (where the Reformers go at this time,) & thence stupidly been sent on to Rye by the person acting for the R.C. porter.[1] (I had not come back from Scotland, & after some brief delay he had so despatched them). When on reaching town (Monday night) I found nothing from you I took a taxi up to your house (Tuesday a.m.) to see if you *were* back—& there learnt you were to return that evening.[2] It seemed to me impossible to assault you at such an hour—travel worn & weary & in the sanctity of your reunion with your household gods, & meanwhile a necessity had arisen, of a very urgent sort, for me to get back here as soon as possible. To wait over & see you tonight, coming home Thursday *as* that 1st moment, had a grave disadvantage for me—so I came off in the afternoon, & found it, on reaching home, well that I did. But I cursed my luck when I also found how I had missed your letters. That had been a sad bungle—but I have only 1/2 come back to practical life. Forgive this long story & believe me all rueful & regretful. Believe, too, with me that I should have had but 1/2 joy of seeing you so indiscreetly & unquietly—& that our meeting is but scantly deferred. I shall have to come up again at an early, a very early day, & if the day doesn't hurry forward I shall give it a great helpful lift. It shall be at the 1st possible hour. I long for our reunion, I hang faithfully about you both, & all, & I am, dear Mrs. Nelly, affectionately yours

Henry James

1. See letter 260.
2. The Gosses returned September 26 from a trip to Savoy and France.

262 / MS Library of Congress   Lamb House, Rye, Sussex.
                                               September 28*th*, 1911

My dear Gosse.

I have written to that best friend of ours who is nearest you—
expressing all my regret for my frustrated visit, which is to be, however, but very briefly delayed.[1] But, apart from that particular immi-
nence, is it unthinkable or impossible to you that you should come
down to *me* for a couple of nights on some early day—as early a one
as possible? You have been on your absences, I know, & you may
have others, more connected with their Lordships, & even with their
Ladyships, in near view; but if you were able none the less to
squeeze me in[,] it would give me the greatest pleasure. Any day
would do—before October 10*th*. Would Saturday 7*th* by any miracle
find you free? The weekend, however, has no *special* advantage for me
if you could manage *any* other pair of nights next week. Note the
hysterical intensity of my italics. A poor couple of hours at "the Terrace" would—& will—be charming in their degree; but for all we
shall have to say after so long a really endless jaw is required, & here
we may achieve it so conveniently. Allons, un bon mouvement, as
they say at Coppet (ah how I want to hear about *that*!)—write me
that I may enjoy you some day (meet you by the 4.25 p.m. down
some day) between this coming Saturday (though that I scarce dare
to hope for)—& October 10*th* as aforesaid. Saturday 7*th* would
indeed be felicitous—though not in the least prescribed. Voyons—!

                                               Yours all faithfully
                                               Henry James

P.S. I have treasures of lurid revelations for you, both oral & docu-
mented, about Fanny Stevenson, "Aunt Maggie," Henley, &c.,
&c.—such as these celibate walls alone may listen to![2] So you see.
Let this fetch you a little.

   1. See letter 261.
   2. For Fanny Stevenson, Robert Louis Stevenson's widow, and William Ernest
Henley, the British poet and editor, see letter 32 and letter 188, note 3, respectively.
"Aunt Maggie" may refer to another member of the Stevenson circle; though Margaret Stevenson was the name of the writer's mother, the reference probably is not to
her. Gosse visited James before October 26. See letter 263.

263 / MS Leeds   Reform Club,
                                                             Pall Mall. S.W. [London]
                                                             October 26*th* 1911.
My dear Gosse.

   I shall rejoice to come on *Monday* evening next, 30*th*, at 9 o'clk; &
then I will tell you all. I haven't yet your letter sent to Rye—but it
will infallibly arrive. I have your cool faint faded *Denmark*—which is
like the reading of very charming old letters, & which I *taste* very
much.[1] But I am still tasting it—in a large spoonful a day, & have but
waited to write to you till I licked the ladle, if not the platter, clean. I
long to *converse* again—better than this, & better than when you were
with me last, for I am another creature now—thanks to the sense of
having broken with that dismal hibernation. *That* was what was the
matter with me, & now I have migrated, & never again—![2] But, as I
say, I will tell you all, & am

                                                             Yours always
                                                             Henry James

   1. Edmund Gosse, *Two Visits to Denmark, 1872, 1874* (London, 1911).
   2. James is thinking of the long period of his illness in 1910 (January to July), of
his hurried trip to America with his dying brother in August, of the long period in
America after William's death (August, 1910, to July, 1911), and of his present
"migration" from Rye. Gosse had apparently visited him earlier in the month. For
James's invitation, see letter 262.

264 / MS Leeds   Reform Club
                                                             Pall Mall. S.W. [London]
                                                             Nov: 6*th* 1911
My dear Gosse.

   I thank you very kindly for your word about Thornycroft's little
studio-flat—which I went this afternoon to see.[1] I am sorry to say
that it is not a practicable, or even very desirable retreat—much too
small for me, practically without a kitchen or accommodation for servants, with only one room to sit & eat & work in, & neither tube nor
train nor cabstand nor omnibus at all near or handy. But I thank you
none the less—experience & observation are so precious; & am on an
excellent footing here for staying as I am till light breaks & ships—
otherwise shillings—come in. I must wait—& am but too thankful to
be able to wait comfortably. I hope you have prospered & enjoyed, &
am yours with renewed acknowledgments, ever,

                                                             Henry James

1. For Hamo Thornycroft, the well-known sculptor and Gosse's old friend, see letter 6, note 1. James was looking for a larger "perch" in London, but was not willing to settle for anything less than what he wanted. He eventually settled in Chelsea in January, 1913. For some of James's difficulties in leasing this flat, see letters 281–83.

265 / MS Cambridge   The Reform Club [London]
                                              [December 18, 1911]

Dear Nelly Gosse.

Alas, alas I've just gone & booked myself—in some uncertainty as to what would become of me.[1] I was (*had* been) thinking of going home, but that collapsed from dreariness, & then I had a genial invitation (for the evening here in town I mean,) & was 2 or 3 days ago formally committed. I'm very sorry indeed that it isn't to *you*, & came within an ace of writing to put it to you. Then I was overridden by the conviction that you would certainly be off somewhere with their lordships & ladyships—& only wanted to spare you the pang of rejecting me. And now you open your arms—& it's all crooked & sad. But I will ask you for a less compromised evening soon—before I go to the country (home for a week or two) on Jan 1st.[2] Express me kindly to Edmund & to the young things—assure them of my vain tears—& let me count on the early compensation aforesaid. I will wire you an appeal at some calmer hour. Yours all & always

Henry James

1. Nevertheless, James dined with the Gosses and "the daughters" on Christmas Eve, as he subsequently informed W. E. Norris on January 5, 1912: "It was very pleasant & peaceful & I came away without a scar—from a perfectly bloodless field. He is the *rarest* person for 'being himself' & striking punctually his very own hour, however, & the mixture in him of ability (that is activity,) & levity is quite indescribable. The levity is as incurable as the activity is irrepressible, & his virtues are like tricks & pranks, though I'm not sure the latter are always like virtues! His great present prosperity goes much to his head, I am told, socially speaking—by which I mean goes exorbitantly to his tongue, & yet there is something in him which keeps that apparently from doing him the last injury. May he come through—for his retirement is more or less within sight—without accident befalling. Your remarks about him are of a perfect justice—he dances the tight-rope (& across Niagara) under a special Providence. His levity, really, most *generally* saves him." Although Lubbock printed part of this letter in *LHJ*, II, 211–13, the above passage was excised and is printed here from the original (Yale).
2. James actually returned to Rye December 30. See the same letter to Norris in *LHJ*, II, 211.

266 / MS Leeds   The Reform Club [London]
                                                          Jan: 30*th* 1912[1]

My dear Gosse.

How sad the situation—with your State captivity (the romance of the old scaffold & axe just tingeing it) & my very *embrouillé* condition for Thursday. I sit to Sargent all that a.m. for a charcoal drawing, & my nephew whom I go to meet this a.m. at Euston—(he arrives with his new bride from N.Y. &, as an aspiring painter will much profit, I hope) is to assist at the sitting.[2] This means that we stop to luncheon afterwards—& that the whole series of hours, to 3 or 3.30, will be much compromised. I much regret it, though not in general good just now for much out-*lunching*—I work in far Chelsea very strenuously till 1.45—& that much interferes.[3] May I not come one of these evenings to join the family circle in the Park? I am keeping as disengaged as possible—I will ask you for a date as soon as the immediate flurry of my care for my young & appealing relations is over. Yours all faithfully

Henry James

1. Printed in *HJL*, IV, 600–601. It is possible that James is wrong about this date, for Monday occurred on January 29 in 1912. See letter 267.
2. John Singer Sargent's charcoal drawing had been commissioned by Edith Wharton. The "aspiring painter" is William James (1882–1961), and his new bride is Alice Runnells. For James's letter to Runnells concerning her engagement to William, see *HJL*, IV, 582–83.
3. Theodora Bosanquet, James's amanuensis, had arranged for two rooms near her flat in Chelsea so that James could dictate his work to her there. The rules of the Reform Club forbade the admission of women to members' rooms. See James's letter to her in *HJL*, IV, 589, 590.

267 / MS Leeds   The Reform Club [London]
                                                          Monday p.m. [January 30? 1912][1]

My dear Gosse.

I'm afraid I incommoded you by some unconscious delay—& even in my note of this a.m. didn't, I fear, explain that I had got it only late yesterday p.m. on my return from a week-end in Surrey spent wholly in bed (so deadly sick was I with a bad cold at going) & which left me unfit & inapt to put pen to paper till this p.m. If your letter had lain here since Saturday p.m. I am sorry—I left on Saturday at 4—& my capture of it was delayed. But above all I regret the impediment of Thursday; I shall soon reach out to you, & am yours always & ever

Henry James

1. Dated by the reference to letter 266. James presumably is wrong about the day. January 30 occurred on Tuesday in 1912. Of course, he may be right about the day and wrong about the date. There is, alas, no envelope to provide a postmark.

268 / MS Leeds   The Reform Club
                                         Pall Mall. S.W. [London]
                                         February 5th 1912[1]

My dear Gosse.

I brace myself—not (for you will frown!) to say No, but literally (& though I quake in every limb as I form the letters,) to say Yes! I hate it but I will do it; I fear it but I will brave it; I curse it but I will wreathe it in smiles: all for *you*—essentially & desperately for You only. I shall make up my distracted mind between 2 things: A shy at the subject of (as who should say) "The Browning of one's Youth"; or, quite differently, a go at "The Ring & the Book as a Novel" (or perhaps better "The Novel in the Ring & the Book.") I predominate toward the latter.[2] I have had & still have a villainous sick cold, & am presently (9. p.m.) going dinnerless to bed; but for which & my feeling thereby a certain lack of confidence in my powers; a nervousness about these immediate next days, I should now name you an evening for the family circle—that is propose you your choice of Thursday or Friday at 9. Suppose indeed you let me do that then if you choose;— & Friday is perhaps safest—I shall know how the case stands in time to notify you promptly—I mean with all solicitude.[3]

Will you please express to Pinero how much I am touched & gratified by his having let his decision depend in any degree on mine?[4] All & always yours

Henry James

1. Printed in *HJL*, IV, 601–602.
2. Gosse, on behalf of the Academic Committee of the Royal Society of Literature, had invited James to speak at the Browning Centenary on May 7, 1912. James eventually decided to call his address "The Novel in *The Ring and the Book*." This piece appeared in *Transactions of the Royal Society of Literature*, 2nd ser., XXXI, Pt. IV (1912), 269–98 (rpr. in *Browning's Centenary*, 1912). A revised text was published in *Quarterly Review*, CCXVII (July, 1912), 68–87, and collected in *Notes on Novelists* (1914).
3. Two days later James had to change his plans. See letter 269.
4. Arthur Wing Pinero (1855–1934), the well-known author of *The Second Mrs.*

Tanqueray (1893) and other plays, was scheduled to talk on Browning and the theater. See *HJL*, IV, 602*n*.

269 / MS Leeds   The Reform Club [London]
                                                       February 7*th* 1912

My dear Gosse.

I have been, alas, most disgustedly unwell since I wrote you, & had yesterday to go to bed, at noon, & really try to get better. My success is imperfect & I must scramble this afternoon down *home* to be there taken care of in better conditions than are possible here.[1] I hope a very few days will serve—but I am meanwhile unable to my great sorrow to come in to you Friday.[2] I must wait till next week— or some easier hour. My Browning matter looms doubly formidable to me under this visitation[3]—but I am hopefully, even while hopelessly, yours

                                                       Henry James

  1. "Down *home*," of course, is Lamb House, Rye.
  2. See letter 268.
  3. See letter 268 and note 2 of that letter.

270 /MS Leeds   The Reform Club
                                                       Pall Mall. S.W. [London]
                                                       2.26.1912

My dear Gosse

I hadn't seen Mrs. Williams for long years, but find myself shocked to think of her distant—but I hope not (in spite of your wife's non-arrival in time) altogether unattended or lonely death.[1] I remember thinking of her, recalling her, with particular satisfaction & sympathy (such was the gentle image she had left me) when you told me of certain things a few years ago. Nelly is indeed now in that vale of the shade where (when one has been of a company or cluster) it becomes only a question of which of the others—? And as these things successively happen there is a great chill. So I think of her with tenderest participation. I could come any night next week after *Monday*. Perhaps she & Tessa will then have come back—if they don't in any case stay. Or had I better wait till they do come back. I am really better—& will come on a sign from you[.][2] Ever your
                                                       Henry James

  1. Emily Epps Williams, Mrs. Gosse's sister, had recently died.
  2. For James's illness, see letter 269.

271 / MS Leeds   The Reform Club [London]
                                          March 13*th* 1912

My dear Gosse.

I rejoice to hear from you that you believe my letter will have
made a difference. But even if it hasn't made enough of one as yet I
suppose there is nothing in the constitution of the A.C. to prevent us
from keeping *at* it.[1] Yes, there is an inevitability, though I don't think
there ought to be an invinceability in the sensitive surface of an
Academy—but it ought to be sensitive to absences as well as pres-
ences, & the thing is here to work *that* sensibility.

I will come in soon again *nuitamment* with great pleasure—when
the others are back.[2] Yours always

                                          Henry James

1. For the efforts of James and Gosse to persuade H. G. Wells (1866–1946) to
accept election as a fellow of the Royal Society of Literature, see letters 272–75.
2. See letter 270.

272 / MS Leeds   The Reform Club [London]
                                          March 20*th* 1912

My dear Gosse.

Wells's attitude is indeed tiresome, & I shall at once go at him on
the subject; but I was more or less suspicious of what he might do—I
was really prepared in advance.[1] I nevertheless hold that we have
done the right & only thing in electing him: we are in the position
not that we would have done so *if* &c—but that we *have* absolutely
done so, & that on *his* head alone therefore &c—. I accordingly
thought it a mistake to sound him in advance, that is to come to him
with any *if*. His reply might have prevented us, & it was not for us to
be prevented. Now we are absolutely *en règle*. I shall write to him
this afternoon—I have waited on purpose till he should be heard
from, & I will do my best & even ask to see him.[2] But I have my fear
that if he is associated with Arnold Bennett in the matter there may
[be] trouble & complication.[3] A.B. *is* a distinct complication. But
you shall hear, & I am yours in a shared disgust

                                          Henry James

1. See also letters 271, 273–75.

2. For James's letter to Wells of March 20, see *HJL*, IV, 607–608.

3. Arnold Bennett (1867–1931), the English novelist, was best known at the time as author of *The Old Wives' Tale* (1908) and the first two books of the Clayhanger series.

273 / MS Leeds   The Reform Club [London]
                                                     March 22*d* 1912

My dear Gosse.

I wrote to Wells just after last writing to you—but this a.m. I have a note from Mrs. H.G. to say that recognising my initialled envelope, she wishes to tell me that he has gone away for "a few days," for quiet & work, & will meantime have no letters—till he comes back.[1] There will thus be a delay in hearing from him—& we must leave it so. I *shall* hear—in time—though exactly to what (perhaps insuperable) tune—I see abysses in it—but I see abysses everywhere—I shall then be able to let you know. Let us live meanwhile as we can (& I'm bound to say I think it's quite horribly interesting!) & me be through everything yours always

Henry James

P.S. I hope *ces dames* are happily back.[2] If so my love to them.

1. For James's letter to Wells of March 20, see *HJL*, IV, 607–608. For more on Wells and the academic committee, see letters 271, 272, 274, 275.

2. Mrs. Gosse and Tessa, her oldest daughter, had attended the funeral of Emily Epps Williams. See letter 270.

274 / MS Leeds   105, Pall Mall, S.W.
                                                     [Reform Club, London]
                                                     March 25*th* 1912

My dear Gosse.

This enclosed is what I have received from Wells this p.m.—very amiable to us in general & to H.J. in particular, but I think inexorable & immutable.[1] It is very much what at bottom I feared—though I also considerably hoped; & I am glad, in spite of it, that we invited him, & did it just as we did: our hands are clean thereby & our position unassailable. The letter, I need scarcely say, is but for your private cognition—& I should be glad if you will return it. You may wonder—but in spite of it (& in spite of my 1*st* letter being copious &, as it were, eloquent,) I have, I almost blush to confess, written this evening *again*.[2] But I expect very little from it—I wrote all privately & individually. The case—for it's a case!—amuses me, so to speak, & I hope it won't aggravate *you*. For when all's said we—you & I, I mean—understand him—though he doesn't *us*! However, good night & yours all faithfully

                                             Henry James

P.S. I think I must now write a little explicatively, to the Secretary. But that will be easy.[3]

1. For Wells's letter to James of March 25, 1912, see Leon Edel and Gordon N. Ray (eds.), *Henry James and H. G. Wells: A Record of Their Friendship, Their Debate on the Art of Fiction, and Their Quarrel* (London, 1958), 159–60.
2. See *HJL*, IV, 608–10.
3. The secretary of the Royal Society of Literature was Percy W. Ames (1853–1919), who held office from 1890 to 1917.

275 / MS Library of Congress   105, Pall Mall, S.W.
                                                [Reform Club, London]
                                                March 26*th*, 1912[1]

My dear Gosse.

This is just a word, on receipt of your note, to conclude the H.G.W. episode—of which absolutely nothing more will come. I wrote him last evening again, in an appealing & remonstrant way—it *interested* me to do so, & I thought there was perhaps a chance, or the fraction of one, of his response to two or three things I could still, with some point, I felt, say to him.[2] But his only response was to come in to this place (Reform Club) today at luncheon time (I think he came on purpose to find me,) & let me see that he is absolutely immoveable. I had a good deal of talk with him—though not, his refusal once perfectly *met*, about that, & without his having answered or met in any way any one of the things my second letter (any more for that matter than any of those my first) had put to him; & my sense that he is right about himself & that he wouldn't at all do among us from the moment our whole literary side—or indeed any literary side anywhere—is a matter of such indifference to him as I felt it to be today—to an extent I hadn't been aware of. He has cut loose from literature clearly—practically altogether: he will still do a lot of writing probably—but it won't be *that*.[3] This settles the matter, & I now agree with you settles it fortunately. He *had* decently to decline, and I think it decent of him to have felt that. My impression of him today cleared up many things. But I will tell you more about it. I won't pretend to speak of other things—to you who are at the centre of the cyclone. How interesting you will be—& how interesting everything else will be (God help all interests!) when you are next seen of yours always

Henry James

1. Printed in Edel and Ray (eds.), *Henry James and H. G. Wells*, 163*n*, and reprinted in *HJL*, IV, 610–11.
2. See *HJL*, IV, 608–10.
3. Wells indicated that he had "insurmountable objections to Literary or Artistic Academies as such" (Edel and Ray [eds.], *Henry James and H. G. Wells*, 160).

276 / MS Leeds

Reform Club
Pall Mall. S.W. [London]
May 1st 1912

My dear Gosse.

I am much obliged to you for your good offices—& Dr. Ames has sent me half-a-dozen cards. It appears indeed that he *had* already sent me a dozen; but to my country address,* a bit obscurely & perversely, as all my recent communications with him had been on *this* basis.[1] However, all is well; the errant ones will come back to me today, & I shall have plenty.

I am torn between the fear of "trying your patience"—collectively—on the 7*th* & not making my remarks constitute a *sufficient* recreational performance—which is wholly what I see them as. Still, I must "jouer le tout" *for* "le tout"—of which I'm so glad you're a helpful part. Yours always

Henry James

* where my servants will have kept them back, by a stupid mistake, as "circulars"—which they never forward—

1. The cards referred to were to admit guests to James's address on Browning at the Royal Society of Literature on May 7. For Dr. Ames, see letter 274, note 3. For James's talk, see letter 268, note 2, and letter 277. For further comment on the occasion by James, see his letter to Edith Wharton of May 12, 1912 (*HJL*, IV, 615).

277 / MS Duke

Reform Club [London]
May 12*th* 1912

My dear Gosse.

George Prothero has asked me for my Browning address to publish *as* an address, as the Centenary address delivered to our body, in the Quarterly; & I shall—for I am sending it to him—of course not dream of its not being accompanied with that definite description of it—which sticks straight out, moreover, of the form & text themselves.[1] So you may indeed "depend" on yours all faithfully—and Academically—[2]

Henry James

1. Sir George W. Prothero (1848–1922) and his wife, Fanny, were good friends to James. Prothero was editor of the *Quarterly Review* from 1899 to 1922. James's address on Browning subsequently appeared in revised form in the *Quarterly Review* in July, 1912. See letter 268, note 2.

2. A reference to the Academic Committee of the Royal Society of Literature, for which the address had been prepared. See letter 268.

278 / MS Cambridge

Reform Club
Pall Mall, S.W. [London]
July 9*th* 1912

My dear Nelly Gosse—

I will come at 8 o'clk. tomorrow Wednesday with the greatest pleasure.

I heard but yesterday (apparently long after the fact,) of the graceful public decoration lately incurred by Edmund; & am impatient (please tell him) to show him how I can match it by private remark.[1] So let his modesty brace itself, & believe me yours & his all faithfully

Henry James

1. Gosse had received the C.B. (Companion of the Bath) earlier in the year. See *EG*, 501. James could "match" Gosse honor for honor, for two weeks earlier, on June 26, Oxford had conferred upon him the honorary degree of doctor of letters (*HJ*, V, 480).

279 / MS Harvard

Lamb House, Rye.
July 12*th* 1912

My dear Gosse.

I brought the last Fortnightly away with me yesterday from town, & it was not till I addressed myself to reading your paper on Rousseau, as I came down here—to find it so interesting & *nourri* & exhaustive of its subject & freshly illustrative of the unspeakable British mind!—that I took in the fact, of which I had no[t] otherwise become aware, that you had but a few days, as it were, ago had the romantic adventure of that journey to Geneva & that brilliant feat of delivery there.[1] No inkling of this had, in all the turmoil [of] those London days & of my own ever-difficult conditions, reached me—which made for my so losing two nights ago the opportunity of turning you on the subject, every item of which I should have liked to hear from you in its vividness & as to which I only ask myself why you didn't guess & feed my latent appetite. I recall that I gave you the chance in saying that I was going to get the Fortnightly—*for* your article; & I rub my eyes with wonder at your withholding from me the rich recital. Let me have it from you yet—I mean on our next meeting, even with whatever lapse of freshness; since I trust I don't attribute to it an interest out of tune with the actual & so conceivable facts. It must have been curious to see the Genevese so handsomely at home; & a great & rare feat in itself your ability to discourse in that idiom in so public & sustained a manner—on the energy & brilliancy of which I congratulate you. Much should I have liked—had you but left me less in the dark—to have from you the "psychology" of such a conscious effort; all of which represents for me great arrears to make up.

Have you read the paper entitled The Five Thousand in the Review?—which is really very prettily & drolly & perceptively done; though there wd. have been so many more morals to point than he *has* pointed.[2] The comparative psychology *there*—! I find myself enchanted to get back here again after 9 months absence; or rather after almost 2 years; & am already much better than I was on Wednesday night. I almost forget, in absence, how sweet this little place really is. It makes me fairly glad that the door of travel is shut to me. I much hope that later on, when London shrinks, or has shrunken, & your time is more spacious, you will be of the mind to come to me for a couple of nights. I shall try to bring you to it. But good-bye now. Yours all-faithfully

Henry James

P.S. In reading this over I am moved to wonder if there be some subtle, or in any degree sinister, mystery in your having let me go unfed, or unbeguiled, with your Geneva news—in the sense, I mean, of its having mislaid any désagrément or discomfort (which heaven forbid!) that has made the reminiscence thankless to you. Please give me so far an account of the matter as to say that that's *not* absurdly the case; I don't ask for more now.[3]

About to address you in the Decorated style I take this out again to tell you of the pleasure with which I heard the other day, for the 1st time (so little do I scan the newspapers,) of its having accrued to you. (Hugh Walpole last Sunday at Ockham let me know of it.)[4] I didn't at once formally felicitate because I was writing at once to Mrs. Nelly about Wednesday—& I therein told her how pleasant a thing I could easily suppose it for your house.[5] Pleasantly & conveniently ornamental & complementary (as well as *i*ment-) I hope you find it in fact: I know naught closely about those baubles, but yours I have always taken for the most chaste & refined. So be delicately saluted!

1. Edmund Gosse, "Rousseau in England in the Nineteenth Century," *Fortnightly Review*, July 1, 1912, pp. 22–28. This is a printing of Gosse's address "delivered, in French, before the Société Jean-Jacques Rousseau, at Geneva, on June 28, 1912, upon occasion of the bicentenary of the birth of Rousseau."
2. James means John F. Macdonald's "The Five Hundred," *Fortnightly Review*, July 1, 1912, pp. 165–72, an essay on the visit of 500 English children to Paris.
3. For James's response to Gosse's explanation (Gosse apparently did *not* deliver the paper himself), see letter 280.
4. In 1909 James had met Hugh Walpole (1884–1941), the son of an Anglican bishop and an aspiring young novelist, through A. C. Benson and had formed an immediate friendship with him. See, for example, James's letter of June 5, 1909, to Benson in *HJL*, IV, 522–23.
5. For James's comment on Gosse's C.B., see letter 278, note 1.

280 / MS Leeds   105, Pall Mall, S.W.
                                    [Reform Club, London][1]
                                    July 15*th* 1912

My dear Gosse.

I thank you for your letter, which so agreeably clears up the mystery. I somehow sniffed in that there was one—& don't think it "rude" if I now say that I am glad it was no worse! I felt my dilemma: on the one hand the note that the address had been "delivered" (though I don't see what less or other term you cld. have used,) & on the other the fact that nothing of the weird or exotic experience overflowed from you, formed the materials of a puzzle—soothingly solved.[2] But it now comes to me that there can't have been much joy in putting together an allocation that you weren't to allocate—though I don't know exactly whether your not dealing with it personally made the more or the less of a sorrow of your having such a story of England to tell. However, all's well that ends well—for the coming up to the scratch of your statement by itself may be called ending well.

I pity you in the torrid town—at least till I think of your vespertinal terrace over the Park. I have nothing here as good as that—& decidedly I wasn't born for high thermometers. I'm affraid [sic] it was high at Cambridge yesterday—& old Lodges don't sound airy. However, the new perspectives are perhaps the very playground of the breezes. What a playground at any rate for those of Arthur's spirit.[3] I gape at all these sumptuous newses of almost everybody—opulence seems so to rage about us!—& quaff again my barley-water.[4] When certain present complications have abated here—& above all when I have got settled to work again, so that it seems to be going on a bit— I shall unfailingly ask you for a couple of nights, & am yours all faithfully

Henry James

1. Although James is using the address of the Reform Club in London, he is writing from Rye, for he had come "down here [Rye] from town but five days ago," as he informed his nephew, Henry James, Jr., on July 16, 1912 (*LHJ*, II, 239). See also letter 279.
2. See letter 279. Gosse apparently did not read the paper himself.
3. For Arthur C. Benson, now fellow of Magdalene College, Cambridge, see letter 107, note 2.
4. James had tried various diets over the years, and barley-water had frequently been a part of his daily regimen.

281 / TLS Virginia   Lamb House, Rye, Sussex.
                                          7th. October, 1912.[1]

Dictated.
My dear Gosse.
Forgive this cold-blooded machinery—for I have been of late a stricken man, and still am not on my legs; though judging it a bit urgent to briefly communicate with you on a small practical matter. I have had quite a Devil of a summer, a very bad and damnable July and August, through a renewal of an ailment that I had regarded as a good deal subdued, but that descended upon me in force just after I last saw you and then absolutely raged for many weeks.[2] (I allude to a most deplorable tendency to chronic pectoral, or, more specifically, anginal, pain; which, however, I finally, about a month ago, got more or less the better of, in a considerably reassuring way.) I was but beginning to profit by this comparative reprieve when I was smitten with a violent attack of the atrocious affection known as "Shingles"— my impression of the nature of which had been vague and inconsid-

erate, but to the now grim shade of which I take off my hat in the very abjection of respect. It has been a very horrible visitation, but I am getting better; only I am still in bed and have to appeal to you in this graceless mechanical way. My appeal bears on a tiny and trivial circumstance, the fact that I have practically concluded an agreement for a Flat which I saw and liked and seemed to find within my powers before leaving town (No. 21 Carlyle Mansions, Cheyne Walk, S.W.) and which I am looking to for a more convenient and secure basis of regularly wintering in London, for the possibly brief remainder of my days, than any I have for a long time had. I want, in response to a letter just received from the proprietors of the same, to floor that apparently rather benighted and stupid body, who are restless over the question of a "social reference" (in addition to my reference to my Bankers), by a regular "knock-down" production of the most eminent and exalted tie I can produce; whereby I have given them your distinguished name as that of a voucher for my respectability—as distinguished from my solvency; for which latter I don't hint that you shall, however dimly, engage![3] So I have had it on my conscience, you see, to let you know of the liberty I have thus taken with you; this on the chance of their really applying to you (which some final saving sense of their being rather silly may indeed keep them from doing.) If they do, kindly, very kindly, abound in my sense to the extent of intimating to them that not to know me famed for my respectability is scarcely to be respectable themselves! That is all I am able to trouble you with now. I am as yet a poor thing, more even the doctor's than mine own; but shall come round presently and shall then be able to give you a better account of myself. There is no question of my getting into the Flat in question till some time in January; I don't get possession till Dec. 25th, but this preliminary has had to be settled. Don't be burdened to write; I know your cares are on the eve of beginning again, and how heavy they may presently be.[4] I have only wanted to create for our ironic intelligence the harmless pleasure of letting loose a little, in a roundabout way, upon the platitude of the City and West End Properties Limited, the dread effulgence of their Lordships; the latter being the light and you the transparent lantern that my shaky hand holds up.[5] More, as I say, when that hand is less shaky. I hope all your intimate news is good, and am only waiting for the new vol. of the Dictionary with your

Swinburne, which a word from Sidney Lee has assured me is of maximum value.[6] All faithful greeting.

Yours always
Henry James

1. Included in *LHJ*, II, 246–48.
2. James had visited the Gosses in London on Wednesday, July 10. See letters 278 and 279.
3. James moved to 21 Carlyle Mansions the following January and subsequently died there February 28, 1916. For the story of his experience with the proprietors of Carlyle Mansions and of Gosse's part in the affair, see letters 282–83 and Gosse's letters to James of October 10, 11, and 12 in *LL*, 335–38. On October 11, Gosse expressed his delight "at having brought the silly landlords fluttering, like pheasants, to your feet" (*LL*, 337).
4. Gosse was still librarian of the House of Lords.
5. Although James often teased Gosse about his social climbing among their "lordships and ladyships," he took advantage of Gosse's position on this occasion and others. See, especially, his appeal to Gosse in 1915 when he sought British citizenship (letter 311).
6. Gosse's sketch of Swinburne appeared in the *DNB Supplement, 1901–1911* (1912). Sir Sidney Lee (1859–1926) was sole editor of the *Dictionary of National Biography* from 1891 on. He was also the author of a life of Shakespeare (1898).

282 / TLS Virginia   Lamb House, Rye, Sussex.
                                          October 10th., 1912.[1]

Dictated.
My dear Gosse,

Your good letter of this morning helps to console and sustain.[2] One really needs any lift one can get after this odious experience. I am emerging, but it is slow, and I feel much ravaged and bedimmed. Fortunately these days have an intrinsic beauty—of the rarest and charmingest here; and I try to fling myself on the breast of Nature (though I don't mean by that fling myself and my poor blisters and scars on the dew-sprinkled lawn) and forget, imperfectly, that precious hours and days tumble unrestrained into the large round, the deep dark, the ever open, hole of sacrifice.[3] I am almost afraid my silly lessors of the Chelsea Flat *won't* apply to you for a character of me if they haven't done so by now; afraid because the idea of a back-hander from you reaching them straight, would so gratify my sense of harmless sport.[4] It was only a question of a word in case they *should* appeal; kindly don't dream of any such if they let the question rest (in spite indeed of their having intimated that they would thoroughly thresh it out.)

I receive with pleasure the small Swinburne—of so chaste and

charming a form; the perusal of which lubricated yesterday two or
three rough hours.[5] Your composition bristles with items and
authenticities even as a tight little cushion with individual pins; and,
I take it, is everything that such a contribution to such a cause
should be but for the not quite ample enough (for my appetite) con-
clusive estimate or appraisement. I know how little, far too little, to
my sense, that element has figured in those pages in general; but I
should have liked to see you, in spite of this, formulate and *resume* a
little more the creature's character and genius, the aspect and effect
of his general performance. You will say I have a morbid hankering
for what a Dictionary doesn't undertake, what a Sidney Lee perhaps
even doesn't offer space for. [6] I admit that I talk at my ease—so far as
ease is in my line just now. Very charming and happy Lord
Redesdale's contribution—showing, afresh, how *everything* about
such a being as S. becomes and remains interesting.[7] Prettily does
Redesdale write—and prettily will O.B. have winced; if indeed the
pretty even in that form, or the wincing in any, could be conceived of
him.[8]

I have received within a day or two dear old George Meredith's
Letters; and, though I haven't been able yet very much to go into
them, I catch their emanation of something so admirable and, on the
whole, so baffled and so tragic.[9] We must have more talk of them—
and also of Wells's book, with which however I am having extreme
difficulty.[10] I am not so much struck with its hardness as with its
weakness and looseness, the utter going by the board of any real self-
respect of composition and expression. Interesting to me, however,
your mention of his civil acceptance of your own reflections on the
matter; which I should have liked to see. What lacerates me perhaps
most of all in the Meredith volumes is the meanness and poorness of
editing—the absence of any attempt to project the Image (of character, temper, quantity and quality of mind, general size and sort of
personality,) that such a subject cries aloud for; to the shame of our
purblind criticism. For such a Vividness to go a-begging—and for a
Will Meredith to stand there as if he were dealing with it! When one
thinks of what Vividness would, in France, in such a case, have
leaped to its feet in commemorative and critical response! But there
is too much to say, and I am able, in this minor key, to say too little.
We must be at it again. I was afraid your wife was having another
stretch of the dark valley to tread—I had heard of your brother-in-

law's illness.[11] May peace somehow come! I re-greet, & regret, you all and am all faithfully yours

Henry James

1. Although included in *LHJ*, II, 248–50, and reprinted in *HJL*, IV, 628–29, I have used the manuscript as text.

2. For Gosse's letter of October 10, 1912, see *LL*, 336–37.

3. For James's shingles, see letter 281.

4. The lessors did apply to Gosse. In the letter mentioned in note 2 above, Gosse reported that "the foolish creatures *have* applied to me!! I have answered them according to their folly," he continued, "expressing in one breath reverence for you and contempt for them" (*LL*, 336).

5. Edmund Gosse, *The Life of Swinburne, with a Letter on Swinburne at Eton by Lord Redesdale* (London, 1912), a privately printed issue of Gosse's contribution to the *DNB Supplement* referred to in letter 281, note 6.

6. For Sidney Lee, see letter 281, note 6.

7. Algernon Bertram Freeman-Mitford, first baron Redesdale (1837–1916), had written Gosse some recollections of Swinburne's experience at Eton.

8. Oscar Browning (1837–1923), another contemporary of Swinburne's at Eton, whose reminiscences were challenged by Lord Redesdale.

9. W. M. Meredith (ed.), *The Letters of George Meredith* (2 vols.; London, 1912). William Maxse Meredith, the son of George Meredith, is the Will Meredith referred to later in the paragraph.

10. "Wells's book" is his novel *Marriage* (1912). Gosse had asked James about it in his letter of October 9 (*LL*, 336).

11. Gosse had mentioned in his letter of October 9 that Mrs. Gosse's "favourite brother, Washington Epps," was "dangerously, and no doubt fatally, ill," and in his letter of October 13, Gosse informed James that Epps "had died last night in his sleep. . . . Poor Nellie," he concluded, "has thus lost, within six months, three of those nearest to her" (*LL*, 338).

---

283 / TLS Virginia   Lamb House, Rye, Sussex.
October 11th., 1912.[1]

Dictated.

My dear Gosse.

Let me thank you again, on this lame basis though I still be, for the charming form of your news of your having helped me with my fastidious friends of the Flat. Clearly, they *were* to be hurled to their doom; for the proof of your having, with your potent finger, pressed the merciless spring, arrives this morning in the form of a quite obsequious request that I will conclude our transaction by a signature.[2] This I am doing, and I am meanwhile lost in fond consideration of the so susceptible spot (susceptible to profanation) that I shall have reached only after such purgations. I thank you most kindly for settling the matter.

Very interesting your note—in the matter of George Meredith. Yes, I spent much of yesterday reading the Letters, and quite agree with your judgment of them on the score of their rather marked non-illustration of his intellectual wealth. They make one, it seems to me, enormously *like* him—but that one had always done; and the series to Morley, and in a minor degree to Maxse, contain a certain number of rare and fine things, many beautiful felicities of wit and vision.[3] But the whole aesthetic range, understanding that in a big sense, strikes me as meagre and short; he clearly lived even less than one had the sense of his doing in the world of art—in that whole divine preoccupation; that whole intimate restlessness of projection and perception. And this is the more striking that he appears to have been far more communicative and overflowing on the whole ground of what he was doing in prose or verse than I had at all supposed; to have lived and wrought with all those doors open and publicly slamming and creaking on their hinges, as it were, than had consorted with one's sense, and with the whole legend, of his intellectual solitude. His whole case is full of anomalies, however, and these volumes illustrate it even by the light they throw on a certain poorness of range in most of his correspondents. Save for Morley (et encore!) most of them figure here as folk too little à la hauteur—! though, of course, a man, even of his distinction, can live and deal but with those who are within his radius. He was *starved*, to my vision, in many ways—and that makes him but the more nobly pathetic. In fine the whole moral side of him throws out some splendidly clear lights—while the "artist," the secondary Shakespeare, remains curiously dim. Your missing any letters to me rests on a misconception of my very limited, even though extremely delightful to me, active intercourse with him. I had with him no sense of *reciprocity*; he remained for me always a charming, a quite splendid and rather strange, Exhibition; so content itself to *be* one, all genially and glitteringly, but all exclusively, that I simply sat before him till the curtain fell, and then came again when I felt I should find it up. But I never *rang* it up, never felt any charge on me to challenge him by invitation or letter. But one or two notes from him did I find when Will Meredith wrote to me; and these, though perfectly charming and kind, I have preferred to keep unventilated. However, I am little enough observing that same discretion to *you*—![4] I slowly mend, but it's absurd how far I feel I've to come back from. Sore and strained has the horrid business left me. But nevertheless I hope, and in fact almost propose. Yours all faithfully

Henry James

1. Printed in *LHJ*, II, 250–52.
2. For Gosse's comment on James's "silly landlords," see his letters of October 10 and 11, 1912 (*LL*, 336–37).
3. Gosse's comment on Meredith is in his letter of October 10 (*LL*, 336–37). John Morley (1838–1923), author and politician, was the editor of the English Men of Letters series; and Leopold James Maxse (1864–1932) was the author of books on Germany and editor of the *National Review*.
4. Gosse had returned some of Meredith's letters for publication in the collection. Moreover, he also reviewed the edition, as he admitted in his letter of October 11 (*LL*, 337), though James did not know about the review when he dictated this letter. See letter 284.

284 / TLS Virginia   Lamb House, Rye, Sussex.
                                        October 13th., 1912.[1]

Dictated.

My dear Gosse.

This is quite a feverish flurry of correspondence—but please don't for a moment feel the present to entail on you the least further charge: I only want to protest against your imputation of sarcasm to my figure of the pin-cushion and the pins—and this all genially; that image having represented to myself the highest possible tribute to your biographic *facture*. What I particularly meant was that probably no such tense satin slope had ever before grown, within the same number of square inches, so dense a little forest of discriminated upright stems![2] There you are, and I hear with immense satisfaction of the prospect of another crop yet—this time I infer, on larger ground and with beautiful alleys and avenues and vistas piercing the plantation.[3]

I rejoice also to know of the M.P. article, on which I shall be able to put my hand here betimes tomorrow.[4] I can't help wishing I had known of it a little before—I should have liked so to bring, in time, a few of my gleanings to your mill. But evidently we are quite under the same general impression, and your point about the dear man's confoundingness of allusion to the products of the French spirit is exactly what one had found oneself bewilderedly noting. There are two or three rather big felicities and sanities of judgment (in this order;) in one place a fine strong rightly-discriminated apprehension and characterisation of Victor Hugo. But for the rest such queer lapses and wanderings wild; with the striking fact, above all, that he scarcely once in the 2 volumes makes use of a French phrase or ventures on a French passage (as in sundry occasional notes of acknowledgment and other like flights) without some marked inexpertness or gaucherie. Three or four of these things are even painful—they cause one uncomfortably to flush. And he appears to have gone to France, thanks to his second wife's connections there, putting in little visits and having contacts, of a scattered sort, much oftener than I supposed. He "went abroad," for that matter, during certain years, a good deal more than I had fancied him able to—which is an observation, I find, even now of much comfort. But one's impression of his lack of what it's easiest to call, most comprehensively, aesthetic curiosity, is, I take it, exactly what you will have expressed your sense of. He speaks a couple of times of greatly admiring a novel of Daudet's, "Numa Roumestan," with the remark, twice over, that he has never "liked" any of the others: he only "likes" this one![5] The tone is of the oddest, coming from a man of the craft—even though the terms on which he himself was of the craft remain so peculiar—and such as there would be so much more to say about. To a fellow-novelist who could read Daudet at all (and I can't imagine his not, in such a relation, being read with curiosity, with critical appetite) "Numa" might very well appear to stand out from the others as the finest flower of the same method; but not to take it as one of them, or to take them as of its family and general complexion, is to reduce "liking" and notliking to the sort of use that a spelling-out schoolgirl might make of them. Most of all (if I don't bore you) I think one particular observation counts—or has counted for me; the fact of the non-occurrence of one name, *the* one that aesthetic curiosity would have seemed scarce able, in any real overflow, to have kept entirely shy of: that of Balzac, I mean, which Meredith not only never once, even, stumbles against, but so much as seems to stray within possible view of. Of course one would never dream of measuring "play of mind," in such a case, by any man's positive mentions, few or many, of the said B.; yet when he *isn't* ever mentioned a certain desert effect comes from it (at least it does to thirsty *me*) and I make all sorts of little reflections. But I am making too many now, and they are loose and casual, and you mustn't mind them for the present; all the more that I'm sorry to say I am still on shaky ground physically; this odious ailment not being, apparently, a thing that spends itself and clears off, but a beastly poison which hangs about, even after the most copious eruption and explosion, and suggests dismal relapses and returns to bed.[6] I am really thinking of this latter form of relief even now—after having been up but for a couple of hours. However, don't "mind" me; even if I'm in for a real relapse *some* of the sting will, I trust, have been drawn. Yours rather wearily

Henry James

P.S. I *am* having, it appears—Sunday 2 p.m.—to tumble back into bed; though I rose but at 10.! [In James's hand]

1. Printed in *LHJ*, II, 252–55.
2. For the figure of the pincushion, see letter 282, and for Gosse's response, see his letter of October 11, 1912: "You crush me by the wit of your comparing my little Swinburne thing to a pincushion! But remember, that a pincushion was all I was asked, or allowed, to make" (*LL*, 337).
3. This is apparently a reference to Gosse's book-length life of Swinburne that eventually appeared in 1917.
4. "The M.P. article" is Gosse's review of the letters of George Meredith for the *Morning Post*, October 14, 1912. See also letters 282 and 283.
5. Alphonse Daudet, *Numa Roumestan* (1881). James knew Daudet and his work very well. For other references to Daudet, see, for example, letter 67, note 1.
6. James has been "ravaged and bedimmed" by a severe case of shingles. See his remarks in letters 281–83.

285 / TLS Virginia   Lamb House, Rye, Sussex.
                                        October 15th., 1912.[1]

Dictated.
My dear Gosse.

Here I am at it again—for I can't not thank you for your two notes last night and this morning received. Your wife has all my tenderest sympathy in the matter of what the loss of her Brother costs her. Intimately will her feet have learned to know these ways. So it goes on till we have no one left to lose—as I felt, with force, two summers ago, when I lost my two last Brothers within two months and became sole survivor of all my Father's house. I lay my hand very gently on our friend.[2]

With your letter of last night came the Cornhill with the beautifully done little Swinburne chapter.[3] What a "grateful" subject, somehow, in every way that gifted being—putting aside even, I mean, the value of his genius. He is grateful by one of those arbitrary values that dear G.M. [George Meredith], for instance, doesn't positively command, in proportion to his intrinsic weight; and who can say quite why? Charming and vivid and authentic, at any rate, your picture of that occasion; to say nothing of your evocation, charged with so fine a Victorian melancholy, of Swinburne's time at Vichy with Leighton, Mrs. Sartoris and Richard Burton: what a felicitous and enviable image they do make together—and what prodigious discourse must even more particularly have ensued when S. and B. sat up late together after the others![4] Distinct to me the memory of a Sunday afternoon at Flaubert's, in the winter of '75–'76, when Maupassant, still *inédit*, but always "round," regaled me with a fantastic tale, irreproducible here, of the relations between the two Englishmen, each other, and their monkey![5] A picture the details of which have faded for me, but not the lurid impression. Most deliciously Victorian that too—I bend over it all so yearningly; and to the effect of my hoping "ever [even?] so" that you are in conscious possession of material for a series of just such other chapters in illustration of S., each a separate fine flower for a vivid even if loose nosegay.

I'm much interested by your echo of Haldane's remarks, or whatever, about G.M.[6] Only the difficulty is, of a truth, somehow, that *ces messieurs*, he and Morley and Maxse & Stephen and two or three others, Lady Ulrica included, really never knew much more where *they* were, on all the "aesthetic" ground, as one for convenience calls it, than the dear man himself did, or where *he* was; so that the whole history seems a record somehow (so far as "art and letters" are in question) of a certain absence of point on the part of everyone concerned in it. Still, it abides with us, I think, that Meredith was an admirable spirit even if not an *entire* mind; he throws out, to my sense, splendid great moral and ethical, what he himself would call "spiritual," lights, and has again and again big strong whiffs of manly tone and clear judgment. The fantastic and the mannered in him were as nothing, I think, to the intimately sane and straight; just as the artist was nothing to the good citizen and the liberalised bourgeois. However, lead me not on! I thank you ever so kindly for the authenticity of your word about these beastly recurrences (of my disorder.) I feel you floated in confidence on the deep tide of Philip's experience and wisdom.[7] Still, I *am* trying to keep mainly out of bed again (after 48 hours just renewedly spent in it). But on these terms you'll wish me back there—and I'm yours with no word more

Henry James

1. Printed in *LHJ*, II, 255–57, and reprinted in *HJL*, IV, 630–31. My text differs in a number of particulars from either printing.

2. For the death of Washington Epps, Mrs. Gosse's brother, see letter 282, note 11. For the death of William James in August, 1910, see letter 259, and for the death of Robertson James (1846–1910), six weeks earlier in July, 1910, see James's letter to Edith Wharton in *HJL*, IV, 557.

3. Edmund Gosse, "Swinburne at Étretat," *Cornhill Magazine*, n.s., XXXIII (October, 1912), 457–68.

4. For Frederick Leighton, the British painter, see letter 130, note 1. Adelaide Kemble Sartoris (Mrs. Edward Sartoris) was the sister of Frances Anne Kemble Butler and a member of the famous acting family, and Richard Burton (1821–1890) was a British diplomat and the translator of the *Arabian Nights* (1885–88).

5. For the story of Maupassant and his tale of the monkey, see letter 286 and Gosse's letter to James of October 16, 1912, in *LL*, 339–40.

6. On October 14, Gosse reported that Richard Burdon, viscount Haldane (1856–1928) and lord chancellor (1912–1915), agreed with James on George Meredith (see letters 283 and 284). For Morley and Maxse, see letter 283, note 3. For Stephen, see letter 207, note 1. James added in his own hand the name of Stephen.

7. James is still having trouble with shingles, and Gosse apparently has discussed the ailment with his son Philip, a physician.

286 / TLS Library of Congress   Lamb House, Rye, Sussex.
                                                   October 17th., 1912.[1]

Dictated.

My dear Gosse.

It's very well invoking a close to this raging fever of a correspondence when you have such arts for sending and keeping the temperature up! I feel in the presence of your letter last night received that the little machine thrust under one's tongue may well now register or introduce the babble of a mind "affected"; though interestingly so, let me add, since it is indeed a thrill to think that I *am* perhaps the last living depositary of Maupassant's wonderful confidence or legend.[2] I really believe myself the last survivor of those then surrounding G.F. [Gustave Flaubert.] I shrink a good deal at the same time, I confess, under the burden of an honour "unto which I was not born"; or, more exactly, hadn't been properly brought up or preadmonished and pre-inspired to. I pull myself together, I invoke fond memory, as you urge upon me, and I feel the huge responsibility of my office and privilege; but at the same time I must remind you of certain inevitable weaknesses in my position, certain essential infirmities of my relation to the precious fact (meaning by the precious fact Maupassant's having, in that night of time and that general failure of inspiring prescience, so remarkably regaled me.) You will see in a moment everything that was wanting to make me the conscious recipient of a priceless treasure. You will see in fact how little I could have *any* of the right mental preparation. I didn't in the least then know that M. himself was going to be so remarkable; I didn't in the least know that *I* was going to be; I didn't in the least know (and this was above all most frivolous of me) that *you* were going to be. I didn't even know that the Monkey was going to be, or even realise the peculiar degree and *nuance* of the preserved lustre awaiting ces messieurs, the three taken together. Guy's story (he was only known as "Guy" then) dropped into my mind but as an unrelated thing, or rather as one related, and indeed with much intensity, to the peculiarly "rum", weird, macabre and unimaginable light in which the interesting, or in other words the delirious, in English conduct and in English character, are—or were especially then—viewed in French circles sufficiently self-respecting to have views on the general matter at all, or in other words among the truly refined and enquiring. "Here they are at it!"—I remember that as my main inward comment on Maupassant's vivid little history; which was thus thereby somehow more vivid to me about *him*, than about either our friends or the Monkey: as to whom, as I say, I didn't in the least foresee this present hour of arraignment!

At the same time I think I'm quite prepared to say, in fact absolutely, that of the two versions of the tale, the two quite distinct ones, to which you attribute a mystic and separate currency over there, Maupassant's story to me was essentially Version No. I. It wasn't at all the minor, the comparatively banal anecdote. Really what has remained with me is but the note of two elements—that of the Monkey's jealousy, and that of the Monkey's death; how brought about the latter I can't at all at this time of day be sure, though I am haunted as with the vague impression that the poor beast figured as having somehow destroyed *himself*, committed suicide through the spretae injuria formae.[3] The third person in the fantastic complication was either a young man employed as servant (within doors) or one employed as boatman, and in either case I think English; and some thin ghost of an impression abides with me that the "jealousy" was more on the Monkey's part toward him than on his toward the Monkey; with which the circumstance that the Death I seem most (yet so dimly!) to disembroil is simply and solely, or at least predominantly, that of the resentful and impassioned beast: who hovers

before me as having seen the other fellow, the jeune anglais or who-
ever, installed on the scene after he was more or less lord of it, and so
invade his province. You see how light and thin and confused are my
data! *How* I wish I had known or guessed enough in advance to be
able to oblige you better now: not a stone then would I have left
unturned, not an *i* would I have allowed to remain undotted; no analysis or exhibition of the national character (of *either* of the national
characters) so involved would I have failed to catch in the act. Yet I
do so far serve you, it strikes me, as to be clear about *this*—that,
whatever turn the dénouement took, whichever life was most luridly
sacrificed (of those of the two humble dependents) the drama had
essentially been one of the affections, the passions, the last *cocasserie*,
with each member of the quartette involved! Disentangle it as you
can—I think Browning alone could really do so! Does this at any
rate—the best I can do for you—throw any sufficient light? I recognise the importance, the historic bearing and value, of the most perfectly worked-out view of it. *Such* a pity, with this, that as I recover
the fleeting moments from across the long years it is my then active
figuration of the so tremendously *averti* young Guy's intellectual,
critical, vital, experience of the subject-matter that hovers before me,
rather than my comparatively detached curiosity as to the greater or
less originality of ces messieurs!—even though with this highly original they would appear to have been. I seem moreover to mix up the
occasion a little (I mean the occasion of that confidence) with
another, still more dim, on which the so communicative Guy put it
to me apropos of I scarce remember what, that though he had
remained quite outside of the complexity I have been glancing at,
some jeune anglais, in some other connection, had sought to draw
him into some scarcely less fantastic or abnormal one, to the necessary determination on his part of some prompt and energetic action
to the contrary: the details of which now escape me—it's all such a
golden blur of old-time Flaubertism and Goncourtism! How many
more strange flowers one *might* have gathered up and preserved!
There was something from Goncourt one afternoon about certain
Swans (they seem to have run so to the stranger walks of the animal
kingdom!) who figured in the background of some prodigious British
existence, and of whom I seem to recollect there is some faint recall
in "La Faustin" (not, by the way, "*Le* Faustin," as I think the printer
has betrayed you into calling it in your recent Cornhill paper.)[4] But

the golden blur swallows up everything, everything, but the slow-crawling, the too lagging, loitering amendment in my tiresome condition, outdistanced by the impatient and attached spirit of yours all faithfully

\ *Henry James*

1. Printed in *LHJ*, II, 257–61, and reprinted in *HJL*, IV, 632–34, but the present text, based upon the original typescript, differs in a number of particulars from either printing.
2. See letter 285.
3. Virgil, *Aeneid*, I, 27.
4. See letter 285, note 3.

287 / TLS Library of Congress   Lamb House, Rye, Sussex
November 19th., 1912.[1]

Dictated
My dear Gosse.

I received longer ago than I quite like to give you chapter and verse for your so-vividly interesting volume of literary Portraits;[2] but you will have (or at least I earnestly beg you to have) no reproach for my long failure of acknowledgement when I tell you that my sorry state, under this dire physical visitation, has unintermittently continued, and that the end, or any kind of real break in a continuity of quite damnable pain, has still to be taken very much on trust.[3] I am now in my 8th. week of the horrible experience, which I have had to endure with remarkably little medical mitigation—really with none worth speaking of. Stricken and helpless, therefore, I can do but little, to this communicative tune, on any one day; which has been also the more the case as my admirable Secretary was lately forced to be a whole fortnight absent—when I remained indeed without resource.[4] I avail myself for this snatch of one of the first possible days, or rather hours, since her return. But I read your book, with lively "reactions", within the first week of its arrival, and if I had then only had you more within range should have given you abundantly the benefit of my impressions, making you more genial observations than I shall perhaps now be able wholly to recover. I recover perfectly the great one at any rate—it is that each of the studies has extraordinary individual life, and that of Swinburne in particular, of course, more than any image that will ever be projected of him. This is a most interesting and charming paper, with never a drop or a slackness

from beginning to end. I can't help wishing you had proceeded a
little further *critically*—that is, I mean, in the matter of appreciation
of his essential stuff and substance, the proportions of his mixture,
etc.; as I should have been tempted to say to you, for instance, "Go
into that a bit *now!*" when you speak of the early setting-in of his
arrest of development etc. But this may very well have been out of
your frame—it might indeed have taken you far; and the space
remains wonderfully filled-in, the figure all-convincing. Beautiful too
the Bailey, the Horne and the Creighton—this last very rich and fine
and touching. I envy you your having known so well so genial a creature as Creighton, with such largeness of endowment. You have done
him very handsomely and tenderly; and poor little Shorthouse not to
the last point of tenderness perhaps, but no doubt as handsomely,
none the less, as was conceivably possible.[5] I won't deny to you that
it was to your Andrew Lang I turned most immediately and with
most suspense—and with most of an effect of drawing a long breath
when it was over.[6] It is very prettily and artfully brought off—but
you would of course have invited me to feel with you how little you
felt you were doing it as we should, so to speak, have "really liked."
Of course there were the difficulties, and of course you had to defer
in a manner to some of them; but your paper is of value just in proportion as you more or less overrode them. His recent extinction, the
facts of long acquaintance and camaraderie, let alone the wonder of
several of his gifts and the mass of his achievement, couldn't, and still
can't, in his case, not be complicating, clogging and qualifying circumstances; but what a pity, with them all, that a figure so lending
itself to a certain amount of interesting *real* truth-telling, should,
honestly speaking, enjoy such impunity, as regards some of its idio-
syncrasies, should get off so scot-free ("Scot"-free is exactly the
word!) on all the ground of its greatest hollowness, so much of its
most "successful" puerility and perversity. Where I can't but feel that
he *should* be brought to justice is in the matter of his whole "give-
away" of the value of the wonderful chance he so continually enjoyed
(enjoyed thanks to certain of his very gifts, I admit!)—give-away, I
mean, by his *cultivation*, absolutely, of the puerile imagination and
the fourth-rate opinion, the coming round to that of the old apple-
woman at the corner as after all the good and the right as to any of
the mysteries of mind or of art. His mixture of endowments and
vacant holes, and "the making of the part" of each, would by them-

selves be matter for a really edifying critical study—for which, however, I quite recognise that the day and the occasion have already hurried heedlessly away. And I perhaps throw a disproportionate weight
on the whole question—merely by reason of a late accident
or two; such as my having recently read his (in two or three respects
so able) Joan of Arc, or Maid of France, and turned over his just-
published (I think posthumous) compendium of "English Literature",
which lies on my table downstairs.[7] The extraordinary inexpensive-
ness and childishness and impertinence of this latter give to my sense
the measure of a whole side of Lang, and yet which was one of the
sides of his greatest flourishing. His extraordinary *voulu* Scotch pro-
vincialism crowns it and rounds it off; really making one at moments
ask with what kind of an innermost intelligence such inanities and
follies were compatible. The Joan of Arc is another matter of course;
but even there, with all the accomplishment, all the possession of
detail, the sense of reality, the vision of the truths and processes of
life, the light of experience and the finer sense of history, seem to me
so wanting, that in spite of the thing's being written so intensely *at*
Anatole France, and in spite of some of A.F.'s own (and so different!)
perversities; one "kind of" feels and believes Andrew again and again
bristlingly yet *bêtement* wrong, and Anatole sinuously, yet oh so
wisely, right!

However, all this has taken me absurdly far, and you'll wonder
why I should have broken away at such a tangent. You had given me
the opportunity, but it's over and I shall never speak again! I wish *you*
would, all the same—since it may still somehow come in your way.
Your paper as it stands is a gage of possibilities. But good-bye—I
can't in this condition keep anything up; scarce even my confidence
that Time, to which I have been clinging, is going, after all, to help. I
had from Saturday to Sunday afternoon last, it is true, the admirably
kind and beneficent visit of a London friend who happens to be at
the same time the great and all-knowing authority and expert on
Herpes; he was so angelic as to come down and see me, for 24 hours,
thoroughly overhaul me and leave me with the best assurances and
with, what is more to the point, a remedy very probably more effective than any yet vouchsafed to me. (I mean Henry Head, F.R.S.,
the eminent neurologist—whose position will be known to Philip.)[8]
When I do at last emerge I shall escape from these confines and come
up to town for the rest of the winter. But I shall have to feel differ-

ently first, and it may not be for some time yet. It in fact can't *possibly* be soon. You shall have then, at any rate, more news—"which," à la Mrs. Gamp, I hope your own has a better show to make.[9] Yours all, and all faithfully,

Henry James

P.S. I hope my last report on the little Étretât legend—it seems (not the legend but the report) of so long ago!—gave you something of the light you desired.[10] And how I shld. have liked to hear about the Colvin dinner & its rich chiaroscuro.[11] He has sent me his printed—charming, I think—speech: "the best thing he has done" [The last two sentences of the postscript are in James's hand.]

1. Printed in *LHJ*, II, 274–78, and reprinted in *HJL*, IV, 637–40.
2. Edmund Gosse, *Portraits and Sketches* (1912), a collection of essays on Swinburne and others, had just been published by Heinemann.
3. James is still contending with shingles. See letter 281.
4. For Theodora Bosanquet, see, for example, letter 266, note 3.
5. Philip James Bailey (1816–1902) was the author of *Festus* (1839, 1845, 1889); Richard Henry Horne (1803–1884), poet and dramatist, was best known for *Orion* (1843); Mandell Creighton (1843–1901), ecclesiastical historian and bishop of Peterborough and, later, of London, penned biographies of Cardinal Wolsey (1888) and Queen Elizabeth (1896); and Joseph Henry Shorthouse (1834–1903) was the author of *John Inglesant* (1880) and other novels and was a good friend of Gosse's.
6. For Andrew Lang (1844–1912), poet, translator, editor, and essayist, see letter 51, note 2. Both James and Gosse, at times, acknowledged the faults James outlines here. See, for example, Gosse's response to these remarks on November 27, 1912 (*LL*, 341).
7. Lang's *The Maid of France* appeared in 1908 and his *History of English Literature* in 1912. Anatole France (1844–1924), French novelist, had also published a book on Joan of Arc in 1908: *Vie de Jeanne d'Arc*.
8. For Henry Head (1861–1940), see also James's remarks to Edith Wharton in his letter of December 4, 1912, in *HJL*, IV, 643–44. Philip Gosse was a physician.
9. Sarah Gamp is in Dickens' *Martin Chuzzlewit*.
10. See letter 286.
11. For Sidney Colvin, see letter 17, note 2. He had just retired from his position at the British Museum.

288 / TLS Leeds   21, Carlyle Mansions,[1]
                                                     Cheyne Walk. S.W.
                                                     June 18*th* 1913.

Dictated
My dear Gosse.
    Saturday, with all thanks (as well as all excuses for this blest machinery) would be very proper for me; save for the fact that I find

myself pledged to be motored in the afternoon, in sore reluctance of spirit, down to Osterley; and that I may not get back absolutely in time to reach you by 7.45.[2] But if you can give me till 8, with a few minutes' grace, I think there will be no difficulty about it; so I take your agreement for granted and gladly engage to come. I salute you all *caramente*, and am yours all faithfully

Henry James

1. James had moved to 21 Carlyle Mansions the previous January. See letter 281, note 3.
2. James had just visited the Gosses on June 16. See Gosse's letter of June 17 to Thomas Hardy in *LL*, 345.

289 / MS Leeds   Lamb House, Rye, Sussex.
                                    Aug. 11*th* 1913.

My dear Gosse.

I hasten to respond to your kind note—& with the liveliest sense of having exactly *yearned* for a pretext to make you a sign of life—of better life, fortunately, than I shld. have been able to make you out of that dread Seasonal, treasonal, pressure of Town, which, for all my precautions & limitations, broke upon me at last in foaming surges. It wasn't that I "did things," or *could* do them; but that, my powers being so shrunken, & my margin so small, the undone vast even left me spent & shaken—so that at the end, just as I was about to return hither, & my servants (female) had already gone I was taken of a sudden with so bad & prolonged an attack of my infirmity that for the 1*st* time in my life I swooned away for pain (I was *consciously* sure I was dying;) & woke up but later on to find the Dr. from round the corner, the *docteur du coin*, bending over me anxiously & backed by my brave little presence-of-mind domestic.[1] My real Dr., from further off, instantly clapped a nurse upon me, my parlour-maid came back, & with 3 days in bed I recuperated sufficiently to come down here on the 4*th* where, after 36 hours, I began to rebound still higher. It is of *that* I have wanted to tell you, my extreme amendment since, rather than of the previous difficulties. Rejoice with me in the former & set me the example of disbelieving with me in the recurrency of the latter sufficiently to exorcise them away. But what a gush of fatuous self-reference! Your own small spurt of this—toward yourself & Nelly—makes me wonder & deplore. You speak clearly of painful things—& how one enters, temporally speaking, the dark zone of these! A German Kur, in the thick dim air, must emit to you, in prospect, almost a genial glow. May you find one that suits you both at once, & you not to have merely to hang about through hers, & *her* to stamp with rage through yours (this, please, with absolutely *no* reflection on her charity!) My very delightful American niece (my brother William's sole daughter, aet. 26) is with me till the September end, & her eldest brother comes over from the Continent presently for a shorter time.[2] They infinitely comfort & sustain me—but if they didn't fill my small house how I shld. like, before you go abroad, to catch you by the sleeve! You must absolutely let me do so after you come back. May your own sky meanwhile very comfortably clear. I wish this to your wife affectionately, & am yours & hers always & ever

Henry James

1. James's infirmity is heart trouble. For other references to angina and pectoral difficulties, see letter 281, for example, and letter 295.
2. Margaret Mary (Peggy, 1887–1952) and Henry (Harry, 1879–1947) James, Jr. According to Edel, however, Peggy and her youngest brother, Aleck (Alexander Robertson James, 1891–1946), were staying at Lamb House in August (*HJL*, IV, 681*n*).

290 / MS Leeds   Lamb House, Rye, Sussex.
                                              October 31*st* 1913.[1]

My dear Gosse.

When some little time since I read in the Times your admirable letter of reply to Galsworthy's portentous allocation on the Propriety of Books I was much moved to write you in lively congratulation—& if I didn't I fear it was because my poor physical consciousness has the effect of keeping all initiative, for me, all doing of anything whatever, extremely low.[2] Here I am doing *this*—but see how long it has taken me to come to it. And I have the incentive that I have more lately read your further remarks on the censorship matter at the Meeting of the other day, & seen thereby you were at home again—I had made out before that you were still on the Continent.[3] Thus I seem in some sense supported & uplifted toward telling you that I find your expressions on the great subject exactly in the right & happy note & tone, incisive without solemnity, & as effectually explosive, even though gently so, of the great Galsworthiness, as need have been desired. Your letter was a charming ironic thing. And

I am somehow brought into touch with you by receiving a notice of
the Dinner to dear old Brandes which has my full sympathy even
though I mayn't hope to be present at it—dinners being impossible
to me now.[4] It gives me pleasure none the less to see you concerned
in it & to think that I may thus a little later on be perhaps able to
give you a message to brave B. This will be helped by the fact that I
am now arranging, so far as I can arrange anything, to get up to
town, for the winter, from one week, or almost one day, to the other.
(I am planning hard for the 15th.) Weren't it for this I should say to
you won't you come down for a couple of nights even yet?—&
should have said it before, on learning, by inference, your return, if I
hadn't been, frankly, so inapt, physically speaking, for any easy or
graceful discharge of the office of host even in the very modest conditions to which it is restricted with me. I have had to live all summer
& autumn with the last unsociability—the fruit of the blighted initiative. But the rigour of this here has now become very depressing &
an early return to Carlyle Mansions quite urgently indicated.[5] I hope
you both have come home much refreshed & reinforced. I am very
eager to hear your story, & shall make a prompt overture for it as
soon as I am in town. I send my best love to Mrs. Nelly & am yours
& hers

all faithfully
Henry James

1. Printed in *TD*, 285–86.
2. For the letter by John Galsworthy (1867–1933), see the *Times*, October 3, 1913,
p. 9. Gosse's reply appeared on October 7, 1913, p. 9. The question concerned the
restriction of the circulation of novels by libraries.
3. The Gosses had returned from Wiesbaden, Germany, Gosse informed James
on October 31, "nearly four weeks ago" (*TD*, 286–87).
4. James had known Georg Morris Cohen Brandes (1842–1927), the Danish critic
and scholar, for many years. James, by the way, did manage to attend a lecture by
Brandes. See letter 292, note 1.
5. James's flat in London.

291 / MS Leeds   Lamb House, Rye, Sussex.
                                                November 1st 1913.[1]

My dear Gosse.

   This is a very sad showing. Yet I am glad not to have remained
longer in ignorance of your troubles. I sounded at one time—a number of years since—the depths of sciatica; but have been pretty well

ever since out of peril of it—so take to yourself the comfort that one *can*, that one does, cast it out. Sweet indeed the uses of starvation & incredible, on occasion, the bliss of barley water. But I greatly rejoice that you climb back to life & liberty even up the steep stair, or whatever it is, of enteric—& I'm not sure I know even what *that* is, in its manifestations.[2] But you will luridly tell me, & you have meanwhile all my sympathy—over your horrid time. I think it must have been inflicted on you a little as a makeweight to the dazzling glory of your ruban rouge, of which I hadn't heard, but which, lest you should go mad with these worldly lusts, a thoughtful providence has been inspired to handle a bit coolingly.[3] It is really very interesting—how graceful is the French tradition, dear old thing! How much you will have to tell me—& how I count the days to it! How solemn indeed, also, are ces messieurs!—were *we* so solemn at their ages? [4] Certainly they won't be so gay at ours. I am the gayer for hearing that your wife made a good cure. Do you now the same. Yours all faithfully

Henry James

1. Printed in *TD*, 287–88.
2. In his letter of October 31, 1913, Gosse had informed James that he had been "attacked by sciatica," had been "felled by an enteric attack," and had concluded that his doctors saw "a gouty condition in all these ailments" (*TD*, 286–87).
3. In the above-mentioned letter, Gosse noted that he had been made an "Officier of the Legion d'Honneur."
4. In his letter of October 31, Gosse had referred to Galsworthy as one of the "clever young men" of the day. See also letter 290, note 2.

292 / MS Leeds   21 Carlyle Mansions
                                         Cheyne Walk S.W.
                                         November 24*th* 1913.

My dear Gosse.

The ticket for tomorrow night is "to hand"; I am sending the money for it; & I heartily thank you for your kind good office in the matter. They appear to have sent me an excellent seat—with a near view of the chair—& the table.[1] I here renew my eager acceptance of your invitation to lunch with you at the House of Lords on Tuesday 2*d* at 1.30 precisely.[2] Yours all faithfully

Henry James

1. Apparently the ticket is for a lecture to be delivered by Georg Brandes, over which Gosse was to preside. See *HJ*, V, 495. For Brandes, see letter 290, note 4.
2. Gosse had been librarian of the House of Lords since 1904.

293 / MS Cambridge   21 Carlyle Mansions
                                         Cheyne Walk S.W.
                                         December 7*th* 1913.

My dear Nelly Gosse.

You have sent me a honeyed card for the 15*th*—but this, alas, is a melancholy word to excuse myself in form. You will easily understand, I think, that if you miss my substantial presence in the glittering throng that will then hang upon your smile, this can only be because my impaired conditions absolutely make the midnight revel, or any kind of nocturnal circulation, impossible for me. But I don't despair of still arranging with you for some more intimate & diurnal round when you won't wholly withhold that smile from yours all faithfully[1]

Henry James

1. James settled for Christmas dinner with the Gosses. See Gosse's letter to Max Beerbohm, "Christmas Night, 1913," in *LL*, 347.

294 / MS Duke   21 Carlyle Mansions
                                         Cheyne Walk S.E.
                                         December 13*th* 1913.[1]

My dear Gosse.

I think it's very kind of you to have diverted to my enjoyment & happy possession one of the so few copies of your charming monograph on Lady Dorothy—which I am delighted to have in spite of my sense of perhaps doing so to the privation of some more immediately entitled candidate.[2] I had known her long, but it was in all the earlier time that I saw her most, & our contacts were more & more interspaced (inevitably,) as the years went on. I greatly liked her—it was impossible, I agree with you, not to do that; & she was probably one of the few cases of so positive a personality to the liking of whom there was (putting rare idiots aside) no exception whatever. I am not sure I am of your mind about the reach & *portée* of her undemonstrable Wit; but this isn't to differ with you explicitly about that. You saw her hundreds of times more often than I, & measured much better her possibilities. The difficult little report to make—difficult for *roundness* of the image—you seem to me to have made so easily & naturally, enumerating *all* her incoherent little marks, & giving her full vividness & colour. She had no *Unity*—any more than the contents of a pocket; & one might have called her the capacious Pocket of Society! But for something now to serve her memory *instead* of the missing fact—I mean of unity—& do as a substitute for it, her friends will have to go to your Letter.

At the moment I received that[,] I was on the edge of writing to you about another matter—in the way of an appeal for a small particular assistance; & now this evening comes in a prompting to another matter *still*—& for the moment more important. But I will speak of the literally prior one first.

I am putting together into a volume some critical papers done at intervals during the last 16 or 18 years, & should like to enclose among them the 2 Introductions furnished some dozen(?) years ago to the Balzac & the Flaubert volumes of a certain Century of French Romance that you edited for Heinemann—if you & he assent to this.[3] I have had no copy of either book since immediately after they were published, but I have got hold of one of the Balzac, & my question is as to whether you happen still to possess one of the *Mme Bovary*, which I am assured in Bedford St. is out of print & almost *introuvable*. If you do possess one & can let me have a sight of it I shall be deeply indebted; in that case I shld. have the Introduction copied & carefully return the volume—in case of there being no obstacle to my reprinting the Prefaces. My impression would be that the Series is this considerable time now an *extinct* actuality (if ever a very living one;) & the unrenewed out-of-print phase of the Flaubert seems to confirm this as well as to remove any objection to a possible *concurrence*. The volumes are not dated, but I see them as at least 10 years old. (I have no date of my Preface-producing.)

The other, the deeply disconcerting, matter is that I just hear from Hugh Walpole of the deplorable & ludicrous blunder committed by the Chiswick Press in sending out the Notices for the 3 days of the Sargent Portrait.[4] I am dismayed & disgusted, & regard the grotesque accident as without excuse on the part of the Press. I went over with Hugh Walpole to the place & was present at his interview & understanding with the employee that we saw there & who professed an absolute competence for the job; & nothing could have been more explicit & emphatic & lucid & detailed than Hugh's instructions to him & than his apparently thorough grasp of them. Percy L. had left with Hugh a definite statement of what was to be done, & Hugh put this before the man in its absolute integrity &

with no sort of superficiality or hurry—we were there a long time over it; after which we departed with the blest sense that all would be right. How wrong the wretched people made it I am infinitely shocked to hear—I haven't seen the thing—& am haunted with the sense that with my presence at the transaction it oughtn't conceivably to have happened. I am therefore possessed with the idea that I ought absolutely, somehow or other, to make up for the accident (fortunately as obvious as a gross misprint in the *Times*—there are so many now!) to the members of the Committee & the recipients. Thinking of *how*, I see 2 courses—one of which is to go over as early as possible tomorrow & have simply new Notices sent out in the correct form; & the other to be present at the Studio on each of the 3 days & personally apologise to each of the Subscribers who come for the ridiculous manner in which their information was given them. If I was physically more fit I wd. at once decide to attend there for this purpose the *whole* of each of the times. As it is, a combination of the 2 forms of reparation strikes me as really possible. Certainly I shall go to Tite St. betimes on *Tuesday* & do my best to propagate my amends.[5] It is *the* thing, I see. And I can go again for a while each other day, & possibly even recruit adjutants.

Sunday. I have kept this over to this p.m., & the interval has confirmed me in the better & more "graceful" of the 2 ideas above mentioned. I shall be at Tite St. on Tuesday as much as possible—& as much as possible after, & there pour over the occasion such explanatory balm, that nothing but the balm will linger in any memory & what it was "about" be quite forgotten. My only regret is that *you* won't, I feel sure, be able to find time to come & be drenched. Perhaps Nelly or Tessa or Sylvia will. Yours & theirs all & ever

Henry James

1. Printed in *SR*, 587–89.

2. Edmund Gosse, *Lady Dorothy Nevill: An Open Letter* (London, 1913). Since the *Letter* was privately printed in a run of thirty-two copies, James is aware that others who had known Lady Dorothy better might be more entitled to a copy than he.

3. James's critical introductions to Balzac's *The Two Young Brides* and Flaubert's *Madame Bovary* had appeared in "A Century of French Romance," a series published by Heinemann and edited by Gosse. Gosse immediately sent a copy of the Flaubert volume (see letter 295), and the two introductions subsequently appeared in *Notes on Novelists* (1914).

4. A group of James's English friends (Gosse had been a chief instigator) had arranged to honor his seventieth birthday on April 15, 1913, by giving him a golden bowl (a silver-gilt porringer) and arranging for a portrait by James's old friend John

Singer Sargent. When Sargent refused any fee for the painting, a bust by Derwent
Wood (1871–1926) was added. Percy Lubbock and Hugh Walpole were handling
many of the details of the affair. At this time Sargent was ready to display the portrait, and the Chiswick Press failed to head the invitations to the exhibition properly.
See also letter 295 and *HJ*, V, 484–89.
  5. Sargent's studio was in Tite Street in Chelsea. James "put himself on exhibition" for three days in "reparation" for the press's blunder.

295 / TC Leeds   21 Carlyle Mansions,
                                                   Cheyne Walk, S.W.
                                                   December 18*th*, 1913.[1]

My dear Gosse,
  The exquisite incident in Tite Street having happily closed, I have
breathing time to thank you for the goodly Flaubert volume, which
safely arrived yesterday and which helps me happily out of my difficulty.[2] You shall receive it again as soon as I have made my respectful
use of it.
  The exhibition of the Portrait came to a most brilliant end to-day,
with a very great affluence of people. (There have been during the
three days an immense number.) It has been a great and charming
success—I mean the View has been; and the work itself acclaimed
with an unanimity of admiration and, literally, of *intelligence*, that I
can intimately testify to. For I really put myself on exhibition beside
it, each of the days, morning and afternoon, and the translation (a
perfect Omar Khayyam, *quoi*!) visibly left the original nowhere. I
attended—most assiduously; and can really assure you that it has been
a most beautiful and flawless episode. The slight original flaw (in the
title) I sought to bury under a mountain of flowers, till I found that
it didn't in the least do to "explain it away" as every one (like the dear
Ranee) said: they exclaimed too ruefully "Ah, don't tell me you
didn't *mean* it!"[3] After which I let it alone, and speedily recognised
that it was really *the* flower—even if but a little wayward wild-
flower!—of our success. I am pectorally much spent with affability
and emissions of voice, but as soon as the tract heals a little I shall
come and ask to be heard in your circle.[4] Be meanwhile at great
peace and ease, at parfect [*sic*] rest about everything.
                                              Yours all faithfully
                                              Henry James

  1. Printed in *LHJ*, II, 348–49.
  2. See letter 294 and note 3 of that letter.
  3. Margaret Brooke, ranee of Sarawak (1850–1936), was the widow of the former
rajah of Sarawak and an old friend of James's.

4. James frequently refers to his heart disease in terms of "pectoral" difficulties. See letter 281, for example.

296 / MS Leeds

21 Carlyle Mansions
Cheyne Walk S.W.
Jan. 21st 1914[1]

My dear Gosse

Have you any recollection of once going down the River to dine with me at Greenwich long years ago?—in company with Maupassant, Du Maurier, & one or two others.[2] One of those others was Primoli, who had come over from Paris with Maupassant; & on whom you made, you see, the ineffaceable impression.[3] He wrote to me the other day to ask your address—it has lasted all these years—& you meanwhile—infidèle—! I have seen him since then from time to time; he is a very amiable & rather singular person—I will tell you more about him some other time. He made on dear du Maurier, I remember, an impression that remained—though not on your sterner nature! He is a Bonaparte (exceedingly so in looks;) that is his Mother was a Bonaparte Princess, & his father, I think, the offspring of the marriage of one (I *believe* they were cousins.) He lives in Paris & in Rome, & if you write him a word in Rome address him M. le Comte *Joseph* P. There is another brother. Voilà.—

I rejoice most heartily in your authentic word for your wife's brave state—I send my prompt blessing on it. Also I take comfort, of the greatest, in Percy L. [Lubbock]'s Viennese cheer. Let us indeed meet again before the year is too sensibly (or senselessly) older. I am waiting to give effect to what we talked of the other day only till I can learn that Hagberg W. is back.[4] When I last inquired he wasn't—it was a few days since. But now—! Yours all faithfully

Henry James

1. Printed in *HJL*, IV, 698–99. The present text, based upon the manuscript, differs in details.
2. The dinner at Greenwich took place on August 12, 1886. See letter 21 and James's letter to Du Maurier in *HJL*, III, 129. For Du Maurier, see letter 2, note 4.
3. Count Joseph-Napoléon Primoli (1851–1927) was the son of Charlotte Bonaparte and the grandson of Joseph Bonaparte, the brother of Napoleon I.
4. Charles T. Hagberg Wright (1862–1940), librarian of the London Library from 1893 to 1940. Gosse was a member of the library committee for many years (*EG*, 321). James may have been trying to make reparation for a "delinquency" he describes in a letter to Wright of October 31, 1913 (*LHJ*, II, 339–41).

297 / MS Leeds   21 Carlyle Mansions
                                                    Cheyne Walk S.W.
                                                    Jan: 29: 1894 [1914?]]¹

My dear Gosse

I should sooner have thanked you for your information about
Hagberg W.—had I not been sick & sore with a bad congested throat
that was blighting to all initiative, & eke to the decently responsive. I
write you as it is in the panting interval between gargle & sprays &
(saving your presence,) vainly-attempted expectoration.

I have seen Hagberg & talked with him, & all is happily settled. I
shall now proceed to the consequent act.²

Your story of R. is curious & I suppose characteristic—but he has
long since become so dim & mythic to me as to have ceased at all to
be a peg for the attribute or the anecdote to hang on: the predicate
offers itself but the nominative is thin air & it therefore drops to the
ground.³ The behaviour would doubtless be extraordinary if it could
only be *his*. And what a pity for such extraordinary behaviour to be
wasted!—though doubtless only for my own dried-up apprehension!

What comes home to me much more is the unspeakably painful
impression of the state of poor tragic Bobby R., who has taken me
(all earnestly sympathetic) into the confidence of his trouble, &
whose nervous demoralization (which he must & his friends must,
absolutely stand up against in him) affects me as rending the heart.⁴
He tells me you have been extraordinarily & admirably kind & helpful to him—& indeed what a state of things when the "authorities"
are open to influence from a man with D.[Douglas]'s infamous history! Its [*sic*] like something of the ugly age of English legal or judi-
cial history—the 17*th*–18*th* century. But you will tell me more about
it, occasion offering, & meanwhile B.R. *haunts* me. What a torture,
truly, is the faculty of pity.⁵ Yours always

Henry James

1. Although James gives 1894 as the year, this letter is dated by letter 296, where-
in Hagberg Wright is mentioned. Other internal references also support the 1914
date.

2. See letter 296, note 4.

3. The reference is presumably to André Raffalovich (1864–1934), the author of a
book on homosexuality who had recently sent his edition of *Last Letters of Aubrey
Beardsley* (1904) to James. See James's letter of November 7, 1913, to Raffalovich and

his comments on Raffalovich in a letter to Logan Pearsall Smith of November 17, 1913 (*HJL*, IV, 691–92 and 693–94, respectively).

4. Robert B. Ross (1869–1918), a Canadian who attended Cambridge University and subsequently became a friend of Oscar Wilde's and eventually his literary executor, was also a friend of Gosse and James's. For Gosse's friendship with Ross during this period, see *EG*, 360–63. In 1913 Ross had begun to have further difficulties with Lord Alfred Douglas. (The Wilde trials had been concluded in 1895.) After various allegations appeared concerning Ross and young boys, Ross brought Thomas W. H. Crosland (1868–1924) to trial in June, 1914, on a charge that he conspired with Lord Douglas to have Ross charged "with having committed certain acts," Lord Douglas being out of the country and unavailable for trial. Crosland was eventually found not guilty, but upon Lord Douglas' return to England the following October, Douglas was arrested for slander on a warrant based on information from Ross. In the trial that followed, the jury could not reach a verdict, Ross pleaded *non prosqui*, Douglas was acquitted and discharged, and Ross, in effect, was ruined. Gosse had testified in behalf of Ross, provided money, and used his influence in behalf of Ross on several occasions. See *EG*, 360–62.

5. See also James's comment on "sympathy" in letter 236.

298 / MS Leeds   21 Carlyle Mansions
                                                                        Cheyne Walk S.W.
                                                                        February 2*d* 1914

My dear Gosse.

The spectre of our demoralized Dreyfus has been haunting me so hard that your news of the Affair is indeed a relief & a recreation. And yet wasn't it a turn of the mad wheel that one felt sure *must* come, by the very law of madness & vice—with whatever other wild revolutions may ensue further? *Pace* poor Dreyfus's alarm there *couldn't* be any consistent keeping-up on ground so quaking as Esterhazy's improvised springboard, or any guarantee of his opulent Egeria's nerve against alarms more felt & menacing than any she could administer. Vicious passion & poisonous petulance haven't *character* enough behind them to go straight, & of the p.p. Egeria must *easily* have provoked an assault, full in her face, from the moment she began in the least to discriminate. *Poor* Egeria, for all her opulence, I think really. But now I hope Dreyfus will really pull himself together a bit—it's important for him.[1]

What various & striking observations you are indeed à même to make! Yours in much envy

H.J.

1. For the Dreyfus affair and James's views of it, see, for example, letter 162, in which James said in 1899 that he lived "in the great shadow of Dreyfus." See also James's letters to Elizabeth Cameron of October 15, 1898, and to William and Alice

James of August 9 [1899] (*HJL*, IV, 82–83, and 113–16, respectively). In 1914 Dreyfus was still trying to clear his name.

299 / MS Leeds   21 Carlyle Mansions
                                                         Cheyne Walk S.W.
                                                         May *1st* 1914

My dear Gosse.

   I thank you kindly for your telegram on the Chantrey purchase—it gives me (the purchase) the greatest pleasure, & my enjoyment of your sympathy is proportionate. When Derwent Wood's work was seen by a great many people in the autumn I didn't quite feel it adequately appreciated, & greatly admiring it myself, was rather disappointed. I was *sure* it was fine, & I now greatly rejoice for him that the judges & even the jealous colleagues have done him such signal justice—besides rejoicing for myself & for the vision of my "long rest" here (or hereabout,) by the Thames-side of which these 2 years have made me so fond.[1]
   Meanwhile the weeks & the months go without our conversing— thanks largely, no doubt, to the fact that the social scene (where we might perchance sometimes meet if the case were other) is more & more out of the question for me. But isn't it thinkable for you that you might on some near day, shaking *yourself* also free of social scenery, squeeze in luncheon with me here alone, at *1.45?*—which wd. bridge a little this constant chasm. Won't you choose some day after Tuesday next if possible—& note that I am telephonable?[2] We really are hugely in arrears, & I am yours always & ever so faithfully
                                                         Henry James

   1. For Derwent Wood, see letter 294, note 4. The bust of James by Wood was purchased by the Chantrey trustees and placed in the Tate Gallery, a museum that is indeed "by the Thames-side."
   2. James had acquired a telephone during this period and about this time included his number on his personal stationery—2417 Kensington.

300 / MS Leeds   Lamb House, Rye, Sussex.
                                                         July *27th* 1914.

My dear Gosse.

   I have but this minute to catch the post with this word. I this a.m. wrote to MacColl that I would associate myself with Robert Ross's friends in any public evidence of their regard that they might offer.[1] I haven't known of other names—till your note comes—save MacColl's own & yours, but I am glad to hear of them, & am yours ever

Henry James

P.S. What an extraordinarily & portentously multitudinous moment! One can't find sufficiently sesquipedalian designations for it![2]

1. Dugald S. MacColl (1859–1948), art critic, editor, and keeper of the Wallace Collection, was seeking signatures of public figures to support Ross after the failure of his case. After the second case was dropped the following autumn, Gosse was instrumental, according to Thwaite, "in raising a public subscription for him"—an effort that produced £700 and 350 signatures, including "those of the Prime Minister and the Bishop of Birmingham" (*EG*, 361).

2. The moment James refers to is the crisis before the beginning of World War I. The Archduke Francis Ferdinand, heir to the Austrian throne, had been assassinated in Sarajevo June 28, 1914. When Servia (later Serbia) with the support of Russia rejected part of the Austrian ultimatum of July 23, the Austrian empire, with the backing of Germany, declared war on Servia July 28, the day after the date of James's letter. Three days later, Russian mobilization precipitated a German ultimatum and a declaration of war on August 1. Germany then declared war on France August 3, and invaded Belgium and Luxembourg. This violation of Belgian neutrality brought Britain into the war. Through his intimate friendship with Richard Burdon, viscount Haldane, lord chancellor (1912–1915), Gosse was privy to state policy at the highest level. For his friendship with Haldane, see *EG*, 453–59.

301 / MS Leeds   21 Carlyle Mansions
                                                        Cheyne Walk S.W.
                                                        Oct. 8*th* 1914

My dear Gosse.

I was struck dumb, like most of us all, ten weeks ago, & you will perhaps have noted that consistently dumb I have remained.[1] To write to you amounted mainly to asking you to write to *me*—& *that* seemed to me anything but fair. And moreover I don't do it even now—telephoning me will serve, for at least I think we can talk, even though everything *is* beyond all words.[2] In short I desire greatly to see you, & only ask you to make it possible. I came back to town the 1*st* of the month; alone in the country I simply ate my heart out & could stand it no longer. Unfortunately I have I have [*sic*] been unwell since my return & have had to spend several days in-doors & in bed—otherwise I should have written you at once. Are you ever at Westminster now at such an hour as that you could come here to lunch at 1.30?[3] That would be *a* way that would give me great pleasure if you could make it possible; or are you ever at home yourself at the tea-hour—when I might see you [,] perhaps all, to whom I send

my love? At any rate I will do anything you propose or recommend
—& I reserve all comment on the abysses over which we shall meet.
I hope you are (what's called) "well"! What an application of the
word!

Yours always
Henry James

1. James has been "struck dumb" by the beginnings of World War I. See letter
300, note 2.

2. James now frequently refers to his "telephonability." See, for example, letters
299 and 302.

3. Gosse had reluctantly retired from his position at the House of Lords on September 26 at the age of sixty-five (*EG*, 460–61). James, though he had been aware of
Gosse's impending retirement, is apparently not sure about Gosse's present routine.

302 / TLS Leeds

21, Carlyle Mansions,
Cheyne Walk. S.W.
October 15*th*. 1914.[1]

Dictated.

My dear Gosse.

Forgive, please, my use of this helpful machinery for expedition of
my thanks. I find it does so expedite a backward and embarrassed
handling of letters that I have ceased to make any apology for it to
myself; so with that pleading victim of our conditions let me associate you.[2]

Your article for the Edinburgh is of an admirable interest, beautifully done, for the number of things so happily and vividly expressed in it, and attaching altogether from its emotion and its
truth.[3] How much, alas, to say on the whole portentous issue (I
mean the particular one you deal with) must one feel there is—and
the more the further about one looks and thinks! It makes me much
want to see you again, and we must speedily arrange for that. I am
probably doing on Saturday something very long out of order for
me—going to spend Sunday with a friend near town; but as quickly
as possible next week shall I appeal to you to come and lunch with
me: in fact why not now ask you to let it be either on Tuesday or
Wednesday, 20*th*. or 21*st*., as suits you best, here, at 1.30? A word as
to this at any time up to Tuesday a.m., and by telephone as well as
any otherhow, will be all sufficient.

Momentous indeed your recall, with such exactitude and authority, of the effect in France of the 1870-71 cataclysm, and interesting

to me as bringing back what I seem to myself to have been then almost closely present at; so that the sense of it all again flushes for me. I remember how the death of the immense old Dumas didn't in the least emerge to the naked eye, and how one vaguely heard that poor Gautier, "librarian to the Empress", had in a day found every-thing give way beneath him and let him go down and down! What analogies verily, I fear, with some of our present aspects and pros-pects! I didn't so much as know, till your page told me that Jules Lemaître was killed by that stroke: awfully tragic and pathetic fact. Gautier but just survived the whole other convulsion—it had led to his death early in '73. Felicitous Sainte-Beuve, who had got out of the way, with his incomparable penetration, just the preceding year! Had I been at your elbow I should have suggested a touch or two about dear old George Sand, holding out through the darkness at Nohant, but even there giving out some lights that are caught up in her letters of the moment.[4] Beautiful that you put the case as you do for the newer and younger Belgians, and affirm it with such em-phasis for Verhaeren—at present, I have been told, in this country.[5] Immense my respect for those who succeed in going on, as you tell of Gaston Paris's having done during that dreadful winter and created life and force by doing.[6] I myself find concentration of an extreme difficulty: the proportions of things have so changed and one's poor old "values" received such a shock. I say to myself that this is all the more reason why one should recover as many of them as possible and keep hold of them in the very interest of civilisation and of the hon-our of our race; as to which I am certainly right—but it takes some doing! Tremendous the little fact you mention (though indeed I had taken it for granted) about the *absolute* cessation of Bourget's last "big sale" after Aug. 1st. Very considerable his haul, fortunately,—and *if* gathered in!—up to the eve of the fell hour.[7] I have heard of him as in his native Auvergne from that time on. All I myself hear from Paris is an occasional word from Mrs. Wharton, who is full of ardent activ-ity and ingenious devotion there—a really heroic plunge into the breach.[8] But this is all now, save that I am sending you a volume of gathered-in (for the first time) old critical papers the publication of which was arranged for in the spring, and the book then printed and seen through the press, so that there has been for me a kind of pain-ful inevitability in its so grotesquely and false-notedly coming out now.[9] But no—I also say to myself—nothing serious and felt and sincere, nothing "good", is anything but essentially in order to-day, whether economically and "attractively" so or not! Put my volume at any rate away on a high shelf—to be taken down again only in the better and straighter light that I invincibly believe in the dawning of. Let me hear however sparely about Tuesday or Wednesday and believe me all faithfully yours

Henry James

1. Printed in part in *LHJ*, II, 409–12, and reprinted in *HJL*, IV, 719–21, but the present text is based upon the manuscript.

2. James consistently apologizes for using the typewriter for letters, but he nevertheless uses it when necessary.

3. Edmund Gosse, "War and Literature," *Edinburgh Review*, CCXX (October, 1914), 313–32. Gosse's essay considers the effect of the Franco-Prussian War of 1870–71 on certain French writers—Victor Hugo, Émile Zola, and Rene François Armand Sully-Prudhomme among them.

4. Alexandré Dumas père, born in 1802, died in 1870; Théophile Gautier, born in 1811, died in 1872, shortly after the war ended, not in 1873; Jules Lemaître, born in 1853, had just died in 1914; and Charles Augustin Sainte-Beuve, born in 1804, died in 1869. George Sand died in 1876. For Sand's letters, see letter 146, note 2.

5. Émile Verhaeren (1855–1916), Flemish poet and dramatist who wrote in French and whose *Hélène de Sparte* (1912) would appear in English in 1916, was characterized by Gosse as "the greatest poet of Europe at the opening of the twentieth century" (p. 315 of "War and Literature," cited in note 3).

6. Gaston Paris (1839–1903), French philologist and a professor at the Collège de France after 1872, continued his work on medieval French literature during the war.

7. Paul Bourget's last novel before the war was *Le Demon de midi* (1914). For other references to Bourget, see letter 10, for example.

8. For Edith Wharton's activities in behalf of the Allied cause during this period, see Lewis, *Edith Wharton*, 339ff.

9. *Notes on Novelists*, a collection of pieces on Stevenson, Zola, Flaubert, Balzac, and Sand, among others, was published in London October 13, two days before the date of James's letter. See *BHJ*, 151, and letter 294.

303 / TLS Leeds   21, Carlyle Mansions,
Cheyne Walk, S.W.
23 Oct. 1914.

[Dictated]

My dear Gosse,

Forgive again this form of thanks, the liveliest, for your kind and most founded imagination of my interest in our two friends.

I rejoice heartily to hear that Rupert Brooke has come safely through what he must have had to "put up with."[1] I don't know exactly what conjunctivitis is (though I shall look it up presently in my huge Webster); but it sounds rather dire when intermixed with

the Antwerp shells and other complications—all of which now make
me want to write to him, bless him, though I don't quite grasp what
he is doing. I find he has the art of inspiring personally (as well as
otherwise) an interest, and would fain testify to that none so-frequent
fact; which is, however, I hasten to reflect, much more frequent now
than it has ever been in all one's days.

From dear W.E.N. I have just, and of course ever so characteristically, heard—which means also of course ever so gallantly.[2] I
am writing to engage with him for after the 28*th*. Apropos of which,
to what a heart-breaking despoilment of all reality that evening of
ours with him last summer seems now to belong!

Yours all gratefully,
Henry James

1. James had met Rupert Brooke (1887–1915), the young British poet, while
Brooke was at Cambridge in 1909, and subsequently had characterized him as
"splendid Rupert." Brooke was in the unsuccessful defense of Antwerp.

2. For W. E. Norris, see letter 95, note 1, for example.

304 / TLS Leeds

21, Carlyle Mansions,
Cheyne Walk. S.W.
December 2nd. 1914.

[Dictated]
My dear Gosse.

Forgive again my resort to this machinery, which has definitely
become, in all these desperate conditions, my one blest dependence.
Admire moreover, freely, the brave character in which I am able to
thank you for your note of a couple of days since, with its promise of
an indication of your hour for Tuesday 8*th*., the prospect of which
evening I cherish, and for your information about the reception of
Boutroux.[1] I didn't know of his being expected here and shall want
exceedingly to be present at his welcome. But I shall have to extract
from you assistance, not to say inspiration, as to the ways and
means, by which I think I must mean the where and how, of this,
and will do so on Tuesday next. No, I haven't been to The Dynasts
—I'm afraid the theatre nowadays is insurmountably forbidding to
me, no matter what the specious seduction.[2] But you will tell me all
about that too.

Yours all faithfully
Henry James

1. Émile Boutroux (1845–1921), well-known French philosopher and author of a book on William James (1911), was to lecture in London at the British Academy on December 10. James attended the conference and reported to his old friend Walter Berry that the lecture was "admirable" and the "audience *vibrant d'emotion*" (*HJL*, IV, 732).

2. Thomas Hardy's *The Dynasts* (1904–1908) was abridged and produced by Harley Granville Barker at the Kingsway Theatre. See the *Times*, December 2, 1914, p. 8.

305 / MS Colby   21, Carlyle Mansions,
                                                   Cheyne Walk. S.W.
                                                   December 17*th* 1914[1]

My dear Gosse.

I am very sorry that your kind invitation does find me, as it happens, definitely committed for Xmas night—when I am to owe my dinner to the benevolence of my next-door neighbour here, Emily Sargent (& her brother John.)[2] Please express to Mrs. Nelly my melancholy regret for this gaucherie.

To make up for it a little I am writing to the young Elizabeth—who appears to have an impression of spacious times, or time, on the part of each of us, that her great original can scarce have attained to—that I *will* try to lash my extinct imagination into five minutes life for her sweet sake, & the cause's—& yours.[3] Yours all faithfully

                                                   Henry James

1. Printed in *CLQ*, 164.
2. Emily Sargent, John Singer Sargent's sister, also lived in Carlyle Mansions and is frequently referred to by James as his neighbor.
3. Possibly a reference to Elizabeth Robins Pennell (1855–1936), a good friend to both Gosse and James. In 1914 Pennell was active in London in supporting the needs of Belgian refugees—a cause also dear to the hearts of James and Gosse. Although she was hardly young at the time, James often referred in an avuncular manner to friends who were not much younger than he.

306 / MS Princeton   21, Carlyle Mansions,
                                                   Cheyne Walk. S.W.
                                                   Dec: 17: 1914.[1]

My dear Gosse.

This is a scratch of postscript to my note this evening posted to you—prompted by the consciousness of not having therein made a word of reply to your question as to what I "think of things."[2] The recovered presence of that question makes me somehow positively *want* to say that (I think) I don't "think" of them at all—though I try to; that I only feel, & feel, & toujours feel about them unspeakably, & about nothing else whatever—feeling so in Wordsworth's terms of exaltations, agonies & loves, & (our) unconquerable minds. Yes, I kind of make out withal that through our insistence an increasing purpose runs, & that one's vision of its final effect (though only with the aid of *time*,) grows less & less dim, so that one seems to find at moments it's almost sharp! And meanwhile what a purely suicidal record for themselves the business of yesterday—the women, & children (& babes in arms) slaughtered at Scarborough & Whitby, with their turning & fleeing as soon as ever they had killed enough for the moment.[3] Oh! I do "think" enough to believe in retribution for *that*. So I've kind of answered you. Ever your

Henry James

1. Printed in *LHJ*, II, 430.
2. See letter 305.
3. For the attack on Scarborough and Whitby, towns on the North Sea coast, see the *Times*, December 17, pp. 5, 8, 9, 10. German cruisers shelled these cities December 16. At Scarborough, fifteen to eighteen people were killed and a hundred wounded.

307 / MS Leeds   21, Carlyle Mansions,
                                                Cheyne Walk. S.W.
                                                February 26*th* 1915

My dear Gosse.

I embrace with eagerness the first opportunity of seeing you & shall be glad to dine with you tomorrow at 8 o'clock. I greatly lament your news of your wife's illness—please assure her of my liveliest sympathy & my hope of seeing her,—down stairs. That you are to be alone will render the occasion all the more welcome to me,[1] & I am yours impatiently & all-faithfully

Henry James

1. Even at this late stage of the friendship and with the assistance of the telephone, James usually felt that he was "in arrears" with the latest news from Gosse. See, for example, letter 299 or 308.

308 / MS Leeds   21 Carlyle Mansions
                                                    Cheyne Walk S.W.
                                                    March *21*st 1915.

My dear Gosse.

   When I dined with you the other week I went away feeling that we
had somehow not half talked, & I have wanted ever since to try &
make up, if possible, our deficiency—even if, given what there
mainly is to talk of at this horrible time, the deficiency be not of
more comfort than the abundance.[1] However, there's nothing of it
that one can keep away from, & one hunts it through even—& above
all with help—to see if some relief doesn't lurk. Which means
couldn't we some day soon converse again? It's a long way for you to
come—this is—for a poor luncheon with me alone, & yet that is my
best possible contribution to the idea of our meeting. Clubs are a little nearer, but in themselves unpropitious. *Could* you come on any
day this week save Tuesday 23*d*? Thursday, Friday or Saturday, at
1.45, in particular—could you manage one of those? If so I am fully
accessible by telephone & should be glad to hear your voice. I greatly
hope Nelly has left even convalescence behind her.[2] Yours & hers all
faithfully

                                                    Henry James

   1. See letters 307 and 309.
   2. See letter 307. The reminder about the telephone now appears rather
consistently.

309 / MS Leeds   21, Carlyle Mansions,
                                                    Cheyne Walk. S.W.
                                                    March 22*d* 1915

My dear Gosse.

   I am delighted you can come on Thursday, & I shall expect you at
1.45, please, if you can stay your proud stomach till then.[1] I *have* to
be a late luncher—to get anything of a morning clear. I start the day
with such difficulty & (imposed) deliberation. But I continue it better, or try to—& [your] advent will help.

   You say you dine with the King "Thursday" & will bring me news
of it; but I take that as a slip of the pen for Wednesday—& so not less
confidently expect the news.[2] Let it, I beseech you, be glorious!

   Yours all faithfully

                                                    Henry James

1. See letter 308.

2. James's tone with regard to Gosse's engagement with the king is quite different from earlier jibes about Gosse's attentions to various lords and ladies. The war, as James notes elsewhere, changed everything. See letter 302.

310 / MS Leeds

21 Carlyle Mansions
Cheyne Walk S.W.
April 25*th* 1915.

My dear Gosse.

This is indeed a dismal damnable stroke, the barren extinction of so beautiful a being & so distinguished a young poet as R.B.[1] It wrings the heart & makes the time still more hideous. But I will none the less be with you on Wednesday 28*th* at 8.15, & am yours all faithfully

Henry James

P.S. What an inspiration for some *other* poet—fine enough; even as Milton was fine enough for Lycidas. Why not try your own fineness?

1. Rupert Brooke died on Scyros on April 23, 1915. For other references to him, see letter 303, note 1, and James's letters to Edward Marsh (April 24, 1915, in *LHJ*, II, 468–69, and October 4, 1915, in *HJL*, IV, 780). James eventually wrote an introduction to Brooke's *Letters from America* (1916).

311 / MS Library of Congress

21 Carlyle Mansions
Cheyne Walk S.W.
June 25*th* 1915.[1]

My dear Gosse.

Remarkably enough, I should be writing you this evening even if I hadn't received your interesting information about Léon Daudet—concerning whom nothing perversely base & publicly pernicious at all surprises me. He is the cleverest idiot & the most poisonous talent imaginable, & I wait to see if he won't somehow swing—![2]

But il ne s'agit pas de ça; il s'agit of the fact that there is a matter I should have liked to speak to you of the other day when you lunched here, yet hung fire about through its not having then absolutely come to a head. It has within these 3 days done so, & in brief it is *this*. The force of the public situation now at last determines me to testify to my attachment to this country, my fond domicile for nearly forty years (40 *next* year,) by applying for naturalization here: the throwing of my imponderable moral weight into the scale of her fortune is *the geste* that will best express my devotion—absolutely nothing *else* will. Therefore my mind is made up & you are the *1st* person save my Solicitor (whom I have had to consult) to whom the fact has been imparted.[3] Kindly respect for the moment the privacy of it. I learned with horror just lately that if I go down into Sussex (for 2 or 3 months of Rye) I have at once to register myself there as an Alien & place myself under the observation of the Police. But that is only the *occasion* of my decision—it's not in the least the cause. The disposition itself has haunted me as Wordsworth's sounding cataract haunted *him*—"like a passion"—ever since the beginning of the War.[4] But the point, please, is this: that the process for me is really of the simplest, & *may* be very rapid, if I can obtain 4 honourable householders to testify to their knowledge of me as a respectable person, "speaking & writing English decently" &c. Will you give me the great pleasure of being one of them?—signing a paper to that effect?[5] I should take it ever so kindly. And I should further take kindly your giving me if possible your sense on *this* delicate point. Should you say that our admirable friend the Prime Minister would perhaps be approachable by me as another of the signatory 4?—to whom, you see, great historic honour, not to say immortality, as my sponsors, will accrue. I don't like to approach him without your so qualified sense of the matter first—& he has always been so beautifully kind & charming to me. I will do nothing till I hear from you—but his signature (which my solicitor's representative, if not himself, would simply wait upon him for;) would enormously accelerate the putting through of the application & the disburdening me of the Sussex "restricted Area" alienship—which it distresses me to carry on my back a day longer than I need. I have in mind my other two sponsors, but if I could have from you, in addition to your own personal response, on which my hopes are so founded, your ingenious prefiguration (fed by your intimacy with him,) as to how the P.M. would "take" my appeal, you would increase the obligations of yours all faithfully

Henry James

1. Printed in *LHJ*, II, 480–81, and reprinted in TD, 288–89, and in *HJL*, IV, 762–63, but the present text differs in particulars with all three.

2. Léon Daudet (1868–1942), the son of James's old friend Alphonse, was a leader in the Royalist party in France and the editor of *Action Française*. James is referring to a newspaper clipping about Daudet's political activities that Gosse had sent him on June 24, 1915 (Harvard).

3. James's solicitor was Nelson Ward. See letter 313. James had also written Henry James, Jr., his executor, on June 24, 1915 (in *LHJ*, II, 477–79, and in *HJL*, IV, 759–62).

4. William Wordsworth, "Tintern Abbey," ll. 76–77.

5. Gosse had also served as a reference when James sought to secure a flat in Carlyle Mansions. See letter 281. For Gosse's reply to this letter, see *TD*, 290. Gosse also intervened with the prime minister, H. H. Asquith.

312 / MS Leeds   21 Carlyle Mansions
                                                    Cheyne Walk S.W.
                                                    June 28*th*, 1915.[1]

My dear Gosse.

I can't sufficiently thank you for your so generous & understanding letter.[2] My decision has brought me a deep & abiding peace. I have written then without hesitation to the Prime Minister, & every instinct tells me that he will be more than kind.[3] This is but a stopgap word—I will write again as soon as I shall have heard from him. Yours all gratefully

Henry James

1. Printed in *TD*, 290.

2. Gosse's letter of June 25, 1915 (*TD*, 290).

3. For James's letter to H. H. Asquith, see *HJL*, IV, 764. "What I presume to ask you," James writes the prime minister, "is whether you will do me the honour to be the pre-eminent one of that greatly guaranteeing group"—the "four honourable householders" who would testify to the respectability of James's character. "Edmund Gosse," he added, "has benevolently consented to join it."

313 / MS Leeds   21 Carlyle Mansions
                                                    Cheyne Walk S.W.
                                                    July 9*th* 1915[1]

My dear Gosse.

I am distressed & dismayed to hear how you have been suffering, & all the more that I can measure with the last competence the force of your visitation. Lumbago of the fiercest temper was my perpetual company for long years—the first *thirty* in fact of my long life in London, & was really an awful blight to me.[2] (I could only little by little *sweat* it out & used to take heroic measures to that end.) But the great thing is that it *goes*, that it will, & that I have been practically exempt from it for several years now. So be of good heart & take my assurance that you will outgrow & outlive it. I have lived with other troubles, but left that one (absit omen!) behind me. I would very gladly have come to see you had you but breathed into the telephone. I heartily hope that you are well on your feet now. As for the Gran Rifiuto—to be [no] longer a child of the West—it is going forward, I think, with all due celerity.[3] I have done my own part, as the law requires, & the P.M. has been most kind about backing me. I am expecting to hear from my Solicitor that he has already—or will have very presently, waited upon you for your kind signed attestation (of *your* knowledge of my respectability & my acquaintance with the Tongue;) & after this has been accomplished with my 2 other backers—with one other, making the 4*th*, it was accomplished 3 or 4 days ago—the affair will be on the march.[4]

Ah, it *is* on the march! for I just receive your note telling me that Nelson Ward has been with you: I do rejoice![5] At this rate we move. Bless you, I will with the greatest pleasure send you my autograph of that Declaration, but shall have 1*st* to see it again to get it straight—I don't absolutely remember it![6] Count on it as soon as I can copy it & believe me again all gratefully yours

Henry James

1. Printed in *TD*, 292.
2. For Gosse's account of his lumbago, see his letter of July 8, 1915, in *TD*, 291. For James's lumbago, see, for example, letter 72.
3. For the course of James's application for naturalization, see letters 311, 312, 314, 315, and 316.
4. The other "honourable householders" were Sir George W. Prothero, editor of the *Quarterly Review* and an old friend, and James B. Pinker, James's literary agent for over fifteen years.
5. Nelson Ward was James's solicitor.
6. See letter 314.

314 / MS Lamb House, Rye

21 Carlyle Mansions
Cheyne Walk S.W.
July [25] 1915[1]

My dear Gosse.

The undersigned applicant for naturalization in this country applied . . . "because of his having lived & worked in England for the best part of forty years; because of his attachment to the country & his sympathy with it & its people; because of the long friendships & associations & interests he has formed here—these last including the acquisition of some property: all of which things have brought to a head his desire to throw his moral weight & personal allegiance, for whatever they may be worth, into the scale of the contending nation's present & future fortune."

Henry James

1. This letter is actually a part of letter 315, but a copy was sent to each of James's sponsors. The passage containing the "reasons" for James's application for citizenship appeared in the *Times* on July 28, 1915, and Gosse's copy was photographically reproduced as an illustration in Hyde's *Henry James at Home*, 266. My text is from the manuscript at Lamb House, Rye, and I am grateful to Sir Brian Batsford for giving me access to it and to the National Trust for allowing me to print it.

315 / MS Harvard

21 Carlyle Mansions
Cheyne Walk S.W.
(July 25*th* 1915.)[1]

The foregoing, my dear Gosse, is the transcript I promised you of the *reasons* figuring in my application as such to the Home Office.[2] I haven't yet received my Certificate of Naturalizaton, but it will doubtless now speedily arrive, as I had several days ago a most kind personal letter from the Home Secretary, Sir John Simon, telling me that he had ordered it at once to "issue" & giving me his blessing on it.[3]

Frankly, I have done this thing so much for the good example that I shall not care who sees this declaration of my grounds—*when the transaction is complete*. My solicitor tells me that the matter quite remains my property & within my discretion. I hope you have had no return of that abominable ill which I last saw you throwing off. Don't you think one has a certain reserve as to so much as speaking of the public situation? I have such a respect for our interest in it!

Yours all faithfully
Henry James

1. This letter is actually a part of 314, but the two parts were separated by Gosse (see note 3). The present letter was printed in *SR*, 590. The parenthesis about the dates is James's own.

2. For Gosse's request for a copy of James's declaration and Gosse's subsequent recognition of it, see his letters of July 9, 1915, and July 26, 1915, in *TD*, 291–93.

3. James received the certificate on July 26 and took the oath of allegiance the same day. See letter 316. Accordingly, Gosse circulated the list of reasons among James's friends and saw to it that the document appeared in the *Times* on July 28.

316 / MS Library of Congress   21 Carlyle Mansions
                                                  Cheyne Walk S.W.
                                                  July 26*th* 1915[1]

My dear Gosse.

Your good letter makes me feel that you will be interested to know
that since 4.30 this afternoon I have been able to say Civis Britannicus sum![2] My Certificate of Naturalization was received by my
Solicitor this a.m., & a few hours ago I took the Oath of Allegiance,
in his office, before a Commissioner. The odd thing is that nothing
seems to have happened & I don't feel a bit different; so that I see not
at all how associated I have become, but that I was really too associated before for any nominal change to matter. The process has only
shown me what I virtually *was*—so that it's rather disappointing in
respect to acute sensation. I *haven't* any, I blush to confess![3]

I shall be in town like yourselves till the very end of next month—
I have let Lamb House for 5 weeks to some friends of the American
Embassy, the E. G. Lowrys—I can't stand in these public conditions
the solitude & sequestration of the country. (E.G.L., ardent for our
cause, is "Attaché to the A.E. for the German Division"—& has been
quartered all winter at the German Embassy.)[4] I thank you enormously for your confidential passage, which is most interesting &
heartening; as is also this evening's news that the Boches have sunk—
torpedoed—another ship; I mean another American one. That affects
me as really charming! And let me mention in exchange for your
confidence that a friend told me this afternoon that he had been
within a few days talking with Captain McBride [,] one of the American naval attachés, whose competence he ranks high & to whom he
had put some question relative to the naval sense of the condition of
these islands. To which the reply had been: "You may take it from
me that England is absolutely impregnable & invincible"—and
McBride repeated over—"impregnable & invincible!" Which kind of
did me good.

Let me come up & sit on your terrace some near August afternoon—I can always be rung up, you know: I *like* it—& believe me
yours & your wife's all faithfully

                                                  Henry James

1. Printed in part in *LHJ*, II, 492–93, and reprinted in *TD*, 293–94, and *HJL*, IV,
772–73.
2. Gosse's letter of July 26, 1915, is in *TD*, 292–93.

3. James, nevertheless, knew that his action would be criticized in America. See, for example, his letter to John Singer Sargent of July 30, 1915, in *LHJ*, II, 493.

4. Edward G. Lowry (1876–1943), an American journalist, was "a special agent of the Department of State attached to the American Embassy in London" (*TD*, 293*n*).

317 / MS Library of Congress   21 Carlyle Mansions
                                                  Cheyne Walk S.W.
                                                  August 25*th* 1915.[1]

My dear Gosse.

I have had a bad sick week, mostly in bed—with putting pen to paper quite out of my power: otherwise I should sooner have thanked you for the so generous spirit of that letter, & told you, with emotion, how much it has touched me. I am really more overcome than I can say by your having been able to indulge in such freedom of mind & grace of speculation, during these dark days, on behalf of my poor old rather truncated edition, in fact entirely frustrated one—which has the grotesque likeness for me of a sort of miniature Ozymandias of Egypt ("look on my *works* ye mighty & despair!")—round which the lone & level sands stretch further away than ever.[2] It *is* indeed consenting to be waved aside a little into what was once blest literature to so much as answer the question you are so handsomely impelled to make—but my very statement about the matter can only be, alas, a melancholy, a blighted confession. That Edition has been, from the point of view of profit either to the publishers or to myself, practically a complete failure; vulgarly speaking, it doesn't sell—that is my annual report of what it does—the whole 25 vols.— in this country amounts to about £25 from the Macmillans; & the ditto from the Scribners in the U.S. to very little more.[3] I am past all praying for anywhere; I remain at my age (which you know,) & after my long career, utterly, insurmountably, unsaleable. And the original preparation of that collective & selective series involved really the extremity of labour—all my "earlier" things—of which the Bostonians would have been, if included, one—were so intimately & interestingly revised. The Edition is from that point of view really a monument (like Ozymandias) which has never had the least intelligent critical justice done it—any sort of critical attention at all paid it—& the artistic problem involved in my scheme was a deep & exquisite one, & moreover was, as I hold, very effectively solved.[4] Only it took such time—*and* such taste—in other words such aes-

thetic light. No more commercially thankless job of the literary order
was (Prefaces & all—*they* of a thanklessness!) accordingly ever
achieved. The *immediate* inclusion of the Bostonians was rather dep- ✓
recated by my publishers (the Scribners, who were very generally &
in a high degree appreciative: I make no complaint of them at all!)—
& there were reasons for which I also wanted to wait: we always
meant that that work shld. eventually come in. Revision of it loomed
peculiarly formidable & time-consuming (for intrinsic reasons,) & as
other things were more pressing & more promptly feasible I allowed
it to stand over—with the best intentions, & also in company with a
small number more of provisional omissions.[5] But by the time it *had*
stood over [,] disappointment had set in; the undertaking had begun
to announce itself as a virtual failure, & we stopped short where we
were—that is when a couple of dozen volumes were out. From that
moment, some seven or eight years ago, nothing whatever has been
added to the series—& there is little enough appearance now that
there will ever. Your good impression of the B.'s greatly moves me—
the thing was no success whatever on publication in the Century
(when it came out,) & the late R. W. Gilder, of that periodical, wrote
me at the time that they had never published anything that appeared
so little to interest their readers.[6] I felt about it myself then that it
was probably rather a remarkable feat of objectivity—but I never was
very thoroughly happy about it, & seem to recall that I found the
subject & the material, after I had got launched in it, under some
illusion, less interesting & repaying than I had assumed it to be. All
the same I *should* have liked to review it for the Edition—it would
have come out a much truer and more curious thing (it was meant to
be curious from the first;) but there can be no question of that, or of
the proportionate Preface to have been written with it, at present—or
probably ever within my span of life. Apropos of which matters I at
this moment hear from Heinemann that 4 or 5 of my books that he
has have quite (entirely) ceased to sell & that he must break up the
plates. Of course he must: I have nothing to say against it; & the
things in question are mostly all in the Edition.[7] But such is "success"! I should have liked to write that Preface to The Bostonians—
which will never be written now. But think of noting now that *that* is
a thing that has perished!

I am doing my best to feel better, & hope to go out this afternoon,
the 1st one for several! I am exceedingly with you all over Philip's

transfer to France.[8] We are with each other now as not yet before over everything & I am yours & your wife's more than ever

H.J.

1. Printed in *LHJ*, II, 496–99, and reprinted in *HJL*, IV, 776–78. Since the manuscript differs in several important particulars from the printed texts, I have followed it. This letter is presumably the last Gosse received from James. The two friends met for the last time, according to Gosse, "on the evening of November 29*th*" (Gosse, *Aspects and Impressions*, 53). Three days later James suffered a stroke, which led eventually to his death on February 28, 1916.

2. Since the New York Edition (1907–1909) had not sold well, James considered it in many ways a failure. The quotation, of course, is from Shelley's sonnet "Ozymandias."

3. There were twenty-four volumes in the edition, not twenty-five.

4. Actually, there had been thoughtful and appreciative considerations by Percy Lubbock, W. Morton Fullerton, and Gosse himself, but James obviously means that the edition had not received adequate "critical justice."

5. For the question concerning *The Bostonians* (1886), see James's letters of July 30, 1905, and May 9, 1906, to Charles Scribner's Sons in *HJL*, IV, 368 and 404, respectively.

6. Richard Watson Gilder (1844–1909) was a member of the editorial staff of *Scribner's Monthly* for a decade, and when *Scribner's* became the *Century* in 1881, he became editor and remained in that position until he died.

7. James had published a total of ten titles with William Heinemann, from *The American: A Comedy in Four Acts* (1891) and *Terminations* (1895) to *Italian Hours* (1909).

8. Philip Gosse had taken a medical degree before the war. During the war, he served until 1917 with a medical unit of the 23rd Division (in France, 1915–1917) and then was posted to India until the close of hostilities.

Index